T0100459

Introduction to Python for Kids

Learn Python the Fun Way by Completing Activities and Solving Puzzles

Aarthi Elumalai

Apress®

Introduction to Python for Kids

Aarthi Elumalai
Chennai, Tamil Nadu, India

ISBN-13 (pbk): 978-1-4842-6811-7 ISBN-13 (electronic): 978-1-4842-6812-4
https://doi.org/10.1007/978-1-4842-6812-4

Managing Director, Apress Media LLC: Welmoed Spahr
Acquisitions Editor: Celestin Suresh John
Development Editor: Laura Berendson
Coordinating Editor: Aditee Mirashi

Cover designed by eStudioCalamar

Cover image designed by Freepik (www.freepik.com)

Distributed to the book trade worldwide by Springer Science+Business Media New York, 1 New York Plaza, Suite 4600, New York, NY 10004-1562, USA. Phone 1-800-SPRINGER, fax (201) 348-4505, e-mail orders-ny@springer-sbm.com, or visit www.springeronline.com. Apress Media, LLC is a California LLC and the sole member (owner) is Springer Science + Business Media Finance Inc (SSBM Finance Inc). SSBM Finance Inc is a **Delaware** corporation.

For information on translations, please e-mail booktranslations@springernature.com; for reprint, paperback, or audio rights, please e-mail bookpermissions@springernature.com.

Apress titles may be purchased in bulk for academic, corporate, or promotional use. eBook versions and licenses are also available for most titles. For more information, reference our Print and eBook Bulk Sales web page at http://www.apress.com/bulk-sales.

Any source code or other supplementary material referenced by the author in this book is available to readers on GitHub via the book's product page, located at www.apress.com/978-1-4842-6811-7. For more detailed information, please visit http://www.apress.com/source-code.

Printed on acid-free paper

Dedicated to My Daughter and to the rest of my family who believed me when no one would and stood by me through everything.

Table of Contents

About the Author

Aarthi Elumalai is a programmer, educator, entrepreneur, and innovator. She has a Bachelor of Engineering degree in Computer Science from Anna University, Chennai.

Since then, she has managed a team of programmers and worked with hundreds of clients. She has also launched a dozen web apps, plug-ins, and software that are being used by thousands of customers online.

She has over 15 years of experience in programming. She started coding in Basics at the age of 12, but her love for programming took root when she came across C programming at the age of 15.

She is the founder of DigiFisk, an e-learning platform that has more than 60,000 students all over the world. Her courses are well received by the masses, and her unique, project-based approach is a refreshing change to many. She teaches the complex world of programming by solving a ton of practical exercises and puzzles along the way. Her courses and books always come with hands-on training in creating real-world projects using the knowledge learned, so her students get better equipped for the real world.

When she is not working on her next course or book, you'll see her researching her next product idea and refining her existing products. She is currently committed to bringing the sheer power of artificial intelligence to make life easier for small business owners.

About the Technical Reviewer

Ashwin Pajankar holds a Master of Technology from IIIT Hyderabad. He started programming and tinkering with electronics at the tender age of 7. BASIC was the first programming language he worked with. He was gradually exposed to C programming, 8085, and x86 assembly programming during his higher secondary schooling. He is proficient in x86 assembly, C, Java, Python, and Shell programming. He is also proficient with Raspberry Pi, Arduino, and other single-board computers and microcontrollers. Ashwin is passionate about training and mentoring. He has trained more than 60,000 students and professionals in live and online training courses. He has published more than a dozen books with many international and Indian publishers. He has also reviewed numerous books and educational video courses. This is his fifth book with Apress, and he is working on more books. He regularly conducts programming bootcamps and hands-on training for software companies in Nashik, India.

He is also an avid YouTuber with more than 10,000 subscribers to his channel. You can find him on LinkedIn.

Introduction

This book is the perfect blend of education and fun for kids 8 years and above looking to learn one of the easiest languages they can use to develop almost everything from websites to desktop apps to games to AI. It will include four big projects (or capstone projects): three games with *Turtle*, *Tkinter*, and *Pygame* and a desktop app with *Tkinter*.

The book starts with an overview of basic programming concepts such as variables, numbers, and strings while creating fun, personalized mini projects like "Print your name" and "Is your mom tipping enough." It then dives right into *Turtle*, a Python library custom-made for kids, where they'll learn how to draw, animate, automate, and eventually make colorful mini projects based on the Python concepts learned. Once they have built a foundation in programming and the Python language, they will learn all about building desktop apps with *Tkinter* and games with *Pygame*.

There is also an entire chapter dedicated to more fun puzzles and activities that come with a step-by-step solution, and another chapter with cool ideas for more puzzles, and a section that gives them advice on where they can go from there. By the end of this book, kids will learn Python from the inside out while creating projects that they can showcase to their friends, families and teachers. They will develop problem-solving skills along with programming skills while doing the puzzles and activities described in the book.

This book is really jam-packed with information, but do not worry, I made sure that you will not be bored. You will not feel like sitting in another one of your boring classes at school, I promise.

I have included a lot of fun activities, mini as well as big projects throughout this book. There are also a lot of puzzles and even more activities at the end of the book, so you will not have a boring minute.

In Chapter 1, I'll give you a brief introduction to Python, its uses, and an overview of what's covered in this book and how to get the most out of it.

In Chapters 2 and 3, I will start by guiding you through the steps required to install Python in your system. It is quite easy to do, do not worry.

Then, you will create your very first program. Yes, you will start coding from the get-go!

In Chapters 4 and 5, you will learn all about numbers, performing mathematical calculations with Python, and the various cool tools Python equips you with to perform your magic with numbers. You will start coding real Python programs in this chapter.

Chapters 6 and 7 are where things get interesting. You will learn how to create a lot of cool graphics with Python's built-in module, *Turtle*. Remember the add-ons I told you Python had to help you make awesome stuff? *Turtle* is one of the best of them. With *Turtle*, you can literally draw on the screen, and it will be automated!

Once I have taught you *Turtle*, I will use it in the next chapters to make things more colorful.

In Chapter 8, you will learn how to play with alphabets, words, and sentences in Python. You will learn how to print things, extract words from sentences, find words in sentences, and a whole lot more.

Chapter 9 is where you will learn about conditions. There is always a cause and effect in life. If something happens, something else will happen because of it. "If I ace my test, my mom will praise me." That is a cause and effect. You will learn how to apply scenarios like that and use it to create fun little mini games (you will see how) in this chapter.

What if you want to print every number from 1 to 100? What if you do not want to write more than four lines of code to do that? You will learn how to do that and use the power of automation to automatically draw your graphics and animations in Chapter 10.

In Chapter 11, you will learn how to store a lot of information in one place. You will start using the real power of Python from this chapter onward.

In Chapter 12, we're going to take a break from all the learning and create fun mini projects based on the concepts we've learned so far.

In Chapters 13 and 14, we will take a long look into real-world programming. We will look at true automation with functions and real-world problem-solving with objects.

In Chapter 15, you will learn how to automatically manipulate files with Python.

From Chapter 16, we will go back to having fun with Python! In Chapters 16, 17, and 18, you will learn all about a powerful package called *Tkinter*. You can use it to create desktop-based apps and games. You will learn how to use the package to create a paint app you can show off to your friends and a tic-tac-toe game you can play with your friends.

In Chapter 19, we will revisit *Turtle* and create a fun project with it. Let us create a snake game, shall we?

In Chapters 20 and 21, I will focus on making you a budding game developer. Let us learn how to use *Pygame* to create awesome games and make a space shooter game you can modify to your heart's content!

In Chapter 22, we will learn the basics of web development with Python. We will not delve too much into it, but I will give you an introduction to get started.

In Chapter 23, we will go back to solving puzzles and activities. We will even make a couple more mini projects!

Chapter 24 is the final chapter. I'll give you ideas on new projects and mini projects you can try with what we've learned in this book and also advice on what you can do next. What is covered in this book is just the starting point. There is a lot more to Python, and I will point you in the right direction to continue your journey.

CHAPTER 1

Did You Know?

I have written the first part of this chapter for parents and the rest for the kids. I hope to convince you of the importance of programming and Python as your kid's first programming language in this chapter. If your kid is older (10+), they can read those topics themselves. In the latter half of the chapter, I'll address the kids and give them a brief overview of all the fun stuff they can do with Python, what they'll learn from my book, and how to use my book to its full capacity.

So, let us get started.

What is programming?

You have your gadget – your laptops, PCs, tablets, mobile phones, and so on – and whenever you ask it to do something, within reason, it does it. How? Well, that is because every time you task your gadget with something, the pre-programmed set of instructions it has pertaining to that task will fire up in the background. Those set of instructions are called *code*.

A. Elumalai, *Introduction to Python for Kids*, https://doi.org/10.1007/978-1-4842-6812-4_1

You will find that your gadgets need a complete set of instructions to perform even the simplest tasks, like opening an application or performing a calculation. They are just machines after all, just 1s and 0s at the base of it all. They cannot think on their own, so with our code, we are making them think.

In other words, programming is the language your computer speaks, and the different programming languages are the different languages it understands/speaks. You might know English, French, and Mandarin, but you might not know Italian or Japanese. Similarly, out of the, literally, hundreds of programming languages out there (Python, JavaScript, C, C++, C#, Ruby, etc.), *your* computer might speak a few, or just one, and not understand the rest.

Why should your kids learn to code?

Now that you know what programming is and how it literally runs the digital world, I shouldn't have to give you a lot of reasons to convince you to teach your kids coding, am I right?

But still, you might be wondering why *your* kid needs to learn programming, and why should they learn *now*. After all, in our time, people learned programming in college and only if they decided to become a programmer.

Well, I think I have a couple of reasons that will convince you why, in this day and age, kids, regardless of their future career aspirations, should learn programming, and why it is prudent that they start now.

Programming is like Math

Thirty years back, no one would have dared make such a statement, but now, times have changed, and yes, programming is, indeed, like Math. It is everywhere, just like Math is.

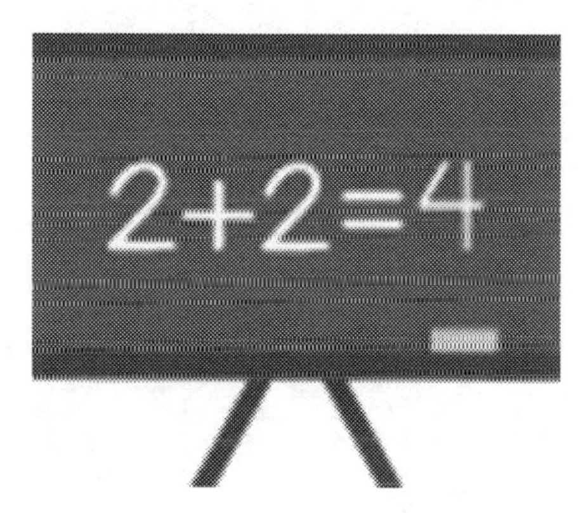

Math was a part of our educational requirement until we were at least 18, but not everyone of us is a mathematician today. Then why was Math forced down our throats? Well, because Math runs everything. We need basic mathematics in our daily life and certainly in most of our careers. So, we learned everything from calculus to algebra to geometry, knowing very well that we would probably not use 90% of our knowledge when we grew up.

That is exactly the case with programming today. Everything is digitized. There is an app for everything from food delivery to stock market prediction. Computers have entered every field, including traditional fields like construction and manufacturing. Most of the construction equipment are digitized nowadays, and what powers them? Programs, and thousands of lines of code.

Even art is digitized. So regardless of the field your kid is getting into, their knowledge in programming is going to give them a leg up.

But apart from that, coding also improves a kid's mathematical capabilities by fostering logical thinking and problem-solving.

Coding improves logical thinking and creativity

A contradictory statement, but true in this case. Every code blocks your child creates will be logically driven.

Logic dictates programming, and once they start coding on their own, they will learn to dissect a problem into bite-sized components, apply logic to solve each component, and then finally combine all the components into a coherent solution.

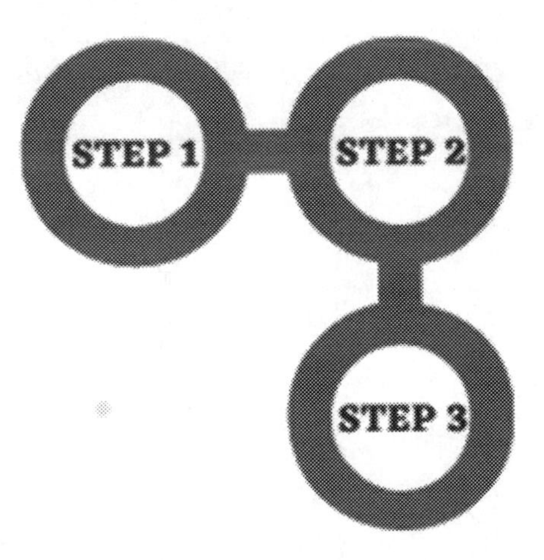

That is how problem-solving works in the real world, regardless of field, and they will learn this invaluable skill as a child.

But let us be honest, your kid would be bored with just logic. That is where creativity comes in. The world runs on both creativity and logic, and the same holds true for programming.

There is no right answer in programming. If they are solving the problem, how they are solving it does not matter. There are best practices, of course, but if you ask two programmers to solve the same problem, chances are, their code blocks will look completely different.

So, while coming up with a solution, and multiple solutions for multiple problems down their programming journey, they will foster creativity as well.

The best of both worlds, don't you think?

Coding is the future

Let us be very honest here. We are moving toward a completely digitized society at an amazingly fast pace. Everything is digitized. Apps are everywhere. Artificial intelligence is making new waves in the world every single day. Before we know it, we will have artificial intelligence–driven technologies cleaning our houses and driving our cars.

It is no wonder that programming has become an invaluable skill in today's world, and the demand for programmers is just going to increase every year.

So, coding is indeed the future, and by learning to code at a young age, your child will have a leg up over their competitor. Sounds good, but why does your kid need coding if they were going to become a mechanical engineer, for example? Or a financial analyst?

This brings me back to my original argument. Everything is digitized, and coding is everywhere, in every single field. So, if your kid has a programming base, then will they not stand out from the rest?

For example, a financial analyst with knowledge in programming can code a stock prediction application themselves and hence save the company tons of resources, or they would at least be fluent enough in tech talk that they'd guide the programmers better and save their boss hundreds of production hours and back and forth.

So, regardless of what your kid is going to study in the future, coding is going to help them out, and in the immediate future, they have a monetizable skill they can use to make extra cash.

In their teenage years, they do not have to flip burgers at minimum wage as a side gig. They can freelance as a software developer and make at least three to four times more money working half the time.

Or better yet, your kid could decide to become an entrepreneur. As you know, almost every startup relates to programming and software in some way, so as a programmer, your kid can code the app themselves and easily save tens of thousands in programmer fees.

I believe those are very convincing arguments as to why your kid needs to start learning to code right now.

Why Python?

Alright, now you are convinced about the benefits of your kids learning to code, but why Python? Out of the tens of popular programming languages out there, why should they start with Python?

I firmly believe that Python should be the first choice of real-world programming for a kid and let me convince you why.

Python is easy

Well, that is pretty much it. Kids want to have fun, and if we want them to learn programming, it needs to be fun *and* easy. Python is both.

Unlike the other older languages where you need to learn a lot of syntaxes and theory before you can create your first program, Python is very straightforward. The syntax is easy to understand and logically sound. "Print" just prints something on the screen. Easy to remember, right? There is not a lot of memorizing to do, and your kid can start coding and creating from the get-go.

It is the perfect programming language for beginners with no prior knowledge of programming, and it is even better for kids because it is also fun.

Python has a lot of built-in kid-friendly modules and libraries that will help them draw graphics and create games and fun apps with just a few lines of code.

It can do a lot of things

Now, do not underestimate Python because it is easy to learn. It can be used in literally everything from web development to desktop app development to artificial intelligence.

The language is immensely powerful, and the libraries and modules that come with it are even more powerful. You have add-ons for everything.

You can create graphics with *Turtle*, beautiful desktop apps with *Tkinter* (like the calculator app you're so fond of using on your laptop), create professional games with *Pygame*, develop full-blown websites and web apps with *Django* or *Flask*, and apply machine learning (artificial intelligence) algorithms with a host of easy to learn libraries. The possibilities are endless with Python.

By starting their programming journey with Python, your kids are not just stepping into the world of coding, they are also equipping themselves with skills in one of the most highly sought-after (and paid) programming languages of this time.

What more? With the rate at which Python's popularity, and its adoption into fast-moving fields like artificial intelligence, is growing, it is obvious that Python is here to stay, so your kids' skills are unlikely to go stale in the future.

From this point onward, I will be addressing the kids.

Python is fun!

Hi there! So, you are here to learn Python. Not only is it easy to get started with, it also comes with a lot of bells and whistles that make programming fun for you. Would you like to know all the cool things you can create with Python?

Games!

Who does not love games, am I right? But what if you can create *your own games* and then play them with your friends? You will be the most popular kid in class if you can do that.

What more? You can change the features of the games as you like. Want five lives instead of three? Great, add two more. Not enough levels and you are bored already? Code more levels into your game! Make those levels extra difficult to give yourself a challenge. You have the freedom to do anything you want with the games you create, and you can even get suggestions from your friends and apply them to your games.

With just a little bit of coding, you will be able to modify the games you have always been dissatisfied with or create a brand-new game you can play with your friends.

So, you will have fun *while coding* and after coding (while playing the games).

Graphics and animation

For me, graphics and animations are the next best thing right after games. What about you?

Imagine running a program that draws a design you created in real time. What about an animation? What if you can create designs and animations and use them in that game you have always wanted to create and play?

Like I always say, the possibilities are endless, and they are only limited by your creativity and imagination. Run wild with Python!

Websites

Do you use the Internet? Then you must have visited at least 100 websites by now. They look great, don't they? What if you can create a website just like your most favorite website?

If you learn Python, you certainly can.

I am not talking about simple websites. I am talking about big, full-blown websites and web apps with a lot of cool features. You could even create websites and apps like Facebook and Instagram with enough practice.

Apps

Python comes with a lot of tools, just like the tools you use in your games. These tools are called libraries and packages in Python. With the help of these libraries, you can create almost anything, including apps.

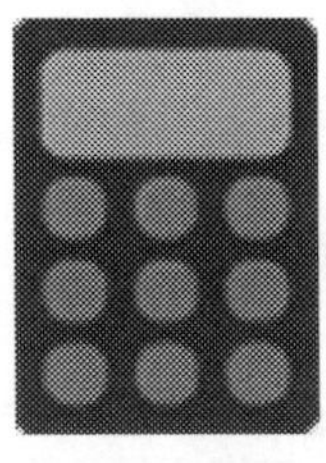

Do you use a laptop or tablet? It comes with a lot of cool apps, right? There is a calculator app, a stopwatch/timer app, paint app, and so on.

What if you can create those exact apps? Well, with Python, you certainly can. In fact, you will learn to create some of those apps right in this book. Are you excited?

Not just that, with packages like *Kivy* and *PyQt*, you can even start creating mobile apps with Python. We will not be talking about those packages in this book, but as you can see, you have a lot of possibilities with Python.

Whew! That was a big list indeed. The world is your oyster with Python, so come and play!

Getting the most out of this book

This chapter (and the last) would be the only two chapters with a lot of text. I have tried my best to keep things interesting and practical in the rest of the chapters.

You will come across a lot of examples that illustrate every topic we cover. There will be a lot of coding, so I recommend you code the examples along with me. Try not to copy and paste. Type everything out so you get familiarized with coding.

Every chapter comes with a lot of activities, puzzles, and mini projects with detailed, step-by-step solutions too. I would recommend following along with the solutions in the first few chapters, but once you are confident enough, try solving the puzzles/activities on your own and then cross-verify with the given solution.

Remember, there are no wrong solutions in programming! If you get the desired result, you are good to go.

This book includes four capstone projects (big projects) as well to solidify your knowledge of Python. I would recommend creating the projects, but do not stop there. Try changing things in every project to make it your own. Of course, do not forget to show your projects to your family, friends, and teachers as well!

That is pretty much it. It is an easy-to-follow along book, so do not get overwhelmed by the size of it. Just get started and start coding.

Summary

In this chapter, which was addressed to the parents (in the first half) and the kids (in the second half), I gave a brief explanation of what programming is and why your kids need to learn to code at such a young age, regardless of their future aspirations. I also gave convincing arguments on why Python should be the first real-world programming language of choice for a kid and what a kid can do with Python. We ended the chapter with a brief overview of everything you will learn from this book and the best way to utilize this book to its full capacity.

In the next chapter, we will learn how to install Python and create and execute our very first Python programs.

CHAPTER 2

Let's Install Python!

In this chapter, we will take a deeper look into what programming is and how it is used to control various gadgets. We will also look at installing Python in our system. Let us get started!

Speak the computer's language

Language is used for communication between two or more people, am I right? But if someone talks to you in a language you do not know, would you understand them? Of course not. I would not either!

Similarly, your computer cannot understand languages it does not speak. So, if you just look at your computer and command it to open the paint program in plain English, it will not understand you. If you talk to it in a language it understands, on the other hand, you will certainly get a response.

Programming languages are languages computers understand. Python is one of them. If you want your computers or mobile phones or GPS or tablets to do something, you need to give them instructions.

When you click the paint app's icon, how does your device know that you have actually clicked it? How does it open that exact app and not something else? That is because a programmer probably wrote a bunch of lines of code that says that when someone clicks the paint icon, the paint app should open. If they changed the code and wrote that clicking that icon should open the Google Chrome browser, then that is what would happen.

A. Elumalai, *Introduction to Python for Kids*, https://doi.org/10.1007/978-1-4842-6812-4_2

Therefore, a programmer's job is extremely important. They make the devices work. They create the device's brain that makes actions possible. Without their code, the devices you use every day would just be a mass of plastic, chips, and wires, and nothing else.

So, if you learn to speak the computer's language, you can give your computer, or any gadget really, instructions like these too. Once you get good at programming, you can create apps like the paint app or games like Minecraft.

Get started – install Python

Now you know what programming is. It is just a set of instructions you give a gadget/device to make it do what you want it to do.

Shall we start programming then? Python is one of the easiest programming languages out there, so that is exactly what we are going to learn in this book.

Before you write Python programs though, you need to install it in your laptop or computer. Remember how I said your computer needs to speak the language to understand what you are saying?

Right now, your computer probably does not speak the Python language. That is because Python is not installed in it. Once you install it, your computer will learn the language in seconds (yes, it is that fast!), and then when you give it instructions in Python, it'll understand you and react accordingly. It is magic!

I will give you step-by-step instructions on installing and running Python on your system, so just follow along with me, alright? I will give separate instructions for Windows as well as Mac, so skip to the one you have on your device.

Installing Python on a Windows computer

Let us look at how to download and install Python on a Windows device first. These steps work for Windows versions 7 and higher.

Download Python

1. Open the following link on your browser: `www.python.org/downloads/`.

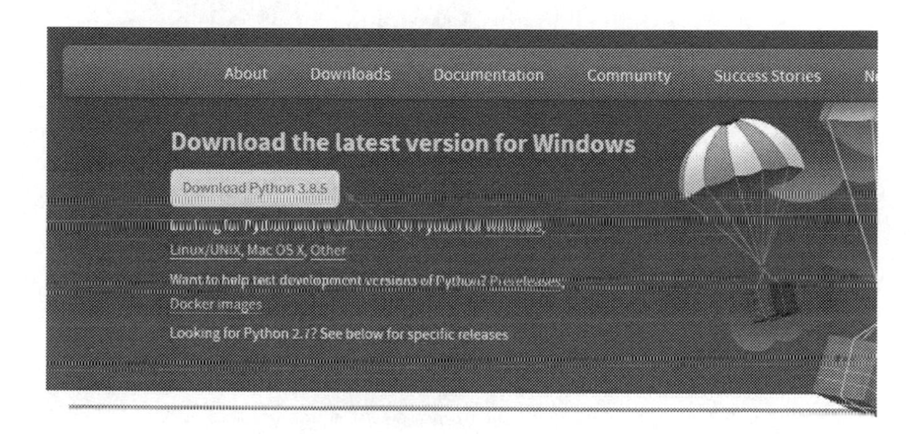

Figure 2-1. *Python Windows download page*

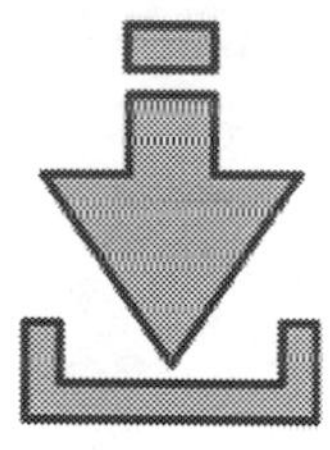

2. Click the **download button** (look at the arrow in Figure 2-1) to download the Python installer. Remember how I told you that coding was magical? You will see that in action now. When you opened the page, it knew you were using a Windows computer without you having to tell it.

I have downloaded **Python 3.8.5** as of writing this book, but you might be downloading a newer version. Do not worry about that. Go ahead and download the latest version.

Install Python

It knows you have a Windows computer, so you will now have to **install** the Windows version of Python. Let us do that:

1. Open the .exe file you just downloaded. You will see a popup like Figure 2-2.

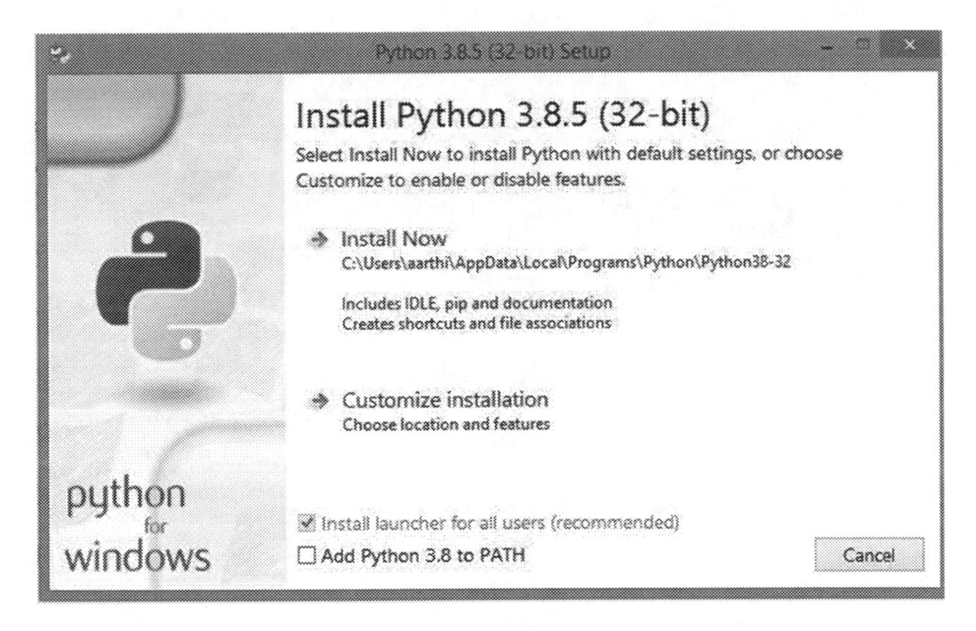

Figure 2-2. *Python installation setup*

2. Do not forget to click the checkbox that says "**Add Python 3.8 to PATH**" (Figure 2-3).

Install launcher for all users (recommended)
Add Python 3.8 to PATH

Figure 2-3. *Add Python to PATH*

3. Once you have ticked the box, click **install now**. The installation will start, and it will look something like Figure 2-4.

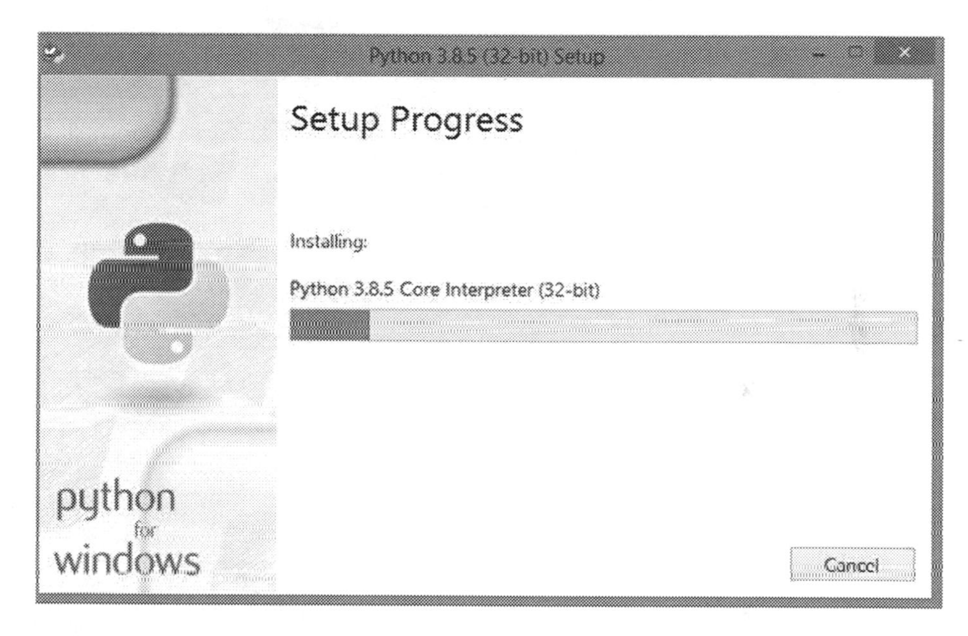

Figure 2-4. *Python installation progress*

4. Wait until the green bar reaches the end, and you will see a message that says "**Setup was successful**" (Figure 2-5).

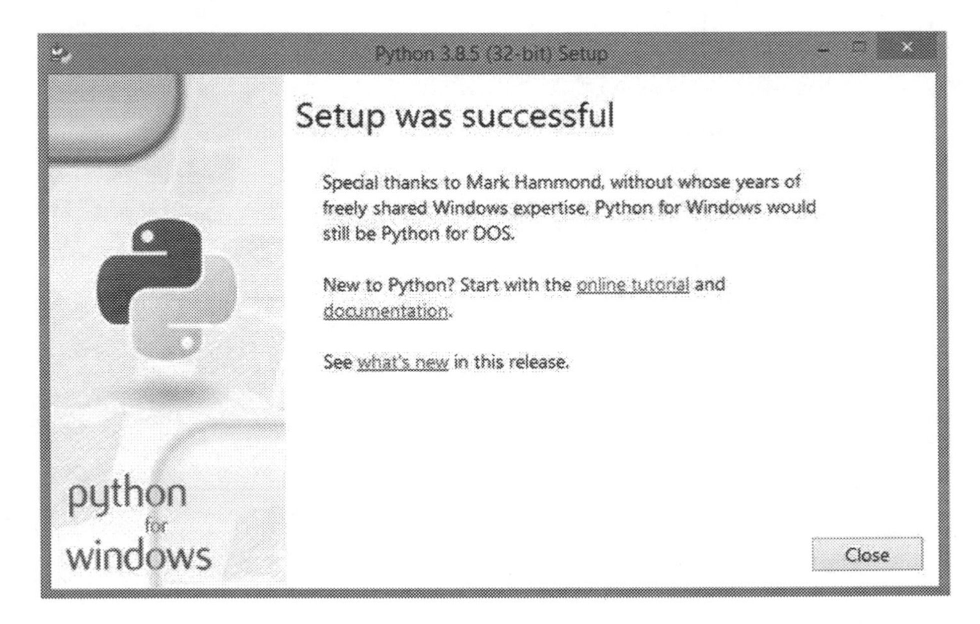

Figure 2-5. *Python setup successful message*

5. Press the **Close** button, and you are done installing Python on your computer. Hurray! ☺

Installing Python on a Mac device

Let us look at how to download and install Python on a Mac device next. If you have a Windows computer, and you have already installed Python following the steps in the last section, you can skip this section.

Python usually comes preinstalled in any Mac device, but chances are you have an older version of Python in your system. It never hurts to have the latest version of any software, so let us update our Python, shall we?

Download Python

1. **Open the following link** in your browser: `www.python.org/downloads/` (Figure 2-6).

Figure 2-6. *Python Mac OS download page*

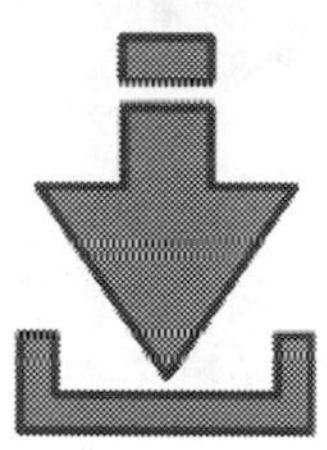

2. Click that big yellow **download button** to download the Python installer. Remember how I told you that coding was magical? You will see that in action now.

Did you notice that when you visited the download page from your Mac device, it automatically says "Download the latest version for Mac OS X"? That is because the Python website's code read which operating system (Windows, Mac, etc.) you are using and gave you the correct version to download automatically. Cool, right?

Your package will download as in Figure 2-7.

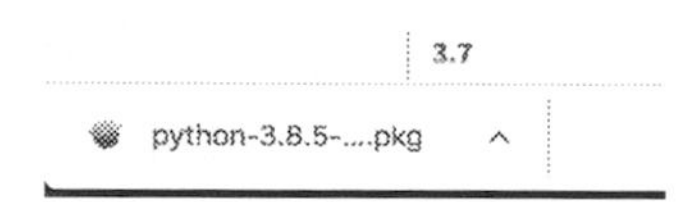

Figure 2-7. *Python 3.8.5 package downloaded*

I have downloaded Python 3.8.5 as of writing this book, but you might be downloading a newer version. Do not worry about that. Go ahead and download the latest version.

Install Python

1. **Open the installer** and you will see a screen like Figure 2-8.

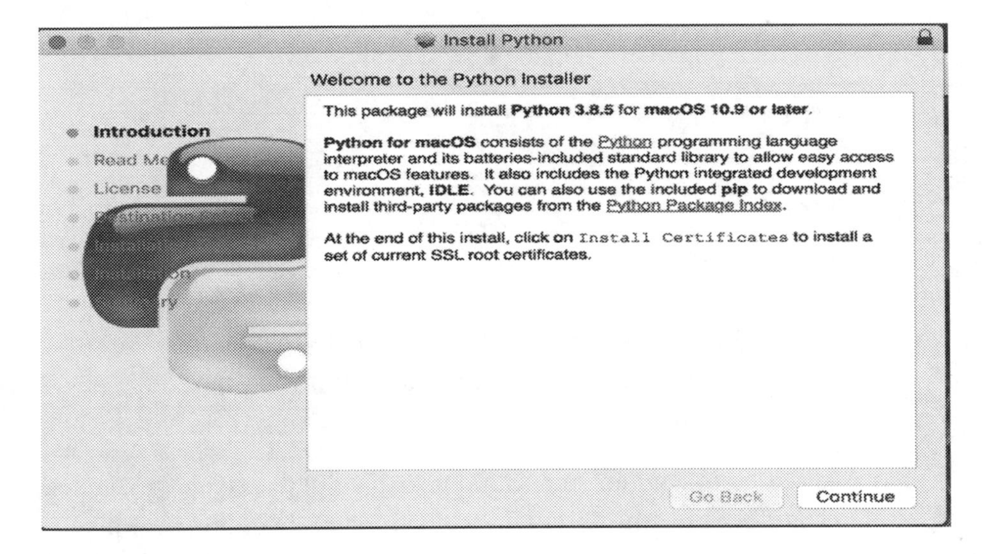

Figure 2-8. *Python Mac installation – Introduction*

2. Click **Continue**, and you will get the following page (Figure 2-9).

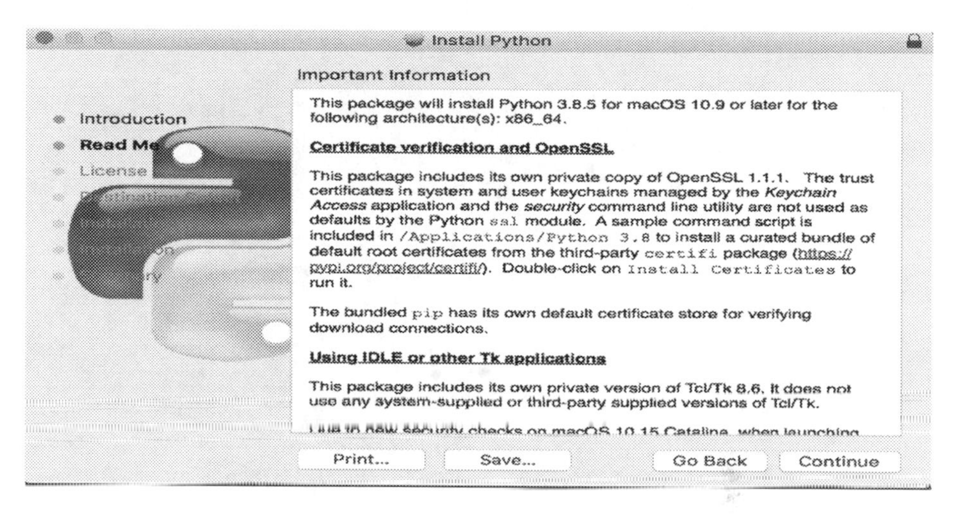

Figure 2-9. *Python Mac installation – Read Me*

3. Click **Continue** again, and you will get the following page (Figure 2-10).

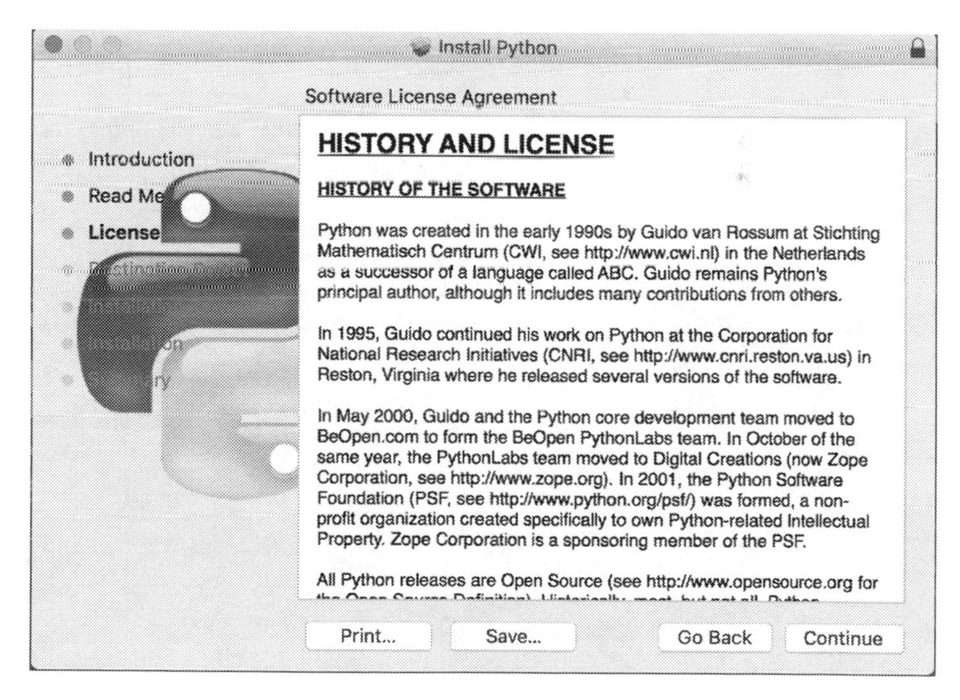

Figure 2-10. *Python Mac installation – License*

4. Click **Continue** again (Figure 2-11).

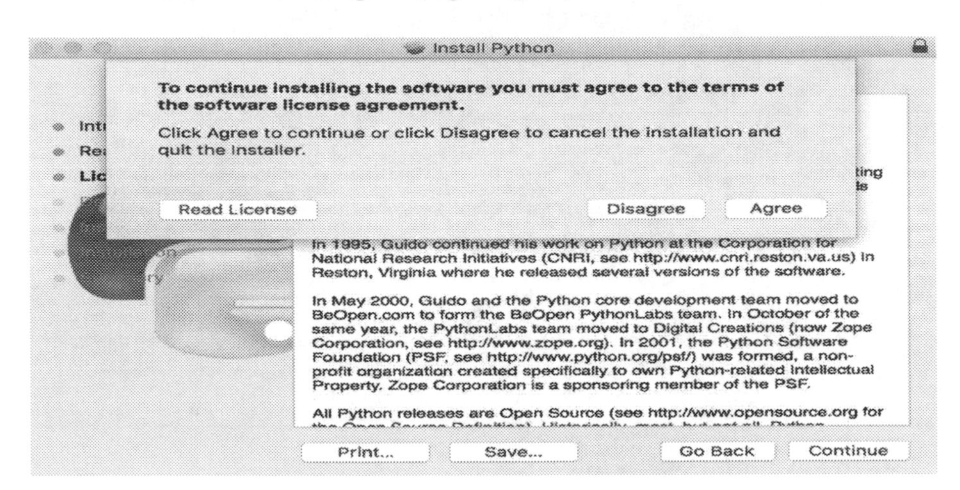

***Figure 2-11.** Python Mac installation – License agreement*

5. While you are at the license page, you might get a **popup** like the preceding one. Click **Agree**, and you will get the Installation Type page (Figure 2-12).

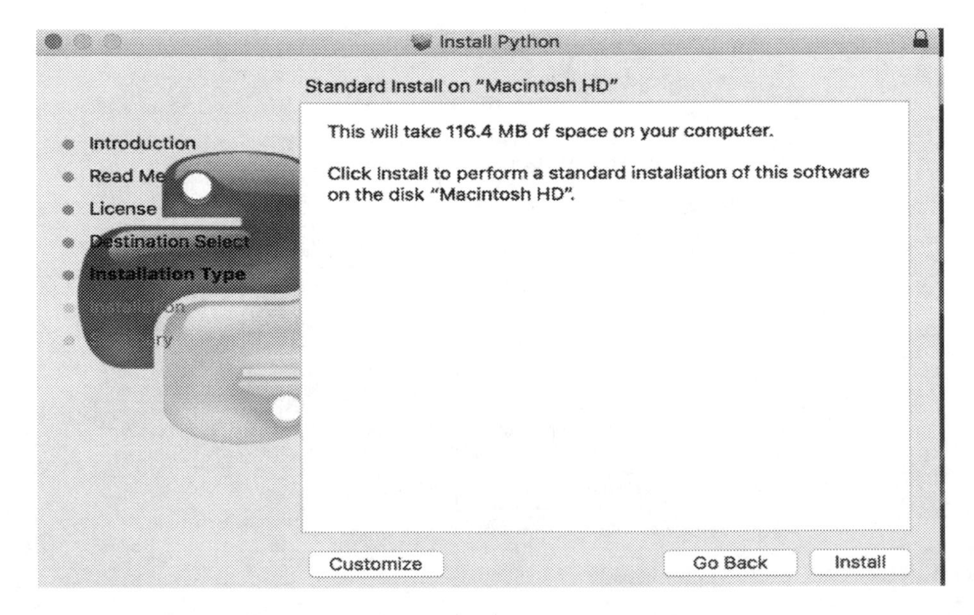

***Figure 2-12.** Python Mac installation – Installation Type*

6. We are almost there! Click the **Install button**, and your installation should start immediately. In certain cases, you might see a popup that asks for your **username and password** like the following one (Figure 2-13).

Figure 2-13. *Python Mac installation – Authentication*

7. Enter your Mac username and password and you'll be good to go. If you're using your parents' system, call them to help you with this step.

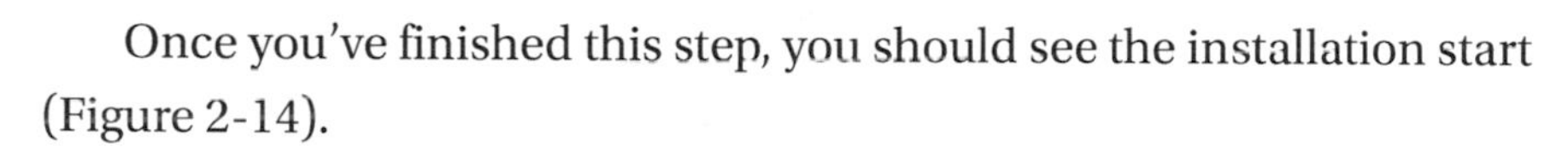

Once you've finished this step, you should see the installation start (Figure 2-14).

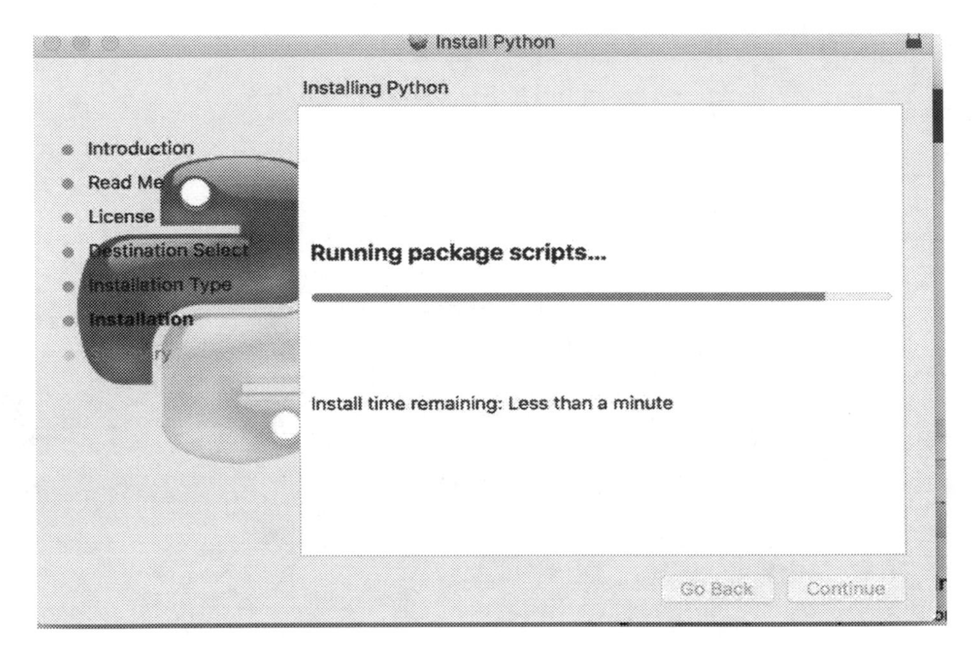

***Figure 2-14.** Python Mac installation – Installing*

8. Wait till the blue bar runs till the end. It shouldn't take more than a few minutes. Once done, your **Python package** should open up (Figure 2-15).

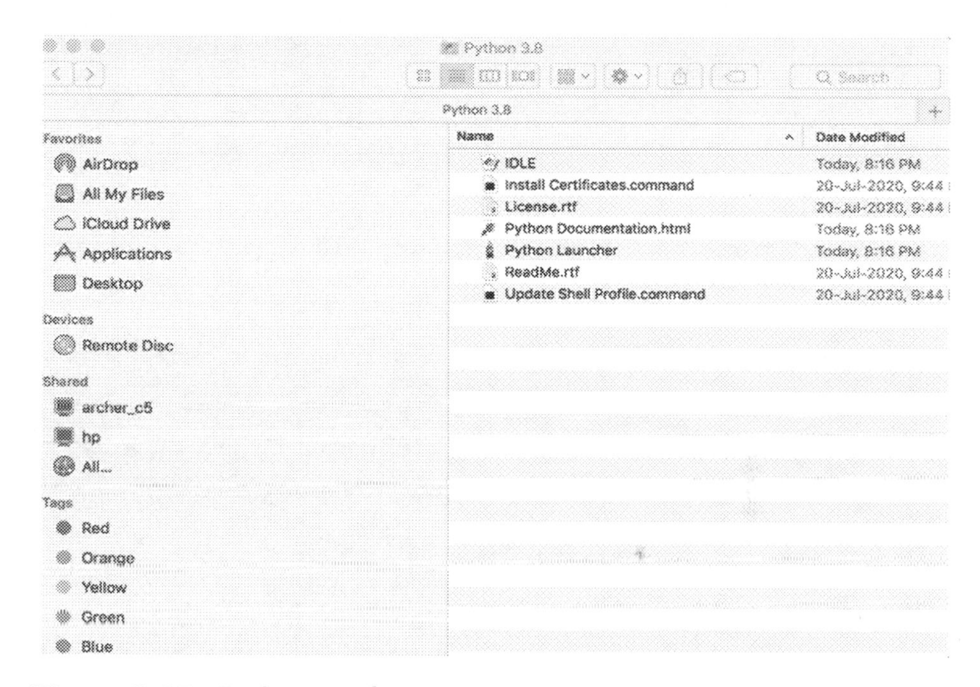

Figure 2-15. *Python package*

Congrats! You've downloaded Python! It wasn't as hard as you thought, was it? Let's have fun with it in the next section. ☺

Summary

In this chapter, we learned how to download and install Python in both Mac and Windows. In the next chapter, let us look at creating our very first program in Python.

CHAPTER 3

Your First Python Program

In this chapter, let us look at creating and running programs in Python, and create our very first Python program.

Creating and running programs in Python

Okay, now that we have installed Python, let us start creating our very first programs. We cannot just write Python programs in MS word or notepad. That is not how it works. We need a specific application that can understand the Python code you write. This application will process your code and give you the desired result.

One of the default Python applications is called **IDLE**. It is **Integrated Development and Learning Environment**, and it was developed by the Python Software Foundation. It automatically gets installed when you install Python (Figure 3-1):

1. Go to your applications (in Windows or Mac) and type IDLE (Figure 3-1).

A. Elumalai, *Introduction to Python for Kids*, https://doi.org/10.1007/978-1-4842-6812-4_3

Figure 3-1. *Python IDLE on Windows*

2. When you open the application, the Python Shell will open. This is where we will type our Python programs and get our outputs (results) (Figure 3-2).

```
Python 3.8.5 (tags/v3.8.5:580fbb0, Jul 20 2020, 15:43:08) [MSC v.1926 32 bit (Intel
)] on win32
Type "help", "copyright", "credits" or "license()" for more information.
>>>
```

Figure 3-2. *Python Shell*

3. You can change the way the text looks in this application. You can increase the font, make the text bold, and change the font style. In order to do that, **go to Options and click Configure IDLE** (Figure 3-3).

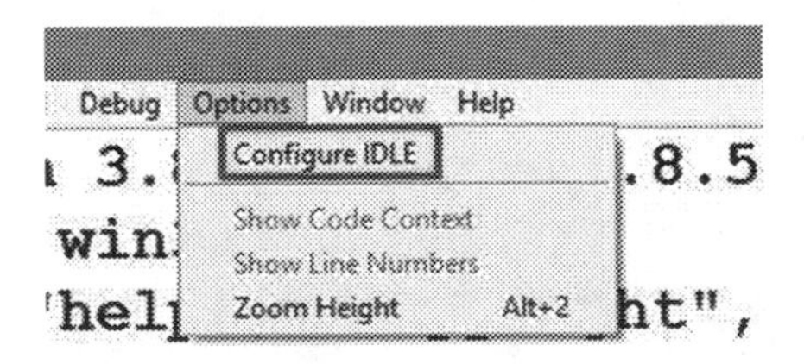

Figure 3-3. *Configure IDLE*

4. When you click it, the following window will pop up (Figure 3-4).

Figure 3-4. Python IDLE configuration window

5. Let us change the font size to 29 (look at the highlighted square) and select the checkbox across "Bold" if it is not already checked.

That is all we are going to change now, but as you can see, you have a lot more options. Play around with them to format your Python Shell's text in any way you want.

Python interactive mode (Python Shell)

There are two ways to run Python programs using IDLE. The default method is by directly typing your code into the Python Shell (Figure 3-5).

```
Python 3.8.5 (tags/v3.8.5:580fb
[MSC v.1926 32 bit (Intel)] on
Type "help", "copyright", "cred
e information.
>>> |
```

Figure 3-5. *Python Shell prompt*

Do you see the >>> the arrow is pointing to? That is called the Python Shell prompt. It is asking you to type your Python code after the prompt so it can run it and give you the result you are expecting.

Every time you type Python code in the Shell, press Enter; it will run that line of code and execute it. It is quite handy because you get immediate results.

Your Shell can do Math

That is right. You can do Math in your Python Shell. Let us try with some basic operations, shall we?

I want to prove to you that Python is not an alien language you are learning for the first time. You can do extremely complicated mathematical calculations and get results for those in the Shell as well. Want to see how that works?

Alright, let us start simple. Type the following in the prompt:

```
3 + 6
```

Press Enter and you should see the following result (Figure 3-6).

```
>>> 3 + 6
9
>>> |
```

Figure 3-6. *A simple Math problem*

Did your Python application just do Math? How cool is that? Let us try something more complicated.

```
(235 * 542) / (564 + 123)
```

Run the preceding mathematical expression and you should see the following result (Figure 3-7).

```
>>> (235 * 542) / (564 + 123)
185.40029112081513
>>>
```

Figure 3-7. *How complicated can it get?*

You could cross-verify the result with your calculator. It is correct. You can make the equation as complicated as you want, and your Shell will spit out the result in less than a second. Try a couple more and see!

But is that all you can do? Math problems? Not even close! You can even print things on your screen, and that is what we are going to look at next. But then again, it does not stop there either. You can do a host of things with Python. I do not want to overwhelm you too much from the get-go though, so we are going to take it slow, alright?

Print with Python

Python is a very easy-to-learn language. Proof? If you want to print something to the screen, just use the "print" command. A pre-defined code/command in Python or any programming language is called a syntax.

So, the syntax to print a message to the screen is as follows:

```
print('Hello there!')
```

You need to start and close parenthesis right after "print" and type your message within quotes. It could either be a single ('message') or a double quoted ("message").

When you run the preceding line of code, this is what you will get (Figure 3-8).

```
>>> print('Hello there!')
Hello there!
```

Figure 3-8. *Print a message*

But be careful here. The "p" in "print" should be a lowercase p. If you use an uppercase p, you will get an error message like in Figure 3-9.

```
>>> Print('Hello')
Traceback (most recent call last):
  File "<pyshell#2>", line 1, in <module>
    Print('Hello')
NameError: name 'Print' is not defined
```

Figure 3-9. *"Print" instead of "print"*

The error message says 'Print' is not defined. That is because as far as Python is concerned, "print" is different from "Print" and the command to print something to the screen uses a lowercase p. In other words, Python is case sensitive. So be sure to use the "commands" or "syntax" as it is.

IDLE script mode

Remember how I said that there are two ways to write programs with your IDLE? We have looked at the first method so far. It looks easy at the first glance, but did you notice a problem with it?

While using the Shell, you get outputs for every single line of code, and that will work as long as you write very simple lines of code. But once you start writing actual programs, you would want an application that processes multiple lines of code together and gives you the final result. You need the script mode to make that happen.

Let us look at how that works. Let us print the same 'Hello there!' statement, but now in script mode.

Go to **File ➤ New File** (Figure 3-10).

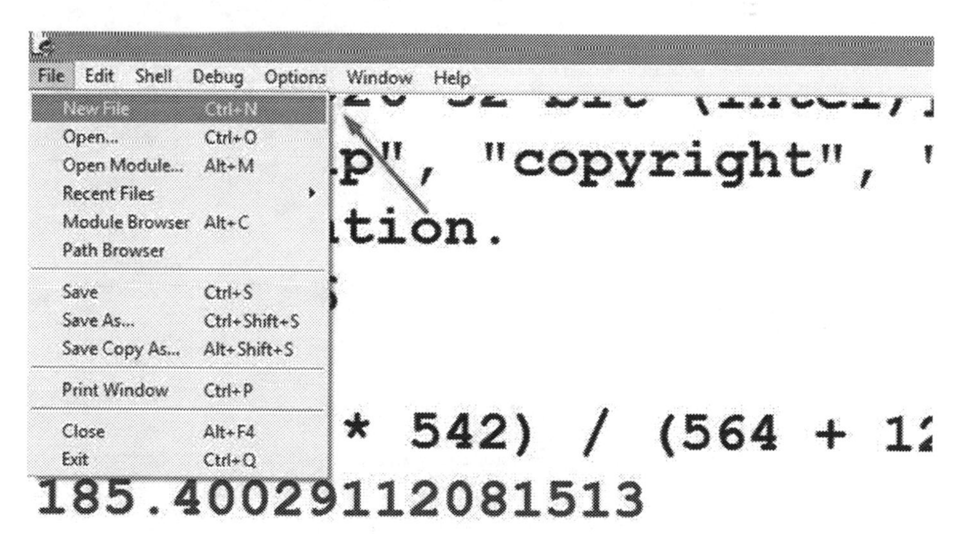

Figure 3-10. *Open a new file*

An untitled document will open like the following one (Figure 3-11).

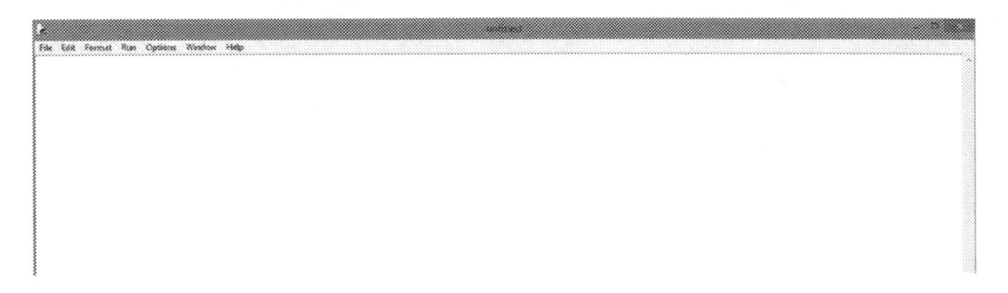

Figure 3-11. *Untitled document*

Go to **File ➤ Save As** (Figure 3-12) and save the document with the **.py extension**. .py denotes that a particular file has Python code in it and needs to be executed as such.

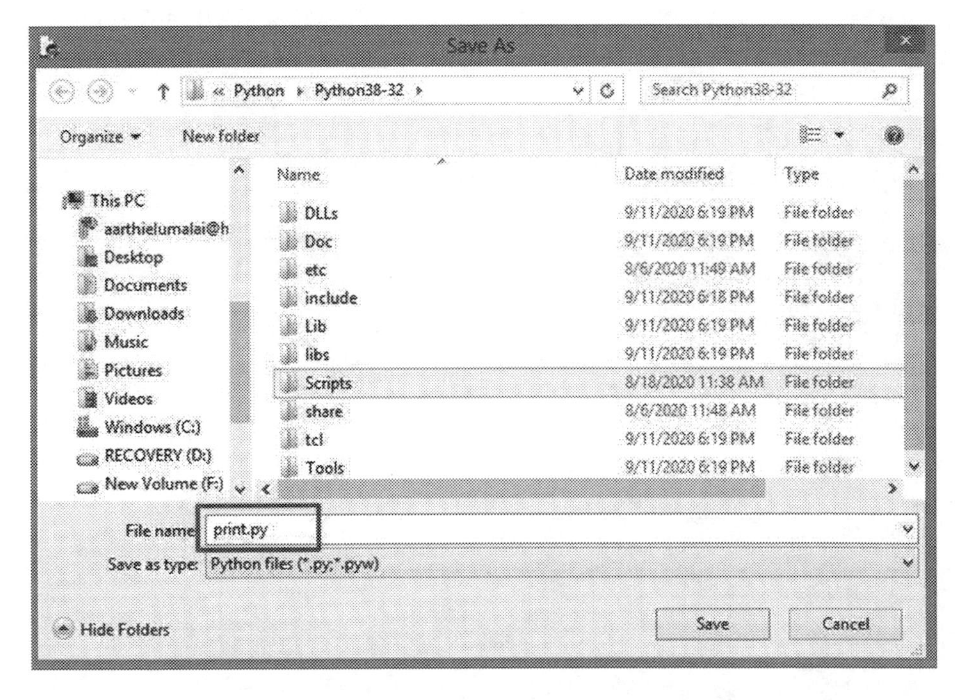

Figure 3-12. *Save your .py file*

We named our file **print.py**. Click **Save**, and you should see the name of your file change from untitled to print.py. Now, you can name your file anything you want, but just make sure that the **Save as type** is **"Python files"** or you give an extension .py or both, alright?

Now, let us type our line of code again (Figure 3-13):

```
print('Hello there!')
```

Figure 3-13. *Write your line of code*

There you go! You have written your very first Python program. Whoohoo! ☺

Let us run it, shall we?

Go to Run ➤ Run Module (Figure 3-14).

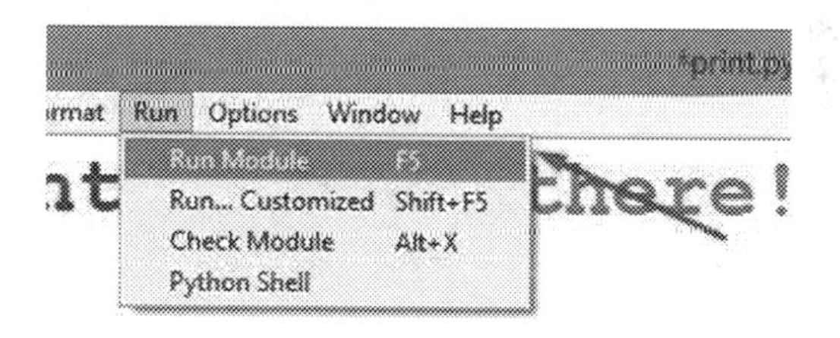

Figure 3-14. *Run the program*

It will ask you to save the code again. Click OK. Your IDLE should open the Shell window again, and in the very last prompt, you should see the result ("Hello there!") printed, like in Figure 3-15.

```
= RESTART: C:/Users/aarthi/AppData/Local/Programs/Python/P
ython38-32/print.py
Hello there!
```

Figure 3-15. *Output (result)*

Now you have run your first Python program and gotten your very first result! Whoohoo again! ☺

Python activity: Print your name (and some more)

We have come to our very first Python activity now. You are going to print your name. Actually, why don't we make it a small introduction? You are going to introduce yourself and print that introduction on the screen.

Do not worry. It is not hard to do. I will teach you how. Let us create an imaginary character and name her Susan Smith. Let us assume that she is 9 years old and she loves puppies. Now let us introduce her to the world!

Open a new file and save it as introduction.py. You know how to do that, don't you?

Now, follow along with me. Type the following into the file:

```
print('Hello there!')
print('My name is Susan Smith.')
print('I am 9 years old.')
print('I love puppies! :)')
```

We need to print out multiple lines on our screen, so we have created multiple print statements. Let us save the code we just created and run it. Go to **Run ➤ Run Module**.

```
= RESTART: C:/Users/aarthi/AppData/Local/Programs/Python/P
ython38-32/introduction.py
Hello there!
My name is Susan Smith.
I am 9 years old.
I love puppies! :)
```

Figure 3-16. *Introduction printed to the screen*

Our introduction is on the screen (Figure 3-16)!

Now, I want you to do the same with your introduction. What is your name? How old are you? What do you like? Print everything on the screen. Go ahead. It is quite easy to do.

Congrats, you are now a budding Python developer. ☺

Summary

In this chapter, we looked at IDLE and its interactive programming environment. We tried a few Math problems in the Python Shell and then created our very first print statement. Then we learned about the script mode and writing and running more than one line of code at a time. We finished the chapter with an activity where we introduced ourselves and printed the introduction to the screen over multiple lines of code.

In the next chapter, we will look at using numbers with your Python code, manipulating them, and a lot more.

CHAPTER 4

Python Loves Numbers

In the previous chapter, we learned how to get started with Python. We looked at downloading the latest version of Python for Windows, Mac, and Linux and then looked at working with IDLE to create our very first Python program.

Let us look at how to play with numbers in this chapter. We'll look at how to store numbers in something called variables and about the different types of numbers you can work with in Python.

Numbers in Python

A. Elumalai, *Introduction to Python for Kids*, https://doi.org/10.1007/978-1-4842-6812-4_4

Numbers play a *very important* role in everything, so it's no wonder that they are important in programming as well. Would you like to become a top game programmer in the future? Then you need to know your numbers. Where do you want the ball to go? How many bullets should your space gun shoot at your aliens? How fast should the bullets be? How fast should your character run, or walk, or do anything at all? You need numbers to determine all of that and a lot more.

Also, once you start programming and creating different kinds of projects, you'll notice that numbers play a big role in pretty much every kind of programming, and not just games.

So, without further ado, let's look at how to create numbers in Python, how to store them, how to use them, and so much more.

Store your numbers

We've already looked at numbers in Python, remember? Type the following in your IDLE Shell:

```
3 + 5
```

Press Enter, and you'll get the following output:

```
8
```

It's that simple to play with numbers in Python. But do you see a problem here? You can't really do much with the result or the numbers. Programming is all about automation, am I right? But there isn't much automation going on right now.

What can we do? Well, what if we can store the numbers somewhere, so we can use them multiple times? What if we store the result somewhere else, so we can use that to do further calculations? Do you see what I'm getting at here?

Unless you start storing your values, be it numbers or alphabets or words, you can't do much with programming.

Okay, that's all well and good, but how do you store them? Is there a secret container in Python that stores all the values you want in it, so you get them out to play when you need them? Not exactly, *but* you can *create* such containers. Even better, isn't it? You can create containers of information called variables that store the values you want in them. You can create unlimited number of containers like that! :O

So, how do you create these variables?

Take a look at your kitchen cabinet. You must see a container for every spice your parents use to cook and even for common cooking ingredients like salt, pepper, and sugar. Your mom probably labeled them as such, am I right?

The container labeled salt has salt, or she probably has a code word for it that she understands.

Similarly, you'll be labeling your variables as well. There are certain rules to label them, but other than that, you have free reign to label your variables in any way you want, so have fun with it. Just make sure that you would understand your labels when you read them later. You would need to know what's inside your container, won't you?

It's as simple as that to create variables. Decide on a label/name and just type it in your Shell or script, and you've created your variable.

But a variable is useless without information stored inside it, and you can do that with the "=" sign. We use the equal to sign to indicate answers in Math, don't we? Similarly, in Python, we use it to assign values to a variable. The variable is on the left-hand side of the "=" and the value is on the right-hand side.

Let me show you some examples so you understand better.

Why don't we store the numbers in our last calculation in two separate variables so we can reuse them as we want?

Let's open a new script file (you know how) and save it as numbers.py. We'll be using this file to try out the examples in this chapter.

```
num1 = 3
num2 = 5
```

I've named them num1 and num2 as short forms of number1 and number2, so I remember what they refer to when I look back at the code.

Let's test if num1 and num2 really have the numbers stored in them. Why don't we print them out and see?

```
print(num1)
print(num2)
```

When we run the preceding four lines of code, this is what we'll get:

```
= RESTART: C:/Users/aarthi/AppData/Local/Programs/Python/
Python38-32/numbers.py
3
5
```

As you can see, the variables do store the numbers. So, your program has now created two containers labeled num1 and num2, just like your mom labeled the salt and sugar containers. "num1" has the value 3 inside of it, and "num2" has the value 5 inside of it.

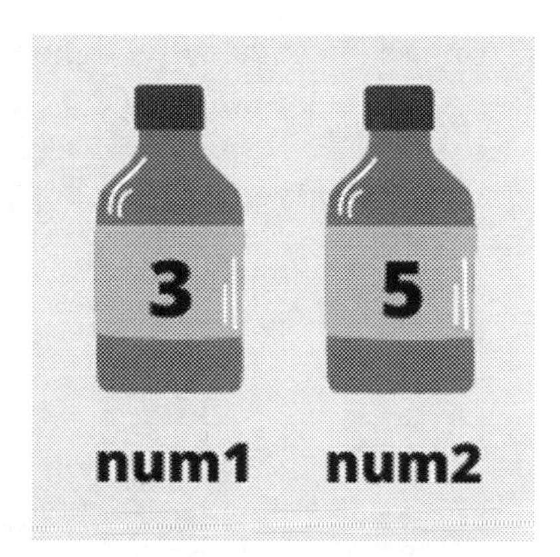

Let's take this one step further. Why don't we create another variable called sum and store the sum of the two numbers in it?

```
sum = num1 + num2
print(sum)
```

When we run numbers.py now, this is what we'll get:

```
= RESTART: C:/Users/aarthi/AppData/Local/Programs/Python/
Python38-32/numbers.py
3
5
8
```

Perfect. "sum" holds the sum of "num1" and "num2" now. Do you see how handy this is? We don't have to stop here. We can actually change the value of any of these variables! Let's try changing num1. I'm going to clear out the script file, and this is what I'm going to be left with:

```
num1 = 3
print(num1)
num1 = 6
print(num1)
```

As you can see in the preceding code, we assigned 3 to num1 first, and then we changed the value stored in num1 to 6. Let's see if that works:

```
= RESTART: C:/Users/aarthi/AppData/Local/Programs/Python/
Python38-32/numbers.py
3
6
```

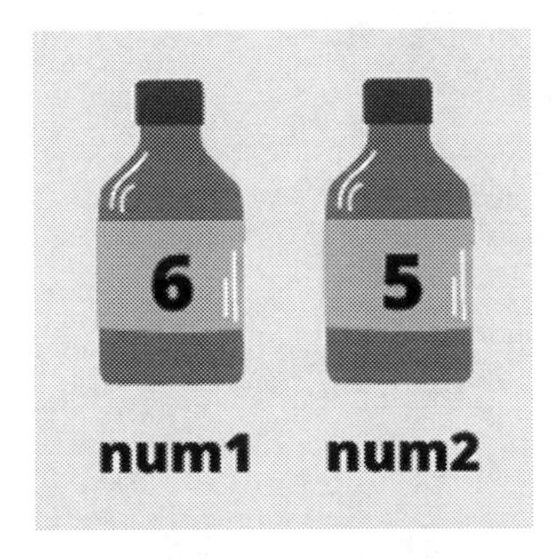

Yes, it does! "num1" originally had 3, but now it has 6 stored inside it, and if you print num2, you'll notice that value is unchanged at 5. So, we can actually change the value stored inside our variables. We have the makings of a real program in our hands now!

But don't get too excited. There are some rules to follow while creating your variables. Don't worry though, the rules are pretty tame. Make sure you follow these rules while creating your variables, or you'll end up with an error.

I'll just list them so you can refer to them later:

1. A variable should start with letters or underscore (_) and nothing else (no numbers or special characters like !, #, $, %, etc.).

2. A variable can only contain letters, numbers, and an underscore (_).

3. Variables are case sensitive. "num1" is different from "Num1".

Pretty simple, don't you think? But we're both not fans of theory, so let's test these rules out to see if they're true. Go back to your Shell prompt. Let's create a variable that follows the rules first, and then let's break them and see what happens.

```
_var5 = 1
```

When I run the preceding code, nothing happens. It looks like the preceding variable was accepted. It started with an underscore, and it only has letters and numbers in it.

What if I break the first rule?

```
1var_ = 1
```

Oops, I get an error that says the following:

```
SyntaxError: invalid syntax
```

What if my variable starts right, but doesn't follow the second rule?

```
var$s = 5
```

Error again:

```
SyntaxError: invalid syntax
```

Let's check if Rule #3 is true as well. Let's go back to our numbers.py for this one. Let's delete everything else in the file and type the following:

```
num1 = 3
Num1 = 7
print(num1)
print(Num1)
```

When you run the preceding lines of code, you should get this:

```
= RESTART: C:/Users/aarthi/AppData/Local/Programs/Python/
Python38-32/numbers.py
3
7
```

Look at that! Num1 and num1 might have the same letters and numbers in them, but the case (N and n) makes all the difference. So, Python variables are indeed case sensitive.

We've successfully verified all the rules. Whew!

Comments

What do "comments" mean in English? You comment on something? Describe something? Something along those lines, am I right?

Similarly, you can write comments on your Python code to describe them. You can write them on, before or after your lines of code. These comments are just for your reference, and Python will neither read nor execute them.

Whenever you add a "#" (hash symbol) before you type anything, that particular line becomes a client. The minute you start a new line though, you're back to your regular coding. So, your "#" creates exactly one line of comment.

```
#This is a comment
```

You can use comments to describe the lines of code, so when you read your script later, you'll understand what's happening. You could also share your code with your friends, and your comments will help them understand it.

When you use the "#" symbol, you create single-line comments. What if you want your comments to span multiple lines?

There's a syntax for that too:

```
'''
This
is
a
multi-line
comment
'''
(or)
"""
This
is
a
multi-line
comment
"""
```

Write your comment within three single/double quotes (without space) and you have yourself a multi-line comment.

Your numbers come in different forms

Now we know how variables work and how to use them to store our numbers. Before we play with them even further, I want to show you something. Did you know that there are different types of numbers in Python?

Oh yes, just like in Math, where there are whole numbers and numbers with decimal points, there are integers (whole numbers) and floating-point numbers (numbers with decimal points) in Python as well. You can even ask Python to check the type of number used in your code or convert one number type to another. Let's look at all of that now.

Integers

Whole numbers are called integers, or int for short.

Let's clear out numbers.py again and start over with the following line of code:

```
num1 = 3
```

"num1" stores an integer 3. Any numbers without decimal points are integers.

You can actually check if a number is of a particular type or not. Python has these things called built-in functions that can be used to do a lot of cool things. Since they're built-in, as in, they were already built into Python, you don't need to know how they actually work in the background. You can just use them to get the result you want.

For example, there's a built-in function called "type", with a small "t", which can be used to find the type of a number. Let's find what kind of number is stored in "num1", shall we?

```
print(type(num1))
```

In the preceding line of code, I asked Python to find the type of num1. The variable or the number, as such, should be inside of the open and close parenthesis, just like we do with the print() statement. Then, I placed the entire thing inside a print statement because I wanted to print the result. Otherwise, I wouldn't get to see what the result of the type checking was.

Let's run the preceding lines of code and see what we get:

```
= RESTART: C:/Users/aarthi/AppData/Local/Programs/Python/
Python38-32/numbers.py
<class 'int'>
```

There you go! It says 'int', which means integer.

This works for negative numbers too.

```
num1 = -3
print(type(num1))
```

The result would still be this:

```
= RESTART: C:/Users/aarthi/AppData/Local/Programs/Python/
Python38-32/numbers.py
<class 'int'>
```

So, both positive and negative whole numbers are called integers.

Let's do the same for the rest of the types now, shall we?

Floating-point numbers

Floating-point numbers have decimal points. Even if it's just one decimal point, it'll be classified as floating point.

```
num2 = 5.5
print(type(num2))
```

If you run the preceding lines of code, you'll get the following output:

```
= RESTART: C:/Users/aarthi/AppData/Local/Programs/Python/
Python38-32/numbers.py
<class 'int'>
<class 'float'>
```

Look at that. The last variable created has a floating-point number stored in it.

Again, both positive and negative decimal point numbers are called floating-point numbers in Python. Let's check!

```
num2 = -5.5
print(type(num2))
```

The result would be this:

```
= RESTART: C:/Users/aarthi/AppData/Local/Programs/Python/
Python38-32/numbers.py
<class 'float'>
```

Yes, it's a floating-point number.

Complex numbers

Now, let's look at complex numbers. Have you learned complex numbers at school? These numbers have a real and imaginary part, am I right? If you haven't learned them at school yet, but you're curious, I'd recommend reading up on them yourself. You could ask your parents to help you with this research. A simple Google search should clear your doubts. It's a very interesting mathematical concept. On the other hand, you could skip the next part. The decision is completely up to you. We wouldn't be using complex numbers much in any of our programs, so don't worry about them.

```
num3 = 2 + 3j
print(type(num3))
```

So, 2 + 3j is the complex number where 2 is the real number and 3 is the imaginary number. If we run the preceding lines of code, the final output would be this:

```
= RESTART: C:/Users/aarthi/AppData/Local/Programs/Python/
Python38-32/numbers.py
<class 'int'>
<class 'float'>
<class 'complex'>
```

There you go! The last number was a complex number. We can actually extract the real and imaginary parts separately. Do you want to see how?

If you want to extract the real number from a complex number, type the number (or the variable that contains the number), then follow that up with a period (.), and then follow that with the keyword "real". Keywords are similar to the pre-defined tools/methods in Python. They do things in the background that we don't know about but give us the desired output in the foreground. In our case, we'll be able to successfully extract the real number.

```
print(num3.real)
```

Similarly, for extracting the imaginary number, type "imag" instead of "real".

```
print(num3.imag)
```

When you run the preceding lines of code, you'll get the following output:

```
= RESTART: C:/Users/aarthi/AppData/Local/Programs/Python/
Python38-32/numbers.py
<class 'int'>
<class 'float'>
<class 'complex'>
2.0
3.0
```

Look at the last two lines in the preceding output. 2.0 is the real number and 3.0 is the imaginary number. They'll be extracted as floating-point numbers.

As I said before, you can give the numbers directly. But you need to take care of something before doing that.

```
print(3 + 4j.imag)
```

If you try to run the preceding line of code, your code will go wonky, like this:

```
= RESTART: C:/Users/aarthi/AppData/Local/Programs/Python/
Python38-32/numbers.py
<class 'int'>
<class 'float'>
<class 'complex'>
2.0
3.0
7.0
```

Python thinks your imaginary number is 7.0 and not 4.0. Why? Well, that's because Python added 3 and 4, got the result 7, and added j to it. So according to it, your complex number is now 7j and not 3 + 4j. I'll teach you all about "order of execution" in the next sections of this chapter, but for now, I want to let you know the importance of parenthesis when working with expressions.

If we wrap the complex number in a (), let's see what happens.

```
print((3 + 4j).imag)
```

Run the preceding lines of code, and get this:

```
= RESTART: C:/Users/aarthi/AppData/Local/Programs/Python/
Python38-32/numbers.py
<class 'int'>
<class 'float'>
<class 'complex'>
2.0
3.0
4.0
```

Great! We got the result we were looking for. So, parentheses preserve the expression as it is.

Type conversion between numbers

You can convert from one number type to another. We will be using more pre-defined functions (methods) to do that.

To convert a floating-point or complex number to an integer, use the int() method. Let's clear out our numbers.py file and start afresh. Alternatively, you could just create and name a new script file whenever we are starting anew, especially if you'd like every example saved.

```
num1 = 3.0
print(num1)
print(int(num1))
```

In the preceding example, I've stored a floating-point number 3.0 in the variable "num1". I've printed the exact number first. Then, I've used the int() function to convert "num1" to an integer and printed that too. Let's look at the result:

```
= RESTART: C:/Users/aarthi/AppData/Local/Programs/Python/
Python38-32/numbers.py
3.0
3
```

Look at that. The decimal point is gone now. But what if we had numbers in the decimal place? What happens then?

Let's edit the value of num1 to 3.45 and test again.

```
num1 = 3.45
print(num1)
#convert the number to an integer
print(int(num1))
```

Run the preceding lines of code, and you'll get this:

```
= RESTART: C:/Users/aarthi/AppData/Local/Programs/Python/
Python38-32/numbers.py
3.45
3
```

Interesting. We're still getting 3, even though the number is close to 3.5 with the decimals added in. Why is that? That's because Python is doing something called rounding off. Regardless of what the decimal point is, when you do integer conversion, it is just going to remove the decimal point and retain the whole number. Let's try with 3.9 and see if that's true:

```
num1 = 3.9
print(num1)
print(int(num1))
```

Run the above lines of code, and get:

```
= RESTART: C:/Users/aarthi/AppData/Local/Programs/Python/
Python38-32/numbers.py
3.9
3
```

We still didn't get 4. ☹ When you do an integer conversion, it just removes the decimal points, no matter how big they are. Don't worry. You'll learn how to do proper rounding off based on what the decimal points have when we look at more built-in Math functions in Python.

Now, let's convert a complex number to int.

```
num1 = 3+4j
print(num1)
print(int(num1))
```

When we run the preceding lines of code, we get the following:

```
= RESTART: C:/Users/aarthi/AppData/Local/Programs/Python/
Python38-32/numbers.py
(3+4j)
Traceback (most recent call last):
  File "C:/Users/aarthi/AppData/Local/Programs/Python/
  Python38-32/numbers.py", line 3, in <module>
    print(int(num1))
TypeError: can't convert complex to int
```

Oh my, we got an error! Why is that? Well, theoretically, it isn't possible to convert a complex number into an integer because, well, which part would you extract?

But, if you were to extract the real or imaginary part, you can convert *that* into an integer. Let's try that.

I'm going to save the real number I extract in another variable called "r" first.

```
num1 = 3+4j
#Find the real part of the number
r = num1.real
print(r)
print(int(r))
```

In the preceding lines of code, I extracted the real number, assigned it to a variable "r", and then converted it to an integer. When we run the preceding lines of code, we'll get the following:

```
= RESTART: C:/Users/aarthi/AppData/Local/Programs/Python/
Python38-32/numbers.py
3.0
3
```

Let's convert an integer to a floating-point number next. We need to use the float() built-in method.

```
num1 = 3
print(num1)
print(float(num1))
```

When you run the preceding lines of code, you'll get this:

```
= RESTART: C:/Users/aarthi/AppData/Local/Programs/Python/
Python38-32/numbers.py
3
3.0
```

Successfully converted!

Would this work with complex numbers? What do you think? Nah, they wouldn't. We'll have to extract the real or imaginary numbers again, but the extractions produce floating-point numbers already, so why would you want to convert them?

Now let's convert both integers and floating-point numbers to complex numbers. You'll have to use the complex() function to do that.

```
num1 = 3
print(num1)
print(complex(num1))
```

Run the preceding lines of code, and you'll get this:

```
= RESTART: C:/Users/aarthi/AppData/Local/Programs/Python/
Python38-32/numbers.py
3
(3+0j)
```

Look at that! It took the whole number as the real part of the complex number and the imaginary part is a 0.

Now let's try with floating-point numbers.

```
num1 = 3.5
print(num1)
print(complex(num1))
```

Run the preceding lines of code, and you'll get this:

```
= RESTART: C:/Users/aarthi/AppData/Local/Programs/Python/
Python38-32/numbers.py
3.5
(3.5+0j)
```

It took the entire floating-point number as the real part of the complex number and the imaginary part is still 0. Interesting!

Mini project – Do you understand numbers?

More than a mini project, this is going to be an activity that's going to test your understanding of the topic at hand. Do you understand numbers in Python? Let's see!

Let me describe the problem statement first. I want you to try it out before you look at my explanation. We're still taking baby steps, so I've made sure that this activity isn't too tough.

Problem statement: Create three variables (num1, num2, and num3) and store the numbers 3, 5.5, and 3 + 5j in them, respectively. Then, convert num1 into a floating-point number and num2 into an integer. Extract the imaginary number of num3 and replace that in num3 and convert that into an integer too. Display the three converted numbers on screen. Describe the important lines of code with comments.

Solution:

It's a pretty simple problem, isn't it? Don't worry, you'll see more complex, yet fun ones once we cover more topics to play with. ☺

Here is the entire program:

```
#Created num1, num2 and num3 and stored the respective values
num1 = 3
num2 = 5.5
num3 = 3 + 5j
#convert num1 into a floating point number
num1 = float(num1)
#convert num2 into an integer
num2 = int(num2)
#Extract the imaginary part of num3 and place it back in num3
num3 = num3.imag
#Convert the imaginary number (floating) into an integer
num3 = int(num3)
#Print everything
print(num1)
print(num2)
print(num3)
```

I've described everything I did in comments, just like the problem asks. The code and the comments are self-explanatory, so I'm sure you understand them. Why don't you try different combinations and conversions to get a better understanding of the topic?

Summary

In this chapter, I gave you an introduction into numbers and how they are used in Python. We looked at storing numbers using variables and the different types of numbers Python lets you create and manipulate.

CHAPTER 5

Let's Play with Our Numbers!

In the previous chapter, I gave you a brief introduction to using numbers in Python, creating, and storing them and the different types of numbers you can play around with.

Let us look at how to play with those numbers in this chapter by looking at how to use your numbers to do calculations and how to have real fun with Python's pre-defined number methods.

Get your numbers out to play

We've looked at creating numbers and storing them and the different types of numbers in Python. But we haven't done anything with them yet, have we?

A. Elumalai, *Introduction to Python for Kids*, https://doi.org/10.1007/978-1-4842-6812-4_5

Would you like to finally play with your numbers? Yes!

You can do pretty much everything you do in Math in Python as well. You can add two numbers or more, multiply numbers, divide them, subtract them, and it doesn't stop there! You can do a little bit more than the usual calculations. What fun is programming if you're stuck doing the same old calculations?

You have operators that can find the remainder of a division. Yes, you read that right. You won't have to find remainders using a long-drawn-out process anymore. I bet your calculator doesn't do that!

You can do exponentiation as well. Want to find the result of 5 * 5 * 5? That is 5 to the power of 3. Python has a single operator you can use to do that. What more? Make the number and power as big as you want, and you'll still get your result immediately.

Basic Math operations

Without further ado, let's look at all the operations you can play around with in Python. I'll be explaining how the operators work with examples for each. Clear out your numbers.py file or create a new script file.

Let's look at addition first. You need to use the "+" symbol to add two numbers. If you want to add three numbers, use "+" twice. It's just like how you add at your Math class.

```
num1 = 5
num2 = 7
add = num1 + num2
print(add)
```

When you run the preceding lines of code, you'll get this:

```
= RESTART: C:\Users\aarthi\AppData\Local\Programs\Python\
Python38-32\numbers.py
12
```

The answer is correct! Let's make things more complicated, shall we?

```
num1 = 55.876
num2 = 100.54
#Add num1 and num2
add = num1 + num2
num3 = 1235.583
#Add the value in num3 to the current value in add
add = add + num3
print(add)
```

We created two numbers, "num1" and "num2", added them, and stored the result in the variable "add". Then, we created another variable "num3" and stored another number in it. We added the current value of "add" with "num3" and stored it back in "add" and printed the final value of "add". Let's see what we get:

```
= RESTART: C:\Users\aarthi\AppData\Local\Programs\Python\
Python38-32\numbers.py
1391.999
```

Cross-verify with your calculator. I'm sure that's the correct answer. As you can see, you can add more than one number. You can also change the value of your variable by doing calculations with its current value and re-storing (it's called re-assigning in programming) it back to that variable.

We've learned addition in Python. The same rules apply for subtraction, multiplication, and division. Let's quickly look at them.

You need to use the "-" symbol for subtraction, "/" for division, and "*" for multiplication. Unlike Math, using "*x*" or "*X*" for multiplication won't work with programming languages.

```
num1 = 20
num2 = 10
#Addition
add = num1 + num2
```

```
print(add)
#Subtraction
sub = num1 - num2
print(sub)
#Multiplication
mul = num1 * num2
print(mul)
#Division
div = num1 / num2
print(div)
```

When your run the preceding lines of code, you'll get this:

```
= RESTART: C:\Users\aarthi\AppData\Local\Programs\Python\
Python38-32\numbers.py
30
10
200
2.0
```

Did you notice something? Every other operation (addition, subtraction, and multiplication) produced an integer as the output, but the result of division was a floating-point number. Take a note of this. Division always produces decimal numbers in Python. If there are no decimal points, it'll just end the result with a "*.0*", but it'll still be a decimal (floating) number.

Special Math operations in Python

We've looked at the common operators. Let's look at the special ones now.

You need to use the multiplication operator twice to do exponentiation. "**" is the operator you're looking for.

So, instead of typing *2 * 2 * 2 * 2*, which means 2 to the power of 4 (2 multiplied by itself four times), you can just type *2 ** 4* and you'd get the same result. If you had to multiply 2 by itself 20 times, just type *2 ** 20*. You'd have saved a lot of time and space with this operator.

Let's look at some examples.

```
exp = 2 ** 4
print(exp)
exp = 2 ** 20
print(exp)
exp = 5.5 ** 3
print(exp)
exp = 5.5 ** 3.5
print(exp)
```

As you can see in the preceding code, exponentiation works with floating-point numbers too. You can have floating-point numbers for both the number and the exponent (the power). Let's look at the result to see if it works, shall we?

```
= RESTART: C:\Users\aarthi\AppData\Local\Programs\Python\
Python38-32\numbers.py
16
1048576
16.5
19.25
```

Yes, it works!

Now, let's find our remainders. Use the modulus operator "%" instead of the division operator "/", and you'll get the remainder of the operation. Remember what happens when you divide a number by another number? You get a quotient and a remainder, am I right? Your modulus operator will do the same, but it'll just return the remainder and not the quotient. If you want to find the quotient of the same operation, use the division operator with the same numbers.

```
#Division
div = 5 / 2
print(div)
#Remainder
r = 5 % 2
print(r)
```

When you run the preceding code, you'll get this:

```
= RESTART: C:\Users\aarthi\AppData\Local\Programs\Python\
Python38-32\numbers.py
2.5
1
```

Did you see what happened? You got the floating-point value of the division as your first result and the remainder of *5 / 2* as your second result.

But what if you just need the quotient and not the complete result with the decimal point? You have an option for that as well!

It's called the floor division operator. Write it with two forward slashes, like this: "//".

It'll divide your numbers and return just the whole number, leaving out the decimal point. Let's try the same with simple and complex examples.

```
floor = 5 // 2
print(floor)
```

When you run the preceding code, you'll get this:

```
= RESTART: C:\Users\aarthi\AppData\Local\Programs\Python\
Python38-32\numbers.py
2
```

Look at that. We just got 2 and not 2.5. 2 is the quotient of the operation 5 / 2. So, if you want the quotient and remainder separately, use the floor division to get the quotient of the operation and the modulus to get the remainder.

Let's look at a more complex example to test if this really works:

```
#Division
div = 100 / 15
print(div)
#Quotient
q = 100 // 15
print(q)
#Remainder
r = 100 % 15
print(r)
```

When you run the preceding code, you'll get this:

```
= RESTART: C:\Users\aarthi\AppData\Local\Programs\Python\
Python38-32\numbers.py
6.666666666666667
6
10
```

When you multiply 15 by 6, you'll get 90. So, the quotient of 100 / 15 is 6 and the remainder is 10. We got the correct answer. It works! ☺

Assignment operations

Python has something called assignment operations to make things easy for us. We've looked at one of them already. Remember the equal to, "=", operator? You can use that operator to assign values to a variable.

Let's quickly look at the rest. They are quite easy to understand.

There is the += operator.

a += 5 basically means *a = a + 5*. So, if you'd like to add a value to a variable and re-assign it back to the same variable, use this operator.

Similarly, you have -=, *=, /=, **=, %=, and //=.

Let's look at examples of all of that now. Read the comments in the following lines of code to understand what each line of code does:

```
num = 5
#Add and re-assign 5
num += 5
#Ans -> 10
print(num)
#Subtract 5 from num
num -= 5
#Ans -> 5
print(num)
#Multiply the current value of num with 2
num *= 2
#Ans -> 10
print(num)
#Divide the value of num by 2
num /= 2
#Ans -> 5.0
print(num)
#Calculate num to the power 2 and re-assign it
num **= 2
#Ans -> 25.0
print(num)
#Find the quotient of num / 3
num //= 3
#Ans -> 8.0
print(num)
#Find the remainder of num / 3
num %= 3
#Ans -> 2.0
print(num)
```

When you run the preceding lines of code, you'll get the following:

```
= RESTART: C:\Users\aarthi\AppData\Local\Programs\Python\
Python38-32\numbers.py
10
5
10
5.0
25.0
8.0
2.0
```

Did you see something weird in the preceding operations? We started with integers, but the minute we performed a division operation, the rest of the results continued to be in floating point, regardless of the operation. We know why we got a floating point in the division operation. Division always results in a floating-point number. But why did it continue to be the case for the rest of the operations?

That's because performing operations on a floating-point number will always result in a floating-point number, even if the other number is an integer.

What comes first?

Python, and any programming really, has something called precedence when it comes to order of executing mathematical operations. You must have learned about this in your math class too.

Remember the BODMAS rule? It basically says that anything within the brackets executes first and then comes the division, then multiplication, then addition, and finally subtraction.

Python does not have the exact rule, but it has something similar.

The rules of precedence in Python are as follows:

- Order of execution happens from left to right.
- Brackets hold the highest precedence.
- Then comes the exponentiation operator **.
- Then your multiplication (*), division (/), floor division (//), and modulus (%) operators. They hold the same level of precedence.
- Finally, you have your addition (+) and subtraction (-) operators, which hold the same level of precedence as well.

Why don't we put the rules to test?

Let's take the following expression: 2 + 3 * 5.

Let's run the preceding expression in our Python Shell and see what we get:

```
>>> 2 + 3 * 5
17
```

Why is it 17? Since order of execution happens from left to right, shouldn't 2 + 3 be executed first to result in 5, and shouldn't the result (5) have been multiplied with 5 to result in 25 and not 17?

That's where the precedence comes in. Even though order of execution is left to right, the operation with the higher precedence (in this case, multiplication) will be executed first, and *then* the result will be added to the first number (in our example).

But what happens if there's a bracket?

```
>>> (2 + 3) * 5
25
```

Now we get a 25 because even though addition has lower precedence to multiplication, brackets hold the highest precedence, so they get executed first.

What if there are two brackets?

```
>>> (2 + 3) * 5 * (1 + 2)
75
```

The preceding expression was done like this: (5) * 5 * (1 + 2) = 5 * 5 * 3 = 75.

When two operations hold the same precedence, the left to right rule is followed. Now that you know how precedence works in numbers, why don't you write down different expressions and guess how they'd be executed in Python? Then you can execute them to verify your results.

Cool stuff with numbers

Python is a well that keeps on giving. You can do pretty much anything you want with numbers and manipulate them in any way you want. How? There's a cool little tool called the Math module. Do you remember me telling you about Python add-ons that let you do cool stuff? This is one of them.

With this module, you can do pretty much everything you want with Python. You can find the power of a number, its square root, floor, ceiling, and so much more. Let's look at some of the most important ones in this section. If you'd like to know more, a quick Google search will give you a list of all the operations you can do with the Math module. You have a bunch of pre-defined methods/functions that'll help you achieve these things.

Let's get started!

You can find the floor and ceiling numbers of decimal numbers. What is that? You can round off decimal numbers to their integer counterparts. But if you use the floor function, it'll round the number to the lowest integer.

Open a new script file or clear out the one you've been using.

Before you use any of the pre-defined methods in the Math module, you need to import it into your script file first. You need to use the "import" keyword to do that.

```
import math
```

The preceding line of code basically tells our program that we're importing the Math module to our file. Did you notice how we've written "math" with a small "m"? Make sure you do that. If you wrote it as "Math", you'd get an error since Python is case sensitive. This applies for any pre-defined function or keyword you use in Python. You need to use them with no change to their spelling or case.

Floor and ceiling of a number

Okay, now that we've imported our Math module, let's do our operations. The syntax to find the floor of a number is `math.floor(num)` where "num" is either the variable that holds the floating-point number or the number itself. The same goes for ceil.

```
import math
print(math.floor(5.6))
print(math.floor(5.3))
print(math.floor(5))
print(math.ceil(5.6))
print(math.ceil(5.3))
print(math.ceil(5))
```

When you run the preceding lines of code, you'll get the following:

```
RESTART: C:\Users\aarthi\AppData\Local\Programs\Python\
Python38-32\numbers.py
5
5
5
6
6
5
```

Look at that! Regardless of what the decimal point is, a floor operation will always result in the lowest integer, which is 5 in this case, and a ceil operation will always result in the highest integer, which is 6. Floor or ceil operations on integers have no effect on the number, and you'll get the same number as the result.

Power and square root

Next, let's look at powers. Remember how we used the "**" operator to find the power of a number? We have a Math operation that does something like that too.

Its syntax is `math.pow(num,power)`.

So, if you'd like to find the value of 5 to the power of 3 (5 * 5 * 5), then you'd do it like this:

```
import math
print(math.pow(5,3))
```

When you run the preceding code, you'll get this:

```
= RESTART: C:\Users\aarthi\AppData\Local\Programs\Python\
Python38-32\numbers.py
125.0
```

The result is a floating-point number. Try working with decimal points and see what you get.

On the same vein, you can find the square root of numbers with the sqrt method. If 5 * 5 is 25, then the square root of 25 is 5. Let's test!

```
import math
print(math.sqrt(25))
```

Run the preceding code, and you'll get this:

```
= RESTART: C:\Users\aarthi\AppData\Local\Programs\Python\
Python38-32\numbers.py
5.0
```

The result is a floating-point number again.

Factorial of a number

Do you know how to find the factorial of a number?

The factorial of 3 is `3 * 2 * 1`, which is 6.

The factorial of 5 is `5 * 4 * 3 * 2 * 1`, which is 120.

Are you seeing the pattern here? You wouldn't have to laboriously calculate factorials anymore though. Python does that for you with the factorial method!

```
import math
print(math.factorial(5))
```

Run the preceding code and you'll get this:

```
= RESTART: C:\Users\aarthi\AppData\Local\Programs\Python\
Python38-32\numbers.py
120
```

Yes, it works!

Sin, cos, tan, and more

If you know how sin, cos, tan, and log work, then you'll find the next part interesting. If you don't know these concepts, don't worry. You can come back to this section once you've learned these concepts in your Math class.

You can find the sin, cos, tan, and log of numbers with the relevant pre-defined methods. Before we start, I want to clarify something. The values/variables we give inside of the brackets () in any pre-defined method are called as ***arguments***, and I'd be referring to them as such.

```
import math
print(math.sin(2))
print(math.cos(5))
```

```
print(math.tan(2))
print(math.log(10,2)) #The first argument is the number and the
second is the base
```

Run the preceding code and you'll get this:

```
= RESTART: C:\Users\aarthi\AppData\Local\Programs\Python\
Python38-32\numbers.py
0.9092974268256817
0.28366218546322625
-2.185039863261519
3.3219280948873626
```

You can verify the results with your scientific calculator, and you'll find that the results are the same.

These are just some of the operations you can do with the Math module. There is at least a dozen more.

Check them out in the official Python documentation and play around with them, if you'd like: `https://docs.python.org/3/library/math.html`.

More numerical operations

Your fun with Math isn't just isolated to the Math module. There are a bunch of stand-alone functions that do cool stuff as well. You won't have to import the Math module to do these operations, but they're just as powerful.

Would you like to find the minimum number among a list of numbers? Then use the "min" method, and give every number you want compared as the argument for that method, separated by commas. The same goes for "max".

```
import math
print(min(-100,100,40,25.64,200.3452,-253))
print(max(-100,100,40,25.64,200.3452,-253))
```

I've given the same list of numbers for both min and max. Let's look at the result:

```
= RESTART: C:\Users\aarthi\AppData\Local\Programs\Python\
Python38-32\numbers.py
-253
200.3452
```

It works! -253 is the minimum number and 200.3452 is the maximum.

If you want to convert a negative number to a positive number in an operation, then use the "abs" method.

```
print(abs(-100))
```

The preceding code will result in this:

```
= RESTART: C:\Users\aarthi\AppData\Local\Programs\Python\
Python38-32\numbers.py
100
```

Working with random numbers

What if you didn't want to come up with a number to use in your calculations? What if you wanted your computer to choose your number for you? Well, Python has got you covered.

Python has yet another module called the "random" module which comes with a bunch of cool functions that'll help your computer choose a random number every time it's run.

Let's look at that now. You need to import the random module first. It's "random" with a small "r".

If you'd like a random number returned between the range you gave, use the randrange() function.

```
import random
print(random.randrange(1,11))
```

"random" is the name of the module, and "randrange" is the name of the function. I've given 11 in the second argument because the random module ignores the last number in the range. So, if I gave 10, then I'll only get random numbers from 1 to 9. Since I wanted to include 10, I gave 11 as my second argument.

Run the preceding code, and you'll get this:

```
= RESTART: C:\Users\aarthi\AppData\Local\Programs\Python\
Python38-32\numbers.py
10
```

When I ran it again, I got this:

```
= RESTART: C:\Users\aarthi\AppData\Local\Programs\Python\
Python38-32\numbers.py
2
```

The next time:

```
= RESTART: C:\Users\aarthi\AppData\Local\Programs\Python\
Python38-32\numbers.py
7
```

When you run the same lines of code multiple times, you'll get different results than mine. Why don't you try out and see for yourself? ☺

We've just scratched the surface of the random module. There's more where that came from. For example, you can ask your program to choose a letter from a word or phrase you specify, with the "choice" method.

```
import random
print(random.choice("Hello there!"))
```

Print the preceding code, and you'll notice that you get one of the letters (including the exclamation point and space), every time you run the program.

You can choose among a list of numbers as well. We'll look at lists in detail in one of the later chapters, but for now, just understand that a list holds a list of a data, and in our examples, a list of numbers, and you should write the numbers within square brackets, separated by commas, like this:

```
import random
l = [1,3,5,7,9]
```

Let's make our program randomly choose from this list now:

```
print(random.choice(l))
```

Run the preceding code; for the first run, I got this:

```
= RESTART: C:\Users\aarthi\AppData\Local\Programs\Python\
Python38-32\numbers.py
3
```

Subsequent runs will give me random selections. Try and see! ☺

There is the "random" method of the "random" module which returns a random floating-point number between 0 and 1.

```
import random
print(random.random())
```

When I ran the preceding code, I got this:

```
= RESTART: C:\Users\aarthi\AppData\Local\Programs\Python\
Python38-32\numbers.py
0.6386828169729072
```

Since randrange only returns integers within a range, I can use uniform to return floating-point numbers within a range. The only difference here is that this function considers both numbers of the range in its results.

```
import random
print(random.uniform(1,10))
```

When I ran the preceding code, I got this:

```
= RESTART: C:\Users\aarthi\AppData\Local\Programs\Python\
Python38-32\numbers.py
3.7563014275306283
```

Mini project – multiples of a number

In this mini project, I'll teach you how to find the multiples of a number with a number method. So, if I want all the multiples of 3 until 100 displayed, for example, then this is what I'd do:

There's yet another pre-defined method in Python called the "range" method. We'd usually only learn about this method when we learn about loops (in a later chapter), but I wanted to introduce it here, since technically, it *is* a number method.

The range function, as the name implies, produces a range. You need to write it as range(num), where everything is written in small letters:

1. Let's print the following line of code in the Python Shell:

   ```
   >>> print(range(5))
   ```

   Run the preceding code, and you'll get this:

   ```
   range(0, 5)
   ```

2. Alternatively, you can give the starting and ending numbers in a range as well, like this:

```
>>> print(range(1,10))
```

Run the preceding code, and you'll get this:

```
range(1, 10)
```

3. Also, you can print the entire range using the "*" operator. No, don't confuse it with the multiplication operator. This operator is used to print when something (in our case, the range) has more than one object (in our case, more than one number).

Let's open our script and do the following:

```
r = range(1,10)
```

Now, the variable "r" contains the range. To print everything inside "r", which is the list of numbers from 1 to 10, use "*", like this:

```
print(*r)
```

4. Specify "*" before the variable so Python knows that you're trying to print everything inside whatever is coming next. Alternatively, you can also write the same print statement like this:

```
print(*range(1,10))
```

Run either of those statements, and you'll get this:

```
= RESTART: C:\Users\aarthi\AppData\Local\Programs\
Python\Python38-32\numbers.py
1 2 3 4 5 6 7 8 9
```

Yup, it works!

5. If I ran this:

   ```
   print(*range(10))
   ```

   I'll get this:

   ```
   = RESTART: C:\Users\aarthi\AppData\Local\Programs\
   Python\Python38-32\numbers.py
   0 1 2 3 4 5 6 7 8 9
   ```

   As you can see, if you don't give a starting range, then it prints from 0 to the number *before* the ending range.

6. You can also skip numbers between ranges by using a third argument. If you give 2 as the third parameter, your program will print every 2nd number in the range. 3 as your 3rd parameter will print every 3rd number, 4 will print every 4th number, and so on.

   ```
   print(*range(0,10,2))
   ```

   When you run the preceding code, you'll get this:

   ```
   = RESTART: C:\Users\aarthi\AppData\Local\Programs\
   Python\Python38-32\numbers.py
   0 2 4 6 8
   ```

   You've printed out only the even numbers between 0 and 10. How great is that? You can skip any numbers you want with the third parameter.

   Now that we know all of this, can you guess how we can apply this to solve our problem? So, we need to find the multiples of the given number within the given range, and we know that we're going to use the range() function to do that.

7. Let's say we want to find the multiples of 3 from 1 to 100 and print them all out. So, that's 3, 6, 9 until 99, am I right? You can do that in a single line of code. Would you like to try it yourself before you check the solution?

Tried? Okay, let's look at the solution now!

```
print(*range(3,101,3))
```

Run the preceding code, and you'll get this:

```
= RESTART: C:\Users\aarthi\AppData\Local\Programs\Python\
Python38-32\numbers.py
3 6 9 12 15 18 21 24 27 30 33 36 39 42 45 48 51 54 57 60 63 66
69 72 75 78 81 84 87 90 93 96 99
```

Whoa! Quite simple, wasn't it?

We just gave the multiple as the first argument since it's anyway going to be the first result – 3 * 1 = 3. Then we specified 101 as the second argument, so 100 would be included if it were a multiple. Finally, we gave 3 as the third argument again because we need to skip three numbers every time. And it worked! ☺

Now, why don't you try with different multiples and ranges and see how it works out for you?

Summary

In this chapter, we continued to look at numbers. We looked at how to use different operators available in Python to manipulate our numbers. We also looked at using the "Math" module and pre-defined functions to further play with our numbers. We finally looked at the "random" module, and we finished the chapter with a mini project as usual.

In the next chapter, let's look at a very interesting concept in Python. We'll be looking at using the *Turtle* module to draw graphics.

CHAPTER 6

Drawing Cool Stuff with *Turtle*

In the previous chapters, we learned how to play with numbers in Python. We looked at the different types of numbers in Python, the various operations you can do, and using various modules and pre-defined methods to have fun with Python!

In this chapter, we're going to look at yet another module in Python, the *Turtle* module. We're going to learn all about *Turtle*, using it to draw graphics, shapes, deigns, text, and so much more. We're going to end the chapter with a bunch of cool mini projects as well.

Let's get started

Are you starting to get bored? Let's take a break from theory, shall we? I promised you fun, and now it's time I delivered on that promise. Let's draw with Python! Are you wondering how?

A. Elumalai, *Introduction to Python for Kids*, https://doi.org/10.1007/978-1-4842-6812-4_6

Well, let me introduce you to the magical world that is "*Turtle*". *Turtle* is a Python module, and it comes with a ton of tools (pre-defined methods) you can use to draw on your screen. The sky is the limit to what you can do with *Turtle*.

In this chapter, let's start with the basics of *Turtle*, and as we move further into the book, I'll show you more advanced tricks you can do with *Turtle* and Python.

No more boring projects! Our mini projects are going to be colorful from this chapter onward. Are you excited? I know I am!

Alright, let's get started.

Why don't you create a new file and name it whatever you want? You can use it for this chapter. Be careful with the naming though! Don't name your file turtle.py because there's already a turtle.py in your Python installation, and naming your file with the same name will cause errors when you run it. Other than that, you can name it pretty much anything you want. I've named my file drawTurtle.py.

Before we get started though, we need to import *Turtle* into our Python script file. *Turtle* is just an add-on, remember? So, it won't be available in your file unless you import it. The process is pretty simple actually. Just type "import" and then "turtle" with a small "t".

```
import turtle
```

Okay great! We've imported *Turtle* into our script file. Let's create our screen next. *Turtle* creates graphics, and if you noticed, your Python Shell doesn't exactly have the right display for images or drawings. So, we're going to create our own screen where our drawings will appear.

Let's create a variable "s" (you can name it anything you want). We're going to get our screen from turtle by using turtle's getscreen() pre-defined function and assign it to *s*, like this:

```
s = turtle.getscreen()
```

Now, the variable “s” contains our turtle screen (Figure 6-1). Let’s run the preceding line of code and see what we get.

Figure 6-1. *Python Turtle screen*

Did you see a popup like the preceding image with a black mark in the middle? That’s our turtle.

Now that we have our screen, let’s create our *Turtle*! Confused? Don’t be. In turtle, a turtle will draw whatever you command on the screen. Literally. It’ll look cool, you’ll see. There’s another pre-defined function Turtle() of the turtle package (too many turtles, I know :D). It has all the tools you need to draw on the screen, like drawing lines, circle, coloring them, and so on. Let’s get that function and assign it to a variable t so we can use it later when we draw.

```
t = turtle.Turtle()
```

Remember that the “T” in the Turtle() function is capitalized.

When you run the code now, you won’t see any change. It’ll still be the same blank screen, but we’ve set everything up now. The first three lines of code (import, getscreen, and Turtle()) are a constant in every program that involves turtle graphics, so always start with those, and I’ll assume you’ve included those lines in my future examples.

Let’s draw next!

Make your *Turtle* move

Now that we have everything ready, let's make our turtle move in the direction we want and draw while it moves. Our turtle is going to draw straight lines, and we're going to give it the distance and direction of those lines. Sounds good? Let's see how that works.

Move forward and backward

Let's test with the basic ones first, forward and backward.

To move forward, you need to use the forward() pre-defined method of the Turtle() function, and inside of the parenthesis, you need to give the distance. So, if you want your turtle to move (and draw) 100 points in the forward direction, you'll give 100 inside the brackets, like this:

```
t.forward(100)
```

We gave `t.forward()` in the preceding example because the forward() function is also inside of the variable t since we assigned everything inside Turtle() to it.

Let's save and run our script, and we'll get this (Figure 6-2).

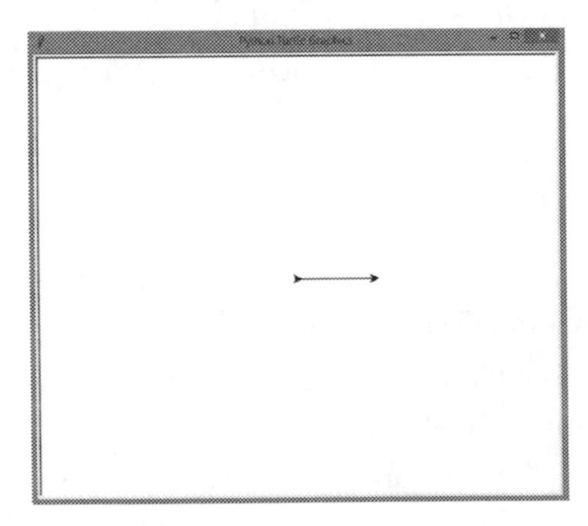

Figure 6-2. *Forward 100 points*

Great! We got a straight line drawn in the forward direction, and it stopped at 100 points, just like we wanted.

How do you make it move backward? Yes, you guessed it right! By using the backward() function. But there's a catch! If you ask your turtle to move backward right now, it'll just draw over the current line and you wouldn't see anything. Let's test that.

```
t.backward(100)
```

Run the preceding code, and you'll get this (Figure 6-3).

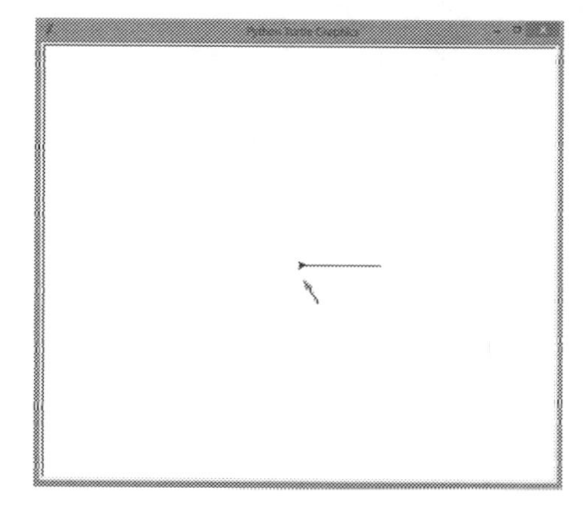

Figure 6-3. *Backward 100 points*

Yep, no change at all. Look at the arrow I drew pointing toward the starting point of the *Turtle*. Our turtle just came back to that starting point, but it didn't draw anything new.

There's a way to get around this issue. There's yet another function called home() which will make your turtle come back home (the starting position). So, before we give the backward command, why don't we use home() to get turtle back into position?

The entire code snippet will be like this:

```
import turtle
s = turtle.getscreen()
t = turtle.Turtle()
t.forward(100)
t.home()
t.backward(100)
```

When we run the preceding code, we'll get this (Figure 6-4).

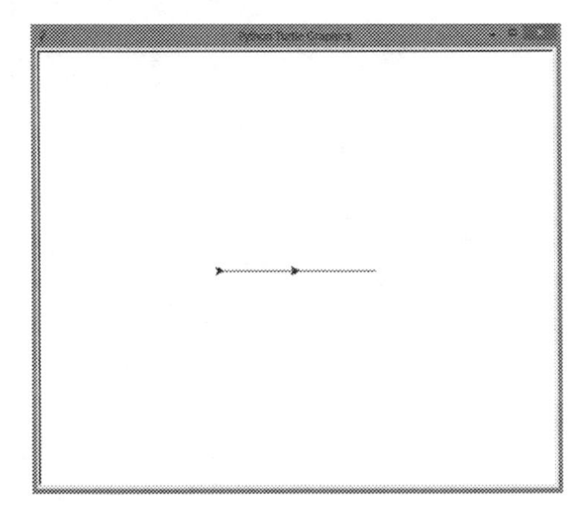

Figure 6-4. *Forward, home, and backward*

Yay! Our *Turtle* started from the starting position, drew a straight line 100 points to the right (forward), then went back to the starting position (it did draw while going back, but you didn't see that since it drew over the original line), and drew another straight line 100 more points to the left (backward). It works perfectly.

Alternatively, you could just give `t.backward(200)` to get the same result.

Did you notice something when you ran the code? *Turtle* literally drew those lines for you in real time. Isn't that awesome? ☺

Make your turtle change directions

You can't keep drawing in the forward and backward direction. You need to change directions to draw proper shapes. This is where the angles come in. Have you learned angles at school yet? If not, don't worry. Let me explain the concept quickly. It's quite easy.

Look at Figure 6-5.

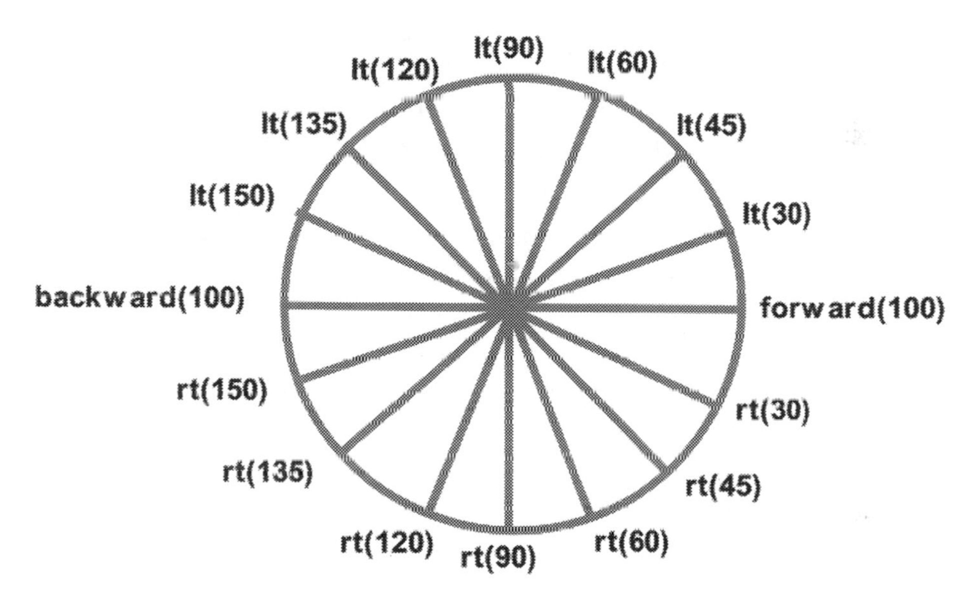

***Figure 6-5.** Using angles to change directions in Turtle*

In Python's turtle module, angles are basically directions. So, if you want your turtle to keep moving forward from the current position (home), then just say forward(100). If you want it to direct straight upward, then first change direction by giving left(45), or lt(45). Now, if you give forward(100) or something similar, you'll get a line upward, just like I've drawn in the preceding image. Similarly, to direct downward, using 90 degrees again, but right(90) this time. For the rest of it, you can refer to the preceding image and decide which line of code you need to use to change directions.

As you can see, if we want our *Turtle* to take complete turns, that is, draw downward instead of toward the right, then we need to give 90 degrees as our angle. Let's test that out now. I'm assuming you've already typed the three mandatory turtle lines of code already. Then, type the following:

```
t.forward(100)
t.right(90)
t.forward(100)
```

We're making our turtle move 100 points in the forward direction first. Then we're making it turn right at 90 degrees, which is a sharp turn (useful for drawing squares and rectangles). Now, our turtle is facing downward, and we're making it move forward 100 points again.

When we run the preceding lines of code, we'll get this (Figure 6-6).

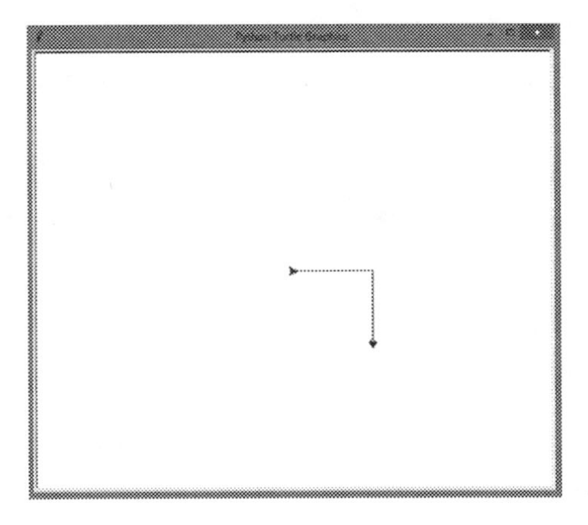

Figure 6-6. *Right(90)*

Let us move 90 degrees to the left now and see what we get.

```
t.left(90)
t.forward(100)
```

When you run the script, you'll get this (Figure 6-7).

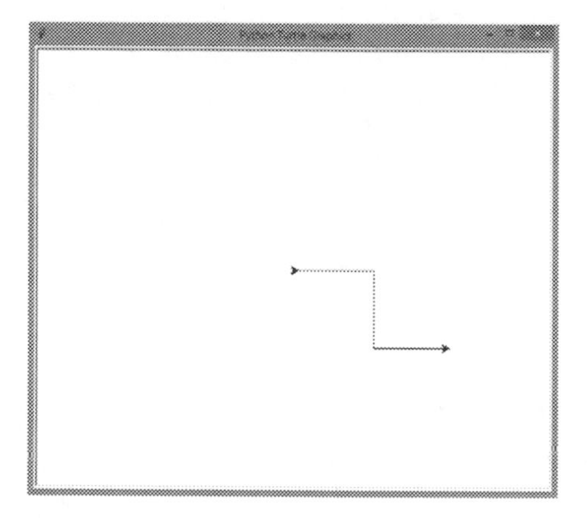

Figure 6-7. *Left(90)*

See, it made a sharp turn to the left.

Congrats! You now have four of the most powerful tools of *Turtle* at your disposal, and you can use them to draw a lot of things. Would you like to start with a couple of cool shapes?

Let's start simple, shall we? What about a square?

Mini project – draw a square

Don't look at the solution immediately. There are plenty of solutions for the same problem in programming, so try to find your own, and *then* look at mine. ☺

Okay, I'm going to make my solution very simple. I'm going to use just forward and right. My square is going to be 100 points in length and height.

These are the steps I'm going to use to draw my square:

1. I'll make the turtle move forward 100 points first and then take a 90-degree right turn.

2. Then move forward 100 points again to draw the second side of the square and another right turn.

3. Forward again to draw the third side and right turn again.

4. Forward again to draw the fourth and final side.

Let's convert the preceding directions to code:

```
import turtle
s = turtle.getscreen()
t = turtle.Turtle()
t.forward(100)
t.right(90)
t.forward(100)
t.right(90)
t.forward(100)
t.right(90)
t.forward(100)
```

Let's run the preceding lines of code. You'll see turtle draw with our commands in real time (Figure 6-8).

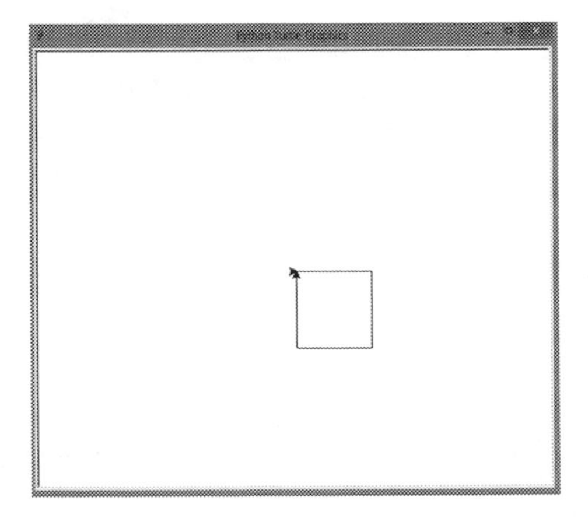

Figure 6-8. *Draw a square*

Yipee! We got our square!

Instead of the last `t.forward(100)`, you could just type `t.home()` and you'll get the same result. Why don't you try and see?

Mini project – draw a hexagon

I'm going to follow the same rules as my square for my hexagon. The only difference is I'm going to make my turtle turn 60 degrees every time, because that's the angle at which the side of a hexagon is placed (Figure 6-9)

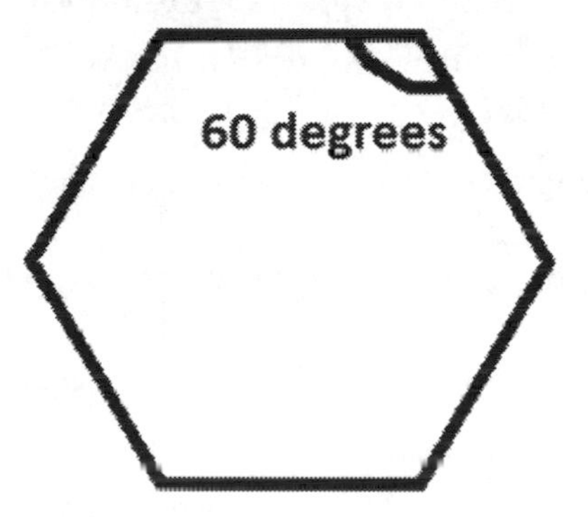

Figure 6-9. *Angle in a hexagon*

Also, I'm going to use the forward function six times instead of four, because I need it to draw six sides.

Look at the following code. It's easy to understand.

```
import turtle
s = turtle.getscreen()
t = turtle.Turtle()
t.forward(100)
t.right(60)
t.forward(100)
```

```
t.right(60)
t.forward(100)
t.right(60)
t.forward(100)
t.right(60)
t.forward(100)
t.right(60)
t.forward(100)
```

It is a bit tedious to type all those lines of code for just one shape, don't you think? Don't worry. When we look at automation, I'll teach you how to draw any shape you want, any number of times you want, with just a few lines of code. It'll be worth the wait, I promise.

When you run the preceding code, you'll get this (Figure 6-10).

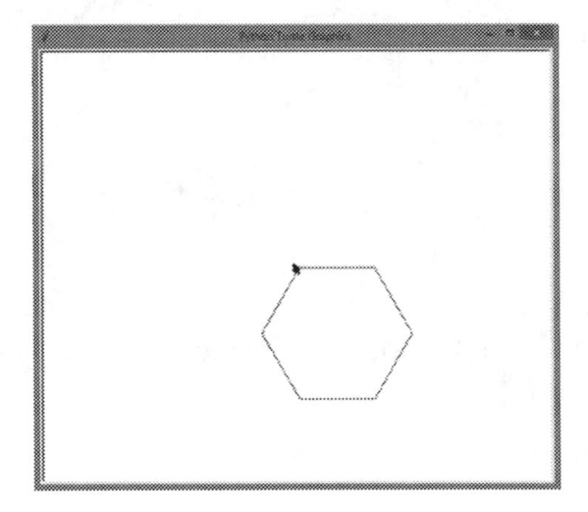

Figure 6-10. *Draw a hexagon*

Yippee again!

Shortcuts

Typing out forward, backward, right, and left every single time is a bit tedious, don't you think? Why don't we shorten everything to make things easy for us? You can write **fd**, **bk**, **rt**, and **lt** instead.

Let's try our shortcuts with our square.

```
import turtle
s = turtle.getscreen()
t = turtle.Turtle()
t.fd(100)
t.rt(90)
t.fd(100)
t.rt(90)
t.fd(100)
t.rt(90)
t.fd(100)
```

Run the preceding code, and you'll get this (Figure 6-11).

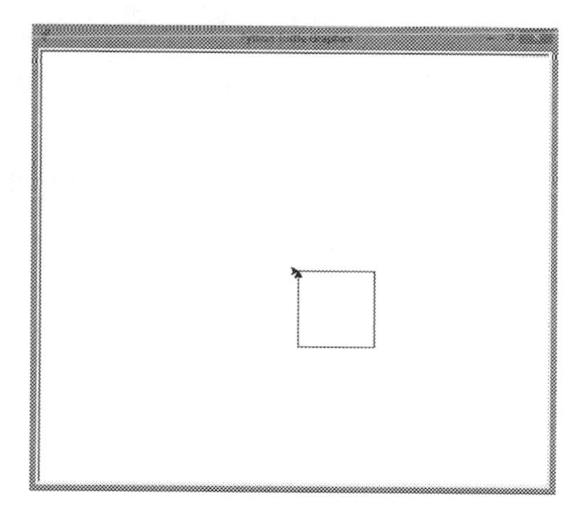

***Figure 6-11.** Shortcuts fd, bk, lt, and rt*

We got it, yay!

Now I want you to let your imagination run free. Draw anything you want. Just type your code, run it, see the results, and modify things. Create as many shapes as you can. Just have fun with it! ☺

Go to random points on the screen

By now, you're probably an expert at making turtle draw straight lines on the screen and manipulating them to get different shapes. But isn't it a tedious process? You're essentially writing two lines of code to draw every single straight line – a forward or backward to draw and then a right or left to change directions.

What if you can just command your *Turtle* to go to a particular position, drawing a straight line while it did, and it did just that? No angles, no forward, nothing. Something like that would save you both time and space, won't it?

You certainly can do something like that with the pre-defined function ***goto***. But, instead of just specifying the number of points you want your turtle to move, like you do with forward and backward, you need to specify the exact coordinate to which you want *Turtle* to move to.

What are coordinates? Have you learned about them at school, maybe when you learned about graphs? If not, don't worry. I'll explain now.

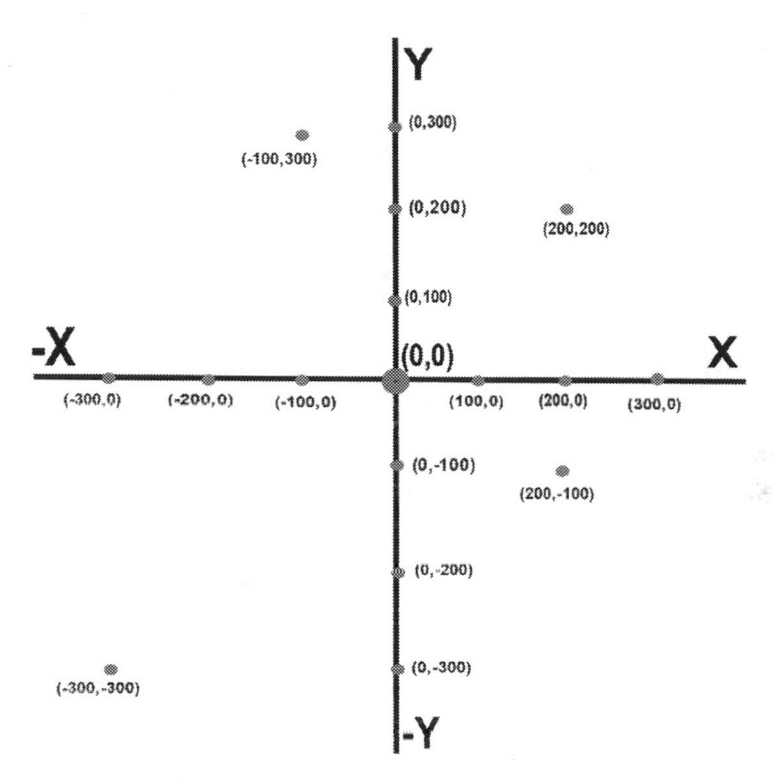

***Figure 6-12.** Coordinates in Turtle*

Look at the preceding image (Figure 6-12). The point *Turtle* starts from usually (home) is the big red dot marked (0,0). The first 0 is the x value, and the second 0 is the y value. Did you notice that the lines are marked X, -X, Y, and -Y? Those are called axis. Don't worry too much about axis and coordinates. If you don't know them already, you just need to know enough to know where to send your turtle to.

The x value positively increases in the right direction and negatively increases in the left direction. The Y value positively increases in the upward direction and negatively increases in the downward direction. Now that you know that, and you also know that (x,y) is how the coordinates are written, take a look at the image again. Do you see how the coordinates are written now?

(200,200) is where it is because x is at positive 200 and y is also at positive 200. So, if you gave goto(200,200), then you'd draw a straight line from (0,0) which is the default starting point for turtle to (200,200), which would be a diagonal line (Figure 6-13).

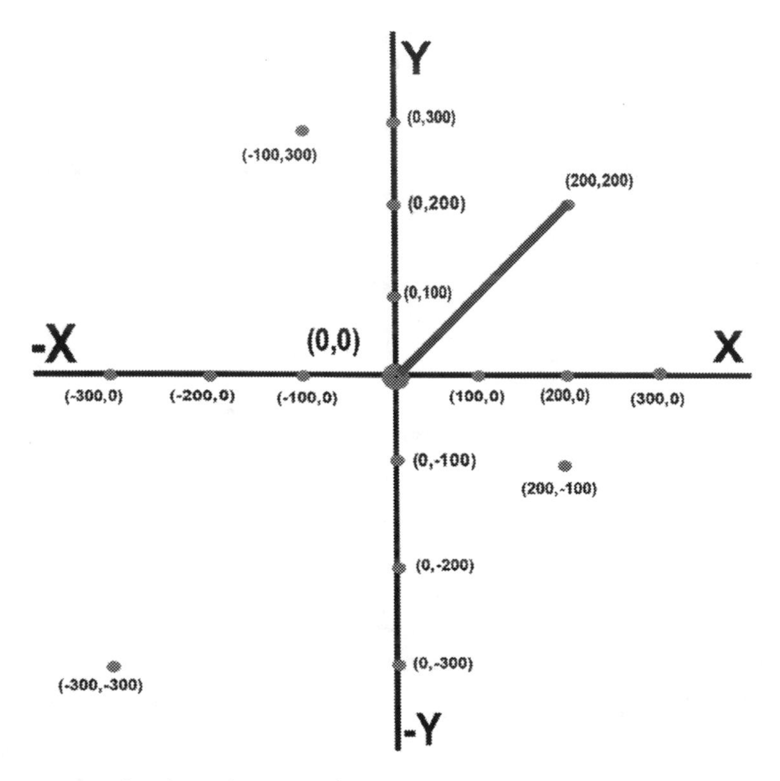

Figure 6-13. *(0,0) to (200,200)*

Draw a square with goto

Alright, now that you know how coordinates work, let's use it to draw something. What about a square?

I'm going to start from the default (0,0). I won't have to mention that because *Turtle* does that by default. Then, I'm going to move upward to (0,100), then right to (100,100), down to (100,0), and finally back home to (0,0). Why don't you refer to the coordinates image to see where each of these points is?

Let's write the code now:

```
import turtle
s = turtle.getscreen()
t = turtle.Turtle()
t.goto(0,100)
t.goto(100,100)
t.goto(100,0)
t.home()
```

t.home() will make the turtle go back to the (0,0) position.

When you run the preceding code, you'll get this (Figure 6-14).

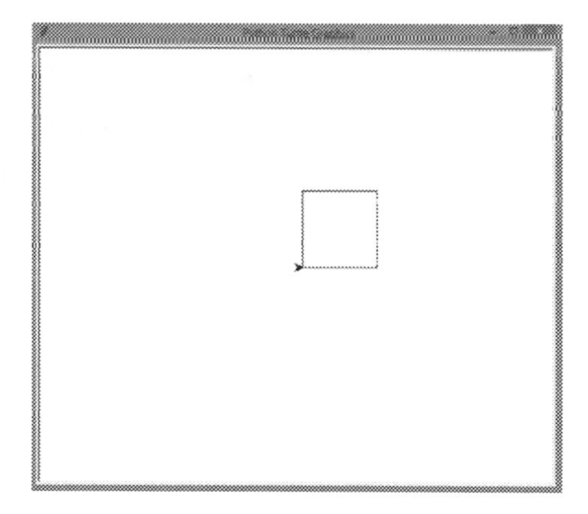

Figure 6-14. *Square with goto*

Look at that, you drew the same thing with just four lines of code instead of seven. Why don't you play around with the coordinates and draw more squares or any other shape?

Mini project – draw a mandala (with just straight lines)

In this mini project, we're going to take your drawing to the next level. We're going to draw a mandala, but with just straight lines. Okay, I admit it. A mandala with only lines is not a proper mandala, but hey, it's still a mandala, so let's go with it. We'll look at drawing more complex mandalas in future lessons, so wait for it! ☺

Let's get started, shall we? To start with, we're going to draw a square at the base and four tilted squares from each side of the square:

1. Let's first get done with the basics.

```
#Mandala with lines
import turtle
s = turtle.getscreen()
t = turtle.Turtle()
```

2. Now, we're going to create our base, our square. It's going to be a square of 100 points on each side, starting from the point (0,0), moving upward to (0,100) for the first side, then right toward (100,100) for the second side, then down to (100,0) for the third side, and going back to home (0,0) for the last side.

```
#Create the square base first
t.goto(0,100)
t.goto(100,100)
t.goto(100,0)
t.home()
```

When we run what we have so far, this is what we'll get (Figure 6-15).

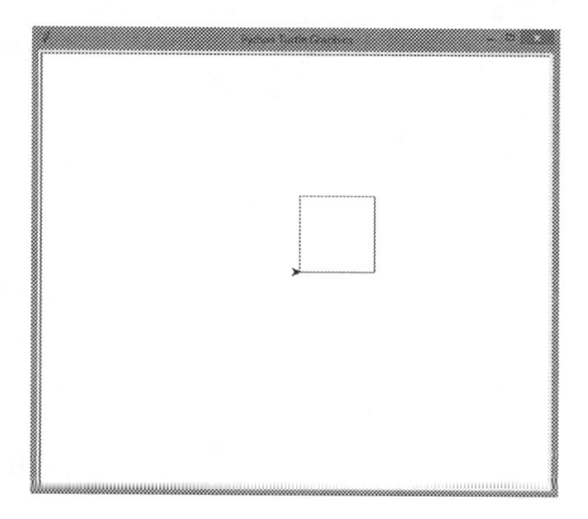

Figure 6-15. *Step 1 – draw the square base*

3. Let's draw the first tilted square next.

   Right now, our pen is at (0,0). We're going to ask it to draw a diagonal line to the point (50,50) (middle of the square) and then meet back at the point (0,100), which would give us a conical shape inside the square.

   ```
   #First tilted square
   t.goto(50,50)
   t.goto(0,100)
   ```

   When we run the preceding code, we'll get this (Figure 6-16).

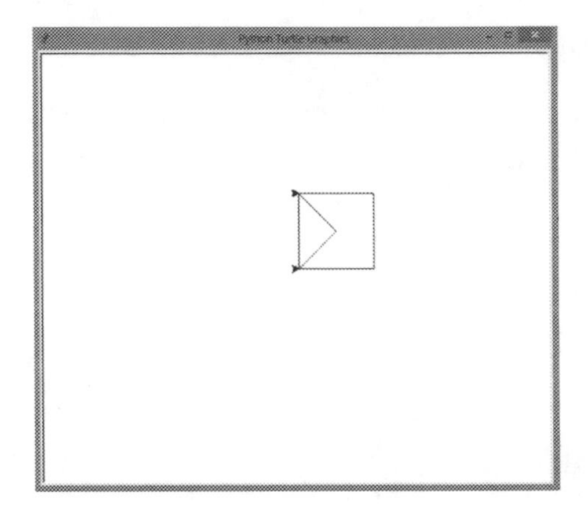

Figure 6-16. *Step 2 – first tilted square, part 1*

4. Now let's draw the same shape outside of the square to complete our first tilted square. Let us have our *Turtle* go to the exact opposite of the point 50,50 which is –50,50 and then again back home.

```
t.goto(-50,50)
t.home()
```

When we're done, we'll get something like this (Figure 6-17).

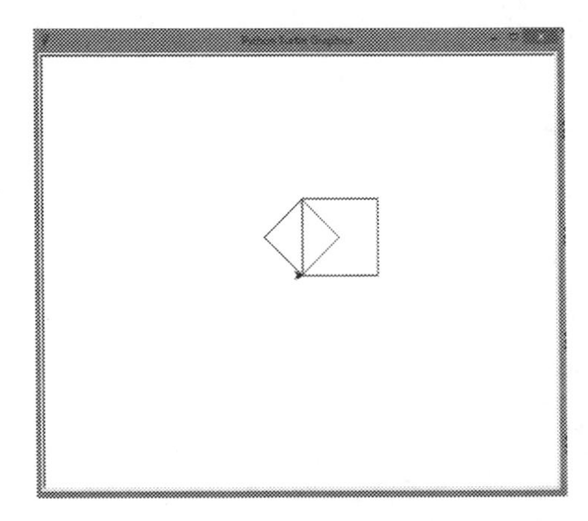

Figure 6-17. *Step 3 – complete the first tilted square*

5. We have our first tilted square! Yay! Now for the next one.

   The second one is quite simple, really. We are just going to the point 50,–50 (below the square) from 0,0 and meet back at 100,0. Then we're going to go to the opposite side of the square to 0,100 to get ready to draw the next square.

```
#2nd tilted square
t.goto(50,-50)
t.goto(100,0)
t.goto(0,100) #Getting ready to draw the next tilted
square
```

   When we run the preceding code, we'll get this (Figure 6-18).

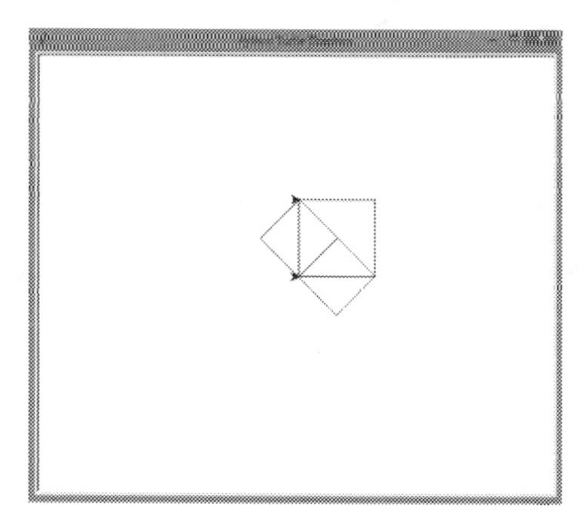

Figure 6-18. *Step 4 – second tilted square*

6. From the point 0,100, let's draw the next tilted side to 50,150. Then let's go back to 100,100 from there, we'll get a conical shape again. Then, when we go to the center of the square to 50,50, we'll have our third tilted square (Figure 6-19).

```
#3rd tilted square
t.goto(50,150)
t.goto(100,100)
t.goto(50,50)
```

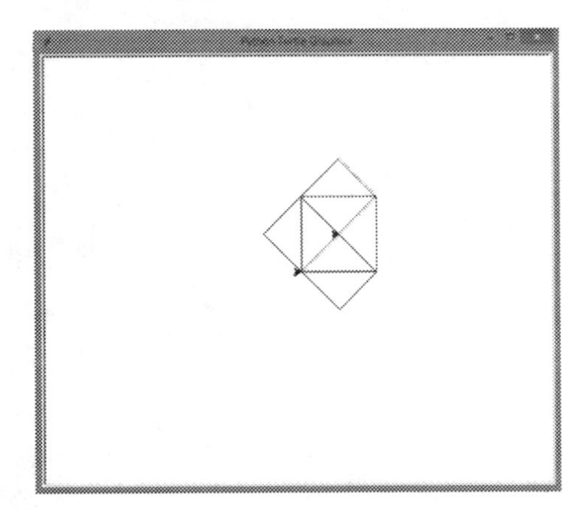

Figure 6-19. *Step 5 – third tilted square*

7. From the center 50,50, go to 100,0 so we can prepare to finish the fourth tilted square. Go to 150,50 to start the conical shape and 100,100 to end the same.

```
#4th tilted square
t.goto(100,0)
t.goto(150,50)
t.goto(100,100)
```

When we run the entire script, we'll get this (Figure 6-20).

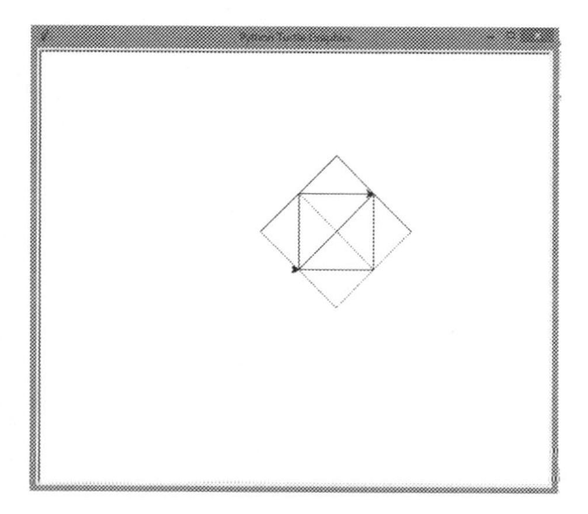

Figure 6-20. *Step 6 – fourth tilted square*

Whoa! We have a basic mandala shape, yes, but when we finish learning the rest of the goodies *Turtle* comes with, you can customize this shape to literally anything you want!

Summary

In this chapter, we looked at Python's graphics module *Turtle*, how to use it to draw lines by using forward, backward, right and left, but also making our turtles go to their respective coordinate points. We also looked at drawing shapes like squares, rectangles, hexagons, and so on in Python, and we ended the chapter with two mini projects.

In the next chapter, let's look further into *Turtle*; learn how to draw circles, dots, semi-circles, and arcs; make things colorful; and code more fun mini projects!

CHAPTER 7

A Turtle Deep Dive

In the previous chapter, you were introduced to the *Turtle* library in Python. We looked at drawing lines and shapes with *Turtle*, and we even learned how to draw a mandala design entirely composed of lines.

In this chapter, we're going to take a deeper look into *Turtle*. You'll learn how to draw colors to your designs and draw circles and arcs of all shapes, sizes, and angles. You'll also learn how to draw text on screen. At the end of the chapter, you'll learn how to change the angles of your drawings and finally draw smileys or drawings of any kind.

Customize your screen

What use are graphics and images without colors? Right now, your screen looks boring. It has a white background, and your screen title is always "Python Turtle Graphics". You can change all of that though.

To start with, you can change your screen title using the title method but remember something. This function isn't a part of t (turtle.Turtle). You need to preface it with turtle, the actual package, like this:

```
turtle.title('Hello Turtle!')
```


A. Elumalai, *Introduction to Python for Kids*, https://doi.org/10.1007/978-1-4842-6812-4_7

The same goes for your background color. You need to use the bgcolor method to change your background color and specify your color, in words, within either single (') or double (") quotes.

I'm going to change my screen's background color to red.

```
turtle.bgcolor('red')
```

Would you like to look at the changes we made? Look at the yellow arrow (I drew that in Figure 7-1). Our title now says "Hello Turtle!" and our screen is red. Perfect!

***Figure 7-1.** Background color set to red*

Try changing your screen to a different color or title.

You're not limited to the basic colors either. Follow this link: `https://en.wikipedia.org/wiki/Web_colors`.

You'll find the names of hundreds of colors on there. Let your imagination run free!

Customize your graphics

You know how to change the background color of the screen. Great! But what about the image color? Colored pens and images filled in color are a staple of any good drawing, aren't they?

So, you can change the color of your pen (outline of your graphics) and your graphic (fill color). You can also set a size for your lines and change the speed of your turtle (pen) if you feel it's too slow.

To change the color of your pen, use the pencolor function (write the function as it is, in all small letters) and give the name of the color as the parameter (what you give within the brackets). I'm going to use one of the colors from the color chart I gave you a link to in the last section.

Similarly, to change your fill color, use the fillcolor function. You can increase the size of your pen (the thickness of your lines) with the pensize function and give a number as its parameter. Specify a number greater than 2 to really see a difference, since 1 is the default pen size. Also, you can increase the speed of your pen by using the speed function. The default speed value is 1, so give anything more than that and you'll see a change.

Let's apply all of this and look at the result.

```
import turtle
s = turtle.getscreen()
t = turtle.Turtle()
turtle.title('Hello Turtle!')
turtle.bgcolor('DarkOrchid')
t.pencolor('Salmon')
t.fillcolor('Chartreuse')
t.pensize(5)
t.speed(7)
t.goto(0,100)
t.goto(100,100)
t.goto(100,0)
t.home()
```

Alright. I've specified the background color as "Dark Orchid", the pen color as "Salmon", the fill color as "Chartreuse", the pen size as 5, and the speed as 7. I've also drawn a square with goto. Let's see if it works (Figure 7-2).

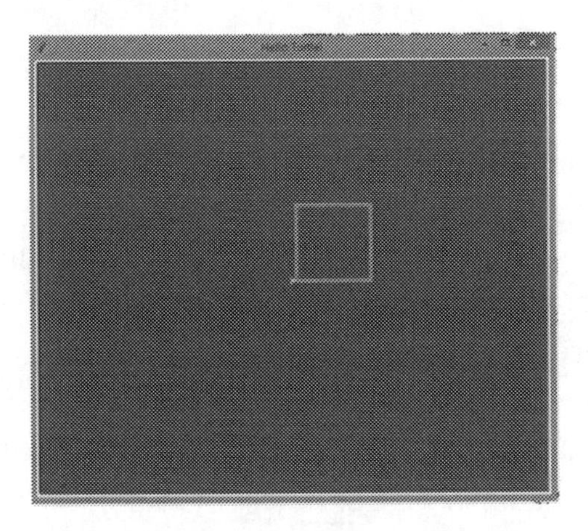

Figure 7-2. *Set speed, size, pen color, and background color*

It has worked to an extent. My pen drew so fast that I didn't see it draw this time (bummer). The lines are thick, the pen color is indeed salmon, but where is the fill color?

That's because *Turtle* wants you to indicate when you want the filling to start and end, so it doesn't accidentally fill something it shouldn't (like just two lines joined at a point).

You need to use the begin_fill() method when you want the fill to start and the end_fill() method when you want it to end.

So, after I've typed out the lines of code required to change the colors, size, and speed, this is what I'd do when I draw the shape:

```
t.begin_fill()
t.goto(0,100)
t.goto(100,100)
t.goto(100,0)
t.home()
t.end_fill()
```

Now, when I run my program, I'll get this (Figure 7-3).

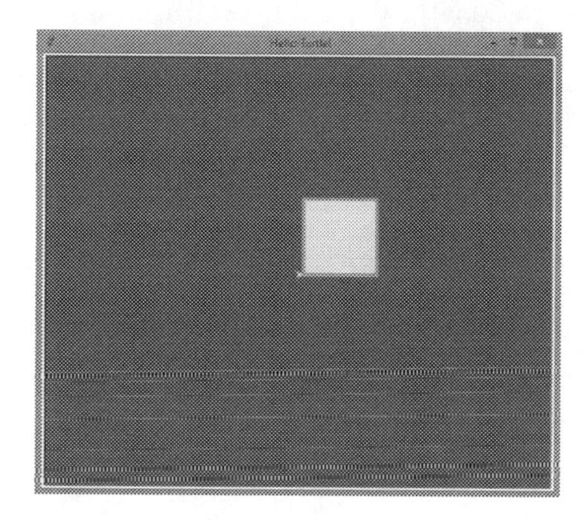

Figure 7-3. *Set fill color of the rectangle*

Yes, it works!

Also, you can use shortcuts for your formatting. Instead of using two lines of code to specify pen and fill color, you can use one, like this:

```
t.color('Salmon','Chartreuse')
```

The first value is for pencolor and the second is for fillcolor.

Or, better yet, you can use a single line for all the four formatting options, like this:

```
t.pen(pencolor='Salmon', fillcolor='Chartreuse', pensize=5,
speed=7)
```

Notice how you didn't have to place the numbers within quote. When you use the preceding line of code in your script, you'll notice that the result has not changed at all.

You can omit any of those arguments (pencolor='Salmon' is an argument) as per your requirement.

Before we end this section, I want you to try something. I want you to specify the value of speed as 0. What do you think will happen? Will turtle start drawing our square at the speed of an *actual* turtle? Or would you be pleasantly surprised? Try and see! ☺

Shapes without lines

We've been looking at drawing lines so far, but what if you want to draw circles? There's a pre-defined function for that as well. It's called "circle", and you have to give just the radius as the argument within the brackets. Radius is basically the size of the circle.

Let's try one, shall we?

Circles

```
s = turtle.getscreen()
t = turtle.Turtle()
t.circle(100)
```

I've kept it simple. Run the preceding code, and you'll get this (Figure 7-4).

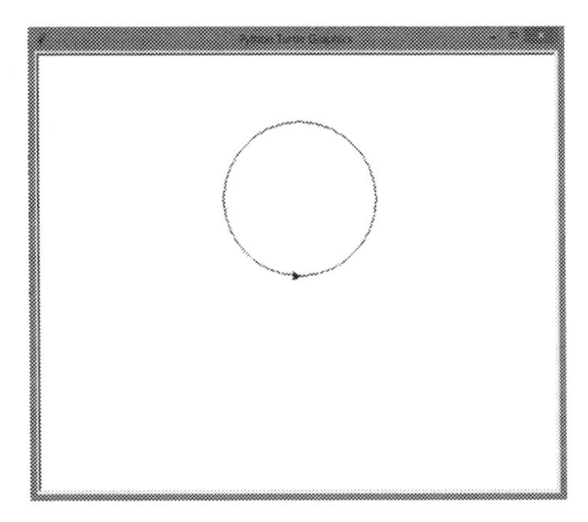

Figure 7-4. *Draw a circle – anti-clockwise direction*

As you can see, turtle started drawing the circle from the default 0,0 position in the anti-clockwise direction (toward the left) so the circle was drawn above the 0,0 position.

If I gave a negative value for radius, it'll draw in the clockwise direction, that is, below the 0,0 position. Let's try.

```
t.circle(-100)
```

Run the above lines of code, and you'll get this (Figure 7-5).

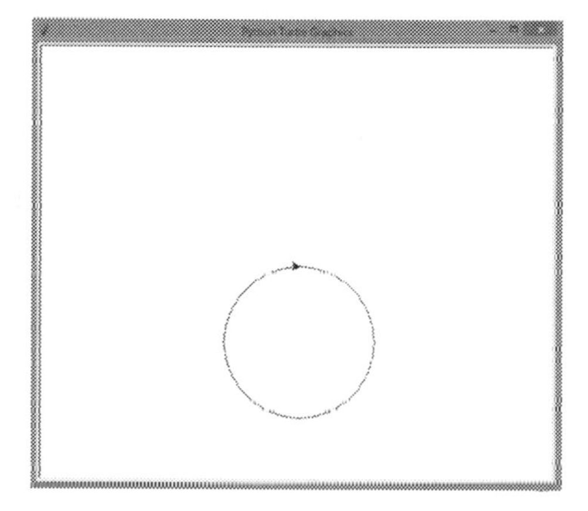

Figure 7-5. *Draw a circle – clockwise direction*

You can use the same coloring and size options you used on your straight lines for your circle.

As a small activity, I want you to draw different colored circles with different colors and see what you get.

Dots

You can draw a dot with the "dot" function. It's just a filled in circle that uses the pen color to fill itself, or you can give a preferred color in the second parameter.

```
t.dot(100, 'Salmon')
```

Run the preceding code, and you'll get this (Figure 7-6).

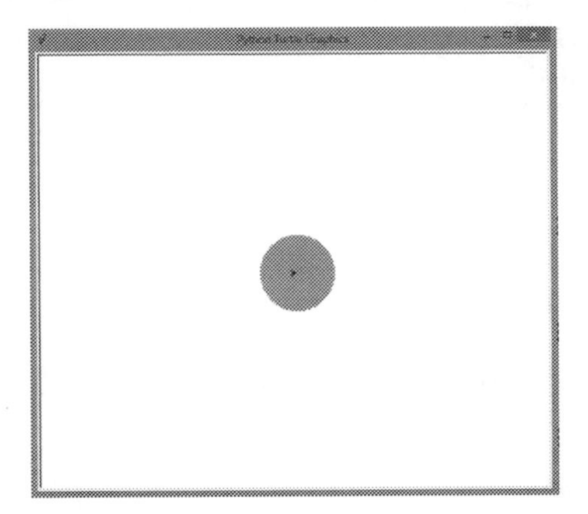

Figure 7-6. *Draw colored dot*

Did you notice something? The size of our circle is considerably bigger than our dot. That is because the value we give inside our dot function is actually the diameter, not the radius. So, your circle, with the same value, is going to be twice as big as your dot.

Arcs

Now, let's draw an arc! Arcs are part of a circle, aren't they? So, we are still going to use the circle function, but we're going to add more parameters to let turtle know that it should only draw a part of the circle (arc).

You know how angles work, don't you? (Figure 7-7)

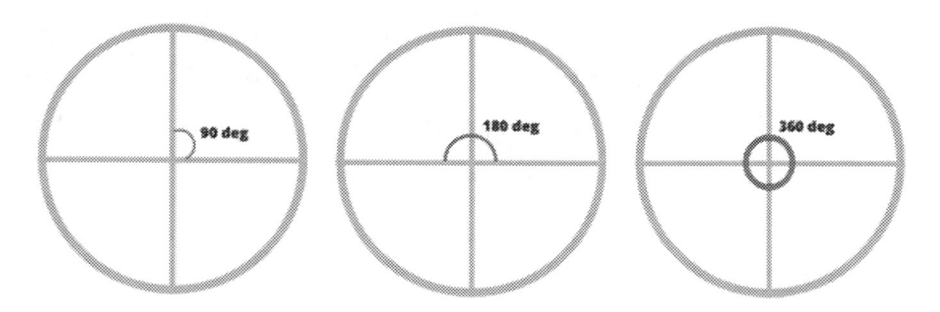

Figure 7-7. *Angles in a circle*

360 degrees makes a circle, so if you want a semi-circle, you need just 180 degrees. To make a quarter circle (arc), you need 90 degrees. We're going to make a semi-circle now.

```
t.circle(100,180)
```

Run the preceding code, and you'll get this (Figure 7-8).

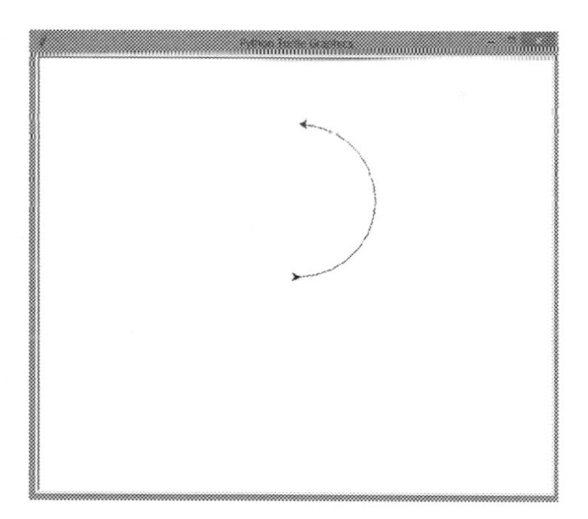

Figure 7-8. *Draw a semi-color*

When you give the values as -100,180, you'll get the same arc, but below. Give 100,-180 and you'll see a mirror image of the first arc, and for -100,-180, you'll see the same mirror image, but below the 0,0 position. Try out and see for yourself!

If you gave the angle as 90 degrees, you'd draw quarter of a circle. Why don't you play around with the angles to get different sized arcs? Don't just stop at 90 or 180. You have angles from 0 to 360 to play around with. Have fun! ☺

More options!

We have a lot more options with *Turtle*, but since we are just covering the basics in this chapter, I'll just talk about a couple more before we move on to the projects. Sometimes, you might want to draw more than one shape or figure on your screen, and they might be in different places. So, you need a way to move your pen to the new location without drawing anything on the move. Once moved, your pen should start drawing again. The penup and pendown methods (all small letters) help you do exactly that.

When you give the "penup" command to your turtle, you're asking it to take the pen off the screen. It won't draw anymore, but it will move positions based on your forward, backward, or goto commands. The command "pendown" does the exact opposite. If you want your pen to draw again, give it the pendown command. This command will only work if the penup command is in effect.

Also, you can use the hideturtle function after your program finishes drawing your graphics to hide the turtle from the screen. I'm sure you'd be relieved to learn of this method. I know I was. Those turtles didn't look good on my images!

I know I just dumped a bunch of random methods on you, and you might be confused. So, why don't we put what we just learned to test? Let's draw a square and then a circle, on different sides of the screen, and hide the turtle at the end, shall we?

1. I'm going to use "penup" when I start the program (after I set up turtle as usual) and then send the pen to the position (-200,200). Once my pen has moved, I'm going to specify pendown because I'm going to draw my square next.

```
import turtle
s = turtle.getscreen()
t = turtle.Turtle()
t.penup()
t.goto(-200,200)
t.pendown()
```

2. Then, I'm going to set the fillcolor to blue for my square.

```
t.fillcolor('blue')
```

3. I'm going to use the usual lines of code to draw my square next.

```
#Draw the square
t.begin_fill()
t.goto(-100,200)
t.goto(-100,100)
t.goto(-200,100)
t.goto(-200,200)
t.end_fill()
```

4. Once drawn, I need to change positions again to draw my circle. So, penup again, go to (200,-200), which is on the opposite side of the screen, and then pendown.

```
#Change positions again
t.penup()
t.goto(200,-200)
t.pendown()
```

5. I'm going to set the fill color as red for my circle.

```
t.fillcolor('red')
```

6. Then, I'm going to draw a 50-point radius circle.

```
#Draw the circle
t.begin_fill()
t.circle(50)
t.end_fill()
```

That's it! We have two shapes on opposite sides of the screen! ☺

7. Finally, I'm going to use the hideturtle() function to hide the turtle (which would still be shown on the circle otherwise).

```
t.hideturtle()
```

When you run the program, you'd get this (Figure 7-9).

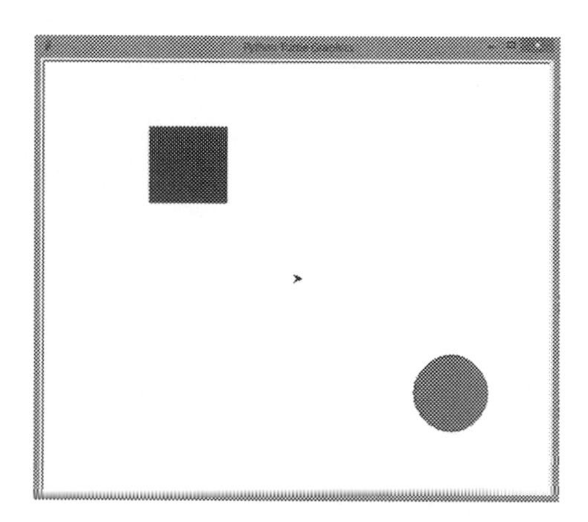

Figure 7-9. *Hide the "t" turtle*

8. Now this is where you'll find things a bit different. If I just use t.hideturtle(), then I'll only hide one of the turtles (why don't you draw and see?). But you must have noticed that there are two turtles. There's one at the home position (0,0), which pertains to the turtle package itself, and there's another (t of the pre-defined function Turtle()) that does the drawing.

So, we need hideturtle() repeated twice. We already wrote hideturtle() for "t". Let's write another one for the "turtle" package in its entirety.

```
turtle.hideturtle()
```

Once I've added the preceding line of code, let's run the script again (Figure 7-10).

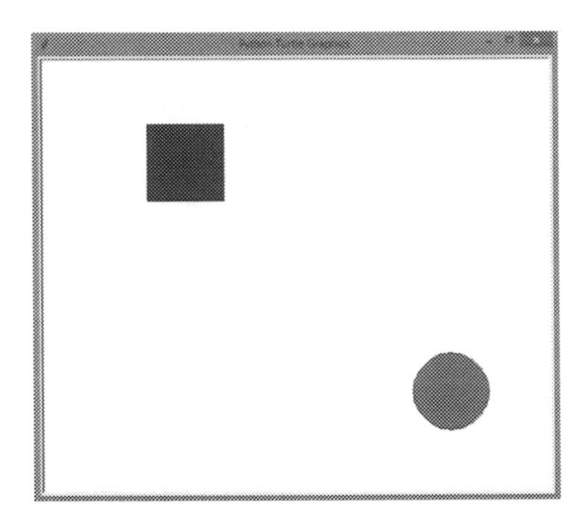

Figure 7-10. *Hide the "turtle" turtle*

Look at that! The turtle in the center of the screen has disappeared as well. Yes!

Draw text on screen

We've drawn all kinds of graphics so far, but no image is complete without a little bit of text, is it? And it's quite simple too. Would you like to see?

To write a simple text, just use the write method of *Turtle*, and specify the text you want displayed, like this:

```
import turtle
s = turtle.getscreen()
t = turtle.Turtle()
t.write('Hello there!')
```

Run it, and you'll get this (Figure 7-11).

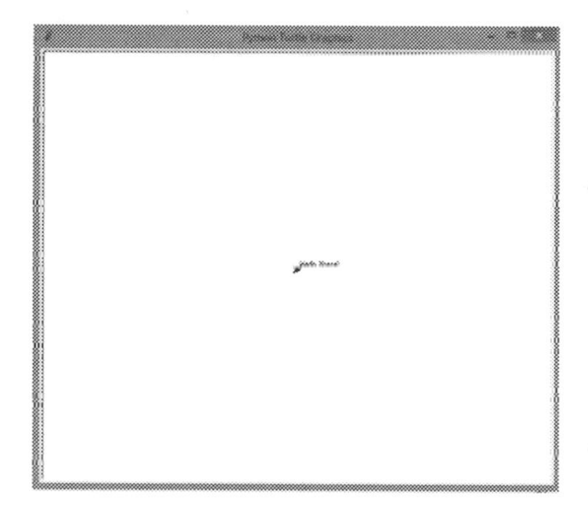

***Figure 7-11.** Draw text on screen*

That looks like chicken scrawl. Aww! Could we manipulate this text in any way? You bet!

Let's position our text somewhere first.

```
t.penup()
t.goto(200,200)
t.pendown()
```

Now, let's draw again, but with a slight change:

```
t.write('Hello there!', move=True)
```

The move argument is False by default. If you make it true, you'll see the arrow below the text being drawn, like this (Figure 7-12).

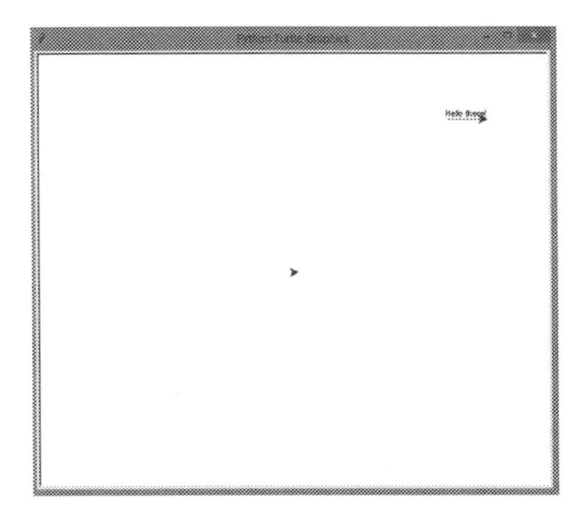

Figure 7-12. *Draw text in a different position*

You might not see much difference now since the text is too small and too short.

Still too small! Let's add some styles, shall we? You know the different font styles you can use on your text, don't you? There's Arial, Calibri, Times New Roman, and a ton of styles like that. A simple Google search will give you a list of them.

I'm going to make mine Georgia. But that's not where it ends. I can also increase or decrease the font size and change the font type. Let's play with them all!

Let's change position again to make room for the "big" text we'll be creating:

```
t.penup()
t.goto(-200,200)
t.pendown()
```

The x position is now –200, instead of 200.

Now, let's draw our text.

```
t.write('Hello there!', move=True,
font=('Georgia',40,'normal'))
```

Did you notice something in the above code? I've mentioned all the styles under "font", and they're within a combined parenthesis. Also, the font style ('Georgia') and type ('normal') are within quotes (can be single or double quotes). Let's run the above code, and we'll get this (Figure 7-13).

Figure 7-13. *Format the text*

You can change the color of your text by using the pencolor tool.

```
t.pencolor('Red')
```

You can also make your text bold, italics, and underlined (or any of those three) by including them as values alongside the rest of the font values, like this:

```
t.write('Hello there!', move=True, font=('Georgia',40,'normal',
'bold','italic','underline'))
```

Run the preceding code, and you'll get this (Figure 7-14).

Figure 7-14. *Change the color of the text*

Looking good! ☺

Mini project – circle within a square

This is going to be a simple project. We're going to draw a circle inside a square in this project:

1. Let's set up turtle first. I've not set up the speed in this program, but you can do so.

```
import turtle
s = turtle.getscreen()
t = turtle.Turtle()
```

2. Next, I've set the fill color of the square to 'Red' and pen size to 5. I'm going to draw the square first and then the circle within it.

```
#Set the color and pen size for the square
t.fillcolor('Red')
t.pensize(5)
```

3. Let's draw the square now. I'm going to go to the position -100,-100 first so I can draw the circle around the center of the screen (0,0). This way, I can draw the circle around the same center point.

```
#Draw the square
t.penup()
t.goto(-100,-100)
t.pendown()
t.begin_fill()
t.goto(-100,100)
t.goto(100,100)
t.goto(100,-100)
t.goto(-100,-100)
t.end_fill()
```

4. Now, to set the circle's center as 0,0, I've asked my pen to go to the position 0,-100, so when I draw a 100-point radius from this point, in the anti-clockwise direction (default), the center would be 0,0. I've set the fillcolor for the circle as 'Blue'.

```
#Set position so the circle's center is 0,0
t.penup()
t.goto(0,-100)
t.pendown()
#Draw the circle
#Color and size
t.fillcolor('Blue')
```

```
#Circle
t.begin_fill()
t.circle(100)
t.end_fill()
```

5. Finally, let's hide the turtles.

```
t.hideturtle()
turtle.hideturtle()
```

Now, let's run the entire code, and see if we get what we want (Figure 7-15).

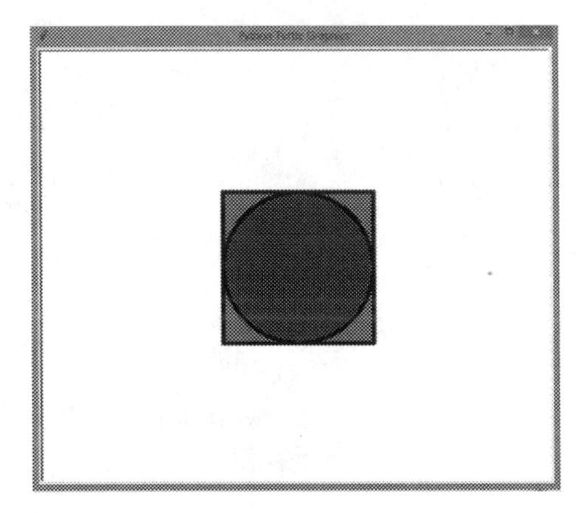

Figure 7-15. *Circle within a square*

Whohoo! :D

Change directions of your drawing

So far, the only way to change directions is by using the right() and left() methods. But, while creating arcs, you might want something else that changes the angle of your pen so you can place the arc wherever you want. What if you want to draw an eyebrow? Or a sideways smile?

Turtle offers you the setheading() method to do just that. Let's look at what a heading is first. The heading() method gives you the angle of the pen at that particular time.

```
import turtle
s = turtle.getscreen()
t = turtle.Turtle()
print(t.heading())
```

When I run the preceding code, I get this:

```
= RESTART: C:\Users\aarthi\AppData\Local\Programs\Python\
Python38-32\drawTurtle.py
0.0
```

Right now, the pen is at an angle of 0, which means it'll draw in the horizontal direction. But with setheading(), I can change the angle.

Let's make it 90 degrees, perhaps. Just mention the angle within the brackets, and you're good to go.

```
t.setheading(90)
```

Now let's check the heading.

```
print(t.heading())
```

Run the preceding code, and you'll get this:

```
= RESTART: C:\Users\aarthi\AppData\Local\Programs\Python\
Python38-32\drawTurtle.py
90.0
```

Okay great, the heading is 90 degrees. What does that mean for us? Shall we draw a line and check?

```
t.pensize(5)
t.forward(100)
```

When we run the preceding lines of code, we'll get this (Figure 7-16).

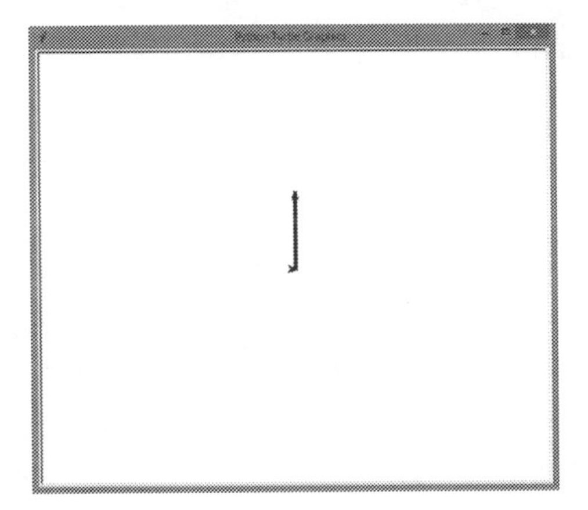

Figure 7-16. *Set heading to 90 degrees*

Look at that! It drew a line upward, so when the heading is 90 degrees, the pen is pointing upward. You already know where each angle is, so you can guess where your pen will point for each angle change you make with setheading(), but let's demonstrate the same with a small program, shall we? We're starting fresh, so please open a new script or clear the one you're currently using.

1. Let me start off with setting up the turtle. I'm going to print the current heading (0 degrees when the program starts running, which points toward the right). I've also increased the pen size to 5 and speed to 5.

```
import turtle
s = turtle.getscreen()
t = turtle.Turtle()
print(t.heading())
t.pensize(5)
t.speed(5)
```

2. Now, I'm going to make the pen draw forward 100 points at the current degree. Once drawn, I'll make the pen write the current degree using the heading() method. Then let's lift the pen and go back to (0,0) to start anew.

```
#0 degrees
t.forward(100)
t.write(t.heading())
t.penup()
t.home()
t.pendown()
```

3. Now, let's change the heading to 90 degrees (point upward) and draw forward and repeat the same as earlier.

```
#90 degrees
t.setheading(90)
t.forward(100)
t.write(t.heading())
t.penup()
t.home()
t.pendown()
```

4. Now, 180 degrees (point toward the left).

```
#180 degrees
t.setheading(180)
t.forward(100)
t.write(t.heading())
t.penup()
t.home()
t.pendown()
```

5. Finally, 270 degrees (pointed downward).

```
#270 degrees
t.setheading(270)
t.forward(100)
t.write(t.heading())
Finally, let's hide all the turtles.
t.hideturtle()
turtle.hideturtle()
```

Run the preceding code, and you'll get this (Figure 7-17).

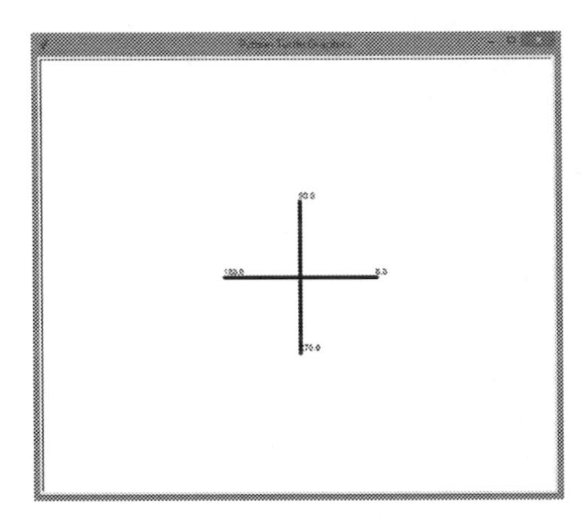

Figure 7-17. *An angle diagram for setheading*

Do you see the significance of using the setheading()? You can set your angle to any point you want. Right now, we've just set it to draw vertical or horizontal lines. Why don't you change to angles and see what you get?

Mini project – smiley

In this project, let's take things to the next level, shall we? Let's draw a smiley face!

1. I've set up the *Turtle* package. You can change the speed if you like.

```
import turtle
s = turtle.getscreen()
t = turtle.Turtle()
```

2. Next, I've asked the pen to go to the position 0, 100 so I can draw a circle, which is our face, with the center of the circle as 0,0. This'll just let me do the calculations for the eyes, nose, and mouth better.

```
#Let's draw a smiley
#Go to the position
t.penup()
t.goto(0,-100)
t.pendown()
```

3. Now, let's draw the face. The fillcolor is going to be yellow, and the pen size is going to be 5 and the circle is going to be of a radius of 100 points.

```
#Draw the face
#Color and size
t.fillcolor('yellow')
t.pensize(5)
#Circle
t.begin_fill()
t.circle(100)
t.end_fill()
```

4. Next, I'm going to draw the eyes. I set the positions based on trial and errors. You can use the same in your program or change the positions to see what you get and create your own (I recommend doing this).

   I'm going to ask my pen to go to the position –40,30 to draw the left eye and draw a black dot with diameter 30.

   ```
   #Draw the eyes
   #First eye
   t.penup()
   t.goto(-40,30)
   t.pendown()
   t.dot(30)
   ```

5. Then, go to the position 40,30 (same horizontal line, opposite X value) and draw the right eye, which is again a dot with diameter 30.

   ```
   #Second eye
   t.penup()
   t.goto(40,30)
   t.pendown()
   t.dot(30)
   ```

6. Next, let's draw the nose. This is where centering the circle at 0,0 comes in handy because our smiley's nose is going to start from 0,0. Let's draw a straight line from 0,0 down to 0,–30.

```
#Draw the nose
t.penup()
t.goto(0,0)
t.pendown()
t.goto(0,-30)
```

7. Finally, the tricky part. Let's draw the smile. We're going to make the turtle go to the x position of the first eye, which is –40, but the y position is also going to be –40. Again, I found this value after a lot of trial and error, and I ended up with a value that gave me the result I want. Try your own! ☺

```
#Draw the smile
#Go to the x position of the first eye but a different
y position
t.penup()
t.goto(-40,-40)
t.pendown()
```

8. A smile is a semi-circle, isn't it? But, if you try to draw a semi-circle as it is right now (try), you'll get a slanted smile, not the only we see on smileys. This is where setheading comes in. We need to change the angle of the pen so we can draw the semi-circle in the exact angle we want. Let's change the angle to –60. Don't be confused! It's the same as setting the angle to 120 (you can use either).

   Next, let's draw a semi-circle with the angle 120, so it's not exactly a semi-circle, but not a quarter circle either – something in between.

```
#Change the direction of the pen (turtle)
t.setheading(-60)
t.circle(40,120)
```

9. Finally, let's hide our turtles!

```
#Finally, hide the turtle
t.hideturtle()
turtle.hideturtle()
```

Whew! That was long. Now shall we run the code and check to see if our efforts bore fruit? (Figure 7-18)

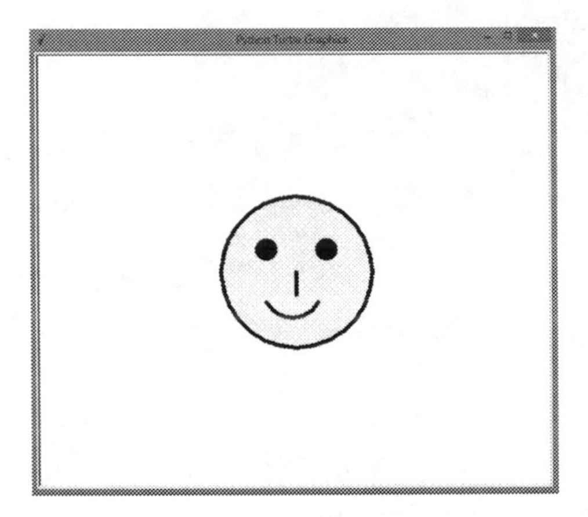

Figure 7-18. *Smiley face*

Yay! That's a cute little smiley! Why don't you try creating different smileys? Maybe a sad smiley? Frowny face, or laugh? You have the tools you need (goto, setheading, etc.) to creating any image now, not just faces!

Summary

In this chapter, we went deeper into the Python *Turtle* module. We learned how to use colors, draw arcs, circles and dots, and manipulate their direction and size, and finally, how to draw text into our screen.

In the next chapter, let's go deep into strings, how to create them and use them, and the various pre-defined string methods Python equips you with, and finally, let's make some magic with them!

CHAPTER 8

Play with Letters and Words

In the previous chapters, we took a break from learning Python basics and we learned all about *Turtle* and using it to draw straight lines, shapes that are formed with straight lines, circles, curves, and even text. We finished the chapter with a bunch of cool and colorful mini projects.

In this chapter, we'll go back to the basics of Python and learn about strings, what they are, how to create them, how to manipulate them using various pre-defined functions available in Python, and getting direct inputs from the users of your programs to make your projects more dynamic. As usual, we'll finish the chapter with some mini projects, but we'll use *Turtle* to make our projects colorful now.

What are strings?

Strings...strings...strings. Such a grown-up word for something so simple. Strings are just letters and number, strung together. Sentences, phrases, and words – they are all strings. Single letters can also be strings.

A. Elumalai, *Introduction to Python for Kids*, https://doi.org/10.1007/978-1-4842-6812-4_8

Do you remember the print statement? When we first started using the print() function, we wrote something within quotes inside the bracket. Was it 'Hello there!'? Yes indeed.

That was a string. Print statements usually have strings inside of them. But that's not where it ends. You can store strings in variables as well, just like you do with your numbers.

Now that you know what strings are, let's learn how to create them next! This is going to be a longer than average chapter, so buckle up! I promise all the exercises and fun projects will make up for the length. 😊

Let's create some strings

I'm going to create a new script file called strings.py and use it for this chapter.

```
a = 'This is a string'
```

The variable "a" now has the string 'This is a string'. You can place the string within double quotes as well.

```
a = "This is a string"
```

Let's try printing this string now, shall we? It's quite simple. You use the print statement again, but instead of typing the string within quotes inside the brackets, you just type the name of the variable that contains the string, without quotes, like this:

```
print(a)
```

Now, if you run the preceding code, you'll get this:

```
RESTART: C:/Users/aarthi/AppData/Local/Programs/Python/
Python38-32/strings.py
This is a string
```

We successfully printed our string. Yay!

Your strings can have numbers as well, and they'd still be considered a string. Anything within quotes is a string. Let me place a number within quotes and check its type by using the type() method.

```
a = "1234"
print(type(a))
```

When you run the preceding code, you'll get this:

```
= RESTART: C:/Users/aarthi/AppData/Local/Programs/Python/
Python38-32/strings.py
<class 'str'>
```

Look at that! Even though "a" has a number, 1234, since it was placed inside quotes, Python automatically considered it a string.

I want lines and lines of strings!

All's well and good with strings as long as you stick to creating single-line strings. What if we need multiple lines? We can't keep creating a separate print statement for each new string line. That's what we did in our very first mini project, where we printed out Susan Smith's introduction, remember? That was very inconvenient!

Why don't we try creating multiple lines inside of string format and see what happens?

```
a = "This is the first line.
This is the second line.
This is the last line."
```

In the preceding example, "a" has three string lines, wrapped inside double quotes. Let's run it and see what happens (Figure 8-1).

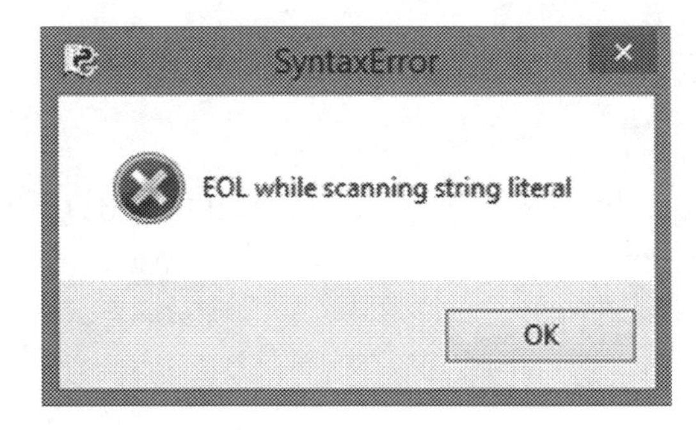

***Figure 8-1.** Multi-line string with double quotes – error*

Uh oh. I can't even run the code. I immediately get a popup with the preceding error. What we wrote previously is not acceptable code at all. So, *how* can we create multiple lines of string? Do you remember multi-line comments in Chapter 3? We used three single quotes, without space before the comment, and the same, after the comment, and that created a multi-line comment.

I have a confession to make. That syntax is actually the syntax of a multi-line string. We just borrowed it to create a multi-line comment because a multi-line string that hasn't been stored in a variable and just stands as it is would be ignored by Python, so it technically acts a comment (though it is not).

Alright, enough chit chat. Let's create a multi-line string now. I'm going to replicate Susan Smith's introduction, but I'm going to use multi-line strings to create and print it.

```
intro ='''Hello there!
My name is Susan Smith.
I am 9 years old.
I love puppies!'''
print(intro)
```

When I run the preceding code, I get this:

```
= RESTART: C:/Users/aarthi/AppData/Local/Programs/Python/
Python38-32/strings.py
Hello there!
My name is Susan Smith.
I am 9 years old.
I love puppies!
```

Simple and neat, don't you think? ☺ Yes!

My string has quotes! :O

Oh my, our string has quotes, and we're getting an error!

```
intro =""Hello!", said Susan"
```

I got this (Figure 8-2).

Figure 8-2. *Single and double quotes in the same string - error*

Bummer. ☹

Well, I could change the quote that wraps around the string.

```
intro ='"Hello!", said Susan'
print(intro)
```

Does it work?

```
= RESTART: C:/Users/aarthi/AppData/Local/Programs/Python/
Python38-32/strings.py
"Hello!", said Susan
```

Yes! ☺

But what if my string has both single and double quotes? Maybe a string like the following one:

"That's my Teddy", said Susan.

I can't just interchange double quotes for single quotes in the preceding string. I need a way to tell Python that the single quote in "That's" is actually a part of the string and not a part of the code. We have something called an ***escape character*** in Python, which is just a backslash, "\". You can use that before the quote that's part of a string (either a single or double quote), and Python will ignore it while running your code.

Let's try.

```
intro = '"That\'s my Teddy", said Susan.'
print(intro)
```

Run the preceding code, and we'll get this:

```
= RESTART: C:/Users/aarthi/AppData/Local/Programs/Python/
Python38-32/strings.py
"That's my Teddy", said Susan.
```

Yes, it works!

Let's join two or more strings

When we used the "+" symbol with two or more numbers, they were added together. Would you like to see what would happen if you do the same with strings? Okay!

I've created two variables str1 and str2 which hold the strings 'Hello' and 'there!'. I've created a third variable "string" and assigned the addition of str1 and str2 to it.

```
str1 = 'Hello'
str2 = 'there!'
string = str1 + str2
print(string)
```

Let's print string and see what we get:

```
= RESTART: C:/Users/aarthi/AppData/Local/Programs/Python/
Python38-32/strings.py
Hellothere!
```

Oh, look at that. It just put the string inside str1 after the string inside str2. That's interesting. Addition didn't take place, even though we used the addition operator.

In fact, there is a name for this string operation. It's called ***string concatenation***. When you use "+" on two or more strings, you add them together, yes, but not in the traditional sense. You just merge them together, in the order they are added in.

Something's bothering me about my result though. "Hellothere!" isn't what I wanted. I wanted a space between those words. That's proper usage of that phrase. So, why don't I just add that?

```
str1 = 'Hello'
str2 = 'there!'
string = str1 + " " + str2
print(string)
```

That was simple! We just created another string that had just one space in it and added it before str2. Let's run the preceding code, and we'll get this:

```
= RESTART: C:/Users/aarthi/AppData/Local/Programs/Python/
Python38-32/strings.py
Hello there!
```

Now, that looks right. So, as you can see, you can concatenate more than two strings, and they can either be inside variables or as is (within quotes). Even a space is a string, if placed inside quotes.

Concatenation in print()

You can apply string concatenation in print() as well.

```
a = 'Hi!'
print('Susan says, "' + a + '"')
```

Does it look a bit complicated? Not to worry. I've wrapped the first part of the string, "Susan says", with a comma, a space, and a double quote at the end in single quotes. The next part of the string is whatever is inside the variable "a", so I concatenated the two strings. The final part of the string is the closing double quote which is also wrapped inside a single quote. Alternatively, I could have just used double quotes throughout and used the escape character to distinguish the string's double quotes.

If I run the preceding code, I'll get this:

```
= RESTART: C:/Users/aarthi/AppData/Local/Programs/Python/
Python38-32/strings.py
Susan says, "Hi!"
```

Nicely done!

Empty string

All these string operations reminded me of something! There's something called an ***empty string***, where you just don't type anything between the quotes, not even an empty space.

```
a = ''
```

In the preceding example, the variable "a" is storing an empty string. If you print that out, you'd get nothing in the output (not even a space). Try and see! ☺

Accessing characters in strings

I want to introduce you to a mind-blowing topic in strings! You can actually access, retrieve, and even modify specific characters (letters) in strings. How cool is that? You can make changes to the string on a character level with this feature.

```
a = 'Hello there!'
```

Look at the following string index chart. Every character in a string has an index. In fact, they have two indices, a positive index and an equivalent negative index. You can access those characters by using those indices.

-12 -11 -10 -9 -8 -7 -6 -5 -4 -3 -2 -1

Hello there!

0 1 2 3 4 5 6 7 8 9 10 11

Figure 8-3. *String index chart*

As you can see in Figure 8-3, the positive indices start from 0 and increase in value toward the left. The negative indices start from the last position at –1. The space has an index, and so does the exclamation point. It isn't just for the letters/numbers.

Okay, that's all well and good, but how do we access these indices? Simple! Type the name of the string and open and close square brackets, and type in the relevant index within the brackets, and you're good to go.

As you can see, the indices start from 0, and the last one is the length of the string subtracted by 1. Spaces in a string also take up indices.

So, if I want to retrieve the first character of the string, "H", this is what I'd do:

```
print(a[0])
```

When you run the preceding code, you'd see this:

```
= RESTART: C:/Users/aarthi/AppData/Local/Programs/Python/
Python38-32/strings.py
H
```

Perfect!

Now, if I were to retrieve the last character of the string, I'd first calculate the length of the string. The length is 12 in this case, including the space. Now let's subtract it by 1, as follows:

```
print(a[12-1])
```

When you run the program, your interpreter (IDLE) will automatically do the calculation to arrive at 11 for the index. The result is this:

```
= RESTART: C:/Users/aarthi/AppData/Local/Programs/Python/
Python38-32/strings.py
!
```

Yup, that's right.

Negative indices

As you saw in the preceding image, you have both positive and negative indices for the same characters in a string. Let's try to access "o", which is in the positive index 4 (fifth position on the string) and -8 in the negative index position.

```
print(a[-8])
```

Run the preceding code, and you'll get this:

```
= RESTART: C:/Users/aarthi/AppData/Local/Programs/Python/
Python38-32/strings.py
o
```

It works perfectly!

So, the first character would be at a[-12], and the last character would be at a[-1].

Slicing a part of a string

You can extract a part of a string and not just a single character with your indices. That's called ***slicing***.

Slicing follows the same pattern as character extraction, but the only difference is you'll have to give a range within the square brackets. If I want to extract the first four characters in a string, I'll give the range as 0:4 because the first character's index is 0 and the fourth character's index is 3. In slicing, the end of the range (4 in our case) would be omitted. Hence, 0:4 and not 0:3. Let's try and see what we get!

```
a = 'Hello there!'
print(a[0:4])
```

Run the preceding code, and you'll get this:

```
= RESTART: C:/Users/aarthi/AppData/Local/Programs/Python/
Python38-32/strings.py
Hell
```

Yup, we got it!

What if we want the last four characters instead? You can do it in two ways. The positive index of the last character is 11, and that of the fourth last character is 8, so we can do the following:

```
print(a[8:12])
```

Run the preceding code, and we'll get this:

```
= RESTART: C:/Users/aarthi/AppData/Local/Programs/Python/
Python38-32/strings.py
ere!
```

Great! So far so good. But what about negative indices? The negative index of the last character is –1 and that of the fourth last character is –4, so we can do the following instead:

```
print(a[-4:-1])
```

Notice how we've given –4 (fourth last character) first, which will be included. But –1 would not be included, am I right? That's how the syntax works, and that's the last index.

Okay, let's run the preceding code and see if it works:

```
= RESTART: C:/Users/aarthi/AppData/Local/Programs/Python/
Python38-32/strings.py
Ere
```

Ah well, it doesn't work. We're missing a "!". ☹

What can we do? Well, in situations like this, where you start from a point and need the rest of the string (fourth last position to the end of the string), you can just leave the last number in the range blank, like this:

```
print(a[-4:])
```

Run the preceding code, and you'll get this:

```
= RESTART: C:/Users/aarthi/AppData/Local/Programs/Python/
Python38-32/strings.py
ere!
```

Perfect!

String methods – magic with strings!

Just like with numbers (Chapter 5), you have plenty of pre-defined methods that'll help you play with numbers. Some of them look magical! You'll see.

There's a complete list of Python string methods and explanation of what they do in the Python official docs. Here's the link: `https://docs.python.org/2.5/lib/string-methods.html`.

You can refer to the preceding doc in the future. I'll try to cover most of the important methods, though I can't cover every single one as that would just make the chapter too long. Don't worry though. Once you learn a few, you'll be able to decipher how the rest work.

Alright, let's get started!

Why don't we start with something simple? The len() method is used to find the length of the string.

The syntax of the method is as follows: len(string)

```
a = 'Hello there!'
print(len(a))
```

When you run the preceding code, you'll get this:

```
= RESTART: C:\Users\aarthi\AppData\Local\Programs\Python\
Python38-32\strings.py
12
```

Count the number of characters in the string (including the space) and you'll notice that its length is indeed 12.

Capital and small

Alright, now let's look at the other methods. The "capitalize()" method capitalizes the first word in the string. It doesn't change the original string. It just creates a copy that you can either assign to a new variable or print.

The syntax is like this: string.capitalize().

The "string" could either be the exact string inside quotes or the variable that's storing the string.

```
a = 'i am here'
print(a.capitalize())
print(a)
```

When you run the preceding code, you'll get this:

```
= RESTART: C:\Users\aarthi\AppData\Local\Programs\Python\
Python38-32\strings.py
I am here
i am here
```

See, the capitalization did not affect the original string.

In the same vein, you can capitalize all the characters (alphabets) of a string using the upper() method. This creates a copy too. All the string methods create copies. They rarely make changes to the original string.

```
a = 'i am here'
print(a.upper())
```

When you run the preceding code, you'll get this:

```
= RESTART: C:\Users\aarthi\AppData\Local\Programs\Python\
Python38-32\strings.py
I AM HERE
```

Similarly, you can change all the capitalized letters to small letters in a string using the lower() method.

```
a = 'I AM here'
print(a.lower())
```

When you run the preceding code, you'll get this:

```
= RESTART: C:\Users\aarthi\AppData\Local\Programs\Python\
Python38-32\strings.py
i am here
```

Did you notice how some of the letters were already small? Those just go unchanged with this method.

Instead of just capitalizing the first letter of the entire string, like in capitalize, you can actually capitalize every first letter of every word in the string using the title() method.

```
a = 'i love chimpanzies!'
print(a.title())
```

Run the preceding code, and you'll get this:

```
= RESTART: C:\Users\aarthi\AppData\Local\Programs\Python\
Python38-32\strings.py
I Love Chimpanzies!
```

Misc methods

Using the count method, you can return the number of times a word or letter or phrase appears in a string.

The syntax is `string.count('word')`.

This method is case sensitive, just like the rest of the methods in Python, so if you want "word", don't type it as "Word".

To test this method, I'm creating a multi-line string like how I taught you:

```
a = '''Susan is a lovely girl.
Barky is Susan's best friend.
Barky plays with Susan'''
```

Let's count how many times 'Susan' and 'Barky' are mentioned in the preceding string, shall we?

```
print(a.count('Susan'))
print(a.count('Barky'))
```

The result is this:

```
= RESTART: C:\Users\aarthi\AppData\Local\Programs\Python\
Python38-32\strings.py
3
2
```

Whoo! ☺

You can trim extra spaces in a string with the strip() method.

```
a = '           Hello there!             '
print(a.strip())
```

When you run the preceding code, you'll get this:

```
= RESTART: C:\Users\aarthi\AppData\Local\Programs\Python\
Python38-32\strings.py
Hello there!
```

No spaces at all!

There are left and ride side versions of the same method. The rstrip() method only strips the whitespaces in the right side of the string. The lstrip() method does the same for the left side of the string. Why don't you try them out and see if they work right?

Remember that big string we just worked with? What if we made a mistake? What if we were going to talk about Ronny and not Susan? We need to swap their names, am I right? You can use the replace method to do that. The syntax is `string.replace('original','replaced')`.

```
a = '''Susan is a lovely girl.
Barky is Susan's best friend.
Barky plays with Susan'''
print(a.replace('Susan','Ronny'))
```

Let's run the preceding code, and we'll get this:

```
= RESTART: C:\Users\aarthi\AppData\Local\Programs\Python\
Python38-32\strings.py
Ronny is a lovely girl.
Barky is Ronny's best friend.
Barky plays with Ronny
```

See, it's Ronny now!

We can also find the positions from which a particular word or letter or phrase starts in a string. Remember, string positions start from 0, so you'll always be one count behind.

```
a = "I love coding. I have fun with coding"
print(a.find('coding'))
```

Run the preceding code, and you'll get this:

```
= RESTART: C:\Users\aarthi\AppData\Local\Programs\Python\
Python38-32\strings.py
7
```

Count the characters, including the spaces, and you'll notice that the first occurrence of "coding" starts at the position 8 (and hence 7 with respect to Python strings).

What if the phrase isn't found?

```
print(a.find('Coding'))
```

You know that "coding" is different from "Coding" in Python, so it wouldn't be found in the string.

```
= RESTART: C:\Users\aarthi\AppData\Local\Programs\Python\
Python38-32\strings.py
-1
```

Oops, the result was a –1.

The index() method does exactly what the find() method does. The only difference is that it returns an error if the phrase is not found, and not -1. Why don't you try to do the same with index()?

With the split method, you can literally split a string into a list. We'll be looking at what lists are in a future lesson. For now, just know that lists hold multiple values within them, separated by commas.

In order to use the split method, you need to give a separator. Let's say I want the string to be taken apart by word. Then I'd give a single space as the separator.

```
a = "I love coding."
print(a.split(' '))
```

When you run the preceding code, you'll get this:

```
= RESTART: C:\Users\aarthi\AppData\Local\Programs\Python\
Python38-32\strings.py
['I', 'love', 'coding.']
```

That's a list and it holds our string, separated by word.

True? False?

Before I move further with the methods, I want to teach you the concept of true and false in Python, or any programming language, really. It's quite simple. If something is true, then your program will return "True". If a condition is false, then you'll get "False". That's it.

For example, let's say I want to see if my string has the words "best friend" in it. I really want to know if Barky is Ronny's best friend or not.

I'll have to use the "in" keyword. Keywords are special words that do something in Python. The "in" keyword checks whether what the word or phrase we want looked up is inside our string or not.

```
string = "Barky is Ronny's best friend."
print('best friend' in string)
```

Run the preceding code, and you'll get this:

```
= RESTART: C:\Users\aarthi\AppData\Local\Programs\Python\
Python38-32\strings.py
True
```

But as you know, Python is case sensitive. So, "best friend" is not the same as "Best friend" or any other versions. So use the words as is, okay?

Let's look at another example, shall we?

```
print('Python' in 'Python is fun')
```

When you run the preceding code, you'll get True.

But if you ask for this:

```
print('Coding' in 'Python is fun')
```

you'll get False because 'Coding' isn't in the string 'Python is fun.'

Similarly, you can test for a lot of other strings in your string.

Would you like to see if your string has both letters and numbers? Use the isalnum() method. It returns true only if every word in the string has both letters and numbers, like this:

```
a = 'number123 number253'
print(a.isalnum())
```

The preceding code will return True, while the below code:

```
a = 'This is a number: 123'
print(a.isalnum())
```

will return False, because most of the words have just letters and not letters *and* numbers.

The isalpha() method returns true if every single character in the string is an alphabet (no number or special characters at all). The isnumeric() method returns true if every single character in the string is a number (no alphabet or special characters).

Islower() returns true if all the characters are small. Isupper() returns true if every character is capitalized.

I want you to use these methods while giving different possibilities and explore how they *truly* work. Deal?

You can refer to the link I gave in the "String methods – magic with strings!" section to get the rest of the methods and use them in your experiments too. Have fun! :P

Hey, I know what you're thinking.

"Oh man, that's a lot of methods. How would I ever remember them all?"

Well, why should you? I'll let you in on a biggg secret...Shhhhhh

Programmers don't try to memorize syntaxes when they start out. That's what Google's for. They just create a lot. They solve a lot of puzzles, create fun projects, and Google for syntaxes when they get stuck. Over time, the syntaxes just get stuck in their head because they've used them so much.

So, forget about memorizing. Use this book as a reference. Solve the puzzles, create the mini projects with your twist, and take the big projects to the next level, and by the time you're done with them all, you'll be a master of Python. Just have fun. ☺

String formatting

The print statement is boring and limiting. ☹ You can't format it the way you want, and if you try, you'll drown in a mess of quotes. But more than that, you can't print numbers (even if they're in variables) with strings! :O

Let me prove that to you.

```
a = 4
b = 5
sum = a + b
```

So now, I want to print the following statement: 4 + 5 = 9, and I want to print it using the variable names and not the actual values, to keep things dynamic. I can maybe change the value of a variable, and my print statement will automatically change too.

We should be able to do that with the concatenation we learned about before, right? Let's try.

```
print('The answer is: ' + a + ' + ' + b + ' = ' + sum)
```

The preceding code should ideally result in this:

The answer is: `4 + 5 = 9`

But this is what we get:

```
= RESTART: C:\Users\aarthi\AppData\Local\Programs\Python\
Python38-32\strings.py
Traceback (most recent call last):
  File "C:\Users\aarthi\AppData\Local\Programs\Python\
  Python38-32\strings.py", line 4, in <module>
    print('The answer is: ' + a + ' + ' + b + ' = ' + sum)
TypeError: can only concatenate str (not "int") to str
```

Essentially, what the error says is you can only concatenate a string (anything within quotes) with a string, and the variables that contain numbers (without quotes) within them are not strings.

Not only was that statement very hard and confusing for me to create, it simply didn't work.

That's where formatting comes in. You can format the way your print statements are written. Just place {} (without space) where your variables come in, and you can fill them later using the format method.

Let's start with something simple.

```
a = 'apple'
```

Let's say I want to print 'This is an apple', where the value 'apple' comes from the variable a.

I'd type the entire string out, but place {} in the place of 'apple', like this:

```
'This is an {}'
```

Next, I'll tag the format method and place the variable "a" inside the parenthesis. Python will automatically replace the {} with the value inside your variable.

```
a = 'apple'
print('This is an {}'.format(a))
```

When you run the preceding code, you'll get this:

```
= RESTART: C:\Users\aarthi\AppData\Local\Programs\Python\
Python38-32\strings.py
This is an apple
```

Very simple, wasn't it? You don't have to mess around with spaces and quotes anymore, whoohoo!

Let's go for a more complex example now, shall we?

```
a = 'Apples'
b = 'Bananas'
```

If I wanted to print "Apples and Bananas are good for your health", this is how I'd do it:

```
print('{} and {} are good for your health'.format(a,b))
```

Run the preceding code, and you'll get this:

```
= RESTART: C:\Users\aarthi\AppData\Local\Programs\Python\
Python38-32\strings.py
Apples and Bananas are good for your health
```

Did you notice how I have the variables inside the format, separated by commas?

You can place the first part of the string inside a variable and use that as well, like this:

```
a = 'Apples'
b = 'Bananas'
s = '{} and {} are good for your health'
print(s.format(a,b))
```

Or, if I want Bananas to be printed first and then Apples, but I don't want to change the order in which they are listed, I can just label them in the string to be printed, like this:

```
s = '{1} and {0} are good for your health'
print(s.format(a,b))
```

Indices start with 0 in Python, remember?

Run the preceding code, and you'll get this:

```
= RESTART: C:\Users\aarthi\AppData\Local\Programs\Python\
Python38-32\strings.py
Bananas and Apples are good for your health
```

Alright. Now that we're experts at using format() to design our print, why don't we go back to our original problem?

```
a = 4
b = 5
sum = a + b
```

Let's format our string!

```
print('The answer is: {} + {} = {}'.format(a,b,sum))
```

Run the preceding code, and you'll get this:

```
= RESTART: C:\Users\aarthi\AppData\Local\Programs\Python\
Python38-32\strings.py
The answer is: 4 + 5 = 9
```

YES! Easy and neat, just the way it should be. ☺

Getting input from the users (start automation)

So far, we've just been fixing the values of our variables. That's so boring! I want automation. That's what programming is all about, isn't it?

I want to give a different number every time I run my addition program, a different string every time I want to print a message. That's what an input is. A user or the person who runs the program gives values that can be used in the program to get a result. Those values are called inputs.

In Python, you can use the input() method to get inputs. Pretty straightforward, isn't it?

When you run a program, it'll ask you for the value, and wait until you give the same. That is called prompting.

I'm going to start simple. I'm going to get a message I can immediately print. It's always good practice to include a message while asking for inputs, so the user know what value they're expected to give. You can include the message within quotes inside input's parenthesis.

```
message = input('Enter your message: ')
print('Here is your message: ' + message)
```

I've prompted the user to enter a message, and I've received the same inside the variable "message". Then I've printed it out. Simple.

When I run the preceding code, this is what I'd get first:

```
= RESTART: C:\Users\aarthi\AppData\Local\Programs\Python\
Python38-32\strings.py
Enter your message:
```

The program has stopped at this stage because it's waiting for my message.

Let me enter it now:

```
Enter your message: I love Python!
```

When I press Enter, I'll get this:

```
Here is your message: I love Python!
```

It works perfectly! My message was printed out in the format I wanted.

String to int or float conversion

We looked at inputs and how we can dynamically get values and use them in our program. Isn't calculation one of the best ways to use dynamic values? I want a different number every time I perform an addition operation.

Let me use input for the same and see if it works.

```
a = input('First number: ')
b = input('Second number: ')
sum = a + b
print('{} + {} = {}'.format(a,b,sum))
```

Everything looks good in the preceding code snippet. It should work, right? Wrong.

When I run it, this is what I get:

```
= RESTART: C:\Users\aarthi\AppData\Local\Programs\Python\
Python38-32\strings.py
First number: 5
Second number: 2
 5 +  2 =  5 2
```

My program prompted me for the two numbers, and I entered them. All good till now. But then, things went wonky with the addition.

Why?

You haven't entered numbers at all. When you give values to an input, your program considers it as a string, not a number. So, what happened here is string concatenation, and not addition.

How do we make Python look at our inputs as numbers? You need to convert them, of course! Remember how we converted different types of numbers? Similarly, you can convert a string to either an integer using the int() method or a floating-point number using the float() method.

Let's modify our code:

```
a = input('First number: ')
#Convert 'a' into an integer and store it back in 'a'
a = int(a)
b = input('Second number: ')
#Convert 'b' into an integer and store it back in 'b'
b = int(b)
sum = a + b
print('{} + {} = {}'.format(a,b,sum))
```

The only thing I changed in the code is the integer conversions after getting each input. I've stored the converted values back in the same variable as well. Let's run this code and see if it works:

```
= RESTART: C:\Users\aarthi\AppData\Local\Programs\Python\
Python38-32\strings.py
First number: 5
Second number: 2
5 + 2 = 7
```

Phew! It works now.

Mini project – take *Turtle* text to the next level!

This is going to be a simple project. We're going to take your user's name as input in real time and print it out, in big, colored font in our *Turtle* screen:

1. Let's set up our *Turtle* first:

```
import turtle
s = turtle.getscreen()
t = turtle.Turtle()
```

2. Next, let's get create a variable name that gets the user's name as input:

```
name = input("What's your name? ")
```

3. We won't have to convert this string in any way, since we're just going to concatenate it with another string. Let's create our customized greeting on *Turtle* now. Before we do that, let's create the exact string we want to print and assign it to a variable "greeting".

```
greeting = 'Hi {}!'.format(name)
```

4. Now, let's set a pen color of, maybe, Dark Violet? And let's also move the pen to the position -250,0 so it draws in the center of the screen.

   ```
   t.pencolor('DarkViolet')
   t.penup()
   t.goto(-250,0)
   t.pendown()
   ```

5. Finally, let's create our text.

   ```
   t.write(greeting,font=('Georgia',45,'normal','bold','i
   talic'))
   ```

   I've placed the variable "greeting" with the text we need in place of the actual text, and I've also set the font style as 'Georgia' and size as 45, and I've made the text bold and italic. I've omitted the move property, so it's going to be "false" by default (no arrow below the text).

6. Finally, let's hide our turtles:

   ```
   t.hideturtle()
   turtle.hideturtle()
   ```

Let's run this program now:

```
= RESTART: C:\Users\aarthi\AppData\Local\Programs\Python\
Python38-32\strings.py
What's your name? Susan Smith
```

It asked for the name. I gave the name as "Susan Smith", pressed enter, and voila! (Figure 8-4).

Figure 8-4. *Colorful greeting*

We have our greeting, and it looks pretty too! ☺

Mini project – shout at the screen

We're going to do what the title says. Let's shout at the screen, shall we? Oh wait...or is the screen going to shout at us? Either way, let's do some shouting! Whoo!

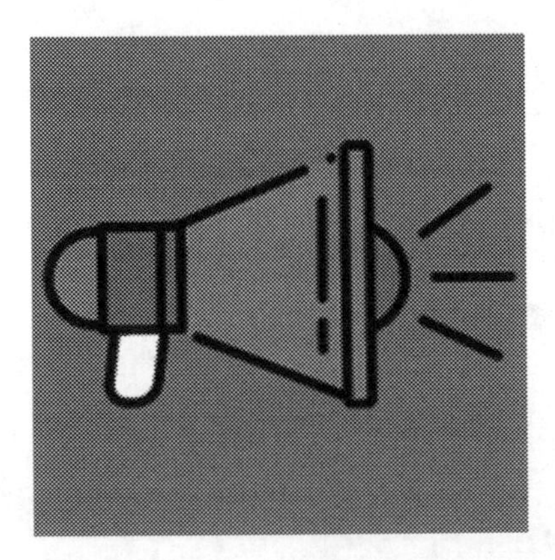

The concept is simple. We're going to get a string input from the user. The message is going to be "Enter what's on your mind in less than 3 words". Less than three words so our text can be displayed in a big enough font in one line. In the later chapters, you'll learn the tools needed to get as many words of input as you want, and make sure you print them all by making space, so don't worry about that right now.

Then, we're going to capitalize the result, add two or more exclamation points at the end, and print everything in *Turtle*. Simple, right? Let's do it!

1. To start, let's set up the *Turtle* package:

```
import turtle
s = turtle.getscreen()
t = turtle.Turtle()
```

2. Then, let's get the input:

```
message = input("Enter what's on your mind in 3 words
or less: ")
```

3. Finally, let's format the message we want to shout! Our "message" is probably in small letters. How do we convert every single letter in our message to uppercase? Yes! The upper() method. Let's use that, and tag on three exclamation points at the end, to make our message more dramatic!

```
shout = '{}!!!'.format(message.upper())
```

4. Now, I'm going to move the pen to -250,0 and change the color of the pen to Red, because nothing says shouting more than Red. ☺

```
t.pencolor('Red')
t.penup()
t.goto(-250,0)
t.pendown()
```

5. Now, on to the main part of the program. Let's create our *Turtle* text. I'm going to use the 'Arial Black' font for this. The size of the font is going to be 45, but I'm going to stop at making the text bold. No italics this time.

```
t.write(shout,font=('Arial Black',45,'normal','bold'))
```

6. Finally, let's hide the turtles.

```
t.hideturtle()
turtle.hideturtle()
```

Let's run everything. My message is going to be "what is this?". Let's see what we get:

```
= RESTART: C:\Users\aarthi\AppData\Local\Programs\Python\
Python38-32\strings.py
```

Enter what's on your mind in three words or less: What is this?

When I press Enter and look at my *Turtle* screen, I get this (Figure 8-5).

Figure 8-5. *Shout at the screen*

Yes! Success!

Mini project – reverse your name

I'm going to teach you something fun while solving this project. So far, we've seen all kinds of ways in which we can manipulate our strings. Why don't we look at one more before we end this chapter?

Did you know that you can reverse your string? Yes, that's right! Complete reversal, with just one teeny tiny line of code. Would you like to try?

Let's create a program that gets the name of the user as input, reverses their name, and displays it in the *Turtle* screen:

1. Let's set up *Turtle*, as usual.

```
import turtle
s = turtle.getscreen()
t = turtle.Turtle()
```

2. And get the user's name and place it in the variable "name".

```
name = input("What's your name?")
```

3. Now comes the interesting part! We're going to format the string we want displayed as usual. We've created a variable "reverse" to store the string. But how do we reverse? Remember how we used to use square brackets to access separate characters, extract parts of the string, and so on? Also, do you remember negative indices? There you go!

   If you use the following syntax, you can reverse your string: string[::-1]. So, that's a double colon, followed by a -1. Simple as that! ☺

```
reverse = '{}'.format(name[::-1])
```

4. Finally, let's change the color of the pen to 'Gold', shift position to -250,0, and draw the reversed string on screen.

```
t.pencolor('Gold')
t.penup()
t.goto(-250,0)
t.pendown()
t.write(reverse,font=('Georgia',45,'normal','bold'))
t.hideturtle()
turtle.hideturtle()
```

Let's run the program:

```
= RESTART: C:\Users\aarthi\AppData\Local\Programs\Python\
Python38-32\strings.py
What's your name? Susan Smith
```

Now, click Enter, and you'll get this (Figure 8-6).

Figure 8-6. *Reverse your name*

Hehe, her name was reversed, alright. :P

Mini project – colorful and dynamic Math

In the numbers chapter, we had to resort to doing boring calculations with pre-defined numbers and no colors! ☹

So, I thought we could have some real fun with numbers before we move on to the next chapter. Shall we?

In this project, we're going to perform addition, multiplication, subtraction, and division on two given numbers. Boring, I know! But this time around, we're going to get the two numbers as dynamic input from the user and display the results, in color, in *Turtle*. Interesting? I know!

1. Let's set up *Turtle* first.

```
import turtle
s = turtle.getscreen()
t = turtle.Turtle()
```

2. Then, let's get the inputs for the first and second numbers we're going to use in our operations. But there's an issue! We can't use them as it is. They are in string formats, remember? So, let's convert them to integers and assign them back to the same variables.

```
num1 = input("Enter the first number: ")
num1 = int(num1)
num2 = input("Enter the second number: ")
num2 = int(num2)
```

3. Now, let's do the addition. We're going to create a variable called display which is going to hold all the formatted strings of the four operations.

```
#Addition
add = num1 + num2
display = "{} + {} = {}".format(num1,num2,add)
```

4. Once formatted, let's position our pen at -150,150 so our drawing is aligned to the middle of the screen. Then, let's change the color of the pen to "Red" and draw the text.

```
t.penup()
t.goto(-150,150)
t.pendown()
t.pencolor("Red")
t.write(display,font=("Georgia",40,"normal","bold"))
```

5. Do the same for subtraction now, except that the position is going to be -150,50 now and the color is going to be "Blue".

```
#Subtraction
sub = num1 - num2
display = "{} - {} = {}".format(num1,num2,add)
t.penup()
t.goto(-150,50)
t.pendown()
t.pencolor("Blue")
t.write(display,font=("Georgia",40,"normal","bold"))
```

6. For multiplication, the position is going to be -150,-50 and the color is going to be "Green".

```
#Multiplication
mul = num1 * num2
display = "{} * {} = {}".format(num1,num2,add)
t.penup()
t.goto(-150,-50)
t.pendown()
t.pencolor("Green")
t.write(display,font=("Georgia",40,"normal","bold"))
```

7. For division, the position is going to be -150,-150 and the color is going to be "Violet".

```
#Division
div = num1 / num2
display = "{} / {} = {}".format(num1,num2,add)
t.penup()
t.goto(-150,-150)
t.pendown()
t.pencolor("Violet")
t.write(display,font=("Georgia",40,"normal","bold"))
```

8. Finally, let's hide the turtles.

```
t.hideturtle()
turtle.hideturtle()
```

9. Now, let's run the program. It asks for inputs first. Our inputs are going to be 10 and 5.

```
= RESTART: C:\Users\aarthi\AppData\Local\Programs\
Python\Python38-32\strings.py
Enter the first number: 10
Enter the second number: 5
```

When we click Enter, this is what we get (Figure 8-7).

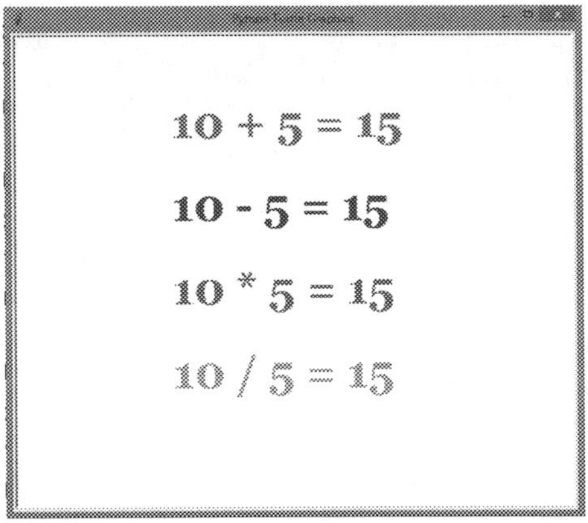

10 + 5 = 15

10 - 5 = 15

10 * 5 = 15

10 / 5 = 15

Figure 8-7. *Colorful and dynamic Math*

Beautiful! ☺

Summary

In this chapter, we looked at strings, what they are, creating single-line, multi-line, and empty strings, creating strings with quotes, concatenating two or more strings, accessing characters in strings, extracting parts of a string, string slicing, how to manipulate strings in different ways, and getting inputs from users and using them in our program.

In the next chapter, let's look at how we can command our program to do whatever we want. We're going to look at "if" statements, creating multiple options with "if else" and "if elif else" statements, and a lot more. It's going to be fun! ☺

CHAPTER 9

Follow My Command!

In the previous chapter, we learned all about strings and how to use them to create strings of letters and numbers, how to manipulate the strings in any way we want, how to get input from the users and convert it into the data type we want, and how to format outputs (especially in print statements) to our preference.

In this chapter, let's look at how to command our computers with "if and else" statements.

True or False

In programming, true or false determines the direction your program goes. If "something" is true, do "something". If it's false, do "something else". You can create a lot of programs with just the preceding "condition".

So, to give commands to your system, you need three things (Figure 9-1).

A. Elumalai, *Introduction to Python for Kids*, https://doi.org/10.1007/978-1-4842-6812-4_9

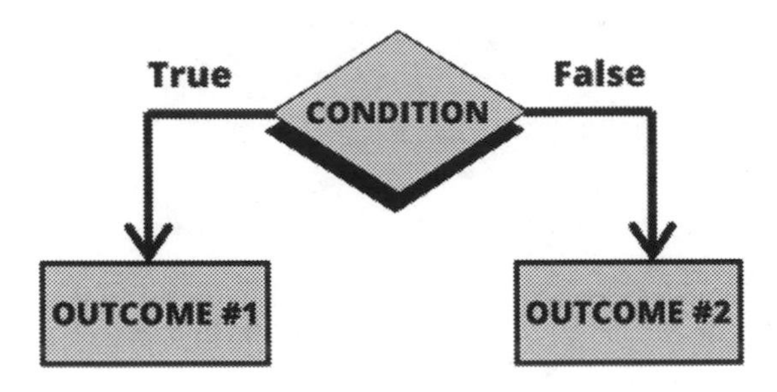

Figure 9-1. *Conditions and their results*

1. A condition that will be evaluated by Python
2. A true or false result
3. A syntax that decides what happens next based on the result, that is, a syntax that directs to either of the two outcomes based on the result

Let's look at the true or false results first. "True" and "False" are also values in Python. They are called Boolean values. Just like we have our strings and numbers, we can assign Boolean values to variables, convert them to another value type, find its type (Boolean), and so on. Would you like to see how to do those?

Let's create a new script file for this chapter. I've created one called condition.py. I'm going to be using and reusing this file throughout this chapter. True and False need to be written with a capital T and F, or you'll get an error, so please remember that.

Let's create variables "a" and "b" and assign them values "True" and "False".

```
a = True
b = False
print('a is {} & b is {}'.format(a,b))
```

When you run the preceding code, you'll get this:

```
= RESTART: C:/Users/aarthi/AppData/Local/Programs/Python/
Python38-32/condition.py
a is True & b is False
```

Okay, so now we know how to use our Boolean values. But what are they really? Did you know that Booleans are actually just 1s and 0s? :O

Oh yes, your True is read by your computer as 1 and False is read by your computer as 0. Your computer is a very simple creature. It converts all of the complicated, weird codes and scripts you send it into very simple 1- and 0-based values. True and False values get converted to the base of them all – a 1 and a 0.

Why don't we verify if that's true? If I convert my Boolean values to an integer, I should get a 1 or 0.

```
a = True
a = int(a)
b = False
b= int(b)
print('a is {} & b is {}'.format(a,b))
```

I've modified the preceding code, and I've inserted integer conversions. Let's see what we get:

```
= RESTART: C:/Users/aarthi/AppData/Local/Programs/Python/
Python38-32/condition.py
a is 1 & b is 0
```

Look at that! True converted to 1 and False converted to 0!

Similarly, you can convert numbers and strings to Boolean values by using the bool() method. Anything that's not an empty string, or the number 0 will return a True. Yes, even negative numbers will return True! Why don't we test that?

I'm going to test the same directly in my Shell.

1 converts to True.

```
>>> bool(1)
True
```

0 converts to False.

```
>>> bool(0)
False
```

A string with something inside it converts to True. That'll be the case for strings with just a space inside it as well.

```
>>> bool('hi there!')
True
```

An empty string converts to False.

```
>>> bool('')
False
```

There is a value "None" in Python. It basically means that there is nothing inside of it. If "None" is assigned to a variable, the value inside that variable will be replaced with nothing. Naturally, "None" converts to False.

```
>>> bool(None)
False
```

We'll be looking at more values called lists, tuples, and sets in a later chapter. When we do, you'll notice that lists, tuples, and sets that hold something inside of them convert to True and empty lists, tuples, and sets convert to false.

Compare and decide

Alright, we've looked at the results. But how do we get them? We need conditions that return those results, don't we? Python has a lot of conditions you can use! Would you like to see? I'm going to remind you again of your Math class here.

Remember the greater than (>) and lesser than (<) symbols? What do they do? They compare two things, usually numbers, and decide if that expression is true or false. Are you seeing what I'm going with this?

Yes, you can use those symbols as your conditions! Why don't we test them in our Shell?

Is 3 greater than 5?

```
>>> 3 > 5
False
```

Nope.

```
>>> 3 < 5
True
```

Is 3 lesser than 5 though? Oh yes!

Look at that, it works! You can even test for equality. Are two numbers equal? Just use two equal to symbols instead of one, and you're good to go!

```
>>> 3 == 3
True
```

Sweet!

You can also see if two values are not equal using the not equal to operator, !=, like this:

```
>>> 2 != 2
False
```

Is 2 not equal to 2? Nope, they're both equal, so you got a False.

You can do this with strings too, you know, not just numbers.

```
>>> 'hello' == 'Hello'
False
```

We got a false. Can you guess why? Yes! Python is case sensitive, so "h" is not equal to "H".

You can shorten things up by checking if something is lesser than OR equal to something else using the <= symbol.

```
>>> 2 <= 2
True
```

The preceding code is true because even though 2 is not lesser than 2, it is certainly equal to 2, and since one of the conditions is true, the result is true.

Similarly, you can check if something is greater than or equal to something else using the >= symbol.

```
>>> 3 >= 5
False
```

3 is neither greater than nor equal to 5 so the result is False.

If this happens, do this (command!)

We know all about "True", "False", and conditions now. What's next? Commands, of course!

You have a nifty little tool in Python to give commands with. It's called the "if" statement. Can you guess what it does? Let me give you a hint: it has something to do with "if". :P

So far, you know how to create conditions and how to interpret their results (true or false), and now let's put it all together to give a command.

It's pretty simple actually. In plain English, this is what an "if" statement does: It checks for a condition, and if that condition is true, then it executes a statement or multiple statements. If it's not true, then those statements won't be executed, and your program will move on to the next line of code.

Let me show a quick illustration of how an "if" statement works so you understand it better (Figure 9-2).

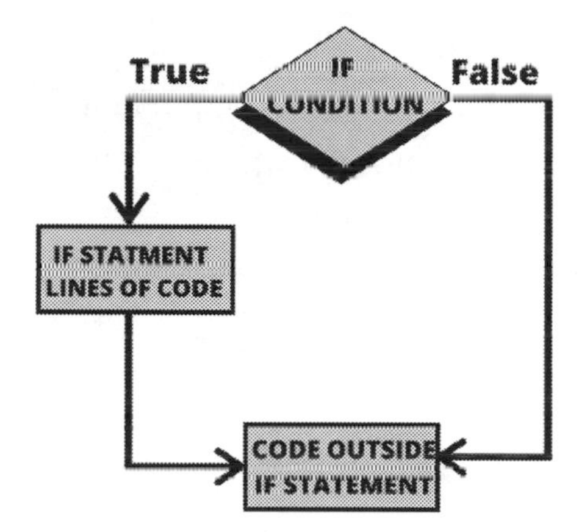

Figure 9-2. *"if" statement*

The syntax of an "if" statement is this:

```
if comparison:
        lines of code
```

"if" has a small "i", and the statements within the if statement should be written with an indentation, which is basically a space/tab. The colon ":" after the comparison is mandatory as well. If you don't indent the "inner" lines of code, then Python wouldn't know that those lines of code belong to the "if" statement and should only be executed if the condition is true. So, remember to indent, okay? ☺

Alright, so now that we know how if statements work, let's put that to test. I want to print "You're a little kid" if someone's age is less than 5. Just that.

How can we do that? Well...the condition could be `age < 5` or something like that. If I want to include 5 years old in this list, then I could make it `age <= 5`. I could include a print statement inside of my statement, which basically says "You're a little kid". That should do it, right? Let's test!

```
age = input("What's your age? ")
age = int(age)
if age <= 5:
    print("You're a little kid :)")
```

I've created a variable age, gotten the input from the user, and converted the default string into an integer so it can be compared with the number.

Run the preceding code, and you'll get this:

```
= RESTART: C:\Users\aarthi\AppData\Local\Programs\Python\
Python38-32\condition.py
What's your age? 5
You're a little kid :)
```

Yay, it works! ☺ You've executed your very first conditional command in Python. Time for a celebration.

Now, I want you to give any number greater than 5 and see what you get.

Did you try? You get nothing, am I right? Well, that's not ideal. Let's fix this issue in the next section!

Else?

We saw that if a condition is true, we can execute the inner statements of the "if" statement. But if it's not true, nothing happens. But what if I want something to happen? If the kid is older than 5 years old, then I want "You're a big kid" to be printed out. How do I do that?

"if" statements have something called "else" statements that accompany them. They basically get executed if the "if" statement is false. Let me illustrate how that works (Figure 9-3).

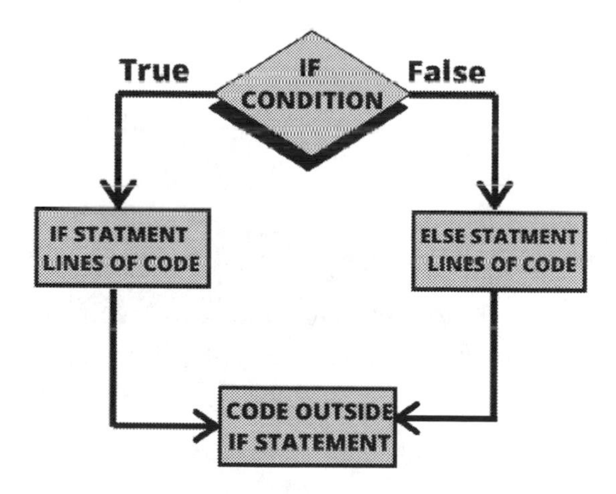

Figure 9-3. *"if else" statement*

The syntax of an else statement is very simple:

```
else:
        inner lines of code
```

You should place a colon right after "else" since we don't need to check for conditions this time around. Also, just like with your "if" statement, place your inner lines of code after an indentation or tab or space.

Let's test how this works now!

```
age = input("What's your age? ")
age = int(age)
if age <= 5:
    print("You're a little kid! :)")
else:
    print("You're a big kid! :)")
```

Now let's give the age as maybe 8 and see what our program does:

```
= RESTART: C:\Users\aarthi\AppData\Local\Programs\Python\
Python38-32\condition.py
What's your age? 8
You're a big kid! :)
```

Whoa!

More than one condition! :O

You know, sometimes, things aren't just black and white, right? If someone is older than 5 years old, they're not necessarily still a kid. If they're older than 12, they'd be a teenager. If they're older than 18, they'd be an adult. But our program isn't considering all of that. Hmm... It's incomplete, don't you think? Let's fix that.

There's something called the "elif" statement that can be inserted between the "if" and the "else" statements. Can you guess what an elif does? It's in the name, isn't it? If something is false, then we're going to check for a second condition to see if *that* is true. You can stack up any number of elif statements like this, one after the other, before ending things with an else statement. Let me illustrate how that works.

The syntax of an elif statement (after an if and before an else) is as follows (Figure 9-4):

```
elif condition:
     Inner lines of code
```

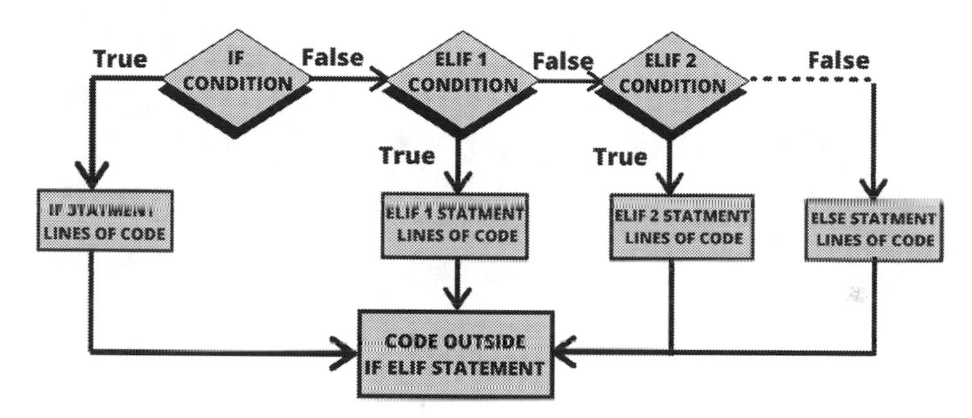

Figure 9-4. *"if elif else" statement*

Let's put our elifs to test now, shall we? I'm going to create a main "if" condition that tests if age `<= 5` (little kid). If that's not true, we'll include another condition that tests if age `<= 12` (big kid). We're going to include a third condition that tests if age `<= 19` (teenager) and finally a fourth condition that tests if age `>= 20` (adult).

Okay, sounds good, but what is the else statement for? Well, the else statement is going to catch everything else. For instance, if your user gave a string or any other non-numerical value as your input by mistake, then your else statement will "catch" that and ask them to re-run the program. Is that clear enough? Shall we write this in code and see if it works? Alright!

```
age = input("What's your age? ")
age = int(age)
if age <= 5:
    print("You're a little kid! :)")
elif age <= 12:
    print("You're a big kid! :)")
```

```
elif age <= 19:
    print("You're a teenager! :)")
elif age >= 20:
    print("Wow, you're an adult already!")
else:
    print("Looks like you've not entered a number. Please re-
    run the program")
```

I'm going to run the preceding lines of code with age as 13.

```
= RESTART: C:\Users\aarthi\AppData\Local\Programs\Python\
Python38-32\condition.py
What's your age? 13
You're a teenager! :)
```

Now, I want you to run the program with different values for age every time (numbers and otherwise) and see what you get. Why don't you try giving a string once too? Have fun! ☺

Mini project – guess the number game

This is going to be a simple little game. We aren't going to use "*Turtle*" for this, but feel free to use it in any part of the game as you'd like.

So, the game works like this: When the game starts, the program will generate a number between 1 and 10 (including both 1 and 10). Then, the user gets three guesses to guess the number right. If they guessed the number right in any of the guesses, they win. If not, they lose. Simple, right? Let's try!

1. Let's import the "random" module first. We need this module because we're going to generate a number between 1 and 10 when the game starts, the number the user needs to guess.

   ```
   import random
   ```

2. Let's start by printing a message that introduces the game. Then, let's generate our random number. We're going to use the randrange() method of the "random" module. Do you remember this method? It generates a random number from within the range, excluding the last number in the range. We need a number between 1 and 10, so the range is going to be 1,11.

   ```
   print('Guess a number and win!')
   number = random.randrange(1,11)
   ```

3. Then, let's get the first guess from the user. Inputs are usually strings, so let's convert them to integers first.

   ```
   guess1 = input('Guess a number between 1 and 10 - Your
   first try: ')
   guess1 = int(guess1)
   ```

4. Now, we're going to start our comparisons. If the first guess is equal to the number, then print a success message. If not, start an "else" statement. In the else statement, start over again. Get the second guess, and inside the "else", start an inner "if" statement that checks if the second guess is the same as the number to be guessed.

```
if(guess1 == number):
    print('You guessed it right! :)')
else:
    guess2 = input('Guess again - Your second try: ')
    guess2 = int(guess2)
    if(guess2 == number):
        print('You guessed it right! :)')
```

5. We're going to do the same thing with the third try.

```
else:
    guess3 = input('Guess again - Your final try: ')
    guess3 = int(guess3)
    if(guess3 == number):
       print('You guessed it right! :)')
```

6. Finally, the last "else" statement. If they've still not guessed after three tries, then the program will run the final "else" statement and print a sad message. ☹ Why don't we also tell them what the number was? They'd probably want to know that, right?

7. And, that's it! A simple little program.

```
else:
    print('Sorry! You used up all your tries! :(')
    print('The number was {}'.format(number))
```

Why don't we see if this game works? Let's run the above code, and we'll get this:

```
= RESTART: C:\Users\aarthi\AppData\Local\Programs\Python\
Python38-32\condition.py
Guess a number and win!
Guess a number between 1 and 10 - Your first try: 5
Guess again - Your second try: 7
You guessed it right! :)
```

I guessed on the second try! Whohoo! ☺

Let's try again:

```
= RESTART: C:\Users\aarthi\AppData\Local\Programs\Python\
Python38-32\condition.py
Guess a number and win!
Guess a number between 1 and 10 - Your first try: 10
Guess again - Your second try: 6
Guess again - Your final try: 3
Sorry! You used up all your tries! :(
The number was 2
```

Oops, I missed it this time around. The number was 2. ☹

The conditions keep stacking up!

Sometimes, you might want to check for more than one condition at the same time. Or you might want your condition to be the opposite of what it is.

Python gives you two options to make that happen. These are called *logical operators*, and you can use them to combine conditional statements (comparisons) and arrive at a final True or False result. Confused? Don't be. I'll explain. ☺

The first one is the ***and*** operator. If you use the "and" operator on two or more comparisons, then the condition will return true *only* if ***all*** the comparisons hold true.

The syntax is as follows:

```
(comparison1) and (comparison2)
```

You can write the comparisons without brackets as well and the execution will still happen properly (comparisons have higher precedence to logical operators), but it's always good practice to include them to make the order of execution clearer.

Let me explain how the "and" operator works. What's the meaning of "and" in English? Inclusion of everything, surrounding the "and", right? So, when you use this statement around two or more conditions, the final result is True only if all the conditions around it are True. If even one of those conditions is False, then you'll end up with a False, even if the other condition is True. Why don't I explain this with an illustration? (Figure 9-5)

AND Statement

Condition 1	Condition 1	Result
True	True	True
True	False	False
False	True	False
False	False	False

Figure 9-5. *"and" statement and its results*

Do you understand how "and" works now?

Next, you have the ***or*** operator. How does that work? Simple, really. In English, "or" means "either or", am I right? So, if either of the conditions around the "or" operator is true, then the entire statement is true.

If you use the “or” operator on two or more comparisons, then the condition will return true if ***any*** of those comparisons hold true.

The syntax is as follows:

```
(comparison1) or (comparison2)
```

Let me illustrate how the “or” statement works as well (Figure 9-6).

OR Statement

Condition 1	Condition 1	Result
True	True	True
True	False	True
False	True	True
False	False	False

Figure 9-6. *“or” statement and its results*

Finally, there is the ***not*** operator. There’s nothing to guess here. It’s pretty simple, isn’t it? The “not” operator just reverses the result. If the result of a comparison is True, then using the “not” operator on that comparison statement returns a False and vice versa.

The syntax is as follows:

```
not(comparison)
```

You can use the “not” operator on other logical statements as well:

```
not((comparison1) and (comparison2))
```

In programming, you need to make sure you always close the brackets. In the preceding syntax, we have two sets of brackets around each of the comparisons with the “and” operator in the middle and another bracket that closes around everything.

Let's finish this chapter by testing these statements in our Python Shell:

```
>>> (5 > 3) and (4 < 3)
False
```

5 is greater than 3, but 4 is not less than 3. If we used the "or" operator instead,

```
>>> (5 > 3) or (4 < 3)
True
```

we get a true because one of the comparisons is true.

Let's combine logical statements now! Why don't we do comparisons with mathematical operations to make things a little bit complicated?

```
>>> ((5 > 3) or (4 < 3)) and ((3 + 2) == 5)
True
```

Take a minute to read the preceding statement carefully. Look at the placement of the brackets first. I have brackets around each operation (greater than, lesser than, and addition) and a bracket that encompasses the "or" statement and one that encompasses the equal to operation. If I'd missed even one of those brackets out, I'd have either gotten an error, or the order of operation would have been messed up and my answer would have been wrong.

Let's test the "not" operator now.

```
>>> not(5 > 3)
False
```

5 > 3 is true, but since I used the "not" operator on the comparison, I got a false.

```
>>> not((5 > 3) or (4 < 3))
False
```

The result of the "or" operation is true because one of the statements is true, but since I used "not" on them all, the final result is false.

```
>>> (5 > 3) and (not(4 < 3))
True
```

Originally, the preceding operation returned false because 4 < 3 is not true. But I used "not" on 4 < 3, which made the final result of the comparison True. So *True and True* is True.

I'm going to stop the tests at this, but I want you to go all out! Why don't you combine all of the mathematical operators you know of with the comparison operators and the logical operators? Try different combinations and see what you get. Programming is all about experimenting. Experiment away! ☺

Summary

In this chapter, we learned all about commanding our computer to do the things we want. We learned about Boolean values and conditions and their results. Then, we moved on to "if", "else", and "elif" statements and how to use them to command our computers. Finally, we looked at "and", "or", and "not" and their uses. As usual, we did a bunch of mini projects as well.

In the next chapter, let's look at automating our programs with loops. You'll find it a welcome relief while creating graphics with *Turtle*.

CHAPTER 10

Automate a Little

In the previous chapter, we learned all about conditions, if, else, and elif statements, and combining multiple conditions to create complex commands.

In this chapter, let's look at automations with loops, how to use for and while loops to automate the creation of graphics, how to pre-maturely end loops with break statements, and so much more. We'll be looking at a lot of colorful and interesting mini projects in this chapter.

Magic loops!

There's no end to Python's magic and wonder, and loops are the best of them! Remember the sheer number of lines of code we wrote to draw a simple little graphic in turtle? Would you like an easier way of doing the same? What if you can draw hundreds of squares, one after the other, in

A. Elumalai, *Introduction to Python for Kids*, https://doi.org/10.1007/978-1-4842-6812-4_10

just four to five lines of code? That's just an example. What if you want to print the numbers 1 to 100 in your turtle, again with just four to five lines of code? That's 100 print statements, but we're making it happen in four lines of code. How? That's the power of loops.

With loops, you can make your program repeat the same actions any number of times. Do you want to print from 1 to 100? You can create an automation code that starts from 1, prints 1, and then increments 1 by 1, which is 2; prints that, and increments again; and so on.

Look at Figure 10-1. We have a bunch of lines of code. There is a range, and as long as that range is true, we run the same lines of code. This range starts from a number and increments by 1 every time the loop is repeated. Once that set number is reached, we stop running the "loop". Every time those same lines of code run, it's called an iteration. In our example, we'll have 100 such iterations to print 1 through 100.

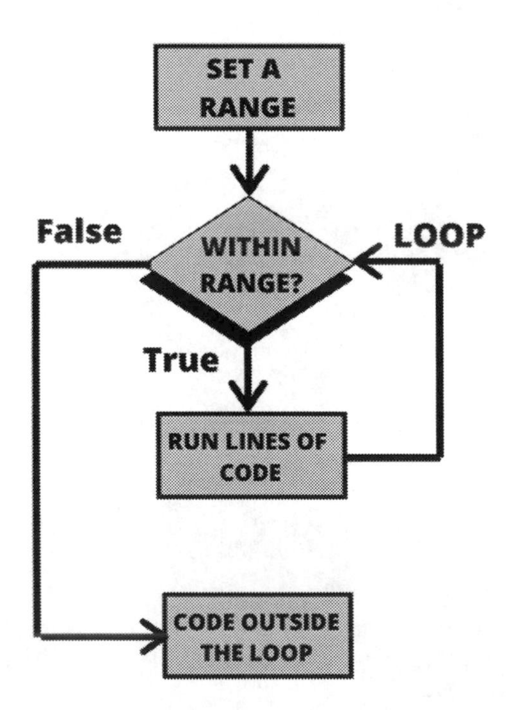

Figure 10-1. *Loops – an illustration*

There are two types of loops in Python, and we'll be looking at both. I'm also going to demonstrate the power of these loops with a lot of mini projects. Are you excited to get started? I know I am! 😊 Loops are the real deal. You're halfway there!

For loops

For loops are the most commonly used loops. They don't just iterate a given number of times. They do that, yes, but you can use the 'for loops' to iterate over strings, lists, and a lot of complex data like that.

In this chapter, we'll just be looking at using for loops within a given number range or a string as the range. Once we look at complex data types like lists and dictionaries in the future, let's revisit for loops and how to use them with those data types, alright? 😊

Okay then, let's get started!

Let's work with our preceding example. I want to print from 1 to 100. You've looked at the illustration. You know what's needed. Let's look at how to write a for loop over a range first, and then let's try to solve our problem, alright?

The syntax is very simple. You have to start the syntax with the "for" keyword, with small letters throughout. Then, you need to create a temporary variable. It could be an "x" (random, unknown number) or an "i" (denoting iteration), or it could be literally any variable name you want it to be. This variable will store your current number in the range for every iteration.

So, if your range was from 1 to 5, and let's say we've named our temporary variable "x".

```
Iteration 1 : x is 1
Iteration 2 : x is 2
Iteration 3 : x is 3
Iteration 4 : x is 4
Iteration 5 : x is 5
```

And when x reaches 5, our loop stops executing. Do you understand how that works?

Also, your numerical range can be anything, really, as long as it has continuity. If you give your range as range(1,6), then that means you want your x value to go from 1 through 5 for every iteration. The last number in the range is ignored.

Don't forget your colon! Just like in your "if" statements, your "for" statement ends with a colon, and the lines of code that come inside of it should be placed after an indentation.

So, the syntax would be something like this:

```
for x in range(1,6):
    lines of code
```

I know, I know. It's all a bit confusing and too theoretical. Let's look at a bunch of examples, shall we?

What was my problem statement again? I wanted to print from 1 to 100, am I right? The range would be range(1,101) since I want 100 to be included, and I just need a print statement inside the loop.

The code would be something like this:

```
for x in range(1,101):
    print(x)
```

Run the preceding code, and you'd get this:

```
= RESTART: C:\Users\aarthi\AppData\Local\Programs\Python\
Python38-32\numbers.py
1
2
3
.
.
.
```

```
97
98
99
100
```

My code printed the entire thing, but I don't think we have space in this chapter to print everything, so here's the "cut" version of it. Did you run the code and see? Amazing, right? You did all that in exactly two lines of code. Nothing more. ***That*** is the power of loops.

This works only if I want everything in the range to be printed. What if I want only the even numbers to be printed? I can give a condition within my range to make that happen.

Let's say my range is something like this: `range(2,101,2)`

I'm basically asking my code to print from 2 through 100, but for every iteration, I want the current value of "x" incremented by 2 and not 1.

So, x would be 2 in the first iteration, 4 in the second iteration, and so on. Shall we test this?

```
for x in range(2,101,2):
    print(x)
```

When I run the preceding code, I'll get this:

```
= RESTART: C:\Users\aarthi\AppData\Local\Programs\Python\
Python38-32\numbers.py
2
4
6
8
10
.
.
.
```

```
94
96
98
100
```

If you want the increment to happen by 3 every time, then give 3 as the third argument and so on.

If statements within for loops

Alternatively, I could just use the modulus operator we learned about in Chapter 5 to just filter out the numbers I don't want. So, if I only want the off numbers printed, then I can do an x % 2 operation, and whenever I get 1 as the result, then I can confirm that the current number is an odd number and print it.

1 % 2 is 1

2 % 2 is 0

3 % 2 is 1 again

Do you see the pattern? Let's try this out!

```
for x in range(1,101):
    if (x % 2) == 1:
        print(x)
```

So now you know how to use if statements within for loops. Similarly, you can use for statements within if loops as well.

```
= RESTART: C:\Users\aarthi\AppData\Local\Programs\Python\
Python38-32\numbers.py
1
3
5
```

```
7
.
.
.
93
95
97
99
```

Nested for loops

You can also create for loops within for loops. These are called nested for loops. To demonstrate how nested loops work, I'm going create a pattern that prints stars for every iteration at the end of this section as a mini project.

But before we start that, I want to introduce a concept in print. Did you notice how every new print statement is written in a new line? That's the default. But what if we don't want that? What if we want the next print statement to be in the same line as the previous one? You can use the "end =" syntax to achieve that.

```
print('Hello', end = " ")
print('there!')
```

If you run the preceding lines of code, you'll get this:

```
= RESTART: C:\Users\aarthi\AppData\Local\Programs\Python\
Python38-32\numbers.py
Hello there!
```

The end = " " told your print statement to end the print statement with a space and instructed IDLE to print the next print statement right after the space and not in a new line.

Now that you know how to manipulate the print statement, let's go back to nested loops.

The syntax is very simple, actually. Let's say I want to print the numbers 123, one after the other, in a row, and repeat that ten times. So, the outer loop will have a range of range(1,11) and the inner for loop will have a range of range(1,4), and the print statement will come only in the inner for loop because we only need 1, 2, and 3 printed out. Let's test this, shall we?

```
for x in range(1,11):
    for i in range(1,4):
        print(i, end = "")
```

In the preceding lines of code, I didn't give a space after end = because I want 1, 2, and 3 printed one after the other. On the other hand, if I gave something like this: end = "," then I'd get something like 1,2,3 in every line. You can design this as you want. Try giving other special characters to manipulate the result.

When I run the preceding code, I get this:

```
= RESTART: C:\Users\aarthi\AppData\Local\Programs\Python\
Python38-32\numbers.py
123123123123123123123123123123
```

Oops, something went wrong! What was it? Well, we never broke the line, did we? We need to do that after every line is completely written, so we can repeat the same thing in the next line, am I right? Let me do that.

There is a piece of code in Python that lets you create a new line. It's called \n and it's similar to the backslash we used when we wanted to exempt single and double quotes from being considered as part of the code, remember? So I just need to add another line of code right after my inner for loop gets over.

```
for x in range(1,6):
    for i in range(1,4):
        print(i, end = "")
    print("\n")
```

Do you see the indentation? The first print is inside of the inner for loop, and the second print statement is inside of the outer for loop. Indentations can make or break your code in Python, so be very careful with them, okay? If I wrote the second print statement in the same line as the first, then Python would have thought I wanted a new line after every number is printed and not after *every line* was printed. That makes all the difference, doesn't it?

When I run the preceding code, I got this:

```
= RESTART: C:\Users\aarthi\AppData\Local\Programs\Python\
Python38-32\numbers.py
123

123


123


123


123
```

Alternatively, you could just end the outer for loop with an empty print(), and you'll just get one new line since print statements produce new lines by default.

Iterating over strings

The beauty of for loops over "while" loops is that they iterate over things and not just range of numbers. You can iterate over every single letter in a string, for example. Would you like to try?

Let me create a variable "a" and place a string 'Hello there' inside of it. Then I'll use the same syntax, but this time, I'll just mention "a", which contains the string, in place of a range.

```
a = 'Hello there!'
for x in a:
    print(x)
```

Let's see what we get:

```
= RESTART: C:\Users\aarthi\AppData\Local\Programs\Python\
Python38-32\numbers.py
H
e
l
l
o

t
h
e
r
e
!
```

Look at that! Every single character was printed in every line. Pretty neat, huh? Think of all the possibilities with something as powerful as this!

While loops

Now that you've explored "for" loops thoroughly, "while" loops are a piece of cake, trust me. Unlike the for loops, while loops keep executing the statements within the loop, as long as a condition is true. Remember your "if" statement? It's similar to that, but there's an added element of iteration in here.

The syntax is very simple:

```
initialize
while condition:
    lines of code
    increment
```

The syntax is a bit confusing, isn't it? Let me explain with an example. It's similar to a for loop, really, but just a bit longer. In a for loop, we give a range. Let's say our range starts from 1, so in our "while" loop, we need to initialize our temporary variable with the start of the range, like this:

```
x = 1
```

Then, we need the condition. Let's say we want the range to end at 11, which means it needs to iterate from 1 to 10, so we can give our condition like this:

```
while x < 11:
```

Alternatively, you could make your condition x <= 10 as well. You have the freedom to do that with your "while" loops.

Finally, you need your lines of code. It could be anything, really, and it could be any number of lines of statements. But just like with your "for" loops, the inner lines of code need to come after indentation.

This is what we have so far:

```
x = 1
while x < 11:
    print(x)
```

But if we end the loop here, we'd create a never-ending loop. "x" would always be 1, and it would always be less than 11, so the condition would always be true, and the loop will never stop executing. That's dangerous. So we need the loop to stop at a point, right? That's where the increment comes in. Increment x by any number you want so at one point, the loop does end.

This is our final code:

```
x = 1
while x < 11:
    print(x)
    x += 1
```

Let's run the preceding code:

```
= RESTART: C:\Users\aarthi\AppData\Local\Programs\Python\
Python38-32\numbers.py
1
2
3
4
5
6
7
8
9
10
```

Perfect! 😊

Abort mission! Break and continue

Break, and continue. It isn't hard to guess what these do, is it? The "break" statement breaks the loop, regardless of your range or condition being true.

```
for x in range(1,11):
    if(x == 5):
        break
    print(x)
print('Loop broke :(')
```

In the preceding lines of code, I'm literally hijacking my for loop in the middle. When x is 5, I'm asking the loop to break and the line of execution would immediately jump to the line right after the loop, which is the print statement that prints "Loop broke ☹". Let's test if this works.

```
= RESTART: C:\Users\aarthi\AppData\Local\Programs\Python\
Python38-32\numbers.py
1
2
3
4
Loop broke :(
```

Look at that. I didn't even get a 5, because my break statement was above my print statement. ☹ This is how "break" works.

But, the "continue" statement, on the other hand, just skips that particular iteration and still executes the rest. Why don't we use the while loop to test things this time? Let's use the same example, but this time, I want a continue when x is 5.

```
x = 1
while x < 11:
    if x == 5:
        x += 1
        continue
    print(x)
    x += 1
print('5 was skipped!')
```

Read the preceding lines of code carefully. Did you notice something? I included another increment statement right before the continue statement. Why? Remember how I told you that we need to be careful of infinite loops in while loops? Now if I just continued the loop, then x would always be stuck at 5, because at every iteration, my program would check if x was 5, and it would always be true, because increment didn't happen. So, while loops can be tricky like that. Be careful.

Let's run our code:

```
= RESTART: C:\Users\aarthi\AppData\Local\Programs\Python\
Python38-32\numbers.py
1
2
3
4
6
7
8
9
10
5 was skipped!
```

Yes, indeed. 5 was skipped!

You're an expert at loops now. Congratulate yourself!

Mini project – guess the number game version 2

We're going to try the "guess the number" game from the last chapter again, but this time, we're going to bring in the magic of automation into it.

The user gets three tries, as usual, but every time they miss, they'll get a hint on whether their guess is higher or lower than the number to be guessed:

1. Let's import the random module first, because we are going to generate the number to be guessed from that.

```
import random
```

2. Let's print out a message and then generate a random integer (whole number) within the range 1 to 10. The last number in the range is 11 because randrange() doesn't consider that.

```
print('Welcome to Guess a Number Game!')
number = random.randrange(1,11)
```

3. Next, let's create a for loop that runs for three iterations (range of 1,4, which runs from 1 to 3). For every iteration, ask the user to enter a number between 1 and 10. Get the input, and convert it to an integer.

```
for i in range(1,4):
    guess = input('Enter a number between 1 and 10: ')
    guess = int(guess)
```

4. Once entered, we're going to start our comparisons. To start with, I need to check for the final iteration because if we've reached the final try and they've still not guessed right, we need to stop the game. So, let's check if the value of "i" is 3 and the guess is still not right. Print a "sorry" message and tell them what the number was.

```
if(i == 3 and number != guess):
    print('Sorry! You used up all your tries! :(')
    print('The number was {}'.format(number))
```

5. But, if they're at the last try but guessed right, then print the success message.

```
elif(i == 3 and number == guess):
    print('You guessed it right! :)')
```

6. Now that we're done with the check, let's create an "else" statement that'll contain the code for the first two tries.

For the first two tries, check if the current guess is wrong. If it is, then print a message after checking if the "guess" is lesser or greater than the number to be guessed. If they've guessed right on any of the tries, then print a success message and break the for loop because we don't need any more iterations.

You didn't need a "break" statement if in third iteration because that was going to be the last iteration of the loop anyway.

```
else:
    if(number != guess):
        if(guess < number):
            print('You guessed a lesser number. Try higher.')
```

```
        else:
            print('You guessed a higher number. Try lower.')
    else:
        print('You guessed it right! :)')
        break
```

That's it! Pretty simple, isn't it? Let's see if it works now.

Run the preceding code, and you'll get this:

```
= RESTART: C:\Users\aarthi\AppData\Local\Programs\Python\
Python38-32\condition.py
Welcome to Guess a Number Game!
Enter a number between 1 and 10: 10
You guessed a higher number. Try lower.
Enter a number between 1 and 10: 5
You guessed a higher number. Try lower.
Enter a number between 1 and 10: 3
You guessed it right! :)
```

I guessed it right on the last try. Whew!

Fun little game, don't you think? Try it with your friends! Increase or decrease the number of tries or the range as you like. Just go crazy on this! 😊

Mini project – automate your square

This is going to be a simple project. We're going to automate our square in *Turtle*.

I'm going to create a for loop. I'm going to give the range as 1:5 so it iterates four times to draw the four sides of a square. I'm just going to repeat forward 100 points and right 90 degrees throughout the loop.

```
import turtle
s = turtle.getscreen()
t = turtle.Turtle()
t.pensize(5)
t.color('Red','Green')
t.begin_fill()
for x in range(1,5):
    t.forward(100)
    t.right(90)
t.end_fill()
t.hideturtle()
turtle.hideturtle()
```

Let's run the preceding code. Look at that! We have our square (Figure 10-2), and we just wrote a fraction of the lines we wrote before.

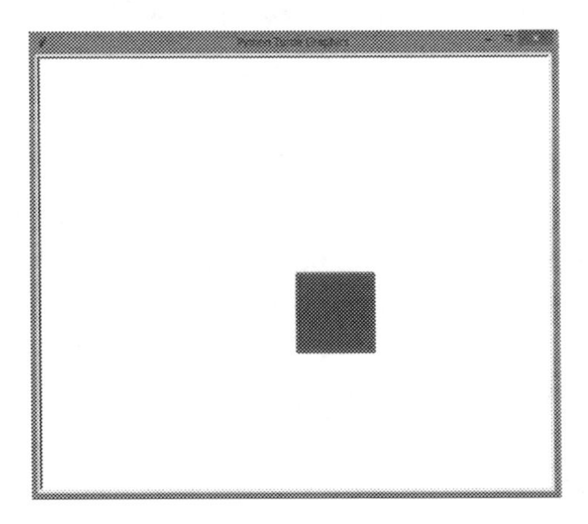

Figure 10-2. *Automated square*

Mini project – automate any basic shape

In this project, we're going to automate any shape we give our program. So, you just input the number of sides and the angle of the sides, and your program will draw the relevant shape for you. Cool, right? Let's get started! 😊

1. Let's set up turtle first.

```
import turtle
s = turtle.getscreen()
t = turtle.Turtle()
```

2. I'm going to make the pen size 5 so our shapes look better. The color of our pen is going to be Blue, and the fill color of the shape is going to be Orange.

```
t.pensize(5)
t.color('Blue','Orange')
```

3. Next, let me get the number of sides and angle as input and convert them to integer.

```
sides = input("How many sides does your shape have?")
sides = int(sides)
angle = input("What's the angle between the sides?")
angle = int(angle)
```

4. Now, let's begin drawing. Start with the begin_fill, and then open a for loop that goes from 0 to sides-1 (give 0,sides as the range). This means, if the value of sides is 5, the loop will run five times and will draw one side for every iteration of the loop.

```
t.begin_fill()
for x in range(0,sides):
```

5. Inside the for loop, let's create an "if" statement that checks if we've reached the last side. If we have, then we're going to take the pen home (0,0) and break the loop.

```
if(x == sides-1):
    t.home()
    break
```

6. In the rest of the iterations, we're going to push the pen forward by 100 points and change the direction of the pen in the right direction with the given angle.

```
t.forward(100)
t.right(angle)
```

7. That's it for the "for" loop. Let's finish the program by ending the fill and hiding the turtles.

```
t.end_fill()
t.hideturtle()
turtle.hideturtle()
```

8. Let's give our inputs as 4 and 90:

```
= RESTART: C:\Users\aarthi\AppData\Local\Programs\
Python\Python38-32\drawTurtle.py
How many sides does your shape have? 4
What's the angle between the sides? 90
```

Click Enter after entering the outputs. Check the *Turtle* screen, and you'll see the image shown in Figure 10-3.

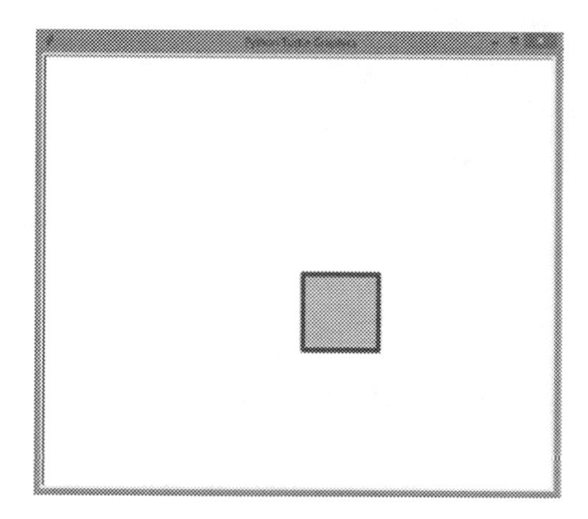

Figure 10-3. *Sides 4 and angle 90 – square*

That's a square!

9. Now, 3 and 60 (Figure 10-4):

```
= RESTART: C:\Users\aarthi\AppData\Local\Programs\
Python\Python38-32\drawTurtle.py
```

How many sides does your shape have? 3

What's the angle between the sides? 60

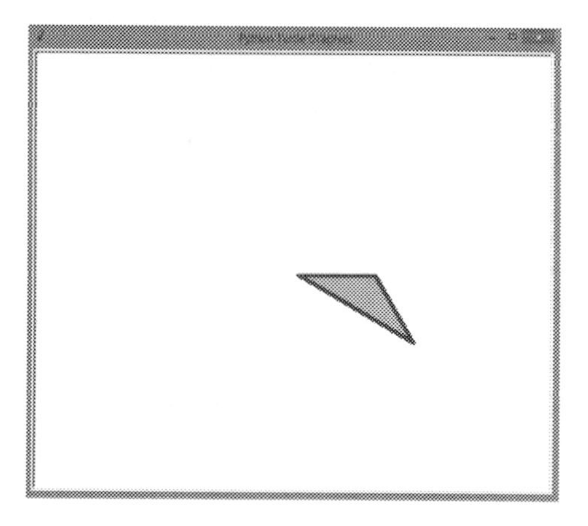

Figure 10-4. *Sides 3 and angle 60 – triangle*

An equilateral triangle!

10. Now, 6 and 60 (Figure 10-5):

```
= RESTART: C:\Users\aarthi\AppData\Local\Programs\
Python\Python38-32\drawTurtle.py
```

How many sides does your shape have? 6

What's the angle between the sides? 60

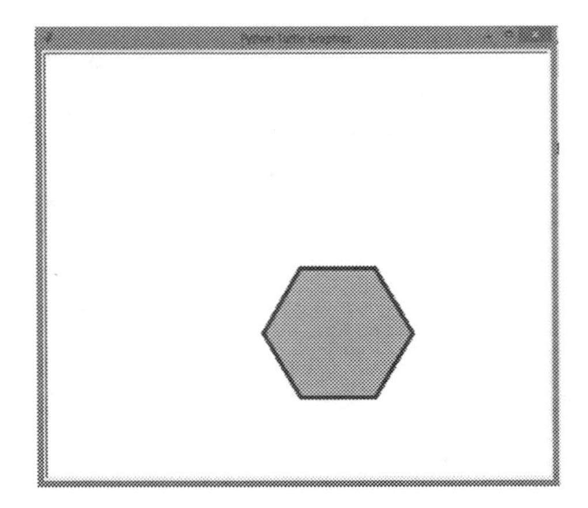

Figure 10-5. *Sides 6 and angle 60 – hexagon*

A hexagon, nice!

Try 5 and 60 to get a pentagon, 8 and 45 to get an octagon, and just experiment with different values to see what you get. Have fun! 😊

Mini project – automatically draw a mandala design

In this project, we're going to automate drawing a proper mandala design. It's quite simple, you'll see!

1. Let's set up turtle first.

```
import turtle
s = turtle.getscreen()
t = turtle.Turtle()
```

2. I'm going to make the speed of the pen 0 so it draws fast. The pen size is going to be 5 and the pen color Red.

```
t.speed(0)
t.pensize(5)
t.pencolor('Red')
```

3. Next, let us open a for loop, and I'm going to make it loop seven times (0,7 in the range). Now, I've arrived at all the values in this for loop by trial and error. You can change them as you want and see what you get, okay? 😊

```
for i in range(0,7):
```

4. In every iteration of the for loop, I'm going to draw a circle of 100 points and turn left at 50 degrees.

```
t.circle(100)
t.left(50)
```

5. That's it! If you run the program now, you'll see your mandala design. But why don't we take it a bit further and draw a circle inside the design? Change the pen size to 7, go to the position -10,-50 (found it by trial and error), change the pen color to Blue, and draw a circle of radius 50. Finally, hide the turtles.

```
        t.pensize(7)
        t.penup()
        t.goto(-10,-50)
        t.pendown()
        t.pencolor('Blue')
        t.circle(50)
        t.hideturtle()
        turtle.hideturtle()
```

Run the preceding code, and you'll get this (Figure 10-6).

***Figure 10-6.** Simple mandala design with loops*

That looks pretty! Try changing the values and the colors and see what you get.

Mini project – arc spirals

In this project, we're going to do a demonstration of the setheading() method in Python. We're going to draw arc spirals! You'll see. 😊

1. Let's set up the *Turtle* first.

```
import turtle
s = turtle.getscreen()
t = turtle.Turtle()
```

2. I'm going to print the current heading (direction) to the Shell to start with. You'll see that it's 0 when we start. Let's also change the pen size to 5 and the speed to 5 so it draws a bit fast.

```
print(t.heading())
t.pensize(5)
t.speed(5)
```

3. I'm going to set the starting angle to 0.

```
angle = 0
```

4. Then, I'm going to open a for loop that runs 12 times, because I want to showcase 12 angles of a circle in the arcs.

```
for i in range(12):
```

5. Every time the loop runs, I'll draw a semi-circle of radius 100. And at the end of the semi-circle, I'll write the current heading. Then I'll move my pen back to the starting point so it'll be ready for the next arc.

```
t.circle(100,180)
t.write(t.heading())
t.penup()
t.home()
t.pendown()
```

6. Finally, I'm going to increase the angle by 30 in every iteration of the loop and set the heading to that particular angle.

```
angle += 30
t.setheading(angle)
```

7. Run the preceding code, and you'll get this (Figure 10-7).

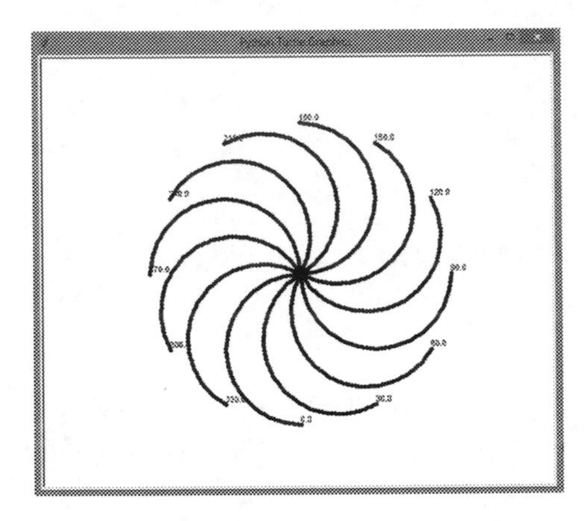

Figure 10-7. *Semi-circle spirals*

8. Change the angle of the circle to 90 degrees to draw quarter circles (arcs), and you'll get this (Figure 10-8).

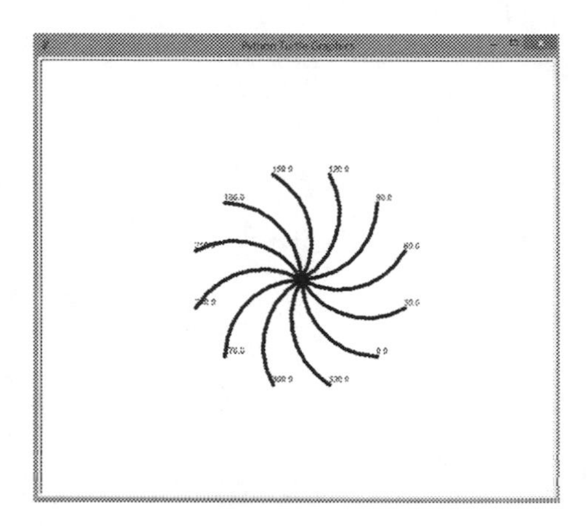

Figure 10-8. *Quarter circle spirals*

You can remove the text if you'd like, draw a circle over everything, and make it a new mandala design too! 😊

Summary

In this chapter, we learned how to do entry-level automation in your programs by using loops. We learned all about for loops, while loops, and ranges and how to manipulate loops with break and continue statements. We also create a lot of mini projects using the concepts we learned in this chapter.

In the next chapter, let's look at how to store more than one value and different kinds of values in a single variable with Python's built-in data structures.

CHAPTER 11

Lots and Lots of Information!

In the previous chapter, we learned all about automating your code with for and while loops. We also looked at the break and continue statements and created a lot of colorful, mini projects.

In this theory-intensive chapter, let's look at the various built-in data structures offered by Python. Let's look at how to use these data structures to store more than one value at a time in a single variable, and let's look at practical examples of using these data structures in real-world programs.

Store more than one value

So far, we've just been storing one value at a time. Of course, we can change the values, but we can't store two values in the same place. Isn't that a little inconvenient? Let's say I want to store six different color values so I can use them in my code, one after the other.

How would I do that? I'd probably do something like this:

```
color1 = 'Red'
color2 = 'Orange'
color3 = 'Blue'
color4 = 'Yellow'
color5 = 'Green'
color6 = 'Violet'
```


A. Elumalai, *Introduction to Python for Kids*, https://doi.org/10.1007/978-1-4842-6812-4_11

Then I'd have to remember and refer each of those values every time I want them used in my code. Whoa...that's a long-drawn-out process.

What if I can store all six colors in the same place, in the same variable? It'll look something like Figure 11-1.

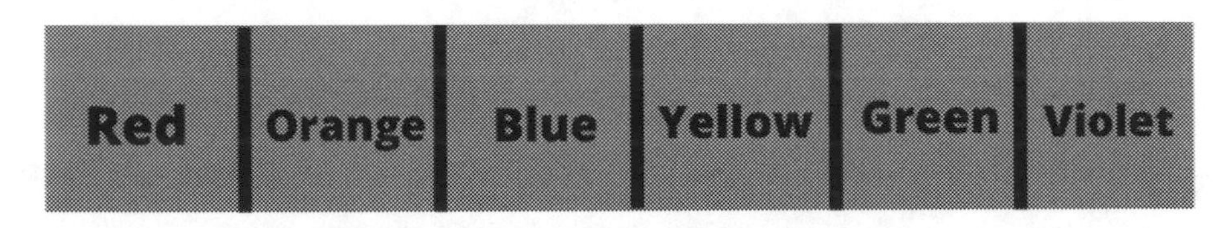

Figure 11-1. *Multiple values in the same variable*

This is called a ***data structure*** in Python. Look at how the data is structured (organized) and stored? Hence the name. There are four such pre-made data structures that can be used to store multiple values in the same location. You save a lot of lines of code, time, and your code is a lot more efficient too. You can store different types of data as well. The same data structure could have strings, numbers, and Booleans stored in them.

Accessing this data is easy too. You'd just have to follow a similar format to the one we use while accessing individual characters in a string. I'll get to that in a bit.

Let me show you the four data structures first:

List: Python is indeed an easy-to-learn language, isn't it? The keywords used in this language are very easy to remember. A list is just that. It's a list of information, but it is ***ordered***. The individual values in a list can be ***changed***, and lists ***allow duplicate values*** inside of them.

Tuple: A tuple is similar to a list. The only difference is that the ***values cannot be changed*** once fixed. That means you can't add or delete values either.

Set: A set, unlike a list of a tuple, is ***unordered***, and there are no indices to access specific values from. It ***doesn't allow for duplicate values*** as well, since the values are unordered.

Dictionary: As the name implies, a dictionary has the values stored in a ***word : description*** format. Dictionaries are unordered as well, but they can be changed and the "word", which is called a "key" in Python, acts as an index through which you can access the values (descriptions).

You're probably squinting at the pages of this book right now. Don't worry at all. At a glance, these data structures look intimidating. They're definitely not. I'll explain them with fun and easy-to-understand examples from the next section, and you'll understand everything in no time. 😊

Lists

Let's look at lists first. It's quite easy to create them. Separate the multiple values you want stored in your list by commas and enclose everything inside of square brackets ([]) and you have yourself a list. Would you like to try?

Let's convert the six lines of code we wrote in the previous example into a list, shall we?

```
colors = ['Red', 'Orange', 'Blue', 'Yellow', 'Green', 'Violet']
```

The preceding example just has strings in them (hence the quotes), but you can create a list of just numbers, or just Booleans, or a combination of two or more of them. Just create what you want based on your need.

You're probably squinting at the pages of this book right now. Don't worry at all. At a glance, these data structures look intimidating. They're definitely not. I'll explain them with fun and easy:

```
a = [1, 'Hello', True, False, 34.5, '*']
```

The preceding code is a list of heterogenous values (different data types).

Accessing values in a list

Okay, so we have a list of values. How do we access them? Would you like to take a guess? You know how already.

Yep, with indices, just like we did for our strings. The first value in the list has an index of 0, the second an index of 1, and so on.

Let's say I want the third value accessed and printed in list "a". It's at the index 2.

```
print(a[2])
```

Run the preceding code, and you'll get this:

```
= RESTART: C:/Users/aarthi/AppData/Local/Programs/Python/
Python38-32/dataStructures.py
True
```

Successfully accessed!

You can do negative indexing just like you did with your strings. So, to access the last element (value) in the list, I'd just have to give -1.

```
print(a[-1])
```

Run the preceding code, and you'll get this:

```
= RESTART: C:/Users/aarthi/AppData/Local/Programs/Python/
Python38-32/dataStructures.py
*
```

It works! Yippee! 😊

Slice a list!

If negative indexing and accessing work, just like with your strings, then extracting a part of a list using ranges should work as well, right? Let's test.

Let's say I want to extract the second through fifth values, with indices 1 through 4. My range should be 1:5 since the last number in the range is not included.

```
print(a[1:5])
['Hello', True, False, 34.5]
```

Oh yes, it works! Then extracting through negative indices should work as well, right? Let's say I want everything from the negative third index extracted.

```
print(a[-6:-3])
```

You already know how negative indices work right? If I run the preceding code, I'll get this:

```
[1, 'Hello', True]
```

You can change values as well. Let's say I want the second value (string) to be changed to a number. Then, I'd have to access the second value (first index) and assign something else to it.

```
a[1] = 100
print(a)
```

Let's print the entire list to see how it's changed now:

```
= RESTART: C:/Users/aarthi/AppData/Local/Programs/Python/
Python38-32/dataStructures.py
[1, 100, True, False, 34.5, '*']
```

List manipulation on fire!

You have a lot of pre-defined methods that can be used to manipulate your list in multiple ways. Remember the methods we saw with your strings? You'll find some of them repeated here as well. Are you ready to play with your list? Yes!

As usual, you can find the length of your string with the len() method:

```
a = [1, 'Hello', True, False, 34.5, '*']
print(len(a))
```

Run the preceding code, and you'll get this:

```
= RESTART: C:\Users\aarthi\AppData\Local\Programs\Python\
Python38-32\dataStructures.py
6
```

Yes! Our list's length is 6. It works.

You have a complete list of methods for each of the data structures we'll be looking at in this chapter. So, I'm just going to link you to the page in the Python docs where all those methods and their explanations are listed.

Here it is: https://docs.python.org/3/tutorial/datastructures.html.

That said, let's just look at some of the most important methods in this chapter, alright?

Copy and append

The append() method appends or adds an element at the end of the list :

```
 a.append('new')
print(a)
```

Run the preceding code, and you'll get this:

```
= RESTART: C:\Users\aarthi\AppData\Local\Programs\Python\
Python38-32\dataStructures.py
[1, 'Hello', True, False, 34.5, '*', 'new']
```

The copy method creates a copy of the list, and this copy can be assigned to any variable to create a copied list:

```
b = a.copy()
print("List b contains: {}".format(b))
```

Run the preceding code, and you'll get this:

```
= RESTART: C:\Users\aarthi\AppData\Local\Programs\Python\
Python38-32\dataStructures.py
List b contains: [1, 'Hello', True, False, 34.5, '*', 'new']
```

Count and clear

Lists can have duplicate values, am I right? Let's say we have a list of numbers where the numbers are duplicated, and I want to check how many times a particular number appears in the list. I can use the "count" method to achieve that.

```
l = [1,2,1,1,4,5,3,5,3,2]
print(l.count(1))
```

I've started the syntax with the name of the list, "l", then the name of the method, "count", and then I've mentioned the value I wanted to count (1). If it were a string, I'd have mentioned the same within quotes. Let's run the preceding code, and we'll get this:

```
= RESTART: C:\Users\aarthi\AppData\Local\Programs\Python\
Python38-32\dataStructures.py
3
```

We got the right answer! The number 1 appeared thrice in the list.

You can clear the entire list using the "clear" method.

```
l.clear()
print(l)
```

Run the preceding code, and you'll get this:

```
= RESTART: C:\Users\aarthi\AppData\Local\Programs\Python\
Python38-32\dataStructures.py
[]
```

We have ourselves an empty list now!

Concatenation

You can use the "extend" method to concatenate or join two lists.

```
list1 = [1,2,3,4,5]
list2 = [6,7,8,9]
list1.extend(list2)
print(list1)
```

As you can see in the preceding code, the elements of the list you want listed first come first, then a period ("."), and then the "extend" method, and then inside the brackets, you can mention the name of the list you want joined to the first list.

Let's run the preceding code, and we'll get this:

```
= RESTART: C:\Users\aarthi\AppData\Local\Programs\Python\
Python38-32\dataStructures.py
[1, 2, 3, 4, 5, 6, 7, 8, 9]
```

Look at that! Perfectly joined, and in the order we wanted as well. 😊

Search inside your list

The "index" method returns the index of the very first instance of the value you are searching for. For example, if you want to find the number 3 in a list, but its duplicated twice, then only the index of the first occurrence of 3 would be returned. Let me show an example:

```
list1 = [1,2,3,2,3,1,3]
print(list1.index(3))
```

When you run the preceding code, you'll get this:

```
= RESTART: C:\Users\aarthi\AppData\Local\Programs\Python\
Python38-32\dataStructures.py
2
```

Look at that! 3 exists thrice in the list, but we only got the index of the first 3. Sweet!

But you can narrow that search down, if you'd like. What if I want to find 3 in the last half of the list, maybe starting from the third index? You can specify the start and end of your search as arguments as well. Let me show you how:

```
print(list1.index(3,3,6))
```

I'm asking my program to search for 3 from indices 3 to 5. You know how these things work right? The last value in the range won't be included. So, if the last value is 5, then your program will only search until the fifth index.

When I run the preceding code, I'll get this:

```
= RESTART: C:\Users\aarthi\AppData\Local\Programs\Python\
Python38-32\dataStructures.py
4
```

Look at that! We got the index of the second instance of 3 in the list. Nice!

Add and remove elements

You know how to add elements to a list using your square brackets, and you can change elements using the same method as well. But what if I want to insert elements in the middle of the list so that the other values still exist, but just move one step further?

You can use the insert method to achieve that. The first argument in the method is the position in which you want the value, and the second argument is the value you want added.

```
colors = ['Red', 'Orange', 'Blue']
colors.insert(1,'Green')
print(colors)
```

I've added the value 'Green' to the first index. Now 'Orange' should be pushed one step further. Let's check, shall we?

```
= RESTART: C:\Users\aarthi\AppData\Local\Programs\Python\
Python38-32\dataStructures.py
['Red', 'Green', 'Orange', 'Blue']
```

Yep, it worked! 😊

The pop() method removes the last element in the list by default. If you give a position (index) though, it'll remove the element at that position.

Let's try removing the second element in the preceding list, which is the element we just inserted, okay?

```
colors.pop(1)
print(colors)
```

When we run the entire code, we'll get this:

```
= RESTART: C:\Users\aarthi\AppData\Local\Programs\Python\
Python38-32\dataStructures.py
['Red', 'Green', 'Orange', 'Blue']
['Red', 'Orange', 'Blue']
```

Look at that! The list originally had four elements, and we successfully removed the second element using the pop() method.

Alternatively, you can use the remove() method as well. The only difference is you can specify the exact element you want removed.

Our list currently has ['Red', 'Orange', 'Blue']. I don't want blue anymore. Why don't we try removing it?

```
colors.remove('Blue')
print(colors)
```

Let's see if it worked:

```
= RESTART: C:\Users\aarthi\AppData\Local\Programs\Python\
Python38-32\dataStructures.py
['Red', 'Orange']
```

Yay! It worked!

It's getting a bit too long, isn't it? Don't worry! We're almost done. Then let's distract us with a fun little project, deal? 😊

Reverse and sort

There's another method called the reverse() method. Can you guess what it does? Exactly! It reverses the elements in a list. Let's try!

```
li = [1,2,3,4,5]
li.reverse()
print(li)
```

Run the preceding code, and you'll get this:

```
= RESTART: C:\Users\aarthi\AppData\Local\Programs\Python\
Python38-32\dataStructures.py
[5, 4, 3, 2, 1]
```

Success!

Finally (yes, finally), there's another method called the sort() method that sorts the elements by alphabetical order.

By default, the sorting happens in the ascending order.

```
colors = ['Red', 'Orange', 'Blue', 'Yellow', 'Green', 'Violet']
colors.sort()
print(colors)
```

Run the preceding code, and you'll get this:

```
= RESTART: C:\Users\aarthi\AppData\Local\Programs\Python\
Python38-32\dataStructures.py
['Blue', 'Green', 'Orange', 'Red', 'Violet', 'Yellow']
```

It's like magic! :O

Does this work with numbers?

```
li = [1,4,3,6,2,8,7,9,5]
li.sort()
print(li)
```

When you run the above code, you'll get this:

```
= RESTART: C:\Users\aarthi\AppData\Local\Programs\Python\
Python38-32\dataStructures.py
[1, 2, 3, 4, 5, 6, 7, 8, 9]
```

Hehe, it works.

But what if I want the sorting done in the descending order? In that case, I'll modify the sort() function call like this:

```
li.sort(reverse=True)
print(li)
```

When you give the argument as reverse=True, your program will sort your list in the descending order. The default is reverse=False, which sorts the list in the ascending order. When something happens by default, you don't need to mention it as an argument.

Let's run the preceding code, and we'll get this:

```
= RESTART: C:\Users\aarthi\AppData\Local\Programs\Python\
Python38-32\dataStructures.py
[9, 8, 7, 6, 5, 4, 3, 2, 1]
```

Nice...my list is in the descending order now. Python lets us do pretty much anything, doesn't it?

More fun with lists!

You can check if something exists in a list using the "in" keyword:

```
print('Hello' in a)
```

In the preceding line of code, we've asked if the string 'Hello' is a part of the list.

```
= RESTART: C:\Users\aarthi\AppData\Local\Programs\Python\
Python38-32\dataStructures.py
False
```

The result is false. We changed the second value from 'Hello' to 100, remember? So, 'Hello' is no longer a part of the list. As with everything in Python, these searches are case sensitive as well. So, 'Hello' is different from 'hello', and if the string was 'Hello there!', then you need to search for the entire thing. Partial searches don't work. Let me show you:

```
a[1] = 'Hello there!'
print('Hello' in a)
```

I've changed the second value to 'Hello there!', and when I search for 'Hello' in the list "a", let me see what I get:

```
= RESTART: C:\Users\aarthi\AppData\Local\Programs\Python\
Python38-32\dataStructures.py
False
```

Look at that. It's still a false because you haven't searched with the correct term.

Now that you know how lists work, I want to get back to a previous topic. Remember "for" loops? And do remember my promise to revisit for loops when I teach you about lists? We're here now!

You can iterate through a list using your for loop. It's quite simple. Just create your list, and then replace that in place of a range, like this:

```
l = [1,2,3,4,5]
for i in l:
    print(i)
```

The result is this:

```
= RESTART: C:\Users\aarthi\AppData\Local\Programs\Python\
Python38-32\dataStructures.py
1
2
3
4
5
```

Alternatively, you can also directly specify the list, like this:

```
for i in [1,2,3,4,5]:
```

Modify and run your code with the preceding line of code and you'll notice that you get the same result.

Apart from the "extend" method, you can also use the "+" operator to concatenate two lists, just like you do with strings, like this:

```
list1 = [1,2,3,4,5]
list2 = [6,7,8,9]
list1 += list2
print(list1)
```

Alternatively, you can create a new variable and assign the value of list1 + list2 to it. Either works.

```
= RESTART: C:\Users\aarthi\AppData\Local\Programs\Python\
Python38-32\dataStructures.py
[1, 2, 3, 4, 5, 6, 7, 8, 9]
```

The "clear" method just clears the list. But if you use the "del" keyword, you can delete the list in its entirety. Would you like to check?

Let's delete the preceding list, shall we?

```
del list1
print(list1)
```

When I try to print list1 after I deleted it, I'll get an error, like the following:

```
= RESTART: C:\Users\aarthi\AppData\Local\Programs\Python\
Python38-32\dataStructures.py
Traceback (most recent call last):
  File "C:\Users\aarthi\AppData\Local\Programs\Python\
  Python38-32\dataStructures.py", line 10, in <module>
    print(list1)
NameError: name 'list1' is not defined
```

Look at that! 'list1' was completely erased from our program.

You can do the same for elements in a list as well.

```
a = [1, 'Hello', True, False, 34.5, '*']
del a[2]
print(a)
```

I've asked my program to delete the third element in the list. Let's print, and we'll get this:

```
= RESTART: C:\Users\aarthi\AppData\Local\Programs\Python\
Python38-32\dataStructures.py
[1, 'Hello', False, 34.5, '*']
```

The third value "True" no longer exists in list "a".

Mini project – multi-colored automated star

In this project, I'm going to draw a star with Python, but each side is going to have a different color. That's where my list comes in. I'm going to create a list of five colors and run a for loop through it. For every iteration of the for loop, *Turtle* will draw a side of the star with a new color from the list.

Let's see how it's done, shall we?

1. I'm going to start with the usual lines of code to set up *Turtle*:

    ```
    import turtle
    s = turtle.getscreen()
    t = turtle.Turtle()
    ```

2. I'm going to set the pen size as 5 so my image looks good.

    ```
    t.pensize(5)
    ```

3. Next, I'm going to create a variable called "colors" and assign a list of five colors, 'Red, 'Brown', 'Green', 'Blue', and 'Orange' to it. I've already given you a link to a list of colors, so choose your preferred set of colors. 😊

    ```
    colors = ['Red', 'Brown', 'Green', 'Blue', 'Orange']
    ```

4. Next, I'm going to create a temporary variable x that iterates, via the for loop, through the entire list:

    ```
    for x in colors:
    ```

5. For every iteration of the loop, my pen color will change to the current color in the temporary variable "x". I'll ask my *Turtle* to move forward by 200 points and turn right by 144 points because a star's outer angle is 144 degrees and I need to turn that much to get a proper star as my result.

    ```
    t.pencolor(x)
    t.forward(200)
    t.right(144)
    ```

6. That ends my for loop and the indentation. Finally, I'm going to hide my turtle.

```
t.hideturtle()
turtle.hideturtle()
```

When you run the preceding code, you'll get this (Figure 11-2).

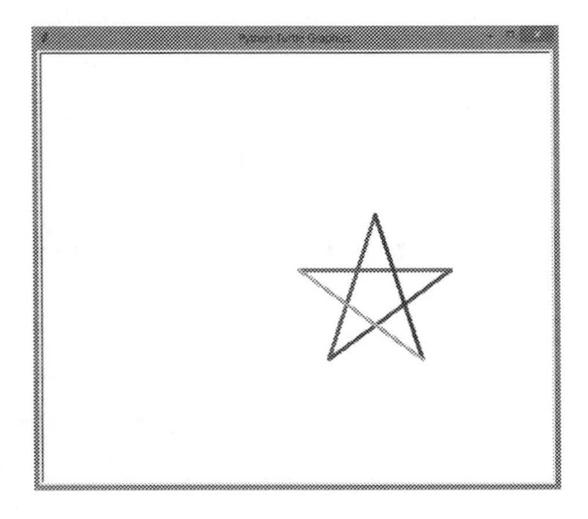

***Figure 11-2.** Multi-colored star*

Yes! We got it! Why don't you try the same with different colors or different shapes? Or maybe, you could try to randomly choose colors for every iteration? You know how to do that already (I've taught you how), so go ahead and try. 😊

Tuples

Now that we've taken a detailed look at lists, you'll find the remaining three data structures easy to understand, so I'll quickly go through them, alright?

As I've mentioned before, a tuple is similar to a list. The only difference is that it's ordered (just like a list, with index and all), but unchangeable (unlike a list). What does that mean for us? Well, it just means that you can't add, delete, or change the elements in the list.

Now that's a bummer! Does that mean a tuple is not as cool as a list? Well, I wouldn't say that, exactly. You know, you might need to create a list that you don't want anyone to manipulate later, am I right? Something like a "read-only" list? In those instances, a tuple is your best friend. Otherwise, go for a list, 100%. 😉

You can create a tuple with parenthesis, with the tuple items separated by commas, like this:

```
t1 = ('Red', True, 2, 5.0)
print(t1)
```

Run the preceding code, and you'll get this:

```
= RESTART: C:\Users\aarthi\AppData\Local\Programs\Python\
Python38-32\dataStructures.py
('Red', True, 2, 5.0)
```

Most of the things in a tuple follow the same format as that of a list, so I'm just going to list them, and I want you to try them out in your computer. It'll be our little activity, okay?

Just like you do with your lists, you can access the elements in a tuple with square brackets.

t1[1] will return the second element, True. Tuples are indexed just like lists, where the first index is 0.

Just like lists, you can use negative indexing to access values in a tuple. So, t1[-1] will return the last element in the list.

You can slice a tuple using indices as well.

If you wanted to extract the second through the fourth value (last), then you can specify t1[1:4]) or just t1[1:], since we want everything from the first index anyway.

If you wanted to write the same with negative indices, you'll do it like this: t1[-3:] because you want everything from -3 to the end of the tuple.

You can use the len(t1) method to get the length of the tuple and use the "in" keyword to check if something is inside a tuple, just like you do with your lists. Why don't you try them out and see?

And then there's your "for" loop. You can loop through tuples as well. The process is the same.

```
for x in t1:
    print(x)
```

Why don't you run the preceding code and check if looping works with tuples?

Ah well, so far, tuples look like lists written within parenthesis. What's their use, anyway? Remember how I told that tuples are unchangeable? And we haven't tried changing elements or adding elements to our tuple yet, have we? Let's try.

I'm going to try changing the value of the second element to False to True.

```
t1[1] = False
```

Let's run our code, and we'll get this:

```
= RESTART: C:\Users\aarthi\AppData\Local\Programs\Python\
Python38-32\dataStructures.py
Traceback (most recent call last):
  File "C:\Users\aarthi\AppData\Local\Programs\Python\
  Python38-32\dataStructures.py", line 4, in <module>
    t1[1] = False
TypeError: 'tuple' object does not support item assignment
```

Oops, we got an error! Tuples don't support item assignment, meaning their elements cannot be changed.

Try adding a new element to the tuple. Access the fourth index (fifth element) and add something. When you do that, you'll notice that you encounter the same error.

This is most important use of a tuple. You can create unchangeable lists that can be used to store sensitive information that shouldn't be changed. What if you create a program to store the id numbers of your classmates? You wouldn't want those changed, would you? Then store them in a tuple. Simple as that!

But, just like in your lists, you can delete the entire tuple using the "del" keyword, like this:

```
del t1
```

If you try to access t1 now, you'll get an error.

Tuples have methods as well, but they only have few methods that can be used to access elements and none that can manipulate the elements or the tuple itself.

The "count" method returns the number of times a value repeated in a tuple. Remember, tuples can have duplicate values, just like lists.

The "index" method returns the position (index) of the value in a tuple.

```
t1 = ('Red', True, 2, 5.0)
print(t1.index(5.0))
```

When you run the preceding code, you'll get this:

```
= RESTART: C:\Users\aarthi\AppData\Local\Programs\Python\
Python38-32\dataStructures.py
3
```

Yes! 5.0 is in the third index (fourth position).

That's it for tuple. It was quite simple, wasn't it? Let's look at the next data structure in the list next.

Sets

Do you remember what I told you about sets? They are unordered and they cannot have duplicate values. It's a double whammy. But sets have their uses too. Would you like to take a look at it?

Great! Well, you write sets within flower brackets, like this:

```
colors = {'Red', 'Orange', 'Blue'}
```

The preceding code is a set of the colors 'Red,' 'Orange,' and 'Blue.'

But! Sets are unordered. So, would those values really appear as we created them? Would you like to check?

```
= RESTART: C:\Users\aarthi\AppData\Local\Programs\Python\
Python38-32\dataStructures.py
{'Blue', 'Orange', 'Red'}
```

Whoa, look at that! The order is changed. Can you run the program again and tell me what you get?

The order changed again, didn't it? How cool is that? 😊

But we do have a problem now. Sets are unordered. So how do we access the elements if we don't know the indices? How do we add elements to the set? How do we insert elements in a particular position? Well, unfortunately, there are certain things you can't do with a set, and anything that pertains to order comes under that.

So, you can't use the square brackets to find an element in a particular position. But, you can use the "in" keyword to check if an element exists in a set:

```
print('Red' in colors)
```

Run the preceding code, and you'll get True.

You can also loop through a set, just like you do with your list and tuple.

```
for i in colors:
    print(i)
```

Run the preceding code, and you'll get this:

```
= RESTART: C:\Users\aarthi\AppData\Local\Programs\Python\
Python38-32\dataStructures.py
Orange
Blue
Red
```

But how would you add elements to the set when you don't know the index? There is the add() method that can be used to add individual elements, though you won't know where they'll end up.

```
colors.add('Green')
print(colors)
```

Run the preceding code, and you'll get this:

```
= RESTART: C:\Users\aarthi\AppData\Local\Programs\Python\
Python38-32\dataStructures.py
{'Blue', 'Green', 'Orange', 'Red'}
```

How interesting it that? We added 'Green' to the set, and it ended up in the second position. Run the program again, and you'll find it somewhere else.

What if I want to add more than one color to my set? I can save space by using the "update()" method.

Create a list of values within square brackets and place that within the parenthesis. Let me try to add both 'Green' and 'Yellow' to my set:

```
colors.update(['Green','Yellow'])
print(colors)
```

Run the preceding code, and you'll get this:

```
= RESTART: C:\Users\aarthi\AppData\Local\Programs\Python\
Python38-32\dataStructures.py
{'Red', 'Yellow', 'Blue', 'Orange', 'Green'}
```

Look at where Green and Yellow ended up. :D

Just like with your lists, you can use the len() method to find the length of a list as well.

Now, let's look at the rest of the methods for manipulating a set, shall we? I'll just list the ones that are similar to the ones we saw with our lists.

In a list, the pop() method removes a random value and not the last one. You can use the remove() method to remove a particular value by mentioning it as an argument.

Alternatively, you can use the "discard()" method to remove a particular element as well. The only difference between discard and remove is that discard doesn't raise an error if the mentioned element doesn't exist. This is important in real-world programming. When running a program, you don't want errors that stop the program execution because one line of code was wonky.

The clear() method clears the set, and the copy() method copies the list.

You can use the "del" keyword to delete the entire set, but you can't use it to delete a particular element since you they don't have fixed indices that you can access.

Finally, let's look at joining sets. You can join two sets using the "union()" or "update()" methods.

```
colors = {'Red', 'Orange', 'Blue'}
colors1 = {'Green', 'Yellow'}
```

Let's say we have two sets, colors and colors1 with their own values, and we want them merged into the colors set.

You can use the union() method. It creates a new set with the values in both the sets.

```
colors2 = colors.union(colors1)
print(colors2)
```

Run the preceding code, and you'll get this:

```
= RESTART: C:\Users\aarthi\AppData\Local\Programs\Python\
Python38-32\dataStructures.py
{'Yellow', 'Green', 'Red', 'Blue', 'Orange'}
```

But update just updates the first set in the syntax with values from both the sets. If you print out the second set in the syntax, you'll notice that it's unchanged. Update just changes the first set.

```
colors.update(colors1)
print(colors)
```

Run the preceding code, and you'll get this:

```
= RESTART: C:\Users\aarthi\AppData\Local\Programs\Python\
Python38-32\dataStructures.py
{'Orange', 'Yellow', 'Red', 'Blue', 'Green'}
```

We're done with sets as well. Yay! You're becoming quite the pro Python programmer now. 😊

Dictionaries

The last data structure in this list is the dictionaries. Let's quickly finish it and go back to some more fun mini projects, so are you with me? Yes!

So, dictionaries are unordered, but they are indexed and can be changed. The thing I love about dictionaries is that they can be used to model real-world stuff. Do you want to see?

Dictionaries are created within flower brackets as well, but inside, you need to mention the values in key:value pairs. The "key" is the index here.

Since I want my dictionaries to model real-world objects, I'm going to create a dictionary that represents a person's characteristics: their name, age, eye color, hair color, and so on.

This is how I'd do that:

```
person1 = {"name":"Susan","age":9,"pet":"Barky","hair":"black",
"eyes":"blue"}
```

I've created a dictionary, "person1". Her name is Susan, she's 9 years old, her pet's name is Barky, and she has black hair and blue eyes. Looks great, doesn't it?

Now, let's manipulate this dictionary. You can access values with the "keys" like this:

```
print(person1["name"])
```

Or

```
print(person1.get("name"))
```

Remember that you have to mention the keys within quotes everywhere.

Run either of these lines of code, and you'll get the same result:

```
= RESTART: C:\Users\aarthi\AppData\Local\Programs\Python\
Python38-32\dataStructures.py
Susan
```

Her name!

You can also change values. Susan is actually 8, not 9! Quick, let's correct her age before she gets sad!

```
person1["age"] = 8
print(person1)
```

Run this, and you'll get the following:

```
= RESTART: C:\Users\aarthi\AppData\Local\Programs\Python\
Python38-32\dataStructures.py
{'name': 'Susan', 'age': 8, 'pet': 'Barky', 'hair': 'black',
'eyes': 'blue'}
```

Nice!

You can also add a new key:value pair the same way. Let's add a key, gender, and make it female.

```
person1["gender"] = 'female'
print(person1)
```

Run the preceding code, and you'll get this:

```
= RESTART: C:\Users\aarthi\AppData\Local\Programs\Python\
Python38-32\dataStructures.py
{'name': 'Susan', 'age': 9, 'pet': 'Barky', 'hair': 'black',
'eyes': 'blue', 'gender': 'female'}
```

It was added, yay!

You can check if a key exists using the "in" keyword.

```
print('pet' in person1)
```

Run the preceding code, and you'll get this:

```
= RESTART: C:\Users\aarthi\AppData\Local\Programs\Python\
Python38-32\dataStructures.py
True
```

Yes, "pet" is one of the keys of the dictionary.

Just like usual, you can find the length of the dictionary using the "len" method.

The following will delete the dictionary:

```
del person1
```

`person1.clear()` will empty the dictionary.

You can use the copy() method to copy the dictionary.

As usual, you can loop through a dictionary, but since our dictionary has a key and a value each, we can do the looping in different ways.

Let's create a smaller dictionary first:

```
person1 = {"name":"Susan","age":8}
```

Let's loop through all the keys first and print them:

```
for i in person1:
    print(i)
```

This should print all the keys:

```
= RESTART: C:\Users\aarthi\AppData\Local\Programs\Python\
Python38-32\dataStructures.py
name
age
```

Yes!

If you want the values, just change the position of "i", like this:

```
for i in person1:
    print(person1[i])
```

Run the preceding code, and you'll get this:

```
= RESTART: C:\Users\aarthi\AppData\Local\Programs\Python\
Python38-32\dataStructures.py
Susan
8
```

We got just the values now. Whoo!

Alternatively, you can loop through both keys and values, like this, using the items() method:

```
for i,j in person1.items():
    print("{} = {}".format(i,j))
```

Run the preceding code, and you'll get this:

```
= RESTART: C:\Users\aarthi\AppData\Local\Programs\Python\
Python38-32\dataStructures.py
name = Susan
age = 8
```

Nice! 😊

Let's just look at one last thing before we end this. pop() removes the given key:value pair, while popitem() removes the last item in the dictionary.

```
person1.pop("name")
print(person1)
```

Run the preceding code, and you'll get this:

```
= RESTART: C:\Users\aarthi\AppData\Local\Programs\Python\
Python38-32\dataStructures.py
{'age': 8}
```

Age is the only key left! ☹

Let's rewrite the dictionary again, and this time, try popitem().

```
person1.popitem()
print(person1)
```

Run the preceding code, and you'll get this:

```
= RESTART: C:\Users\aarthi\AppData\Local\Programs\Python\
Python38-32\dataStructures.py
{'name': 'Susan'}
```

Now, 'name' is the only key left!

That's it for dictionary! 😊

Mini project – never-ending colors

Another simple project with a twist! 😊 We are going to randomly change the background colors after an interval of 1 second while printing the current color on the turtle screen.

The twist? We're going to use a new package called "time" to make the turtle screen pause between each color change. Ready? Let's get going!

1. So, as I said, we need both the "time" and the "turtle" modules. Let's import both.

    ```
    import time
    import turtle
    ```

2. Next, let's set up turtle as usual.

    ```
    s = turtle.getscreen()
    t = turtle.Turtle()
    ```

3. Once set up, let's move the pen we just created to the position from where we want it to write the colors. That's going to be the point -80,0.

```
t.penup()
t.goto(-80,0)
t.pendown()
```

4. Now, let's create a dictionary of colors. I'm creating a dictionary and not a list this time, because I'm going to make the keys capitalized versions of their values (colors) so I can write them on the screen.

```
colors = {'RED':'Red', 'BROWN':'Brown',
'GREEN':'Green', 'BLUE':'Blue', 'ORANGE':'Orange'}
```

5. Before we start drawing, let's hide the turtles. You'll see why when you run the program. 😉

```
t.hideturtle()
turtle.hideturtle()
```

6. Now, here comes the fun part. We want this program to be never ending, remember? So, it's obvious that we need a loop, but what kind of loop? How do we create a never-ending loop? Remember how I said "while" loops can literally run forever if we're not careful? That is, if the condition doesn't become false at one point.

   What if we do exactly that? What if we make the while loop's condition "True" and just that? Then, if there's no break statement anywhere within the while loop, it really will run forever.

```
#never ending loop
while True:
```

7. Simple! Next, let's create for loop that'll loop through the "colors" dictionary.

   ```
   for x in colors:
   ```

8. For every iteration, let's change the background color of the turtle screen to the next color in the for loop (the value). Also, let's write the key value (x) in Arial, 50 pt, bold text.

   ```
   turtle.bgcolor(colors[x])
   t.write(x,font=('Arial',50,'bold'))
   ```

9. Now, after every color change, we need a 0.5-second delay, or gap, before the next color change (for loop iteration) happens. This is where the "time" package comes in. It has a built-in function called sleep() which will literally pause the loop for the number of seconds mentioned. In our case, it's going to be 0.5.

   ```
   time.sleep(0.5)
   ```

10. Okay, this should technically be it, but if we leave it at this, then you'll notice that your turtle writes the next text on top of the old text, and things will continue to get messy. Why don't you try and see?

Your turtle package comes with a clear() function that clears the screen. So, why don't we clear the screen before we change the next color and draw the next text?

```
t.clear()
```

That's it! Let's run this now, and we'll get this (Figure 11-3).

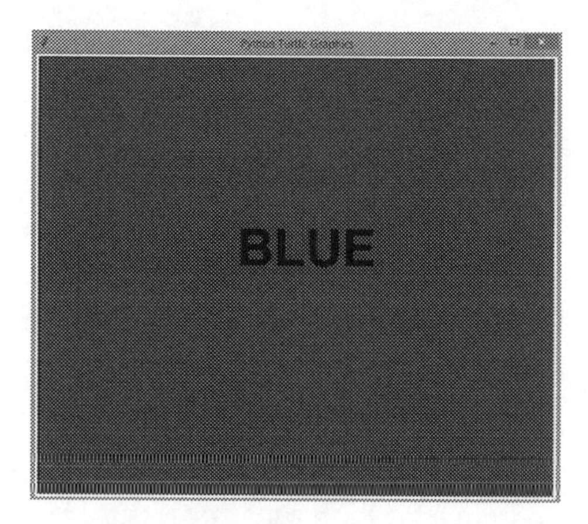

Figure 11-3. *Never-ending colors*

You'll notice that the program loops through the "colors" dictionary, infinitely. Sweet, huh? 😊

Mini project – first and last name reversal

In this project, this is what I want happened: When I enter a name, for example, Susan Smith, I want my program to return the reversal of it, that is, Smith, Susan.

It's more of a puzzle than a mini project. The logic is very simple:

1. Let's start the program by getting the name as the input. The condition is their first and last name needs to be separated by a single space. This is important. You'll see why.

```
name = input('Please Enter your first and last name, separated by a space: ')
```

2. As I said, the format of the string input is important to make this program work. So, I'm going to count the number of single spaces in the string. If it's none, or more than one, then the program stops with an error message.

   Let's create a variable count and assign it to 0 to start with.

   ```
   count = 0
   ```

3. Next, let's create a for loop that loops through the string we just got. Whenever there's a single space, let's add 1 to count.

   ```
   for i in name:
       if i == ' ':
           count += 1
   ```

4. If count is just 1, then we're good to go. Let's convert the string to a list by using the split method, where the first and last names are separated into separate list items with the single space as the delimiter used.

   ```
   if count == 1:
       #Convert string to list, where the condition is
       the space
       l = name.split(' ')
   ```

5. Next, let's reverse the list.

   ```
   #Reverse list
   l.reverse()
   ```

6. Finally, let's insert a comma with a space to the first position of the list, so when we join everything, we get the exact format we want.

```
#Add a comma, with a space, in the first position of
the list
l.insert(1,', ')
```

7. Now let's join the list into a string with an empty string as the join condition. This way, everything gets stuck together, and the only thing separating the last and first names is ", ".

```
#Join a list into a string
name = ''.join(l)
```

8. Finally, print everything.

```
print('Your reversed name is: {}'.format(name))
```

9. If the count isn't 1, print an error message.

```
else:
    print('Please Enter your name in the correct format')
```

Now, let's run the program!

```
= RESTART: C:\Users\aarthi\AppData\Local\Programs\Python\
Python38-32\dataStructures.py
Please Enter your first and last name, separated by a space:
Susan Smith
Your reversed name is: Smith, Susan
```

Perfect! 😊

Summary

In this chapter, we took a deep dive into the four pre-defined data structures offered by Python, namely, list, set, tuple, and dictionary. We looked at how to create them, delete them, manipulate them, and so much more. Finally, we looked at how to use them in programs and why they're useful in real-world programming scenarios.

In the next chapter, let's take a small break from all the learning and start creating! We'll be creating a lot of mini projects. 😊

CHAPTER 12

Fun Mini Projects Galore!

In the previous chapter, we took a deep dive into the four pre-defined data structures offered by Python, namely, list, set, tuple, and dictionary. We looked at how to create them, delete them, manipulate them, and so much more. Finally, we looked at how to use them in programs and why they're useful in real-world programming scenarios.

In this chapter, let's take a small break from all the learning and start creating! We'll be creating a lot of mini projects. You can brush up the topics you learned so far by creating these mini projects. So, code along with me. Have fun! 😊

Project 12-1: Odd or even

Let's start this chapter with something simple. This is a classic puzzle in any programming language.

We're going to complete this project in two parts. In part 1, we're going to check if a given number is even or odd. In part 2, we're going to get a number range from the user and print either the even or odd numbers within that range.

A. Elumalai, *Introduction to Python for Kids*, https://doi.org/10.1007/978-1-4842-6812-4_12

But before we get to the programs, let me ask you a question. How are we going to decide if a number is odd or even? Well, any number that gets divided by 2 without any remainder is an even number, am I right? Numbers that return a 1 when divided by 2 are odd numbers.

The concept is quite simple. Do you remember the modulus operator, the one that returns the remainder of a division operation?

When you divide an even number by 2, what do you get? 0

When you divide an odd number by 2, what do you get? 1

That's it! So, if the modulus of the number and 2 returns 0, we have ourselves an even number. If not, we got an odd number.

Now, shall we create our program?

Part 1 – Is your number odd or even?

1. Get the input and convert it to an integer.

```
num = input('Enter a number: ')
num = int(num)
```

2. Then, check the modulus. If it's 0, it's an even number; otherwise, it's an odd number.

```
if((num % 2) == 0):
    print('{} is an Even number'.format(num))
else:
    print('{} is an Odd number'.format(num))
```

3. Let's run the program. My input is going to be 45.

```
= RESTART: C:\Users\aarthi\AppData\Local\Programs\
Python\Python38-32\dataStructures.py
Enter a number: 45
45 is an Odd number
```

Part 2 – print odd or even numbers within a range

Now, for the second program, let's get a range from the user, and whether they want even or odd numbers printed in the range, and print the same.

1. Get the range and convert them to integers. Get the "choice" too.

    ```
    start = input('Enter the start of the range: ')
    end = input('Enter the end of the range: ')
    start = int(start)
    end = int(end)
    choice - input('Even or Odd? Enter e or o: ')
    ```

2. Before we loop through the range, let's check if it's correct. The "start" value should be lesser than the "end" value.

    ```
    if(start < end):
    ```

3. If it is, let's create a for loop that loops through the range. If the choice is odd, print only when the result of the modulus is 1. If the choice is even, print only when the result of the modulus is 0. If it's neither, they've given an invalid choice and print an error message.

    ```
    for i in range(start,end+1):
        if(choice == 'o' or choice == 'O'):
            if((i % 2) == 1):
                print(i)
        elif(choice == 'e' or choice == 'E'):
    ```

```
        if((i % 2) == 0):
            print(i)
    else:
        print('Enter a valid choice and try again')
```

4. Finally, print an error message for the range too.

```
else:
    print('Enter a valid range')
```

5. Let's run this program. My range is going to be 1 to 10, and I'm going to want to print the odd numbers within this range.

```
= RESTART: C:\Users\aarthi\AppData\Local\Programs\
Python\Python38-32\dataStructures.py
Enter the start of the range: 1
Enter the end of the range: 10
Even or Odd? Enter e or o: O
1
3
5
7
9
```

Sweet! 😊

Project 12-2: Is your mom tipping enough?

In this project, we're going to create a tipping calculator that inputs the total bill and the tip their mom gave the waiting staff. Calculate the percentage of tip their mom gave and say Okay if 10–15%, good if 15–20%, and great if 20+%. If less than 10%, say their mom is not tipping enough.

Let's create it, shall we?

1. Get the bill amount and tip and convert them to integers.

```
bill = input('What was your bill? ')
tip = input('How much did you tip? ')
bill = int(bill)
tip = int(tip)
```

2. Let's calculate the percentage of the tip. To do this, multiply the tip by 100, and divide by the bill amount. This is just a reverse of how you calculate percentages. Let's convert the percent (which would be a floating number because of the division) to an integer.

```
percent = (tip * 100) / bill
percent = int(percent)
```

3. Now, let's use if elif else to print out the right message. Simple! 😊

```
if((percent >= 10) and (percent <= 15)):
    print('{}%. You tipped Okay'.format(percent))
elif((percent >= 15) and (percent <= 20)):
    print('{}%. That was a good tip!'.format(percent))
elif(percent >= 20):
    print('{}%. Wow, great tip! :)'.format(percent))
else:
    print("{}%. You didn't tip enough :
    (".format(percent))
```

Run the program, and you'll get this:

```
= RESTART: C:\Users\aarthi\AppData\Local\Programs\Python\
Python38-32\dataStructures.py
What was your bill? 400
How much did you tip? 45
11%. You tipped Okay
```

Works! 😊

Project 12-3: Draw a Christmas tree

Did you know that you can draw a Christmas tree with just your basic Python syntax? No packages or modules, just Python. Shall we try?

So basically, given the height of the tree, I want my program to draw a tree of that height. Simple enough, right?

As you probably guessed, we need loops to do this, and the tree will look something like Figure 12-1.

Figure 12-1. *Christmas tree of height 5*

How does this program work?

So, we need one loop that loops through each row of the tree and one that loops through its height. This is called nested looping. In this nested loop, the loop that goes through the tree's height is the outer loop, and for each iteration of the outer loop, we'll use an inner loop to draw the relevant row.

Let's do this!

Whenever we try to draw puzzles, or problems of any sort, it's always best to write an algorithm that'll help us write our program better. In this case, I'm going to use the preceding tree to reverse engineer my algorithm. Would you like to see how?

Algorithm:

1. In Figure 12-1, the height of the tree is 5. So, we need five rows of leaves and one stump at the end (in the middle of the tree).

2. The first row has 1 star, the second row has 1 + 2 (3) stars, the third row has 3 + 2 (5) stars, and so on until the end.

3. If you count the number of spaces before the first star is drawn (first row), it's four, which is the height of the tree minus one. For the second row, the number of spaces is three, and it reduces by one for every subsequent row.

4. The stump is drawn after four spaces again, so it's the same as our first row. We'd need a separate for loop to draw the stump because it's not a part of the tree's given height.

Okay, now that we've arrived at an algorithm, let's get cranking!

Let's create our program!

1. Let's get the height of our tree first and convert the string to an integer.

```
n = input("What's the height of your tree? ")
n = int(n)
```

2. Next, let's assign our variables. I'm going to create a variable sp, which is going to denote the number of spaces. It's going to start at n-1. I can reduce the value inside the loop.

   Similarly, I'll be creating another variable star, which is going to start at 1.

```
sp = n-1
star = 1
```

3. Now, let's draw our tree! The main for loop is going to loop through the entire height of the tree (0 to n-1 so the range is 0,n)

```
#draw the tree
for i in range(0,n):
```

4. We need two inner for loops inside the main outer for loop, one to draw the spaces and one to draw the stars.

   We need to loop from 0 to sp, and for every iteration of the loop, print a single space. But here's the catch. Print statements end at new lines, so if you want to be on the same line, you need to use an attribute called end and give it an empty string as its value. This will make sure that the next space is drawn right next to the first space.

```
#draw spaces
for j in range(0,sp):
    #By default, a print function ends with a newline.
    Use the end='' to make it end with an empty string
    instead, so we can draw the star next
    print(' ',end='')
```

5. Now, let's draw our stars. We need to loop through the range 0,star–1 for that. Use end='' again to make sure they are drawn on the same line.

```
for k in range(0,star):
    print('*',end='')
```

6. We're done with the inner for loops now. Before we start the next iteration of the outer for loop (our tree's next row), let's change our variable's values. Let's increment star by 2 and decrement sp by 1. Let's place an empty print() at the end because we're done with the row, and we need a new line for the next row.

```
star += 2
sp -= 1
print() #so there's a new line
```

7. That's it for the tree! Now, for the stump. Do what you did in the first row. Make a single for loop run from 0 to n–2 (range 0,n–1), and print a space with end=''. Once the loop is done, print a single star, and we're done! 😊

```
#draw the stump
for i in range(0,n-1):
    print(' ',end='')
print('*')
```

Whoo! That took some time. Shall we run the program?

```
= RESTART: C:/Users/aarthi/AppData/Local/Programs/Python/
Python38-32/mini_projects.py
What's the height of your tree? 10
```

Press Enter, and you'll get this (Figure 12-2).

Figure 12-2. *Christmas tree of height 10*

Yay! It works! 😊

Project 12-4: Spirals!

In this project, we're going to make different kinds of randomly colored spirals. It's going to be real fun! 😊

Square spiral

1. To start off, let's create a square spiral. Since we need to randomly select colors, we need to import both the turtle and random modules.

```
#Square spiral
import turtle, random
```

2. Let's set up the turtle screen first and set the pen size to 5 and speed to 0.

```
s = turtle.getscreen()
t = turtle.Turtle()
t.pensize(5)
t.speed(0)
```

3. Since this is going to be a square spiral, I'm going to make the length 4. You'll see why.

```
length = 4
```

4. Let's also create a list of colors from which we'll be randomly choosing in our loop.

```
colors = ['Red', 'Brown', 'Green', 'Blue', 'Orange',
'Yellow', 'Magenta', 'Violet', 'Pink']
```

5. Now, let's create our loop and make it go from 1 to 149 (so 1–150 in the range). I've chosen this number after a lot of trial and error. Then, I'm going to use the random.choice method which randomly chooses items from a list and assign the chosen item to the variable "color".

```
for x in range(1,150):
    color = random.choice(colors)
```

6. Change the pen color to that color and make your pen move forward by "length" and move right at 90 degrees. Then, add 4 to the current value of length, so in the next iteration, the pen moves forward by four more points. This keeps repeating, and so, we've created a spiral that keeps increasing in size (because of the increase in the value of length and because we're turning 90 degrees right after every line is drawn).

```
t.pencolor(color)
t.forward(length)
t.right(90)
length += 4
```

7. Finally, hide the turtles.

```
t.hideturtle()
turtle.hideturtle()
```

Run the preceding code, and you'll get this (Figure 12-3).

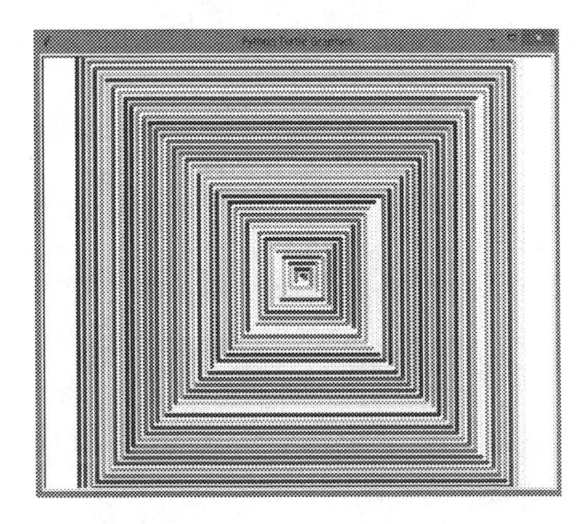

Figure 12-3. *Square spiral*

Change the range and the initial value (and increment) of length, and you'll get differently sized square spirals. Try and see! 😊

Random spiral

Since we realize that our spiral's shape depends on the length and the angles, what would happen if we change the angle to something else, maybe 80? We'll create a randomly shaped spiral, of course!

This would be almost like a pentagon, but not quite, since the exterior angle of a pentagon is 72, and we've given 80 here. Just to show that you can let your imagination run wild and get awesome results!

```
#Spiral pentagon
import turtle, random
s = turtle.getscreen()
t = turtle.Turtle()
t.pensize(5)
t.speed(0)
length = 4
colors = ['Red', 'Brown', 'Green', 'Blue', 'Orange', 'Yellow',
'Magenta', 'Violet', 'Pink']
for x in range(1,200):
    color = random.choice(colors)
    t.pencolor(color)
    t.forward(length)
    t.right(80)
    length += 2
t.hideturtle()
turtle.hideturtle()
```

Run the preceding code, and you'll get this (Figure 12-4).

Figure 12-4. *Random spiral*

Triangular spiral

Since the exterior angle of a triangle is 120 degrees, change the angle to 120 and you've gotten yourself a triangular spiral!

```
#Triangular spiral
import turtle, random
s = turtle.getscreen()
t = turtle.Turtle()
t.pensize(5)
t.speed(0)
length = 4
colors = ['Red', 'Brown', 'Green', 'Blue', 'Orange', 'Yellow',
'Magenta', 'Violet', 'Pink']
for x in range(1,120):
    color = random.choice(colors)
    t.pencolor(color)
    t.forward(length)
    t.right(-120) #-120 so we get a triangle facing upward
```

```
    length += 4
t.hideturtle()
turtle.hideturtle()
```

Run the preceding code, and you'll get this (Figure 12-5).

Figure 12-5. *Triangular spiral*

Star spiral

Since the exterior angle of a star is 144 degrees, give your angle as 144 and you've gotten yourself a star spiral!

```
#Star spiral
import turtle, random
s = turtle.getscreen()
t = turtle.Turtle()
t.pensize(5)
t.speed(0)
length = 4
colors = ['Red', 'Brown', 'Green', 'Blue', 'Orange', 'Yellow',
'Magenta', 'Violet', 'Pink']
```

```
for x in range(1,130):
    color = random.choice(colors)
    t.pencolor(color)
    t.forward(length)
    t.right(144)
    length += 4
t.hideturtle()
turtle.hideturtle()
```

Run the preceding code, and you'll get this (Figure 12-6).

Figure 12-6. *Star spiral*

Circular spiral

A circular spiral is going to be a little different to the rest. Our length is still going to be 4, but we're only going to move forward by one point at a time to get a circular shape, and I've made the angle 20 in this case. You can change the angle to make your spiral closely knit and further apart.

```
#Circular spiral
import turtle, random
s = turtle.getscreen()
```

```
t = turtle.Turtle()
t.pensize(5)
t.speed(0)
length = 4
colors = ['Red', 'Brown', 'Green', 'Blue']
for x in range(1,100):
    color = random.choice(colors)
    t.pencolor(color)
    t.forward(length)
    t.right(20)
    length += 1
t.hideturtle()
turtle.hideturtle()
```

Run the preceding code, and you'll get this (Figure 12-7).

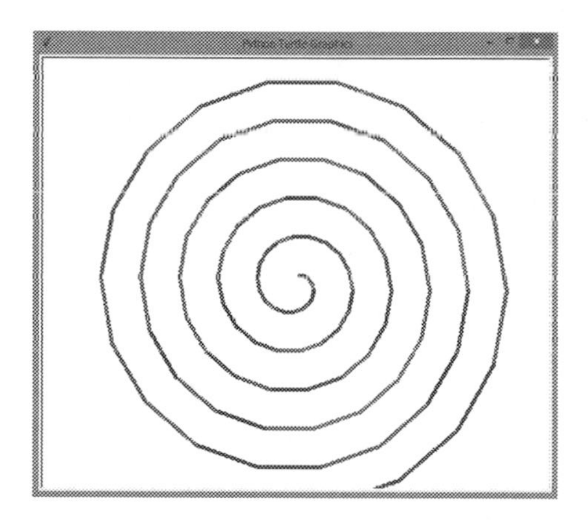

Figure 12-7. *Circular spiral*

Project 12-5: Complex mandala – completely automated

In this project, let's draw a complex mandala with a for loop. This is going to be randomly colored too. It's going to look epic!

1. Let's import the random and turtle modules and set up the turtle screen and pen first. Next, let's change the pen size to 5 and speed to 0.

```
#Mandala
import turtle, random
s = turtle.getscreen()
t = turtle.Turtle()
t.pensize(5)
t.speed(0)
```

2. Let's create a list of colors next.

```
colors = ['Red', 'Blue', 'Green']
```

3. Then, we're going to make our loop loop through the 1 to 24 (1,25 as the range).

```
for x in range(1,25):
```

4. Let's choose our random color and change the pen to that color.

```
color = random.choice(colors)
t.pencolor(color)
```

5. Now comes the fun part. Mandalas are usually complexly drawn circles, am I right? So, let's draw 100-point circle for every iteration, but shift the angle by a slight 15 degrees every time, so we get a closely knit mandala design (you'll see).

```
t.circle(100)
t.right(15) #closely formed mandala
```

6. Finally, hide the turtles.

```
t.hideturtle()
turtle.hideturtle()
```

Run the preceding code, and you'll get this (Figure 12-8).

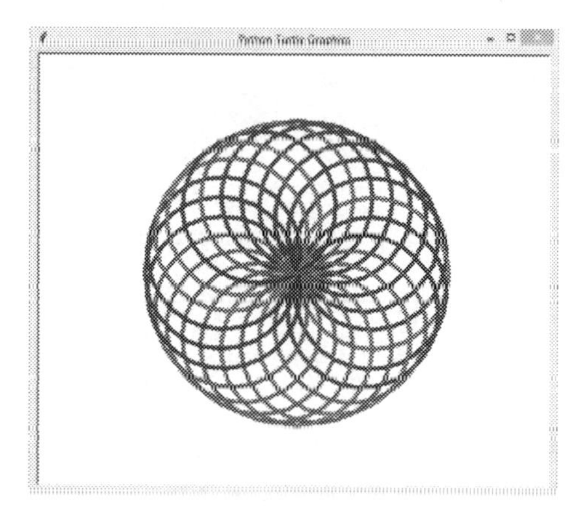

Figure 12-8. *Complex mandala*

Try changing the loop's range, the radius of the circle, and the angle to get different types of mandalas. You can literally create hundreds of designs like this! 😊

Project 12-6: *Turtle* race with loops

This is going to be a fun little game that demonstrates the sheer power of for loops and Python's random package. We're also going to learn a bunch of *Turtle* methods we skipped in the *Turtle* chapters. Excited? Me too!

So, the concept is simple. We're having three turtles, and we're going to conduct a race between them. That's about it. When we're done, it'll look like an actual, live race happening on our screen. How do we do that?

To start off, we need our players, and lucky for us, *Turtle* makes it easy to create "turtles".

1. Let's import the turtle and random packages and set up our screen first.

```
#Turtles
import turtle, random
s = turtle.getscreen()
```

2. Now, for our turtle, we aren't going to go about this the usual way. We're going to create three separate turtles with the turtle.Turtle() command, named red, blue, and green. *Turtle* lets us do that. We can create as many turtles as we want and place them anywhere we want and make them draw different things at the same time. Pretty cool, don't you think?

3. Once we create a player (turtle), we're going to change its pen size to 5, the color of the 'turtle' using the color() method, and the shape of the turtle to 'turtle' using the shape() method. You'll see how these works in just a second.

```
red = turtle.Turtle()
red.pensize(5)
red.color('Red')
red.shape('turtle')

blue = turtle.Turtle()
blue.pensize(5)
blue.color('Blue')
blue.shape('turtle')
```

```
green = turtle.Turtle()
green.pensize(5)
green.color('Green')
green.shape('turtle')
```

4. Finally, let's hide the main turtle that's at the center of the screen.

```
turtle.hideturtle() #hide the main turtle at the center
```

5. Right now, if you run the program, you won't see much. You'd only see the green turtle because that was drawn last. To see the turtles separately, let's move them to their race positions. I chose arbitrary values after trying out a lot of them. You can choose any starting point you want.

```
#Make turtles move to position
red.penup()
red.goto(-250,150)
red.pendown()

blue.penup()
blue.goto(-250,0)
blue.pendown()

green.penup()
green.goto(-250,-150)
green.pendown()
```

6. Now, let's run the program, and we'll get this (Figure 12-9).

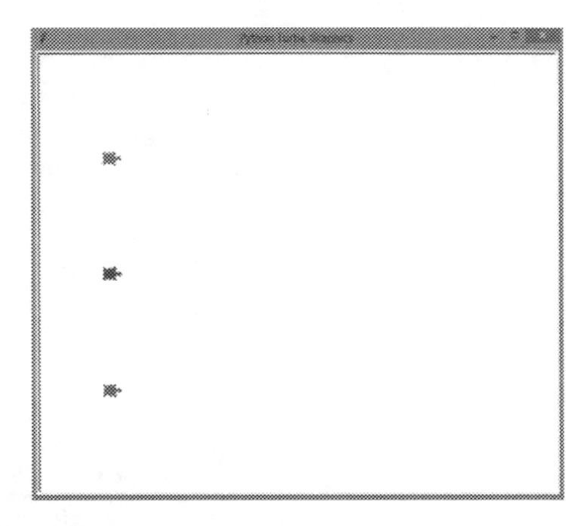

Figure 12-9. *Turtles in position*

We have three turtle players, and they are in position. Perfect!

7. Finally, let's make them race! Create a for loop that runs for 100 iterations. For every iteration, make each of the turtle move forward by a random number from 1 to 10. This way, we don't know how further any of the turtle will move, and there's a real-world racing feel to it.

```
#Make the turtles move
for i in range(100):
    red.forward(random.randint(1,10))
    blue.forward(random.randint(1,10))
    green.forward(random.randint(1,10))
```

That's pretty much it. If you run the programs now, you'll see three differently colored lines moving at different paces on the screen and stop in different points. There you have it. Your race (Figure 12-10)! 😊

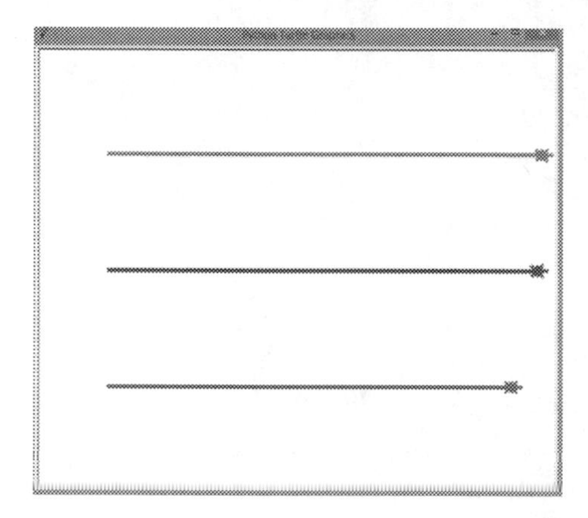

***Figure 12-10.** Turtles racing*

That's it for our mini projects! Hope you had fun creating them. 😊

Summary

In this chapter, we looked at six different, interesting and fun, mini projects. We brushed up the concepts we learned in the previous chapters while creating colorful mini projects. We also learned about creating algorithms to solve problems and puzzles in programming.

In the next chapter, let's learn how to do True automation with functions, how to get arguments to our user-defined functions, how to save time and a lot of lines of code with functions, and a lot more.

CHAPTER 13

Automate with Functions

In the previous chapter, we took a break from all the learning and creating more fun mini projects. Now that we're energized, let's go back to learning for a couple more chapters, shall we? 😊

In this chapter, we'll be looking at a very interesting concept. We had an introduction to automation in Python using loops, but in this chapter, let's look at True automation with functions. It works like magic. You'll see.

True automation

A. Elumalai, *Introduction to Python for Kids*, https://doi.org/10.1007/978-1-4842-6812-4_13

Why do I call it that? We already looked at loops, and they did plenty of automation on their own. We created full-blown shapes with just a few lines of code, am I right? So, why do we need functions?

Well, what if you need to repeat the code? For example, let's bring back the code we wrote in our loops chapter. Remember how we created a program that creates a shape based on the inputs we give it? We had to run the program multiple times to draw different shapes. What if I want to draw different shapes from the same run of the program? What if I want to give multiple inputs, so my program draws each shape, one after the other, while erasing the previous shape? How would you do that?

You'd probably have to write the same code multiple times, with different inputs for angle and sides, am I right? So, if you wanted to draw five shapes, you need five for loops, one after the other, with a clear() method between each loop. That's too long! What if we can shorten this as well?

With functions, you certainly can! You can create your "for loop" with something called a "function". We've been using a lot of functions so far. It's just that, we call them pre-defined methods because they were already created in Python. But now, you can create your own functions. How exciting is that? You've become such an experienced programmer that you can now create your own functions, call them, send arguments, automate, and so on.

Now that your "for loop" is within your function, you can do something called "calling the function" and give different values every time to make sure that your for loop draws a different shape every time. I'll teach you how to do exactly that in just a moment.

But for now, let's learn how to write a basic function.

Our first function

Every function has two parts. There's the function definition, which has the code that you want executed multiple times. Then, there's the function call, which is the line of code that literally "calls" the function definition. It might send arguments/values that serve as input to your function.

But to start with, let's create a function without arguments so you understand how they work at their base.

So, functions have a definition, don't they? So far, we've noticed that Python is very intuitive. Its syntax makes sense. "if" means the English word If; and "while" means something is going to go on for a while, hence a loop; and so on. Similarly, "def" means you're creating a function definition.

Just mention "def", the name of the function you are creating, followed by parenthesis and a colon, as usual. Then, in the next line, add your lines of code after an indent. It's as simple as that!

Let's create a function that prints 'Hello there!' when we call it. We name our functions so we can call them later on. We've called many pre-defined functions like len() and join(), right? The concept is the same for the functions you create: the user-defined functions. I'm going to name my function greet() because that's what it's going to do, greet the person who calls it. 😊

```
def greet():
    print('Hello there!')
```

Great! We have our function. Let's run it.

Crickets...nothing happens. ☹ Why?!

Ah right, we haven't called it yet! How do we do that? Well, how did we call our pre-defined functions? The format is the same. The function's name, followed by parenthesis. That's it!

Let's do things properly now. A function definition, followed by a function call, just like it should be.

```
def greet():
    print('Hello there!')
greet()
```

Run the program now, and you'll get this:

```
= RESTART: C:/Users/aarthi/AppData/Local/Programs/Python/
Python38-32/functions.py
Hello there!
```

Ahah! We got it.

Why do we need functions?

But what's the use of a function? I'm confused. Are you? It does what we've been doing all the while without adding extra lines of code to create and call the function.

Well…what if I want to greet my user five times and not one time. Maybe there are five people in the group? Before now, I would have added five print statements. But now, I can just add five function calls, like this, and the function will be called, and "Hello there!" would be printed every single time. Cool!

```
greet()
greet()
greet()
greet()
greet()
```

Run the preceding code, and you'll get this:

```
= RESTART: C:/Users/aarthi/AppData/Local/Programs/Python/
Python38-32/functions.py
Hello there!
Hello there!
Hello there!
Hello there!
Hello there!
```

We got it! Or did we? What's the use of this either? We still created five lines of code. We would have done that anyway. We saved neither time nor space. Bummer!

Do different things every time!

You'll understand the true use of function when you send different values to it every time you call it. Let's change our greet() program in such a way that it greets a person every time it calls.

Now that I want the function to greet the person with their name every time, I need to let my function know what their name is, am I right? How do I do that? Maybe my function can receive it while it's being called? Yes! You can include the name of the parameter or parameters (you can send as many as you want) you send inside of the parenthesis while you create your function.

Okay, pause! Parameter? Argument? Which is which? Not to worry. It's all the same, really, but if you want to be specific, the values you send from your function call are called parameters, and the values you receive in your function definition are arguments. Simple, right? You'll understand better once we look at our example.

Create (define) your functions

Let's see how that works:

```
def greet(name):
    print('Hello {}!'.format(name))
```

Look at that! I received the parameter "name" within my parenthesis, and then I used it in my print statement. This is not a variable, per se, but it acts like it. You can name your parameter anything you want. Once we're done with this example, why don't you change the name of your parameter from "name" to "n" and see if it still works the same?

Now that we've created our definition, let's create the rest of the program. Let's create a variable name and get the input. Then, let's call the greet() function, but this time with the name of the argument "name" inside the parenthesis.

```
name = input("What's your name?")
greet(name)
```

Nice! Don't be confused by the same "name". I just made the name of the variable and the name of the parameter the function receives the same, so you don't get confused. But the parameter name can be anything you want, and your program would still work the same.

Run the preceding code and you'll get this:

```
= RESTART: C:\Users\aarthi\AppData\Local\Programs\Python\
Python38-32\functions.py
What's your name? Susan
Hello Susan!
```

Look at that! It works!

You can reuse your code!

Now, I'm going to show you the real use of functions. The real use of functions lies in the fact that you don't need to repeat the same lines of code over and over again.

So, let's create a function called "calculation" that calculates the addition, subtraction, division, and multiplication of any two numbers it receives. Alright?

So, it's going to receive two numbers, n1 and n2, as parameters. I'm going to do the calculations and print the results in four separate lines:

```
def calculate(n1,n2):
    n1 = int(n1)
    n2 = int(n2)
    add = n1 + n2
    sub = n1 - n2
    div = n1 / n2
    mul = n1 * n2
    print('''Addition: {}
Subtraction: {}
Multiplication: {}
Division: {}
          '''. format(add,sub,mul,div))
```

In the preceding lines of code, I received the two numbers as the parameters n1 and n2. Then I converted them to integers because I'm going to receive the numbers using the "input()" method, and those values are strings by default. Then, I've done the calculations and finally printed everything out using the multi-line string quote.

Now comes the part I was talking about. Now that we've created the calculate function, we can call it any time we want. What if we want the calculations done three times? Before we discovered functions, we would have written the same lines of code multiple times because there is no other way to receive different inputs and do the same calculations with different values.

But now, we have a way!

```
calculate(input("Enter the first number"),input("Enter the second number"))
calculate(input("Enter the first number"),input("Enter the second number"))
calculate(input("Enter the first number"),input("Enter the second number"))
```

I've created three function calls where each of the function calls has two arguments which are nothing more than input statements.

Let's run those:

```
= RESTART: C:\Users\aarthi\AppData\Local\Programs\Python\Python38-32\functions.py
Enter the first number 10
Enter the second number 5
Addition: 15
Subtraction: 5
Multiplication: 50
Division: 2.0

Enter the first number 5
Enter the second number 10
Addition: 15
Subtraction: -5
Multiplication: 50
Division: 0.5

Enter the first number 100
Enter the second number 20
```

```
Addition: 120
Subtraction: 80
Multiplication: 2000
Division: 5.0
```

Look at that! With the same few lines of code, I was able to do three different set of calculations without resorting to running the program three times like we usually do.

Now this is the *true* use of a function. ***True automation!***

No arguments?

But be careful while sending arguments in your function calls. If you don't send the number of arguments your function definition is expecting, you'll end up with an error while running the function. This holds true if you send lesser number of arguments or more arguments.

```
def greet(name):
    print('Hello {}!'.format(name))
```

For the above function:

```
greet()
```

a call with no argument will give this error:

```
= RESTART: C:\Users\aarthi\AppData\Local\Programs\Python\
Python38-32\functions.py
Traceback (most recent call last):
  File "C:\Users\aarthi\AppData\Local\Programs\Python\
Python38-32\functions.py", line 3, in <module>
    greet()
TypeError: greet() missing 1 required positional argument:
'name'
```

The function call is missing one required argument.

A call two arguments on the other hand:

```
greet(name1,name2)
```

You'll receive the following error:

```
= RESTART: C:\Users\aarthi\AppData\Local\Programs\Python\
Python38-32\functions.py
Traceback (most recent call last):
  File "C:\Users\aarthi\AppData\Local\Programs\Python\
Python38-32\functions.py", line 3, in <module>
    greet(name1,name2)
NameError: name 'name1' is not defined
```

The argument is not defined! So, always make sure that the number of arguments matches the number of parameters in the function definition.

Give an answer

So far, we've just printed things out. But what if we need an answer? Let's say I have an expression, and I'm using the add() and mul() functions to get the result of addition and multiplication on my numbers. But then, I want to, let's say, divide them all. How can I do that when I don't know the result of the operation? Printing the result isn't always enough, is it?

Python has a simple solution for this as well! Just return the result. Simple as that. Use the "return" statement, and return your result, and it'll be received in your function call. Then, you can either assign the function call to a variable and use the result or use the function call as a value in itself.

Confused? Don't be, my dear. Yet another fun activity is on its way to make you understand the concept.

Let me first create two functions, addition() and multiply(). They receive parameters n1 and n2, respectively, and perform addition and multiplication of the two numbers.

```
def addition(n1,n2):
    add = n1 + n2
def multiply(n1,n2):
    mul = n1 * n2
```

But I can't use these values, can I? So, let me return them.

```
def addition(n1,n2):
    add = n1 + n2
    return add
def multiply(n1,n2):
    mul = n1 * n2
    return mul
```

Now, I've returned the results of the addition and multiplication of the numbers. Alternatively, you can just perform the operation in the return statement, like this:

```
def addition(n1,n2):
    return n1 + n2
def multiply(n1,n2):
    return n1 * n2
```

You'll save lines of code if you do it like this. This will only work if your entire function just has one line of code.

Alright, now that we have our functions ready, let's use them!

```
num1 = input("Enter your first number: ")
num1 = int(num1)
num2 = input("Enter your second number: ")
num2 = int(num2)
mul = multiply(num1,num2)
add = addition(num1,num2)
calc = mul /add
print("{} / {} = {}".format(mul,add,calc))
```

In the preceding lines of code, I received two numbers as inputs and converted the strings to integers. And then, I created a variable called "calc" which divides the results of the multiplication of those numbers by the addition of those numbers.

Instead of performing the operation on there, I just received the values in the variables mul and add. Technically, this is all we need because the return statements in those functions will return the result of the operations to the function calls, and then they can be used in the "calc" operation.

Shall we check if this works?

```
= RESTART: C:\Users\aarthi\AppData\Local\Programs\Python\
Python38-32\functions.py
Enter your first number: 10
Enter your second number: 5
50 / 15 = 3.3333333333333335
```

Yes! It works! Why don't you try the same with different operations? Make it as complicated as you want to and have Math fun! 😊

No arguments? What to do!

Sometimes, you might not know what arguments to send. Maybe you just want to test the function? But sending no arguments when the function expects arguments will give us an error! What can we do?

Default arguments to the rescue!

You can assign "default" values to your arguments when you define your function, so they work even if you forget to send any arguments when you call your function. Would you like to test it?

In the following example, I've created a printName function that just prints out the given name. I've called the function twice, once with an argument and once without. Let's see what happens.

```
def printName(name='Susan'):
    print('My name is {}'.format(name))

printName('John')
printName()
Run, and:
= RESTART: C:\Users\aarthi\AppData\Local\Programs\Python\
Python38-32\condition.py
My name is John
My name is Susan
```

It works exactly as we expected. The default argument gets ignored when we actually send an argument from our function call. If we forget, it's used. Perfect! 😊

Too many arguments!

Function hasn't stopped making your programming life easy just yet. What if you don't know how many arguments you're going to send? But you want to receive all of them, without any error.

Arbitrary arguments will help you do that. Instead of the name of the argument, receive them with *listName and you can access each argument as you'd access a list item. Let me show you how.

Let's say I want to print the sum of the numbers sent by my function call, but I don't know how many I'd need added, so I'll just receive them as an arbitrary argument.

Since *listName is essentially a list, we can loop through it like we would in a list.

```
def addNums(*nums):
    sum = 0
    for num in nums:
        sum += num
    return sum
```

Let me call my function with my arbitrary arguments now.

```
print(addNums(1,5,3,7,5,8,3))
print(addNums(1,3,5,7,9))
print(addNums(1,2,3,4,5,6,7,8,9))
```

When I run the program, I get this:

```
= RESTART: C:\Users\aarthi\AppData\Local\Programs\Python\
Python38-32\condition.py
32
25
45
```

Wow, this single feature gives so much freedom to do whatever I want in my programs!

On the other hand, you can just send a list as an argument. That'll work too. Why don't you try modifying the preceding program to send and receive a list of numbers?

Did you try? Did it look something like this?

```
def addNums(nums):
    sum = 0
    for num in nums:
        sum += num
    return sum
print(addNums([1,5,3,7,5,8,3]))
print(addNums([1,3,5,7,9]))
print(addNums([1,2,3,4,5,6,7,8,9]))
```

Great! 😊

Global vs. local

So far, we've seen that once you create a variable, you can't re-define it. You can re-assign values to it, yes, for example:

```
for i in range(1,10):
    print(i,end='')
print()
print(i)
```

Look at the preceding program. I've created a variable "i" that prints numbers from 1 to 9 in the same line. After the for loop is done, we print a new line and the current value of "i".

Let's run the program, and we'll get this:

```
= RESTART: C:\Users\aarthi\AppData\Local\Programs\Python\
Python38-32\condition.py
123456789
9
```

Look at that! It's 9 and not an error because once the "i" was created, even though it was created inside for loop, it becomes accessible to the entire program.

Variables within functions

But that's not the case with functions. Let's create the same inside a function now:

```
def printNum():
    for i in range(1,10):
        print(i,end='')

printNum()
print()
print(i)
Run the above, and:
>>>
= RESTART: C:\Users\aarthi\AppData\Local\Programs\Python\
Python38-32\condition.py
123456789
Traceback (most recent call last):
  File "C:\Users\aarthi\AppData\Local\Programs\Python\
Python38-32\condition.py", line 7, in <module>
    print(i)
NameError: name 'i' is not defined
```

Look at the preceding output. Things were fine while the function was still being executed. It printed out our numbers in the order we wanted. But then, when we tried to print the current value of "i" outside the function, we get a "not defined" error. How's that possible? The variable "i" was defined inside the for loop in the function, was it not?

Yes, it was, but it was ***local*** to that function and cannot be used outside. So, any variable created inside of a function is called a local variable.

Return local variables

If you want to use it outside of a function, you need to return it, like this:

```
def printNum():
    for i in range(1,10):
        print(i,end='')
    return i

i = printNum()
print()
print(i)
```

Now, run the program, and you'll get this:

```
= RESTART: C:\Users\aarthi\AppData\Local\Programs\Python\
Python38-32\condition.py
123456789
9
```

It works! 😊

Global variables

Similarly, any variable created outside of a function is called a ***global*** variable, and if you want to use it inside a function, you need to use the global keyword, like this:

Let's say I want to create a global variable "sum". Every time I send a list of numbers, they get added to the "current" value of sum, so we essentially get a sum of multiple lists. How do we do that?

I've created a variable "sum" and assigned it a 0 at the start of the program. Next, let me define the function. If I want to use the same "sum" from outside the function, then I need to mention it as "global sum" (without quotes) at the start of the function. It's always good practice to mention the global variables at the very top of a function definition.

That's it. The rest of the program is similar to the one we wrote before.

```
sum = 0


def addNums(nums):
    global sum
    for num in nums:
        sum += num
    return sum

print(addNums([1,5,3,7,5,8,3]))
print(addNums([1,3,5,7,9]))
print(addNums([1,2,3,4,5,6,7,8,9]))
```

Run this code, and you'll get the following:

```
= RESTART: C:\Users\aarthi\AppData\Local\Programs\Python\
Python38-32\condition.py
32
57
102
```

The old value of sum was preserved, and it gets added to the new values sent in the subsequent function calls. Sweet!

Note *Order of creation and usage* is very important in Python. Before you call a function, define it. So, the *function definition* should always be above the function call or you'll get an error. Similarly, before you use a variable, create it. So, your *global variables* should be created before the function definitions inside which you want them used.

Lambda

A lambda is an anonymous function. It has no name, it can take any number of arguments, but can only have one line of code. Sounds very simple, doesn't it? Why would we ever need it when we have our glorious functions to work with?

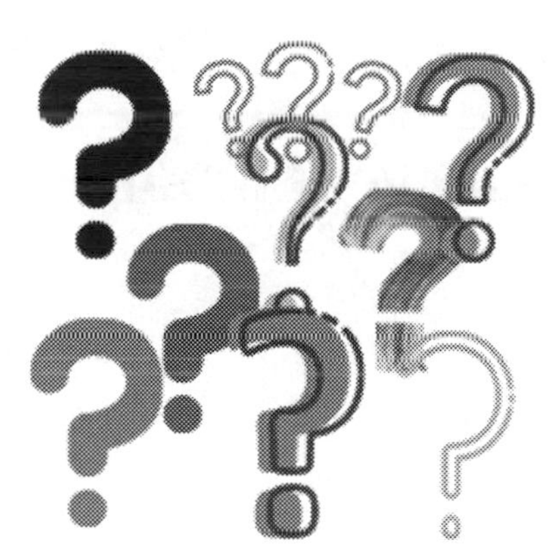

In the future chapters, we'll be working with events. These events will let you call functions when you click a button on an app, press your mouse button, click a keyboard button, and so on. Lambdas are very much needed in those cases, so let's look at them now (even if right now they're not of much use to us).

A lambda's syntax is quite simple:

```
variable = lambda arguments: line of code
```

Why do we assign our lambda to a variable? So we can call it, of course! Let's look at an example now:

```
sum = lambda num1,num2: num1 + num2
```

Now, we can call the lambda by calling sum(), like this:

```
print(sum(3,5))
print(sum(100,240))
```

Run the preceding lines of code, and you'll get this:

```
= RESTART: C:\Users\aarthi\AppData\Local\Programs\Python\
Python38-32\condition.py
8
340
```

Mini project – do your Math homework with Python

We're going to make this project simple. If we used a package like *Tkinter*, we could make this a proper app. But we haven't covered *Tkinter* yet, so let's just do it in the Shell.

Our calculator is going to be designed like this:

1. Different functions for each of the operations – addition, multiplication, division, subtraction, and modulus.

2. We're going to get input from the user. We'll be getting two numbers to start with and their choice on which operation they want to perform.

3. Then, we're going to print the result and ask them if they want to continue using the calculator.

4. If the answer is "y" or "Y", then we'll ask them if they want the previous result as one of the numbers in the calculation. If "y" or "Y" for that as well, then we'll just ask one more input and ask for the operation they want again.

5. The calculator can go on like this forever. When the user answers "n" for continuation, we'll break out of the loop and end the program.

Interesting? Excited to get started? Me too! 😊

1. Let's create the functions that do the operations again. Since the function definitions need to be created before they are called, let's finish that first.

```
#Addition
def add(n1,n2):
    return n1 + n2
#Subtraction
def sub(n1,n2):
    return n1 - n2
#Multiplication
def mul(n1,n2):
    return n1 * n2
```

```
#Division
def div(n1,n2):
    return n1 / n2
#Modulus
def mod(n1,n2):
    return n1 % n2
```

2. Now, let's create a never-ending while loop, which means the condition is always true until we break out of the loop with a "break" statement.
3. Inside the while loop, we'll ask the user to enter the two numbers as inputs and convert the strings to integers as always.
4. Then, we'll ask for the operation. We'll use an if...elif...else statement to call the relevant function and get the result.

```
#create a result globally
result = 0 #default value
repeat = 0 #if the user decided to reuse the result of
previous operation, this becomes 1

while(True):
    #if this is the first/new operation
    if(repeat == 0):
        #number1
        num1 = input('Your first number: ')
        num1 = int(num1)
        #number2
        num2 = input('Your second number: ')
        num2 = int(num2)
```

```
    #If the user asked to use the result of the last
    operation in this one
    else:
        #number2
        num2 = input('Your second number: ')
        num2 = int(num2)
    #get the operator
    op = input('''Enter any of the following numbers,
    that correspond to the given operation:
Just the number, not the period.
1. Addition
2. Subtraction
3. Multiplication
4. Division
5. Modulus
''')
    op = int(op)
    #Call the relevant function
    if(op == 1):
        result = add(num1,num2)
    elif(op == 2):
        result = sub(num1,num2)
    elif(op == 3):
        result = mul(num1,num2)
    elif(op == 4):
        result = div(num1,num2)
    elif(op == 5):
        result = mod(num1,num2)
```

```
        else:
            print('You entered an invalid operation. Please
            run the program again')
            break
        #print the result
        print('Answer: {}'.format(result))
        again = input('Do you want to do another operation?
        Enter Y or N: ')
        if((again == 'y') or (again == 'Y')):
            reuse = input('Do you want the result of the
            current operation to be the first number of the
            next? Y or N: ')
            if((reuse == 'y') or (reuse == 'Y')):
                num1 = result
                repeat = 1
            else:
                repeat = 0
        else:
            print('Ok bye!')
            break
```

Mini project – automated shapes – next level

Loops were automation, but functions are supposed to be True automation, aren't they? Why don't we see what they can do to our automated shapes mini project?

I'm going to create a function called draw_shape() and place my code inside. I'm going to accept two arguments inside my function: sides and angle.

If the sides are equal to 1, I'm going to draw a circle. Otherwise, I'm going to draw a polygon. Simple as that.

For this project, I'm going to use another package called the time package. With this, I can give a small delay of around 300 milliseconds before the next shape is drawn so the user can see what's going on:

1. Let's import the turtle and time packages first.

```
import turtle
import time
```

2. Then let us set up turtle. I'm going to set the pen color to red and fill color to yellow.

```
s = turtle.getscreen()
t = turtle.Turtle()
t.pensize(5)
t.color('Red','Yellow')
```

3. Then, I'm going to define the draw_shape() function. At the start of the function, I'm going to use the sleep() method of the time package to basically stop the program for 0.3 seconds (300 milliseconds). Then, I'm going to clear the turtle so any previous shape is erased before I draw the next one.

```
def draw_shape(sides,angle):
    time.sleep(0.3)
    t.clear()
    t.begin_fill()
    #If sides are greater than 1, then it's a polygon
    if sides > 1:
        for x in range(0,sides):
```

```
            if(x == sides-1):
                t.home()
                break
            t.forward(100)
            t.right(angle)
    elif sides == 1:
        #circle
        t.circle(100,angle)
    t.end_fill()
    t.hideturtle()
    turtle.hideturtle()
```

4. I'm going to give multiple values in various function calls. When you run this program, you'll see these shapes drawn in succession, with a 0.3 delay in between.

```
draw_shape(4,90)
draw_shape(3,60)
draw_shape(5,50)
draw_shape(6,60)
draw_shape(8,45)
draw_shape(1,180)
draw_shape(1,360)
```

The images you'll get are shown in Figure 13-1.

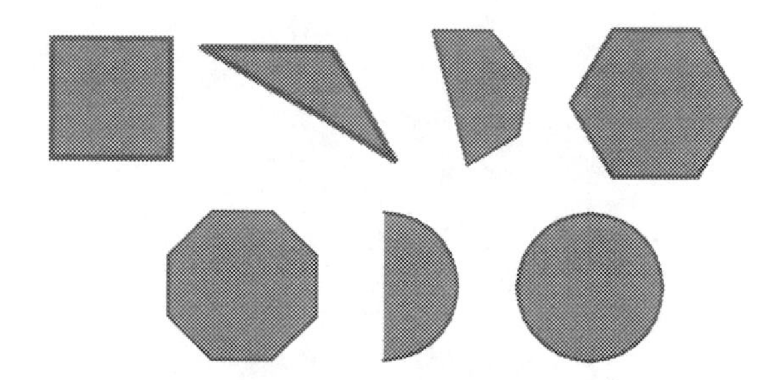

Figure 13-1. *Automated shapes*

Neat! 😊

Summary

In this chapter, we looked at True automation with functions. We learned all about defining functions, calling them, sending arguments to make our functions dynamic, returning values back to the function calls, accepting arbitrary arguments, and so much more. We also automated some of the projects we did in the previous chapters.

In the next chapter, let's do real-world programming like the pros do it! We're going to look at objects and imitating real-world scenarios in programming.

CHAPTER 14

Let's Create Real-World Objects

In the previous chapter, we looked at True automation with functions. We looked at saving time, space, and lines of code with functions, defining functions, calling them, sending arguments to our functions, using default arguments, returning values back to our calling statement, and accepting arbitrary arguments and lists as arguments. b

In this chapter, let us look at how to do real-world programming with object-oriented programming (OOPs). We'll be looking at classes, the initialization function, self, user-defined properties and methods, and creating objects on our classes. We will also look at accessing our properties and functions and changing the values of our properties.

A. Elumalai, *Introduction to Python for Kids*, https://doi.org/10.1007/978-1-4842-6812-4_14

What is object-oriented programming?

Everything in Python is an object. It has its properties and methods remember? This is how things are in the real world. Let's take us, humans, for example. We have properties, or attributes, like our height, weight, eye color, hair color, and so on. Similarly, we have "methods", as in we run, walk, talk, do stuff, am I right?

Everything in Python mirrors our real-world objects. For example, strings have properties like length, but methods like splitting, capitalizing, and so on. Humans are a "group" under which there are individual human beings with their own values (different hair color, weight, height, etc.). Similarly, "strings" as such are a group under which you can create your own individual strings with their own properties and methods.

That's object-oriented programming in its core: real-world programming. Instead of using the pre-defined objects and their methods and properties, you can create your own objects for your projects. Do you see the possibilities here? The world is your oyster now!

But this is a vast topic, and it's impossible to cover everything in a single chapter. I don't want to confuse you too much either. You're here to learn Python and create fun projects, and we can create the projects in this book without OOPs (object-oriented programming). But I'll give you an introduction to OOPs so you understand the basics of it. Sounds good? Alright then, let's do it! 😊

Let's prove it!

I just said that everything is an object in Python, didn't I? Why don't we prove it?

Let's start with an integer (a number) and check its type.

```
num = 10
print(type(num))
```

Run the preceding code, and you'll get this:

```
= RESTART: C:\Users\aarthi\AppData\Local\Programs\Python\
Python38-32\oops.py
<class 'int'>
```

Interesting. In the next section, you'll see that classes are how you create objects in Python, so essentially, an integer is a class and the variables that hold integers are objects. Alright, but what about the remaining data types?

```
s = 'Hello'
print(type(s))
b = True
print(type(b))
f = 1.0
print(type(f))
def fName():
    pass
print(type(fName))
```

Run the entire program, and you'll get this:

```
= RESTART: C:\Users\aarthi\AppData\Local\Programs\Python\
Python38-32\oops.py
<class 'int'>
<class 'str'>
<class 'bool'>
<class 'float'>
<class 'function'>
```

Whoa! They're all classes! So everything is indeed an object in Python. 😊

Classes

Remember the groups I talked about earlier? If you want to create your own objects, you need to create a group under which you can create those objects. "Humans" are a group, and each human being is an individual objects. Every human has a set of properties and methods that are common to us, right?

Similarly, every group of objects will have a set of properties and methods that are common to it, so let's create a blueprint of that group and create every object separately with its own set of values.

Confused? Don't be. It'll all be clear in a minute.

You need ***classes*** to create these blueprints.

To model the real world, let's create a "Human" class with properties and methods that mirror us, humans.

```
class Human:
    sample = 'Sample property value'
```

That's it! You have your first class. It's not compulsory, but when naming your classes, capitalize the first letter, so when you create your objects, you can distinguish them better.

Alright. We have a class, but what next? Where are our objects? Well, you need to create them. Why don't we create a "human1" object?

```
human1 = Human()
```

It's as simple as that. Now, you can access the property values inside the class, like this:

```
print(human1.sample)
```

Run the preceding code, and you'll get this:

```
= RESTART: C:/Users/aarthi/AppData/Local/Programs/Python/
Python38-32/oops.py
Sample property value
```

It works! 😊

Objects with their own values

So far, we've not created dynamic classes that change their property values based on the objects we're creating on them.

To do that, you need to use a pre-defined method of "class" called the __init__() function. That's two underscores before and two underscores after init, followed by ().

With this method, you can send individual values for your objects as you create them, so they get assigned to your class's properties. Let's see how:

```
class Human:
    def __init__(self,name,age,hair,eye,pet):
        self.name = name
```

```
        self.age = age
        self.hair = hair
        self.eye = eye
```

So, define the init function and accept the attributes you need when creating the objects. Our attributes are going to be name, age, hair (hair color), eye (eye color), and pet (name of their pet).

But that's not all. There's this special attribute at the start, "self". What's that? Would you like to guess? What's self? Yourself? Then it should be the object that's being created, shouldn't it? Absolutely!

"Self" is the object being created, and we're creating properties for that object and assigning the accepted values to it. You can name it anything you want, as long as you follow the variable naming convention. Programmers use "self" so they know what it is.

Alright, now that we've created a "proper" class, let's create our object.

```
human1 = Human('Susan',8,'brunette','blue','Barky')
```

Our first object is "human1" and it's going to be an object of the "Human" class, and we've sent a bunch of properties for the same. Make sure to send the properties in the order your init() function expects them, or you might end up with an error.

You can create any number of objects like that. Let's create another one.

```
human2 = Human('Johny',10,'blond','green','Boxer')
```

This looks similar to a regular function call so far. Why use classes then?

Well, for one, you don't need to return anything to access the properties.

```
print(human1.name)
print(human2.eye)
```

Your object's name, followed by a period and the property, and you're good to go.

Let's run this, and we'll get the following:

```
= RESTART: C:/Users/aarthi/AppData/Local/Programs/Python/
Python38-32/oops.py
Susan
green
```

Yes! We got what we wanted.

Manipulate your objects

Unlike functions, we can change the property values of your objects as well.

```
human2.eye = 'brown'
print('Eye color: {}'.format(human2.eye))
```

Run everything, and you'll get this:

```
= RESTART: C:/Users/aarthi/AppData/Local/Programs/Python/
Python38-32/oops.py
Susan
green
Eye color: brown
```

Look at that. The value changed.

So, objects are a mix between dictionaries and functions. They're the best of both worlds, and more! 😉

Just like you do in dictionaries, you can use the "del" keyword to delete properties of objects, or just the entire object, like this:

```
del human2.eye
del human1
```

But unlike your data structures (lists, dictionaries, etc.), you can't loop through an object. ☹

Objects do stuff

When I started this chapter, remember what I said? Objects have properties (just like we do), and they do stuff or stuff is done to them (just like it is with us). So, why don't we add a bunch of "methods" that make our objects do stuff?

You'll be creating your regular old functions, but just inside your class this time.

Let's make our objects talk, walk, and run, okay? Or just simulate the same.

```
class Human:
    def __init__(self,name,age,hair,eye,pet):
        self.name = name
        self.age = age
        self.hair = hair
        self.eye = eye

    def talk(self):
        print('{} talking'.format(self.name))

    def green(self):
        print('Hello there!')
```

```
    def walk(self):
        print("{} is walking".format(self.name))

human1 = Human('Susan',8,'brunette','blue','Barky')
human2 = Human('Johny',10,'blond','green','Boxer')
```

Did you notice how we used "self.name" to access the object's name from within the class? "self" is the object that's calling the function. Every function needs to accept "self" to indicate the object calling it, regardless of whether you use its property values inside the function or not, or you'll get an error when you run the program.

Let's call our functions now and see what we get:

```
human1.talk()
human1.greet()
human2.walk()
```

Run the preceding code, and you'll get this:

```
= RESTART: C:/Users/aarthi/AppData/Local/Programs/Python/
Python38-32/oops.py
Susan talking
Hello there!
Johny is walking
```

Whoa, nice! 😊

Turtle race with objects

Now that we know how classes work and how to create objects with them, why don't we try to replicate our turtle race with them? I'm sure we can make our code simpler now.

We're going to create a *Turtle* class that creates our turtles, with a user-defined move() method that moves the turtle randomly (within the range 1–10).

1. Let's start by importing the turtle and random modules and setting up the turtle screen. Let's also hide the main turtle while we're at it.

```
import turtle, random
s = turtle.getscreen()
turtle.hideturtle()
```

2. Let's create a *Turtle* class. The initialization function will accept color, x, and y to change the turtle color and move the turtles to the starting positions.

```
class Turtle:
    def __init__(self,color,x,y):
```

3. Then, let's define self.turtle. Why self.turtle and not self? Well, "self" refers to the object we're creating, so if we want a turtle created on that object, we need to create a wrapper object, which in my case is self. turtle. You can name it anything you want.

   This way, the original object won't be re-assigned and we still get to create a turtle.

```
self.turtle = turtle.Turtle()
```

4. Let's change the pen size, color, and shape next.

```
self.turtle.pensize(5)
self.turtle.color(color)
self.turtle.shape('turtle')
```

5. Finally, let's move the turtle to the given position.

```
self.turtle.penup()
self.turtle.goto(x,y)
self.turtle.pendown()
```

6. Now that we're done with the init() function, let's create a move() function. It's just going to move the turtle forward randomly, just like we did in the original program.

```
    def move(self):
        self.turtle.forward(random.randint(1,10))
```

That's it for our class!

7. Now, let's create our objects. I'm going to create three objects, red, blue, and green, with their relevant values.

```
red = Turtle('Red',-250,150)
blue = Turtle('Blue',-250,0)
green = Turtle('Green',-250,-150)
```

8. Now, within a range of 0–99 (100 iterations), let's call our move() function on all three of our turtles for every iteration.

```
for i in range(100):
    red.move()
    blue.move()
    green.move()
```

That's it! Does our program work (Figure 14-1)?

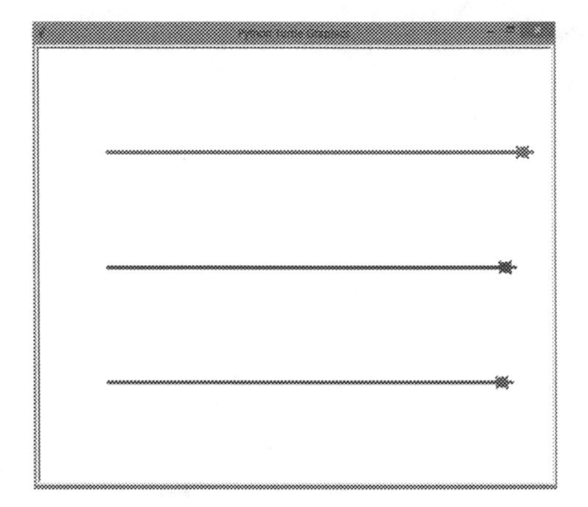

Figure 14-1. *Turtle race with classes*

Of course, it did, and red won! ☺

Summary

In this chapter, we looked at how to do real-world programming with object-oriented programming (OOPs). We looked at classes, the initialization function, self, user-defined properties and methods, and creating objects on our classes. We also looked at accessing our properties and functions and changing the values of our properties.

In the next chapter, let's look at files, how to create them, open them, and modify them.

CHAPTER 15

Python and Files

In the previous chapter, we learned how to create real-world objects in Python using classes. We learned how everything was an object in Python. Then, we learned how to create classes in Python and use those classes to create similar objects without writing too many lines of code.

In this chapter, let's look at file handling in Python. We'll look at creating, reading, writing, and manipulating the files in your system right from inside your Python code.

Why files?

I can hear you groaning. Yet another boring theoretical topic, you're probably saying. Well, don't dismiss files so quickly. It's a very easy topic, and it can open up too many possibilities to count.

A. Elumalai, *Introduction to Python for Kids*, https://doi.org/10.1007/978-1-4842-6812-4_15

Once you learn this, real-world programming is yours for the taking. You can start including the files in your system in your programs, and you can create them from within your program, read them, manipulate them, erase them completely, and so much more. If you want to create full-on apps that work on your laptops and computers, then you'd do well to learn files.

This is a quick chapter, so don't worry much, and as usual, we'll end it with a fun and, this time, easy mini project. Also, from the next chapter, you'll be creating all the big projects, mini projects, apps, and games you could ever want to create, so all the more reason to finish this chapter fast, don't you think? 😉

Opening and reading existing files

Let's start simple. Before you do something with a file, you need to retrieve it and save it in a variable, so you can later read it, write to it, and so on and so forth.

Use the "open" method and specify the file name inside of either double or single quotes. You need to specify the entire file name, including the relevant extensions like .py, .txt, and so on.

But, if the file exists in the same folder as your script, then you can get away with just mentioning the name of the file with its extension, like I'll be doing in our example.

I'm going to ask my program to retrieve the introduction.py file, and since that's in the same folder as the files.py file I created for this chapter, I don't need to specify the entire path.

But what if my path is in a different folder? How can I get it? :O

It's a very simple process. Go to your File explorer in Windows, or its equivalent in Mac, as shown in Figure 15-1.

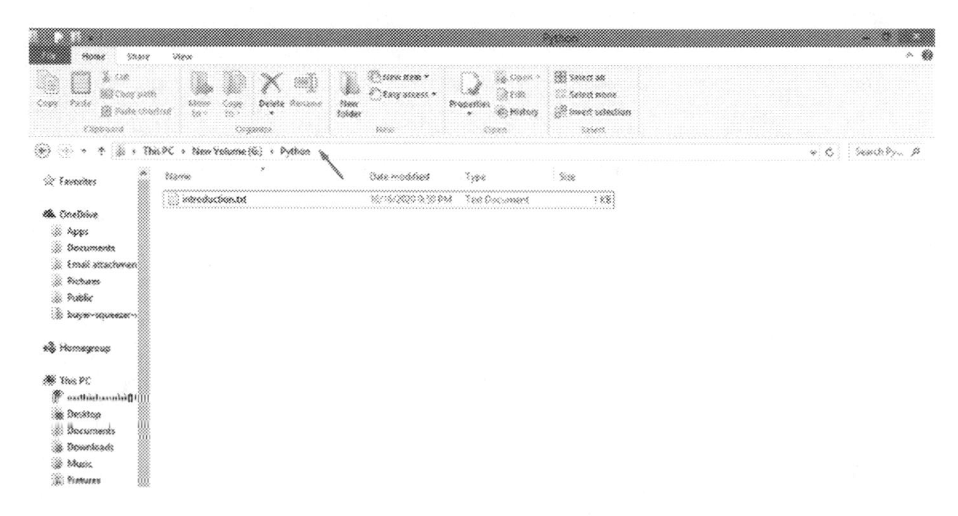

Figure 15-1. *Locate your file*

Click where I've placed the arrow, that is, right after the last folder name. You'll get the path, like this (Figure 15-2).

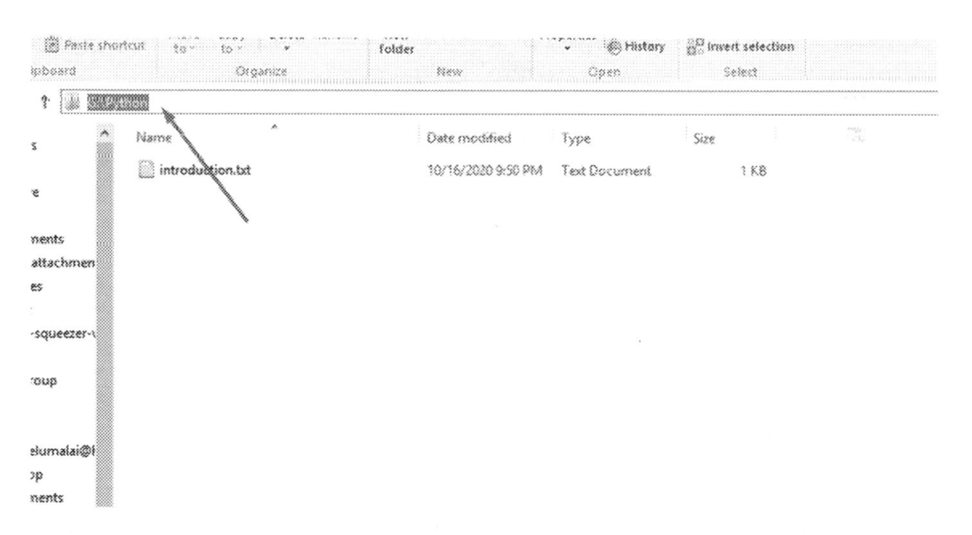

Figure 15-2. *Get your file path*

Now, you can copy the path. But you can't use it as it is. You need to format the path, along with the file name, in the following format. In the preceding example, we're trying to get the path of the file "introduction.txt" which is in the path G:\Python. To use it in my program, I'll format it like this:

```
G:\\Python\introduction.txt
```

And then, I'll place the entire thing within quotes and use it. It's as simple as that! ☺

Once you have the open() method ready, assign the same to a variable. Why? You'll see in just a minute!

```
file = open(' introduction.py')
```

Now that we have our file stored in the variable "file", we can start manipulating it.

What do you want to do first? Shall we read it? Print what's inside? Okay, let's do that!

Can you guess how reading a file will go? Maybe Python has a read() function we can use? Yes, you're right! That's exactly what we have.

But, before you can use the read function, you need to specify to your program that that's exactly what you'll be doing. So, while you're retrieving your file, you need to add a second argument that specifies that you're retrieving it in a read-only format and that you'll be reading and possibly printing what's inside later.

Let's change our line of code:

```
file = open(' introduction.py','r')
```

As you can see in the preceding code, I've included a second argument 'r' within quotes. That'll let my program know that I'm just retrieving the file to read it, and nothing else.

Now, we can actually read our file and print it. Do you want to try?

```
file.read()
```

Let's run the above code, and...

Crickets....

Nothing happened. :O Why?! Well, you asked your program to read it, and it did just that. You didn't ask it to print the results, did you? You need to be very clear with computers. They need exact instructions.

So, let's print our read operation:

```
= RESTART: C:/Users/aarthi/AppData/Local/Programs/Python/
Python38-32/file.py
print('Hello there!')
print('My name is Susan Smith.')
print('I am 9 years old.')
print('I love puppies! :)')
```

Look at that! The entire content (code) inside the introduction.py file was printed out. Did you notice something? Even though the file contains code, and it was printed in the Shell, those print() lines weren't executed. They were printed as such.

Why is that? Well, in this instant, your file is considered a normal text file, and the lines of code are content inside your file. That's all. If you want the preceding code executed, you need to go about it the usual way and not open or read it via the file operations.

You can ask your program to print just a specified number of characters, rather than the whole thing too. Let's say I want only the first 50 characters (individual letters, numbers, special characters, and spaces) printed out, and nothing else. Then all I have to do is specify 50 within the parenthesis, like this:

```
print(file.read(50))
```

Run the preceding code, and you'll get this:

```
= RESTART: C:/Users/aarthi/AppData/Local/Programs/Python/
Python38-32/file.py
print('Hello there!')
print('My name is Susan Smith.')
```

Count the characters in the preceding result, and you'll come up with 50, including the spaces and the new line as separate characters.

Why don't you try with different numbers and see what you get?

Line by line

What if you don't want the entire file printed and you don't want to count characters either? What if you just want the first line? Then, you can use the readline() method to read through lines. Let's replace read() with readline().

```
print(file.readline())
```

Run the preceding code, and you'll get this:

```
= RESTART: C:/Users/aarthi/AppData/Local/Programs/Python/
Python38-32/file.py
print('Hello there!')
```

Yay! Just the first line.

What if I want more lines printed? Can I specify 2 within the parenthesis like I did with read()?

```
print(file.readline(2))
```

Run the preceding code, and you'll get this:

```
= RESTART: C:/Users/aarthi/AppData/Local/Programs/Python/
Python38-32/file.py
pr
```

Ah, bummer. It thought I was asking for two characters again. I guess the only way to go about it is to specify another readline(). Shall we try?

```
print(file.readline())
print(file.readline())
```

We have two readline() methods now. Does it work?

```
= RESTART: C:/Users/aarthi/AppData/Local/Programs/Python/
Python38-32/file.py
print('Hello there!')

print('My name is Susan Smith.')
```

Yes! We have two lines now, with a huge space between them because they were printed in two different prints.

If you'd like to read and print out the entire file, then just loop through it, like you would loop through a list. For every iteration of the loop, your program will print one line from your file.

```
file = open('introduction.py','r')
for i in file:
    print(i)
```

Run the preceding code, and you'll get this:

```
= RESTART: C:\Users\aarthi\AppData\Local\Programs\Python\
Python38-32\file.py
print('Hello there!')

print('My name is Susan Smith.')

print('I am 9 years old.')

print('I love puppies! :)')
```

That's the entire file!

Create new files

You can use either "x" or "w" attributes in the open() method to create new files. "w" just creates a file if it does not exist but opens an existing file, but "x" is exclusively for creating new files. "x" returns an error if you try to "create" an existing file.

Let's create a file newFile.txt now.

```
file = open('newFile.txt','x')
```

Our file was just created! Run the program again, and you'll get an error, since the file now exists.

Manipulate files

You can add to files using the write method. In order to do that, you need to open the file you want to add text to in either the write, "w", or append, "a", mode.

The "write" mode will overwrite any text currently on the file. The append mode will append the given text at the end of the file.

Let's try both, shall we?

I've opened the file we created in the last section in the "write" mode.

```
file = open('newFile.txt','w')
```

Now, let's use the "write" method to add a few lines of text to our file, separated by new lines "\n".

```
f.write('Hi there!\nThis is a new file.\nWe just added text
to it!')
```

Now, let's read our file to see if we get the same.

```
file = open('newFile.txt', 'r')
print(file.read())
```

Run the preceding code, and you'll get this:

```
= RESTART: C:\Users\aarthi\AppData\Local\Programs\Python\
Python38-32\file.py
Hi there!
This is a new file.
We just added text to it!
```

Whoo! 😊

Let's try appending now.

```
file = open('newFile.txt','a')
file.write('\nThis is the last line')

file = open('newFile.txt','r')
print(file.read())
```

Run the preceding code, and you'll get this:

```
= RESTART: C:\Users\aarthi\AppData\Local\Programs\Python\
Python38-32\file.py
Hi there!
This is a new file.
We just added text to it!
This is the last line
```

This is a very powerful feature that can make programming desktop apps, or any apps at all, very easy for you!

Mini project – introduce with files

This is going to be a very simple project. We are going to create a text file called introduction.txt in a folder of your choice. We are going to write our introduction to that file via our Python code, and finally, we're going to print that introduction in our Shell. Simple! 😊

Shall we get started?

1. I'm going to create my file in the following path: `G:\\Python\introduction.txt`

   I can also use "x", but I'm using "w" so I wouldn't have to open the file in write mode again.

   ```
   f = open('G:\\Python\introduction.txt','w')
   ```

2. Then, I'm going to write Susan's introduction to it:

   ```
   f.write('''Hi, I'm Susan.
   I'm 9 years old.
   My puppy's name is Barky.
   He loves me very very much! :)''')
   ```

3. Now, let's print it. Let's open our file again, but this time in read mode, read it while printing its contents, and finally close it.

```
f = open('G:\\Python\introduction.txt','r')
print(f.read())
f.close()
```

Now, when we run the program, we'll get this:

```
= RESTART: C:\Users\aarthi\AppData\Local\Programs\Python\
Python38-32\file.py
Hi, I'm Susan.
I'm 9 years old.
My puppy's name is Barky.
He loves me very very much! :)
```

Perfect! 😉

Summary

In this chapter, we learned all about files, creating them from your Python code, reading them, storing them in variables, manipulating files from inside your programs, and so much more.

In the next chapter, let's learn about *Tkinter*, a Python package that lets you create desktop apps.

CHAPTER 16

Create Cool Apps with *Tkinter*

In the previous chapter, we learned all about creating, opening, and manipulating your computer's files in Python. In this chapter, we're officially back to having fun with Python. You're going to learn about *Tkinter*, which is a package that can be used to create desktop apps (GUI - graphical user interface) with Python. You'll learn how to create buttons, labels, boxes, and so much more.

Tkinter – let's set it right up!

Remember what we did when we worked with *Turtle*? Some of the processes of working with *Tkinter* are the same. You're a pro programmer now. You know the basics of Python already. You've finished an entire chapter of mini projects.

So, in this chapter, I want you to wear your big boy/girl pants. I'm not going to give a lot of hands-on explanations because you know a lot of this stuff already. We'll be covering a lot in this chapter, and at the end of it, you'll have beautiful apps just like the ones you see in your system, and you'll be armed with the tools to create more of them. Excited? Me too! Let's get started. 😊

A. Elumalai, *Introduction to Python for Kids*, https://doi.org/10.1007/978-1-4842-6812-4_16

Just like with turtle, we need to import *Tkinter* first. Let's open a new script file. Don't save it as "tkinter.py". There's already a file like that in your Python installation, and it contains the code for all the pre-defined methods you'll be using to create your apps. I'm going to save my file as tkPrograms.py.

Let's first import *Tkinter*.

```
from tkinter import *
```

I've asked everything to be imported from the *Tkinter* package. "*" means everything. Now, we need to create a window that would contain our app. I'm going to call mine w, and the function I need to call is Tk():

```
w = Tk()
```

Let's run this and see what we get (Figure 16-1).

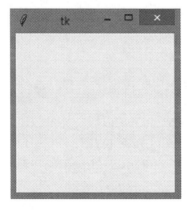

Figure 16-1. *Tkinter screen*

Look at that! A nice little window. It also has buttons you can use to minimize, maximize, and close the window. Why don't you try them out?

The title is a bit strange, isn't it? It just says tk. I don't like it! I want mine to say "My first *Tkinter* app". How do I change that? Well, by calling the title() method on the window we just created, of course!

```
w.title('My first Tkinter app')
```

Run this again, and see what you get (Figure 16-2):

Figure 16-2. *Title change*

Look at that! It says what I wanted now. I resized the window a bit so I could see the entire title. This is beautiful. I just wrote three small lines of code, and I have a nifty little window now. Can you see how powerful *Tkinter* is? :O

Alright then, that's it for the setup. Next, let's see how to create widgets and place them on this window. This is where things get interesting!

Labels, buttons, and packing them

Tkinter has a lot of "widgets" you can create to make the app come alive. These widgets range from buttons to text boxes to radio buttons. Once you create a widget, you need to place it on the window. So, there are usually two steps to the process. Let's look at how to create labels and buttons now, shall we?

To create labels, you need to use the "Label()" method and mention the window you want the label placed it in the first attribute and the text you want in the label within the "text" attribute. I'm going to create a variable label1, and I'm going to place my label inside of it.

```
label1 = Label(w,text='My Label')
```

If I run this, I'll end up with a blank window again. Why? Remember what I told you earlier? Widgets need to be placed inside the windows to be visible. How do we do that?

One of the simplest ways to do that is by using the pack() method. It just packs or shoves the widget you create into the window, and it resizes the window to the size of that widget.

This is why I placed my label inside a variable, so I can call the pack() method on the variable. It just looks neat that way.

```
label1.pack()
```

Now run everything, and see what you get (Figure 16-3).

Figure 16-3. *Label*

There you go! A tiny little window with just my label in it.

If you don't want two lines of code, you can write the same like this, and it'll work:

```
Label(w, text='My Label').pack()
```

I'm going to stick to the first method because it'll look neat once we start designing the label and adding a lot of attributes to it. I can also reference the same label later on to change its attribute values. It's just more dynamic in a real-world sense.

But did you notice something? Whenever I run the program, my shell does open my window, but then it goes back to its next prompt (<<<), which means it considers the output shown. That's not good! When the window's open, I want my program still running. Otherwise, I might not be able to run real-world apps later. So, there's something you can do to make sure your prompt is open until you actually close the window. You can call the mainloop() function on your window to do this. Add this piece of code to the very end of your script.

Now, run again, and you'll notice that our Shell hasn't moved on to its next prompt. Good!

Alright. Can we spruce things up a bit now? Why don't we play with my label's size and colors?

Before we get started though, let's look at our options as far as colors are concerned. *Tkinter* recognizes a ton of color names, and you can find a list of them here, in their official site: `www.tcl.tk/man/tcl8.5/TkCmd/colors.htm`.

If you want to visualize the colors though, you can use this site: `www.science.smith.edu/dftwiki/index.php/Color_Charts_for_TKinter`.

The second link is to a third-party site, but still useful.

So, now that we've armed ourselves with the colors, let's get started!

You can change the size of the label by using the width and height attributes. They change the width and height of your label, respectively. But, you'll notice something different when you use these attributes. Let's say the values of both these attributes are 10, but you'll notice that the height of the label is bigger than the width of the label. That's because the values aren't considered in pixels, but by the size of the character "0". Its width is twice as small as its height, isn't it? That's what you're seeing. So, consider this while giving your values.

Also, you can change the color of the label with the bg attribute and the color of your label text with the fg attribute. Let's combine them all together and design our label now!

```
label1 = Label(w, text='My Label', bg='Salmon4', fg='gold2',
width=10, height=5)
label1.pack()
```

I've changed the background color to 'Salmon4,' the text color to 'gold2,' the width to 10 character units, and the height to 5 character units. Now let's run the program (Figure 16-4)!

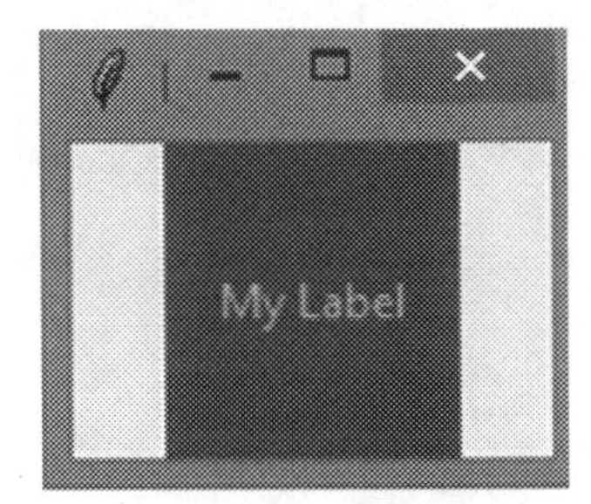

Figure 16-4. *Change the label's size and colors*

Whoo! Look at how the window expanded to encompass my new label. It's perfect. 😊

There are other attributes you can use, but let's look at that in the later section of this chapter. Now, what about buttons? It follows the same procedure. Use the Button() method, and the attributes are the same.

```
button1 = Button(w, text='My Button', bg='steel blue',
fg='snow', width=10, height=5)
button1.pack()
```

Run everything, and see what you get (Figure 16-5).

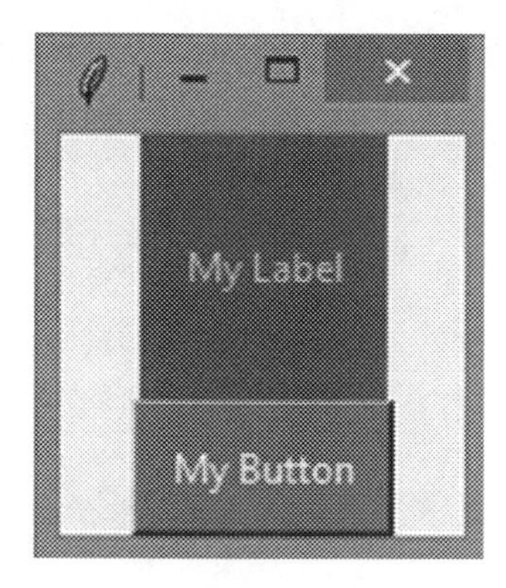

Figure 16-5. *Button*

You'll find that you can actually click the button. It's animated, unlike the label.

But that's not where it ends. You can make your system do something when you click the button. Using the command attribute, I can call a function whenever my button is clicked.

```
def buttonClick():
    print('You just clicked the button! :)')

button1 = Button(w, text='Click Me!', bg='steel blue',
fg='snow', width=10, height=5, command=buttonClick)
button1.pack()
```

As you know, in Python, the function definition should always come before the function call, in our case, the button. Let's create a function buttonClick() that prints a message. That's it.

Now, in our button, we've added a new attribute, "command", and the value is the name of our function. Just the name, you don't have to add the brackets. Now, pack the button and run the program, and you'll get the button, as usual. Click it, go back to the Shell, and you'll see this:

```
= RESTART: C:\Users\aarthi\AppData\Local\Programs\Python\
Python38-32\tkPrograms.py
You just clicked the button! :)
```

Whoa! It works! 😉

Packing in detail

So far, things look ugly. Let's be honest here. This is not how we create an app. Don't panic though. The pack() method has a few more tricks up its sleeves.

Before we look at those though, let's look at something called the "Frame". The frame isn't exactly a window. We already created one of those. But with frames, you can group your widget and then organize them in the way you want.

Let's create a frame around our label and button. We can give a background color (bg), width, and height for the same as well, but the width and height are in pixels in this case, so make the numbers bigger.

```
frame1 = Frame(w)
frame1.pack()

label1 = Label(frame1, text='First button')
label1.pack()

button1 = Button(frame1, text='Button1')
button1.pack()
```

```
label2 = Label(frame1, text='Second button')
label2.pack()

button2 = Button(frame1, text='Button2')
button2.pack()
```

As you can see in the preceding code, I created a frame and then two labels and two buttons within that frame. So, the root window of frame1 is "w", the original window, but the root window of the remaining widgets is our frame1. This way, we can create as many frames as we want within the same window. For now, let's just run this, and see what we get (Figure 16-6).

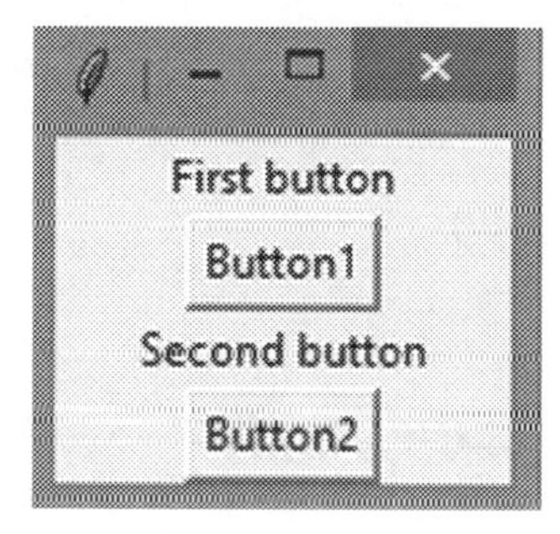

Figure 16-6. *Pack geometry method*

Nothing seems to have changed. ☹ The pack() method to the rescue!

The pack() method is a geometry manager, and it packs your widgets within its parent window (frame1 in our case) in rows and columns.

To start, let's look at the fill option. You can make your widget fill the parent widget with this option.

Right now, the window that pops up looks like its encompassing the entire frame (Figure 16-7), but it's not. If I resize it, it'll add padding around the frame.

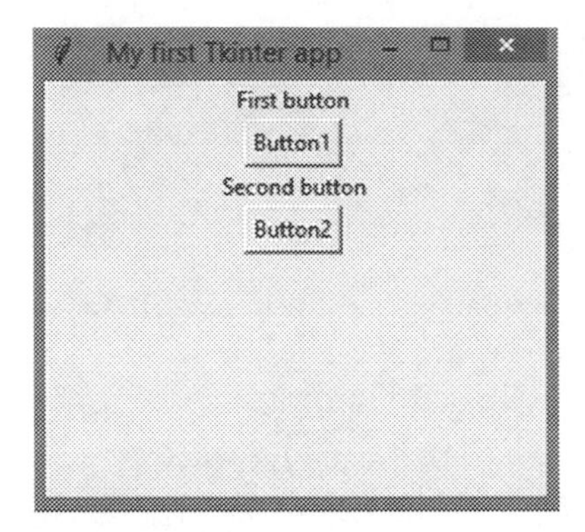

Figure 16-7. *Pack() resize issue*

But if I want the frame to fill the main window, then I can use the fill and expand options. Let's start with "fill". I can give three values here, X, Y, or BOTH.

X fills up main window the horizontally and Y vertically, and BOTH just fills the entire widget. Let's see all three.

```
frame1 = Frame(w, bg='black')
frame1.pack(fill=X)
```

I've given the frame a background color so we can see the frame separately.

Next, I'll fill to Y:

```
frame1.pack(fill=Y)
```

Finally, I'll change it to BOTH (Figure 16-8):

```
frame1.pack(fill=BOTH)
```

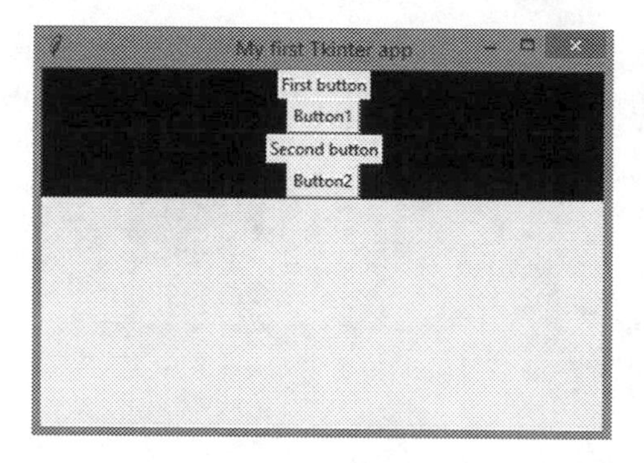

Figure 16-8. *Frame with fill*

Fill works to an extent, but it still does not expand when the window resizes. That's because fill just lets Python know that it wants to fill the entire area given to it. If we give BOTH, it'll fill the entire area both horizontally and vertically.

But, if we want it to fill the entire parent, that is, expand when the parent expands, then we need the "expand" option. Make it True, and see the magic.

```
frame1 = Frame(w, bg='black')
frame1.pack(fill=BOTH, expand=True)
```

Let's try the same for X and Y:

```
frame1.pack(fill=X, expand=True)
```

and finally,

```
frame1.pack(fill=Y, expand=True)
```

Now, run the program with the different fill values and resize the window to get this (Figure 16-9).

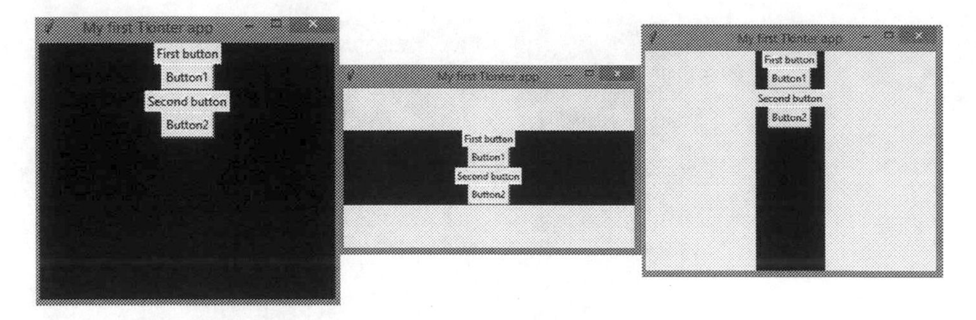

***Figure 16-9.** Fill options in Tkinter*

Fascinating, isn't it?

Okay, now we know how to fill the parent window, but how does that help our little widgets? We have four of them, and I want the first label and button in the first row and the second label and button in the second row. How do I do that? That's where the "side" option comes in.

Let me first explain how the side option works. Let's create two widgets and try to pack them with the different options of "side".

```
label = Label(w, text='My Label')
label.pack(side=TOP)
button = Button(w, text='My Button')
button.pack(side=TOP)
```

I've given the side as TOP to start with, which is the default. You'll notice that the widgets get packed one after the other.

Now, change the values of both to LEFT. It'll pack everything side by side. When you give BOTTOM, it'll pack everything from the bottom to the top, and RIGHT does the exact opposite of LEFT.

When we run the four variations of the preceding code, we get the following four outputs (Figure 16-10).

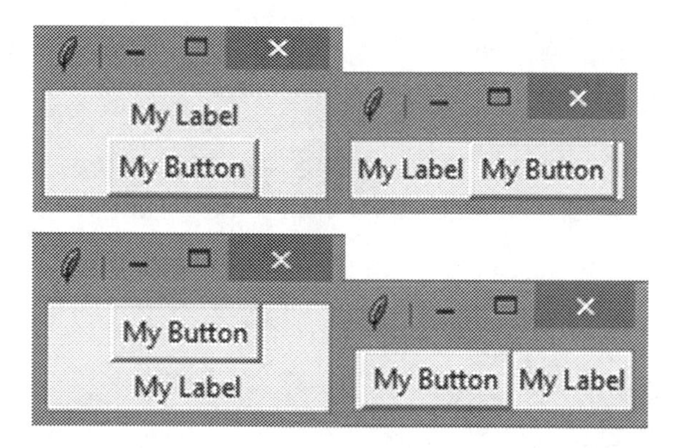

***Figure 16-10.** Side options in Tkinter*

Look at how in the third image the button comes first and then the label. That's what BOTTOM does. It reverses TOP. Similarly, RIGHT is a reverse of LEFT.

Looks great, yes, but this still doesn't seem complete. That's because you need all three options to properly align your widgets the way you want.

So now, let's combine all the options and create something that looks aligned. I'm going to create two frames, and each of these frames is going to be packed at the TOP (one after the other), where they fill the parent window from both sides and expand is True.

Similarly, I'm going to create a label and a button under the first frame and pack both LEFT (side by side), but make them encompass the entire parent frame (fill is BOTH and expand is True). Let's repeat the same for the second frame.

Now, let's see what we get:

```
frame1 = Frame(w, bg='black')
frame1.pack(side=TOP, fill=BOTH, expand=True)

label1 = Label(frame1, text='First button')
label1.pack(side=LEFT, fill=BOTH, expand=True)

button1 = Button(frame1, text='Button1')
button1.pack(side=LEFT, fill=BOTH, expand=True)
```

```
frame2 = Frame(w, bg='white')
frame2.pack(side=TOP, fill=BOTH, expand=True)

label2 = Label(frame2, text='Second button')
label2.pack(side=LEFT, fill=BOTH, expand=True)

button2 = Button(frame2, text='Button2')
button2.pack(side=LEFT, fill=BOTH, expand=True)
```

Run the preceding code, and you'll get this (Figure 16-11).

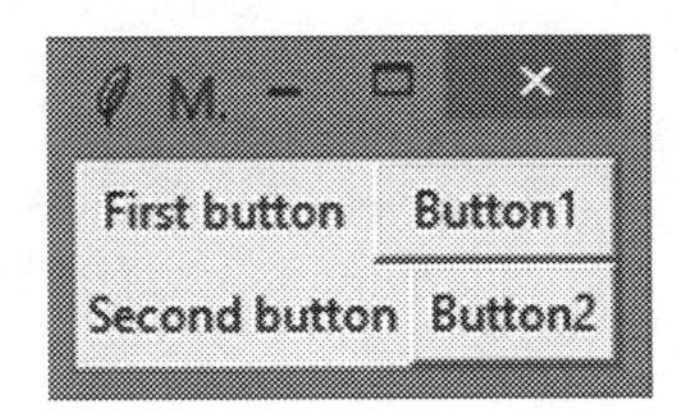

Figure 16-11. *Pack organized label and button*

Whoa! That's exactly how I wanted to place things when I first created these widgets together. Done! 😊

Now expand this window, and you'll notice that the widgets expand with them. Since the child widgets completely encompass the frames, you don't see their background colors, which means we've done our job right!

Lots of inputs

Now that you know how to use the pack() method to align your widgets properly, let's go back to quickly looking at more widgets. *Tkinter* offers a ton of widgets that get input from the user.

One line of text

You can get a single line of text input from your user by using the Entry() method.

```
entry = Entry().pack()
```

Run the preceding code, and you'll get this (Figure 16-12).

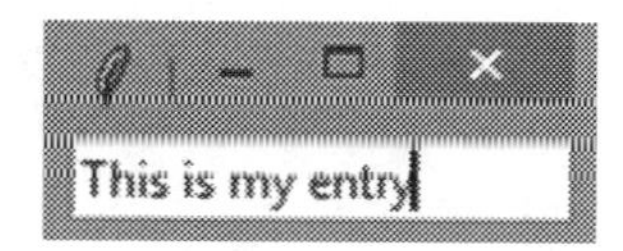

Figure 16-12. *Entry widget*

Look at that! I can give a single-line entry now.

Also, apart from the usual attributes like fg, bg, and width, your entry widgets also have methods that can be used to manipulate the entry.

Why don't we see how to do that? We can use the get() method to retrieve what we type in the entry, and we can use it however we want.

So now, let's create a label "name" and an entry box and finally a button that says "Enter". When the user clicks the button, it calls the greet() function, which "gets" the input from the entry box and prints out a "Hello" message. Simple enough? Let's try!

```
def greet():
    name = entry.get()
    print('Hello {}'.format(name))

label = Label(w,text='Your name?')
label.pack(side=LEFT)
entry = tkinter.Entry(w)
entry.pack(side=LEFT)
button = Button(w,text='Enter',command=greet)
button.pack(side=LEFT)
```

Let's run everything, and we'll get this (Figure 16-13).

Figure 16-13. *Name box with entry*

Now, when I press Enter and look at the Shell, I get this:

```
= RESTART: C:\Users\aarthi\AppData\Local\Programs\Python\
Python38-32\tkPrograms.py
Hello Susan
```

Yay!

Also, you have the delete() method that deletes text and the insert() method that inserts text in any position you want.

Let's look at insert first. The syntax is pretty simple.

```
entry.insert(pos, ‘text’)
```

So, just give the position at which you want to insert the text. The first position is 0, and it increases from there, just like with your strings. The second argument is either the direct text you want inserted or the variable that contains your text.

Would you like to see how this works? Let's modify our program. Now, when the user enters their name, they have to click the "Insert Hello" button, that, when clicked, literally inserts Hello and a space before their name.

```
def insert():
    entry.insert(0,'Hello ')

label = Label(w,text='Your name?')
label.pack(side=LEFT)
entry = tkinter.Entry(w)
entry.pack(side=LEFT)
```

```
button = Button(w,text='Insert Hello',command=insert)
button.pack(side=LEFT)
```

Let's run the program (Figure 16-14).

Figure 16-14. *Insert into an entry box*

And when we click the button, we get this (Figure 16-15).

Figure 16-15. *Inserted*

Whohoo!

Similarly, you can delete. If you just give one argument, it'll just delete that character. 0 deletes the first character, 1 the second character, and so on.

But, if you give a range, it'll delete a range of characters.

As usual, the last number in the range is not considered. For example, the range 0,4 deletes the characters in indices 0 to 3 (not including 4).

But if you want to delete everything, then just give END as your last argument, and you're done. Shall we try?

```
def insert():
    entry.delete(0,END)

label = Label(w,text='Your name?')
label.pack(side=LEFT)
entry = tkinter.Entry(w)
entry.pack(side=LEFT)
```

```
button = Button(w,text='Clear',command=insert)
button.pack(side=LEFT)
```

When I run the program, I get this (Figure 16-16).

Figure 16-16. *Delete from an entry box*

I've entered Susan, and when I press the Clear button, I get this (Figure 16-17).

Figure 16-17. *Entry box cleared*

A clean slate! 😊

Line after line

Now, let's see how we can enter and manipulate multiple lines of text! You can use the Text() method to do that.

```
text_box = Text()
text_box.pack()
```

Run this, and you'll get a big text box, and when you type some lines of code in the same, it'll look like this (Figure 16-18).

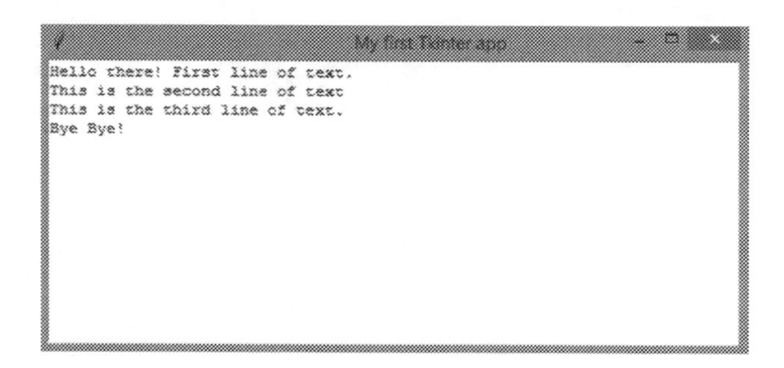

Figure 16-18. *Text box – multiple lines of text*

You can retrieve the text from this text box with the get() method, but you need to specify the line number and the character number in a range.

"1.0" will retrieve just the first character in the first line.

"1.0", "1.9" will retrieve the first character through the ninth character in the first line.

"2.0", "2.5" will retrieve the first character through the fifth character in the second line and so on.

"1.0", "2.10" will retrieve until the tenth character in the second line, so you can span multiple lines like this.

To get the entire text, just give "1.0", END.

Do you understand how this works now? Let's try to retrieve the entire piece of text.

```
text_box = Text(w)
text_box.pack()

def get_text():
    t = text_box.get(1.0,END)
    print(t)

button = Button(w,text="Get data",command=get_text)
button.pack()
```

Let's run the program again and type the same text and see what we get (Figure 16-19).

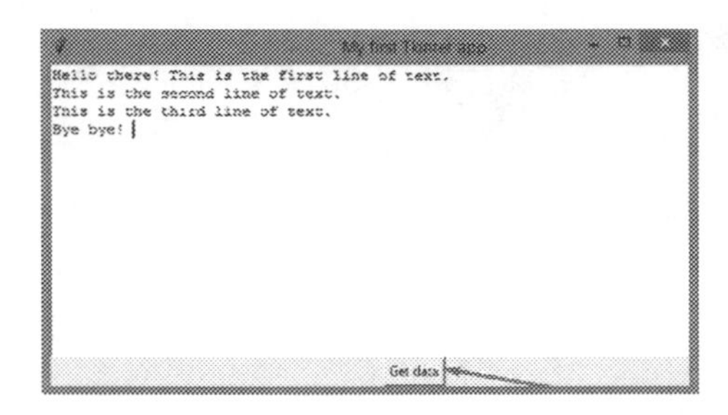

Figure 16-19. *Get data from text box*

Now we have a big text box, with a little button at the end, since that's how we packed it. Let's click the button, and we get this:

```
>>>
= RESTART: C:\Users\aarthi\AppData\Local\Programs\Python\
Python38-32\tkPrograms.py
Hello there! This is the first line of text.
This is the second line of text.
This is the third line of text.
Bye bye!
```

It works! 😊

Similarly, you can insert text into the text box.

```
text_box.insert(1.0,"Welcome! ")
```

The preceding code will insert "Welcome!" and a space to the beginning of the first line. Text, checkbox, entry, radio button, menu button, check button, list box.

To insert something at the end of the text, use END as the first parameter, but if you want the text to be in a new line, add the \n (newline character) at the beginning of the second parameter, like this:

```
text_box.insert(END,"\nYou're great!")
```

To delete the entire piece of text, do this:

```
text_box.delete("1.0",END)
```

You can use the same format you used with get() to delete pieces of text.

So, that's a quick look at text boxes. Now, on to the next widget!

Tkinter variables

But before we do that, I want to talk about *Tkinter* variables. Remember how we had to directly enter the text and not use variables for the same? That's not very dynamic. What if I wanted to change a label text, or a button text, based on something that happened in my app/game? I need a variable. That's where *Tkinter* variable classes come in. They work pretty much similar to our normal variables.

There are five kinds of variables you can create: Integer, String, Boolean, and Double (floating point).

```
num = IntVar()
string = StringVar()
b = BooleanVar()
dbl = DoubleVar()
```

Assign them to an actual variable to make that variable a *Tkinter* variable. Also, make sure that you maintain the upper- and lowercase of the syntaxes as it is.

Now that you have the variables, you can assign values to them using the "set" method. If you assign a wrong value to a variable, you'll get an error. So, only an integer to an integer variable and so on.

To get the variable's value back, use the get() method. So, let's combine both and see what we get.

```
num.set(100)
string.set("Hello there!")
b.set(True)
dbl.set(150.14)

print(num.get())
print(string.get())
print(b.get())
print(dbl.get())
```

Run the preceding code, and you'll get this:

```
= RESTART: C:\Users\aarthi\AppData\Local\Programs\Python\
Python38-32\tkPrograms.py
100
Hello there!
True
150.14
```

But this is still not dynamic right? Can we set dynamic variables to our *Tkinter* variables? The answer is yes!

Just get an input, place it in a variable, and set that as your string (or any type). That's it.

```
i = input('Enter a string: ')
string.set(i)
print(string.get())
```

Run the preceding code, and you'll get this:

```
= RESTART: C:\Users\aarthi\AppData\Local\Programs\Python\
Python38-32\tkPrograms.py
Enter a string: Hello there!
Hello there!
```

So now, we can dynamically set our label text.

```
i = input('Label text: ')
string = StringVar()
string.set(i)
label = Label(w, text=string.get())
label.pack()
```

Run the preceding code, and you'll get this:

```
= RESTART: C:\Users\aarthi\AppData\Local\Programs\Python\
Python38-32\tkPrograms.py
Label text: Hello there!
```

Press Enter after giving the input, and you'll get (Figure 16-20):

Figure 16-20. *String variable*

Yippee! Our first dynamic label! 😉

Lots of options!

If you want to give your user choices, then checkboxes and radio buttons are the way to go, don't you think? *Tkinter* has those widgets too!

You can create a checkbox using the Checkbutton (small "b") widget. It works similar to the other widgets, except for the fact that you can give onvalue and offvalue that specify that "value" when the check button is clicked or not.

But a simpler way to get a check button state is by assigning a *Tkinter* integer variable to its "variable" attribute, and whenever the box is checked, the variable's value changes to 1, and 0 when it's unchecked.

We're going to create two checkboxes, so let's create two integer variables to store their "state" (whether they were checked or not).

```
c1 = IntVar()
c2 = IntVar()
```

Let's create a label 'Grocery list' and pack it.

```
Label(w,text='Grocery list').pack()
```

Now comes our checkboxes. The only difference is we have our "variable" attribute with the integer variable assigned to them.

```
Label(w,text='Grocery list').pack()
check1 = Checkbutton(w,text="Milk",variable = c1)
check1.pack(side=LEFT)
check2 = Checkbutton(w,text="Flour",variable = c2)
check2.pack(side=LEFT)
```

Now, how do we retrieve the values? We need a button, which, when clicked, will call the check() function that checks which boxes were clicked.

```
def check():
    if(c1.get() == 1):
        print('We bought Milk.')
    if(c2.get() == 1):
        print('We bought flour.')

button = Button(w,text='Check',command=check)
button.pack()
```

Simple! Let's run the program, and we get this (Figure 16-21).

Figure 16-21. *Checkbox*

Press the "Check" button, and you'll get this:

```
= RESTART: C:\Users\aarthi\AppData\Local\Programs\Python\
Python38-32\tkPrograms.py
We bought Milk.
We bought flour.
```

For radio buttons, we just need one variable because we'd just be selecting one of the choices. It has a "value" attribute, which, when set with an integer value, will assign the same to the variable you assigned to the "variable" attribute.

You can add a "command" within the radio button as well.

Let's create a program that asks if the user likes dogs or not and prints a message based on what they chose!

For this example, I'm going to command directly from the radio button, so let's create the "check" function first.

We're going to create a string that'll hold the message we need to display after a person clicked a checkbox. Now, we're going to set two values in our radio button, 1 if the person likes dogs and 2 if the person does not like dogs.

Once we've set the string, create the label.

```
def check():
    string = StringVar()
    if var.get() == 1:
        string.set('You love dogs! :)')
```

```
    else:
        string.set("You don't love dogs :(")

    label = Label(w,text=string.get())
    label.pack()
```

Now, let's create an integer variable that'll hold our radio buttons' value. Next comes a label that asks if they love dogs.

```
var = IntVar()
Label(w,text='Do you love dogs?').pack()
```

Finally, the radio buttons with the relevant text, the variable "var" assigned to them, a value for each and a command that calls the "check" function if the button is selected.

```
radio1 = Radiobutton(w,text="Yes!",variable = var, value=1,
command=check)
radio1.pack()
radio2 = Radiobutton(w,text="Nope",variable = var, value=2,
command=check)
radio2.pack()
```

That's it!

Run the program, and you'll get this (Figure 16-22).

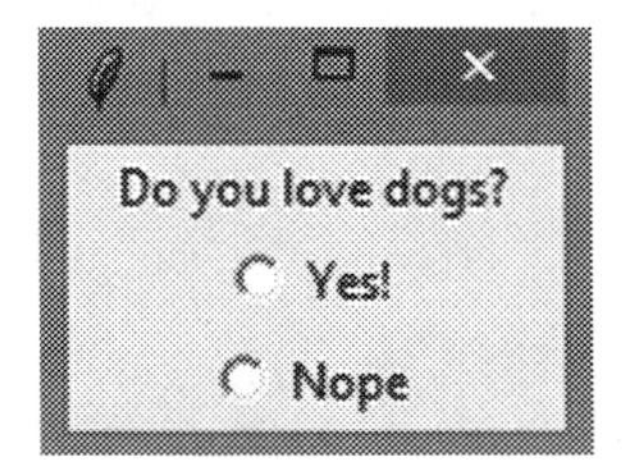

Figure 16-22. *Radio button*

Select an option (Figure 16-23):

Figure 16-23. *Radio button selected*

Perfect!

Menus

With *Tkinter*, you can create menus like you see in your applications! You can use the Menu() method to create them.

You can create a main menu and configure it to the top of your window, and you can add as many submenus as you want to them.

Let me create a main menu "main".

```
from tkinter import *
w = Tk()

main = Menu(w)
```

Let's add a submenu in that main menu. I'll call that fileMenu.

```
fileMenu = Menu(main)
```

Now, I'm going to use the add_cascade() method and add a label to my first submenu and place it in main.

```
main.add_cascade(label='File',menu = fileMenu)
```

Now, let's add items to our main menu.

```
fileMenu.add_command(label='New File', command=lambda:
print('New File clicked'))
fileMenu.add_command(label='Open', command=lambda: print('Open
clicked'))
```

As you can see, we can attach a command to these items like we do with our buttons.

If you run this program now, you won't see anything. That's because once you create all your menus, submenus, and items, you need to configure that main menu to the window (like you pack your widgets) so it's displayed.

Use the config() method to do that.

```
w.config(menu=main)
```

Now, run your program and you'll be able to see your menu (Figure 16-24).

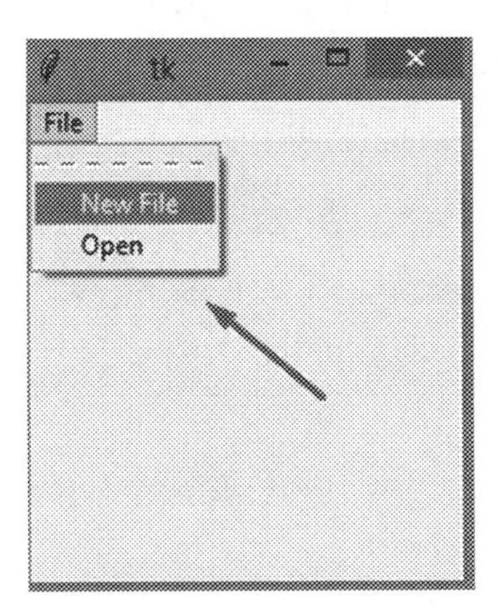

Figure 16-24. *Menu*

Click the New File menu item, and you'll get this:

```
>>> New File clicked
```

I get the message I expected. Perfect! ☺

The perfect layout – grid

I think the pack geometry manager is a teeny bit limiting in its functionalities. Don't you think so as well?

That's why *Tkinter* has the **grid** geometry manager that's leagues apart from the pack manager. You can perfectly align your widgets based on rows and columns.

The rows and columns are arranged like they are shown in the following image (Figure 16-25). The widgets will be placed inside cells, and each cell has a row and column number that starts from 0. You can extend the cells to any number you want.

Row0 Column0	Row0 Column1	Row0 Column2
Row1 Column0	Row1 Column1	Row1 Column2
Row2 Column0	Row2 Column1	Row2 Column2

Figure 16-25. *Rows and columns in a grid*

You can mention the exact row and column of the widget and also where you want it to be sticky.

There are multiple values of sticky: E for East, W for West, N for North, S for South, NE for North East, NW for North West, SE for South East, and SW for South West.

If you give "E" for a widget, it'll (usually the text) stick to the right most part of its column and so on.

The rows and columns start from 0 as shown in the illustration. You can use padx and pady to give padding around the widgets, so they don't stick together.

So, let's put it all together to arrange a bunch of labels, shall we?

```
from tkinter import *
w = Tk()
w.title('My first Tkinter app')

#first row, first column, east sticky
label1 = Label(w,text='Label1')
label1.grid(row=0,column=0,sticky='E',padx=5,pady=5)

#first row, 2nd column, east sticky
label2 = Label(w,text='Label2')
label2.grid(row=0,column=1,sticky='E',padx=5,pady=5)

#first row, 4th column, west sticky
button1 = Button(w,text='Button1')
button1.grid(row=0,column=2,sticky='W',padx=5,pady=5)

#second row, first column, east sticky
label3 = Label(w,text='Label3')
label3.grid(row=1,column=0,sticky='E',padx=5,pady=5)

#first row, 2nd column, east sticky
label4 = Label(w,text='Label4')
label4.grid(row=1,column=1,sticky='E',padx=5,pady=5)

#second row, 4th column, west sticky
button2 = Button(w,text='Button2')
button2.grid(row=1,column=2,sticky='W',padx=5,pady=5)
w.mainloop()
```

Run the program, and you'll get this (Figure 16-26).

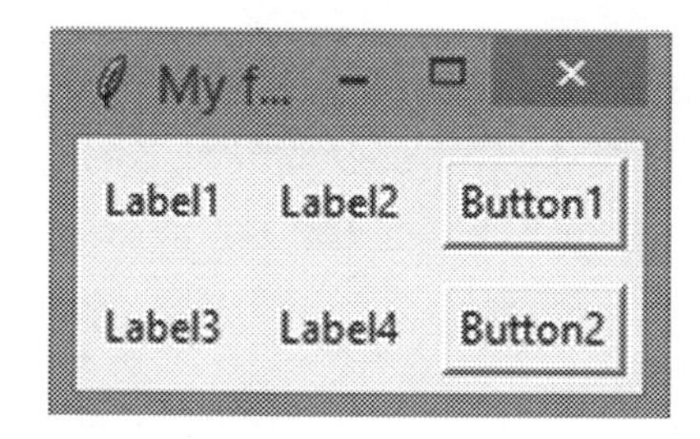

Figure 16-26. *Widgets arranged in a grid*

Beautiful! ☺

Mini project – tip calculator app

Let's put together everything we learned so far and create a tip calculator in *Tkinter*, shall we?

This is what we need:

1. Two entry boxes to enter the bill amount (floating point) and the tip amount.
2. Next, we need a button that gets those values and calls the tip_calculator() function.
3. This function is going to calculate our tip and display the result in a label at the bottom of the screen.

Simple enough? Let's do this!

1. Let's set up *Tkinter* first.

```
from tkinter import *
w = Tk()
w.title('My first Tkinter app')
```

2. Then, let's get the bill (a label, and an entry, arranged properly on the screen).

```
#Get the bill amount
bill_label = Label(w,text='What was your bill? ')
bill_label.grid(row=0,column=0,sticky="W",padx=5,pa
dy=5)
bill = Entry(w)
bill.grid(row=0,column=1,sticky="E",padx=5,pady=5)
Next, let's create the label and entry widgets to get
the tip.
#Get the tip
tip_label = Label(w,text='What did you tip? ')
tip_label.grid(row=1,column=0,sticky="W",padx=5,pady=5)
tip = Entry(w)
tip.grid(row=1,column=1,sticky="E",padx=5,pady=5)
```

3. Before we create the button, we need to define the tip_calculator function. It's going to get the entry values from tip and bill and convert those to integers (entries are usually strings). Next, we're going to calculate the percentage of the tip.

```
#Tip calculator function
def tip_calculator():
    t = tip.get()
    t = int(t)
    b = bill.get()
    b = int(b)
    percent = (t * 100) / b
    percent = int(percent)
```

4. Let's format an appropriate string based on the value of "percent".

```
if((percent >= 10) and (percent <= 15)):
    string = '{}%. You tipped Okay!'.format(percent)
elif((percent >= 15) and (percent <= 20)):
    string = '{}%. That was a good tip!'.
    format(percent)
elif(percent >= 20):
    string = '{}%. Wow, great tip! :)'.format(percent)
else:
    string = "{}%. You didn't tip enough :(".
    format(percent)
```

5. Finally, let's create a *Tkinter* string variable and set the formatted string in it and create a label with this text and place it on the screen.

```
str_var = StringVar()
str_var.set(string)
label = Label(w, text=str_var.get())
label.grid(row=3,column=0,padx=5,pady=5)
```

6. Finally, let's create a button and make it call the function when it's clicked.

```
#Enter button
button = Button(w,text='Enter',command=tip_calculator)
button.grid(row=2,column=0,sticky="E",padx=5,pady=5)
w.mainloop()
```

Let's run the program, and we'll get this (Figure 16-27).

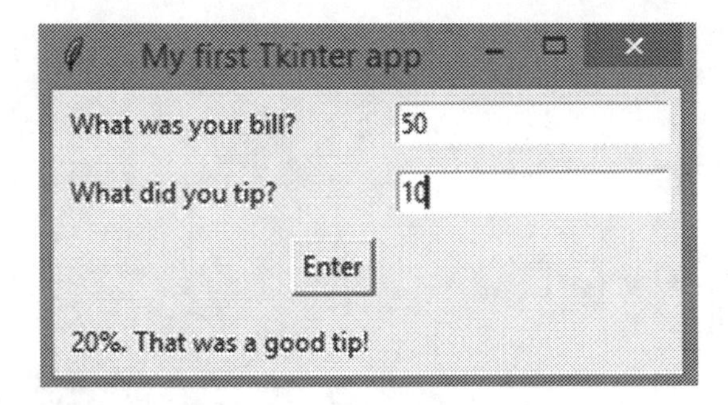

Figure 16-27. *Tip calculator app*

Our app works perfectly! You can further beautify it by adding colors and font. 😊

Summary

In this chapter, we looked at how to use the *Tkinter* package to create desktop apps in Python. We learned how to create different widgets, including buttons, labels, checkboxes, radio buttons, and menus. We learned about frames as well. Then we learned how to style our widgets and execute commands when our widgets are clicked. Finally, we learned how to organize our widgets on our screen using the pack() and grid() geometry methods.

In the next chapter, let's learn about executing functions when events like click, mouse click, and keyboard press happen on our widgets.

CHAPTER 17

Project: Tic-tac-toe Game with *Tkinter*

In the previous chapter, we learned the basics of *Tkinter*. We learned how to create buttons, labels, frames, menus, checkboxes, radio buttons, and so on with *Tkinter*. We also learned how to design our widgets and make our widgets do stuff based on events (click, mouse move, keyboard press, etc.). Finally, we learned how to draw using canvas.

In this chapter, let's apply what we learned in the last chapter and create our very first big project: a tic-tac-toe game! We'll also learn about events and binding them to our widgets.

Bind events – make your apps dynamic!

In the last chapter, we learned a lot about *Tkinter*. I'm sure you're bored of learning all the concepts, and you'd rather create a project now. Bear with me for a few minutes, okay? Let's quickly learn how to bind events to our widgets and get started with our tic-tac-toe game.

So, what's binding? Well, let's say you click your button (with your left mouse button), and you want to execute a function when that happens. What would you do? You'd use "command", yes, but what if you want to distinguish between the left and right mouse button clicks? Open different functions according to which mouse button was clicked or which keyboard key was pressed?

A. Elumalai, *Introduction to Python for Kids*, https://doi.org/10.1007/978-1-4842-6812-4_17

Events help you do all of that and more.

Let's look at the button click events first. Let's create binds that execute separate functions when the left and right mouse buttons are clicked on a button widget.

```
from tkinter import *
w = Tk()

def left_clicked(event):
    print('Left mouse button clicked')
    return

def right_clicked(event):
    print('Right mouse button clicked')
    return

button = Button(w,text='Click here!')
button.pack()
button.bind('<Button-1>',left_clicked)
button.bind('<Button-3>',right_clicked)

w.mainloop()
```

Look at the preceding code snippet. We created the button, packed it, and then used the bind() method to create two binds. The first argument denotes the event we want to bind to our button, and the second argument is the function that needs to be called when the event happens.

The events need to be specified within quotes, and <Button-1> denotes the left mouse button click and <Button-3> is the right mouse button click because <Button-2> is the middle mouse button click.

Now, in the function definition, we've accepted an argument, event, even though we didn't send any arguments from the function call. How is that possible? Well, whenever an event is bound to a widget, your program automatically sends an event object to the function. This "event" will have a lot of information on the event that just happened.

For example, we can find the x and y coordinate positions of the left mouse button click by using event.x and event.y. Let's try that on a frame.

```
from tkinter import *
w = Tk()

def click(event):
    print("X:{},Y:{}".format(event.x,event.y))

frame = Frame(w,width=200,height=200)
frame.pack()
frame.bind('<Button-1>',click)

w.mainloop()
```

Now, let me click a random position on the frame (Figure 17-1).

Figure 17-1. *Left mouse button click event*

I clicked somewhere in the middle, and the result was this:

```
= RESTART: C:\Users\aarthi\AppData\Local\Programs\Python\
Python38-32\tkPrograms.py
X:93,Y:91
```

That's an x of 93 and y of 91. Sweet!

Similarly, you can look for keyboard key presses too. You need to use the <Key> bind for that, and you can use the event.char property to print out the exact key that was pressed. This only works for keys that are printable and not for keys like space, F1, and so on. There are separate event binds for that.

You can use the <Motion> event to run functions when you move the mouse cursor over your widget. The <Return> event fires when the user presses the Enter key and so on.

Okay, now that you've learned how events work, let's start working on our tic-tac-toe game! 😊

Tic-tac-toe game – explanation

We've just been creating mini projects so far. But in the real world, you need to do a lot more than draw a few shapes or run a bunch of loops. In the real world, you'll create games and apps that are used in people's everyday life.

So in this chapter, we're going to create our very first such game. Let's create the classic tic-tac-toe game. Our app will look something like this (Figure 17-2).

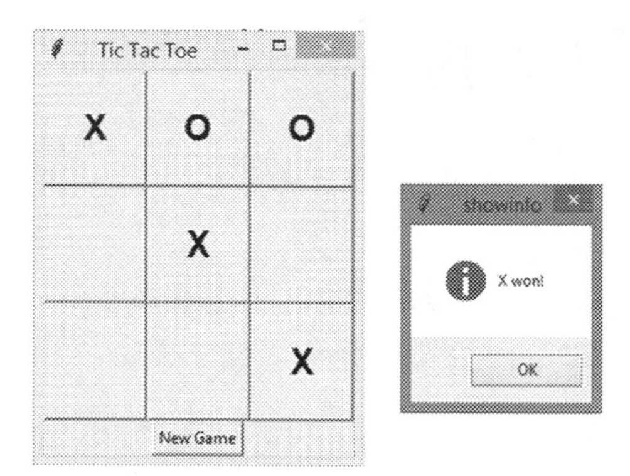

Figure 17-2. *Tic-tac-toe game in Tkinter*

We have our game board with nine boxes on which you can draw. There are two players: X and O, who get alternate turns to draw on the board. If a player draws on three consecutive boards (vertically, horizontally, or diagonally), then that player wins. If no one achieved that and all nine boards are filled, the game is a draw.

It's a simple game. I'm going to be introducing "messagebox" which will help you create the message popups you see in your laptop's programs.

Set up *Tkinter*

Let's start by importing everything from *Tkinter*, as usual. But we also need to import messagebox because when you use *, you're just importing the outside classes and functions, not exactly "everything".

```
from tkinter import *
from tkinter import messagebox
```

Let's set up our window next. I'm going to change my window's title to 'tic-tac-toe'.

```
w = Tk()
w.title('Tic Tac Toe')
```

Create global variables

We looked at global variables in the function chapter, remember? Global variables can be used to keep track of changes happening across multiple functions. We need multiple global variables in this case.

For instance, we need to keep track of the overall changes happening to the "turn" variable that counts the number of turns used up by the players (tic-tac-toe offers nine turns in total).

```
turn = 0
```

Next, we need a list that'll keep track of who's played on which box. This list will have nine pre-defined items that currently hold empty strings. We'll replace them with either "X" or "O" depending on who plays on which box.

```
state = ['','','','','','','','','']
```

Next, we need a two-dimensional list (lists within a bigger list) that'll hold all the win states (Figure 17-3). We'll compare these win states after every player plays to check if someone won the game.

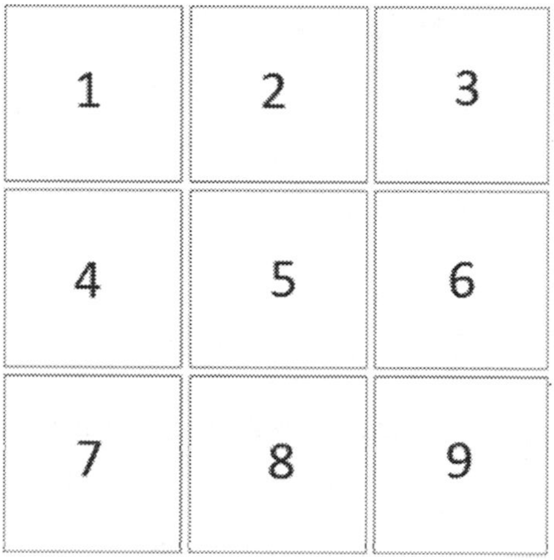

1	2	3
4	5	6
7	8	9

Figure 17-3. *Tic-tac-toe boxes (numbered)*

Look at the preceding image. In tic-tac-toe, a player wins if they draw their symbol on three consecutive boxes, either vertically, horizontally, or diagonally. 1,4,7 is the first vertical win state. 1,2,3 is the first horizontal win state. 1,5,9 is the first diagonal win state and so on.

There are three vertical win states, three horizontal win states, and two diagonal win states. A total of eight win states.

Let's store them in our list. But since we're working with lists here, and their index start from 0, let's convert 1,2,3 to 0,1,2. Do the same for the rest of the win states, and you'll get something like this:

```
winner = [[0,1,2], [3,4,5], [6,7,8], [0,3,6], [1,4,7], [2,5,8],
[0,4,8], [2,4,6]]
```

Finally, let's create a variable "game" that'll store the state of the game. It'll be True when we start the game, and if someone won, or if the game ends in a draw (all nine boxes were used up but no one won), we will change the value of "game" to False so no one can draw on the boxes.

```
game = True
```

Create the buttons

We need nine boxes on which the players can "draw", am I right? Why not make things simple and create buttons? We can make their text a single-spaced string to start with, and every time a player plays, we can change the text to either "X" or "O". That'll work!

Before we create the buttons, let's define a variable "font" that'll store the fonts we need for the button text (what our players "draw" on the buttons). "Helvetica", 20 for the text size, and "bold" font.

```
font = ('Helvetica',20,'bold')
```

Next, let's create nine buttons, one for each box. We're going to make the text a single space, height 2, and width 4. Let's assign the "font" variable we created to the font.

Finally, we're going to see some real use of the "lambda" functions we learned about in the functions chapter. So far, whenever we used the command property on a button, we didn't have to send arguments to the function being called.

But now, we need to send two arguments: one being the actual button that was clicked and the other being the number of the button that was clicked (starting from 1).

If you want to send arguments an event like that, you need to wrap the function call around a lambda, like you'll see in the following. You don't need any arguments for the lambda in itself because it's serving as an anonymous function now. And your one line of code will be the function call to the buttonClick() function with the arguments b1 and 1 sent inside it.

Let's repeat this process for the rest of the buttons. Let's also place the buttons in the grid parallelly. It's a normal grid arrangement.

```
#9 buttons
b1 = Button(w, text=' ', width=4, height=2, font = font,
command = lambda: buttonClick(b1,1))
```

```
b1.grid(row=0,column=0)
b2 = Button(w, text=' ', width=4, height=2, font = font,
command = lambda: buttonClick(b2,2))
b2.grid(row=0,column=1)
b3 = Button(w, text=' ', width=4, height=2, font = font,
command = lambda: buttonClick(b3,3))
b3.grid(row=0,column=2)

b4 = Button(w, text=' ', width=4, height=2, font = font,
command = lambda: buttonClick(b4,4))
b4.grid(row=1,column=0)
b5 = Button(w, text=' ', width=4, height=2, font = font,
command = lambda: buttonClick(b5,5))
b5.grid(row=1,column=1)
b6 = Button(w, text=' ', width=4, height=2, font = font,
command = lambda: buttonClick(b6,6))
b6.grid(row=1,column=2)

b7 = Button(w, text=' ', width=4, height=2, font = font,
command = lambda: buttonClick(b7,7))
b7.grid(row=2,column=0)
b8 = Button(w, text=' ', width=4, height=2, font = font,
command = lambda: buttonClick(b8,8))
b8.grid(row=2,column=1)
b9 = Button(w, text=' ', width=4, height=2, font = font,
command = lambda: buttonClick(b9,9))
b9.grid(row=2,column=2)
```

Create a buttonClick() function definition on top of the buttons and just place a pass on it (so you don't get an error saying that the function is empty). We'll fill the function definition with the relevant code in the next part.

Let's run the program, and we get this (Figure 17-4).

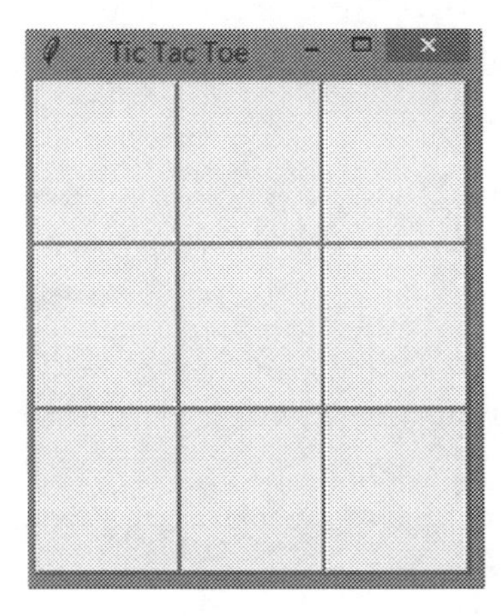

Figure 17-4. *Nine boxes - created*

This is what we have so far. Nice!

When the button is clicked, draw on it

Now let's define our buttonClick() function. This should come above the block of text where we created our buttons (function definition before function call rule).

We'll be accessing the global variables turn, state, and game in this function, so let's load them first.

```
#When a button is clicked
def buttonClick(b,n):
    global turn,state,game
```

Next, before drawing on the particular box, let's check if the box is currently empty. If it is occupied (a player already drew on it), we shouldn't draw on it again, and instead, your game has to pop up an error message.

Also, check if the game is still True (no one won, and the nine tries aren't used up yet).

```
if b['text'] == ' ' and game == True:
```

If the conditions hold true, then check who's currently playing. Player "X" starts the game, and since we started our "turn" at 0, whenever it's X's turn, the value of "turn" will be an even number. You know how to check for an even number, right? Do that. 😊

```
#hasn't been clicked on yet
if turn % 2 == 0:
```

So, if it's X's turn, then change the button's text to "X", increase the value of turn by 1, and change the value of state[n-1] to "X". Why n-1? Well, a list's index starts from 0, and our buttons' number started from 1, so we need to decrease the value by one before using it in "state".

```
#player X's turn
b['text'] = 'X'
turn += 1
state[n-1] = 'X'
```

The minute you draw on a box, call the winner_check() function and send "X" as the parameter. We'll define the winner_check() function shortly. If you're coding along with me, for now, just type pass inside the function so you don't get an error for not defining it, but calling it. Also, create the winner_check() function above the buttonClick() function because we're calling from buttonClick.

```
#winner check
winner_check('X')
```

Okay, now that's done, let's check if turn is even, that is, if it's O's turn. If it is, do the same as earlier, but just for "O".

```
elif turn % 2 == 1:
    #player O's turn
    b['text'] = 'O'
    turn += 1
    state[n-1] = 'O'
    winner_check('O')
```

Let's run what we have so far and see if we can "draw" on our boxes (Figure 17-5).

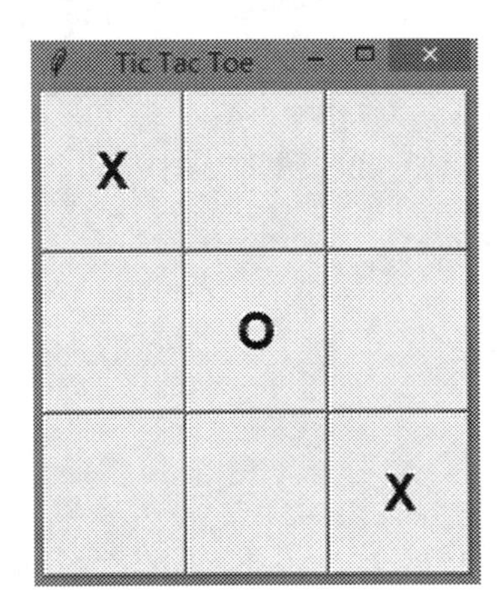

***Figure 17-5.** "Draw" on the boxes*

Yes, we can!

Finally, check for the "else" condition. Either the game is already over, or someone already drew on the box, and you don't want a repeat.

In messagebox, you have a showinfo method that can be used to, yup, you guessed it, print a message. Let's use that.

If the "game" variable is False (game over), print 'Game over! Start a new game.' If the box was already drawn on, print 'This box is occupied!'.

```
else:
    if game == False:
        messagebox.showinfo('showinfo','Game over! Start a new
        game.')
    #because even when the game is over, the buttons will be
    occupied, so check for that first
    elif b['text'] != ' ':
        messagebox.showinfo('showinfo','This box is occupied!')
```

Let's check if the error boxes work now (Figure 17-6).

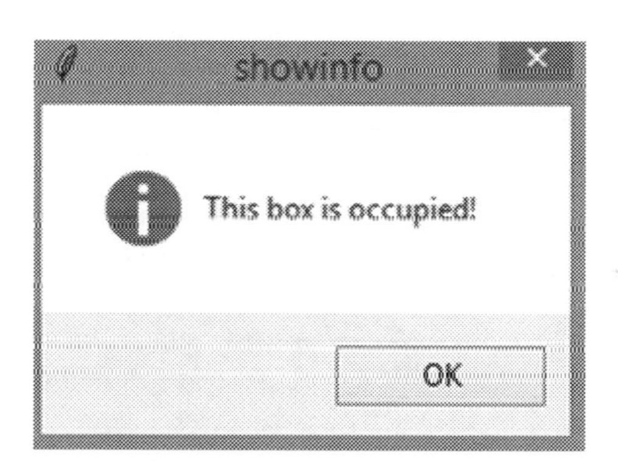

Figure 17-6. *Box is occupied*

I tried drawing on an occupied box, and this message popped up. Great! The other condition isn't relevant right now because we haven't checked for winners yet, so the game won't get "over" yet.

It looks like the program is almost over, right? We've drawn on it. We've even created the winner_check() function to work on next. But are we really done with buttonClick()? Nope.

We still need to check for the draw condition! What if the value of turn is greater than 8 (players have played nine times) and the value of "game" is still true? If "game" is still True, that means no one has won yet because when we call the winner_check() function, if we find someone has won, we immediately change "game" to False.

So, the only reason we're out of turns and the game is still True is because we're at a draw. Let's print that message and end the game (change "game" to False).

```
#game ended on draw
if turn > 8 and game == True:
    messagebox.showinfo('showinfo','The match was a Draw')
    game = False
```

That's it for buttonClick()! Whew. That was big.

Let's run the program, and check if the "draw" condition works (Figure 17-7).

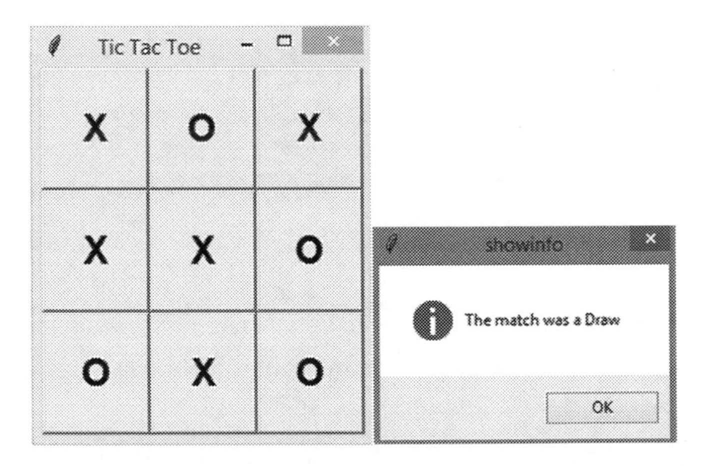

Figure 17-7. *Match was a draw*

Yup, it works! But we need the winner_check() to make everything work properly.

Let's look at winner_check() next.

Check if a player won during each turn

Every time a player plays, we need to check if that player just won the game at that turn. This function accepts the player ("X" or "O") as its argument.

```
#Every time a button is clicked, check for win state
```

```
def winner_check(p):
```

Let's also import the global variables state, winner, and game, because we'll need them.

```
global state,winner,game
```

Now, we need to loop through the winner. So for every iteration of the loop, "i" will have one of the "win" state lists.

For every iteration, let's check if state[i[0]], state[i[0]], and state[i[0]] hold the same value of player ("X" or "O").

For example, the first inner list is [0,1,2], so we're checking for state[0], state[1], and state[2], and if they all hold the string "X", then plalyer "X" won. If they all hold "O", "O" won. That's it!

```
for i in winner:
    if((state[i[0]] == p) and (state[i[1]] == p) and
    (state[i[2]] == p)):
```

If the condition holds true, then create a string that basically says "X won!" or "O won!" and create a message with it. Finally, change the value of "game" to False.

```
string = '{} won!'.format(p)
messagebox.showinfo('showinfo',string)
game = False
```

Let's run our program now, and we get this (Figure 17-8).

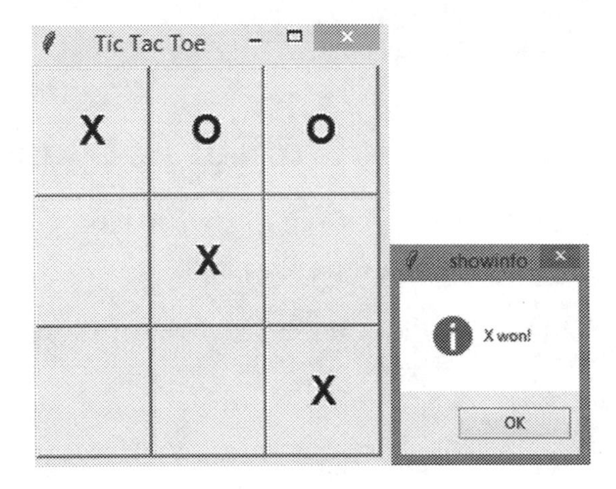

Figure 17-8. *X won!*

Whoa! It works!

Does the "Game over" condition work? Let me close the current message box and try to draw on one of the empty boxes by clicking it (Figure 17-9).

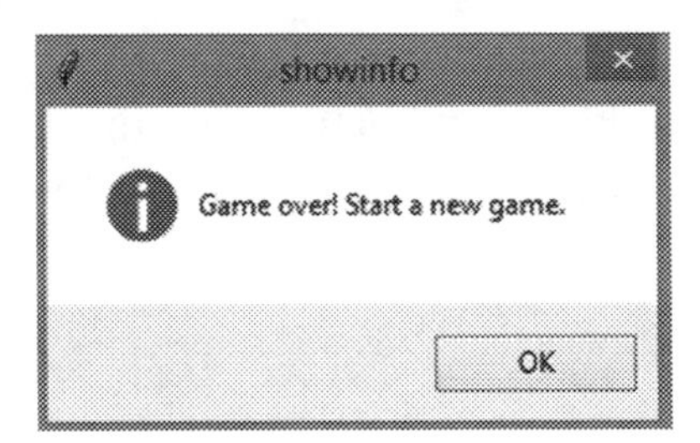

Figure 17-9. *Game over!*

Look at that! Our "Game over!" message just popped up. Our game works perfectly!

New game button

Why don't we add a "New game" button to our game? Right now, our game just hangs after it's over. We have to run the program again to start a new game. If we had a button that just reset everything, that'd be great, won't it?

Let's do that. Let's create a button first.

```
new = Button(w,text='New Game',command=new_game)
new.grid(row=3,column=1)
```

This button will execute the new_game() function when clicked.

Now, let's create the new_game() function above the "new" button.

Before we define the function, let's create a list of all our buttons. We'll need this to loop through the buttons and clear them (so we can draw on them again).

```
#create a list of the buttons so  we can change their text
boxes = [b1,b2,b3,b4,b5,b6,b7,b8,b9]
```

Our new_game() function needs the global variables state, game, turn, and boxes. We need to import state, game, and turn so we can reset them back to their original values.

```
#New game
def new_game():
    global state,game,turn,boxes
```

Let's reset turn, state, and game.

```
turn = 0
state = ['','','','','','','','','']
game = True
```

Finally, let's loop through "boxes" and change the text value of each box to a single space.

```
for b in boxes:
    b['text'] = ' '
```

That's it for our program! I'm sure you'd have done that already, but if you forgot, add a mainloop() at the end of your program.

```
w.mainloop()
```

Let's run the program now, and we get this (Figure 17-10).

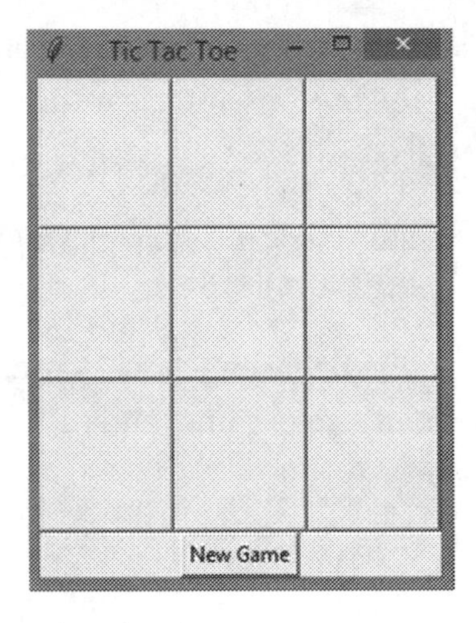

Figure 17-10. *New Game button*

We have our "New Game" button now. Try testing it. It works perfectly!

Did you have fun creating the game? I know I had fun creating it and teaching you how to create it. Tinker with the game. Change fonts, colors, and so on. All the best! 😊

Entire program

Now that you've learned how to create a tic-tac-toe game in *Tkinter,* here's the entire program in the order in which it should be written. Use it for your reference.

```
from tkinter import *
from tkinter import messagebox

w = Tk()
w.title('Tic Tac Toe')

turn = 0
state = ['','','','','','','','','']
winner = [[0,1,2], [3,4,5], [6,7,8], [0,3,6], [1,4,7], [2,5,8],
[0,4,8], [2,4,6]];
game = True

#Every time a button is clicked, check for win state
def winner_check(p):
    global state,winner,game
    for i in winner:
        if((state[i[0]] == p) and (state[i[1]] == p) and
        (state[i[2]] == p)):
            string = '{} won!'.format(p)
            messagebox.showinfo('showinfo',string)
            game = False

#When a button is clicked
def buttonClick(b,n):
    global turn,state,game

    if b['text'] == ' ' and game == True:
        #hasn't been clicked on yet
        if turn % 2 == 0:
```

```
            #player X's turn
            b['text'] = 'X'
            turn += 1
            state[n-1] = 'X'
            #winner check
            winner_check('X')
        elif turn % 2 == 1:
            #player O's turn
            b['text'] = 'O'
            turn += 1
            state[n-1] = 'O'
            player = 'X'
            winner_check('O')
    else:
        if game == False:
            messagebox.showinfo('showinfo','Game over! Start a
            new game.')
        #because even when the game is over, the buttons will
        be occupied, so check for that first
        elif b['text'] != ' ':
            messagebox.showinfo('showinfo','This box is
            occupied!')

    #game ended on draw
    if turn > 8 and game == True:
        messagebox.showinfo('showinfo','The match was a Draw')
        game = False

font = ('Helvetica',20,'bold')

#9 buttons
b1 = Button(w, text=' ', width=4, height=2, font = font,
command = lambda: buttonClick(b1,1))
```

```
b1.grid(row=0,column=0)
b2 = Button(w, text=' ', width=4, height=2, font = font,
command = lambda: buttonClick(b2,2))
b2.grid(row=0,column=1)
b3 = Button(w, text=' ', width=4, height=2, font = font,
command = lambda: buttonClick(b3,3))
b3.grid(row=0,column=2)

b4 = Button(w, text=' ', width=4, height=2, font = font,
command = lambda: buttonClick(b4,4))
b4.grid(row=1,column=0)
b5 = Button(w, text=' ', width=4, height=2, font = font,
command = lambda: buttonClick(b5,5))
b5.grid(row=1,column=1)
b6 = Button(w, text=' ', width=4, height=2, font = font,
command = lambda: buttonClick(b6,6))
b6.grid(row=1,column=2)

b7 = Button(w, text=' ', width=4, height=2, font = font,
command = lambda: buttonClick(b7,7))
b7.grid(row=2,column=0)
b8 = Button(w, text=' ', width=4, height=2, font = font,
command = lambda: buttonClick(b8,8))
b8.grid(row=2,column=1)
b9 = Button(w, text=' ', width=4, height=2, font = font,
command = lambda: buttonClick(b9,9))
b9.grid(row=2,column=2)

#create a list of the buttons so  we can change their text
boxes = [b1,b2,b3,b4,b5,b6,b7,b8,b9]
```

```
#New game
def new_game():
    global state,game,turn,boxes
    turn = 0
    state = ['','','','','','','','','']
    game = True
    for b in boxes:
        b['text'] = ' '

new = Button(w,text='New Game',command=new_game)
new.grid(row=3,column=1)

w.mainloop()
```

Summary

In this chapter, we started with comments in Python and how to create single and multi-line comments. Then we moved on to variables, how to create them, their naming conventions, and what you can store in them. Then we looked at the vast number of data types available in the Python programming language and how to use them. Then we looked at type checking in Python, and finally we looked at getting inputs in Python and displaying them in your output.

In the next chapter, let's go deep into strings, how to create them and use them, and the various pre-defined string methods Python equips you with.

CHAPTER 18

Project: Paint App with *Tkinter*

In the previous chapter, we learned how to create a tic-tac-toe app with *Tkinter*. We also learned all about events and how to use them to make our app respond to external events (mouse click, keyboard key press, etc.).

In this chapter, we'll learn all about "drawing" on your *Tkinter* screen using "canvas" and use that to make a paint app. You'll be able to draw with a pen and draw circles/ovals, straight lines, and squares/rectangles. You'll also be able to change the size of your pen and your shapes' outline colors and fill colors. It's a simple, but complete app!

Paint app – explanation

A. Elumalai, *Introduction to Python for Kids*, https://doi.org/10.1007/978-1-4842-6812-4_18

Our paint app is going to be awesome! You're going to be able to do free-hand drawing and draw straight lines, squares, rectangles, ovals, and circles. You can also choose from hundreds of different color shades. Cool right?

Once we're done, it'll look something like Figure 18-1.

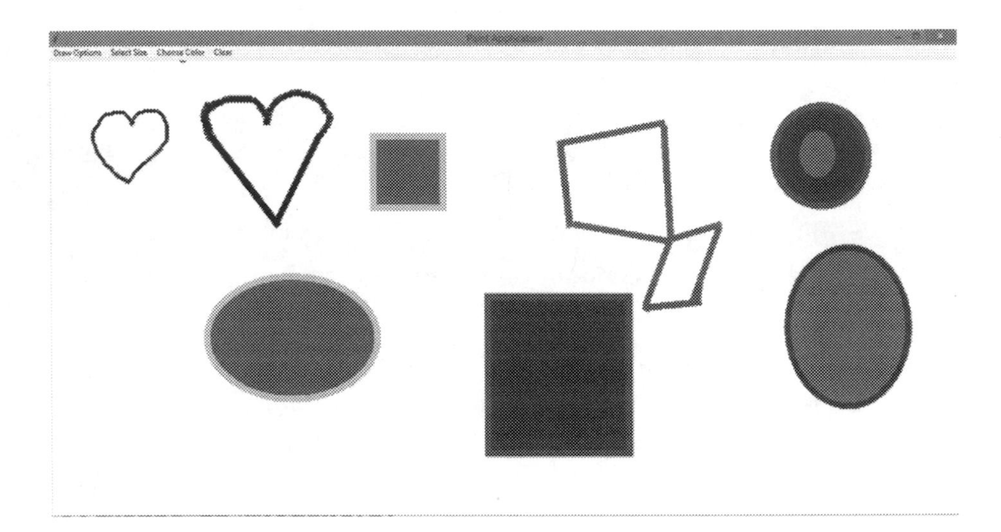

Figure 18-1. *Final app*

I'm no artist, so please forgive my basic drawings, but you can see how powerful this app is, right? And the best part is that this is just the starting point. You can expand this app, add more features, and make it into anything you want.

Share it with your friends, have paint competitions, or just have fun! 😊

Get started

Let's start by importing *Tkinter*. Let's import everything, as usual, but doing so will only import the "outer" classes. It won't import the inner ones, like the colorchooser, for example. We need the color chooser to create color palettes for our app. So, let's import that as well.

```
from tkinter import *
from tkinter import colorchooser
```

Now, let's create and initialize our variables. To draw on the screen, you need coordinates, the x and y points of where your mouse pointer is clicking on the screen. Let's create x and y variables and assign them 0 each to start with.

I've used a new way of assignment now. Makes things easy, doesn't it?

```
x, y = 0,0
```

Next, let's create a variable "color" and make it None (no value) to start with. You can make it an empty string as well. This variable will hold our shapes' fill colors in the future. We also need a color for our "pen" or our shapes' outline, so let's create a variable "outline" and make it black as default. We also need a pen size. It's going to be 1 by default.

```
color = None
outline = 'black'
sizeVal = 1
```

Set up the screen

Now, let's set up our screen. We're going to make the state of our screen "zoomed" by default, so it expands to the full screen. Also, we're going to configure our rows and columns in such a way that the first cell (row 0 and column 0) is going to expand to the full width and height of the screen. We can place our canvas inside this cell, so it expands to the full screen as well.

```
w = Tk()
w.title('Paint Application')
w.state('zoomed')
w.rowconfigure(0,weight=1)
w.columnconfigure(0,weight=1)
```

We've given the weight as 1 to let our program know that this particular row and column should expand to its maximum capacity.

Let's run our program, and we get this (Figure 18-2).

Figure 18-2. *Our Tkinter screen*

Great!

Create the canvas

Now, let's create our canvas. We need to use the Canvas method to do that and place it in the window "w". Let's also make our canvas' background "white" by default.

```
#create a canvas
canvas = Canvas(w, background='white')
```

Next, I'm going to place my canvas in the first row and column (0) and make it sticky in all directions (north, south, east, and west) so it expands in all directions and takes up the entire space (which is our entire screen as of now).

```
canvas.grid(row=0,column=0,sticky="NSEW")
```

Let's run the program now, and we get this (Figure 18-3).

Figure 18-3. *Canvas*

Perfect! We have our white canvas now.

Create your first menu (shapes)

If you looked at the completed app, you'd have noticed that we had multiple menus to choose from. The first one is the shape menu. You'll be able to choose between drawing with a pen and drawing a line, square, or circle. Let's create that menu now.

You already know how to create menus. Let's create a main menu that'll hold all our menus. Our "Draw Options" menu is going to be the first submenu in our "main" menu. Let's add a cascade to it and label it.

```
main = Menu(w)
menu1 = Menu(main)
main.add_cascade(label='Draw Options',menu = menu1)
```

Finally, let's add four commands, 'Pen', 'Line', 'Square' and 'Circle'. But we need to send the selection values to the "select" function, which will in turn call the relevant function that'll do the respective drawing. Let's use a lambda to do that. We're going to number our options, pen is 1, line is 2, square is 3, and circle is 4.

```
menu1.add_command(label='Pen', command=lambda: select(1))
menu1.add_command(label='Line', command=lambda: select(2))
menu1.add_command(label='Square', command=lambda: select(3))
menu1.add_command(label='Circle', command=lambda: select(4))
```

Finally, let's configure our "main" menu to our window. In the future, this line should come after we've created all four of our menus.

```
w.config(menu=main)
```

If you run your program now, and try clicking the menu items, you'll get an error because your "select" function isn't defined yet, but still, you'll see your menu, like this (Figure 18-4).

***Figure 18-4.** First menu (draw options)*

Whoa! First step is a success! 😉

Let's make our draw options work!

Now that we have our draw options menu, let's make it work. Let's first create the "select" function that binds the canvas with the relevant mouse clicks. Create this function above the menus (function calls). We need two kinds of binds.

For the free-hand drawing, we need a <B1-Motion> bind that draws a line every time our left mouse button clicks and drags on the screen. So, we'll essentially get tiny lines between every 2 minute points, so essentially hundreds of tiny lines that join are joined together to make our free-hand drawing.

Then, we need a <ButtonRelease-1> bind that draws either a line, square, or circle whenever our left mouse button releases after it clicks and drags on the screen. So, the result would be a line, square, or circle from the point where it clicked to the point where it released.

Let's do that now. Let's receive our number as "options". If options is 1, then unbind <ButtonRelease-1>, so if we'd previously selected the other options, it'll be unselected now, and we won't get a shape or line after we release the pen. Then, let's bind <B1-Motion> and call the draw_line function.

```
def select(options):
    if options == 1:
        #selected Pen, create bind
        canvas.unbind("<ButtonRelease-1>")
        canvas.bind('<B1-Motion>',draw_line)
```

Similarly, for 2, unbind <B1-Motion> so the pen is no longer active and bind the <ButtonRelease-1> and call the draw_line function.

```
if options == 2:
    #selected line, create bind
    canvas.unbind("<B1-Motion>") #so pen is no longer active
    canvas.bind('<ButtonRelease-1>',draw_line)
```

For 3, call the draw_square function.

```
elif options == 3:
    #selected square, create bind
    canvas.unbind("<B1-Motion>")
    canvas.bind('<ButtonRelease-1>',draw_square)
```

For 4, call the draw_circle function.

```
elif options == 4:
    #selected circle, create bind
    canvas.unbind("<B1-Motion>")
    canvas.bind('<ButtonRelease-1>',draw_circle)
```

Get the mouse position

Before we create the draw_line functions, we need to get our mouse position. We can do that using our "event", as you know. So, let's create another bind outside of our functions (right above our menus and below the function definitions) that binds any left mouse button click to the canvas.

So, every time your user clicks the canvas, we're going to make note of the x and y positions of the same in the background.

We won't draw anything until the user selects a draw option, but let's still make note in anticipation of that, alright?

```
canvas.bind('<Button-1>',position)
```

Now, define the function above the bind. Receive "event" in the function definition. Let's also load the global x and y values and assign the event.x and event.y values (x and y coordinate positions of the mouse click) to the x and y global variables.

Get the current position of the mouse on each left mouse button click on the canvas.

```
def position(event):
    global x,y
    x,y = event.x,event.y
```

That's it! You could print out x and y and see this function in action. Let's make that our little activity, shall we? 😊

Let's draw our lines

Now, let's create the function that'll draw both our mini lines for our free-hand drawing and our straight lines. What do we need here?

There's a create_line function in canvas which can be used to, yup, you guessed it, draw straight lines! You just need to give the start and end coordinate points. You can also specify the "fill", which is essentially the line's color.

We'll be using the "outline" color for this because we want line colors and shape outline colors to be uniform. You can also specify the width of the line. Let's give sizeVal as the value for this property.

You need to be careful how you mention the coordinate values though. Mention the x and y coordinates of the starting point first and then the x and y coordinates of the ending point. More importantly, mention all four values inside of a tuple, or you'll get an error.

```
def draw_line(event):
```

Let's load our x and y values, which is the point where the mouse first clicked, which we calculate constantly using the position() function. Let's also load sizeVal, which is currently at 1. It'll automatically get updated once we write the lines of code that'll let the user manually change the width of the lines.

```
global x,y,sizeVal
```

Now, the starting x and y positions are the x and y positions that contain the point where the mouse clicked (the position() function). The ending x and y positions are the event's x and y positions.

In case of a free-hand drawing, every time the mouse is dragged (while the left mouse button is still pressed down), we get a new event, and new x and y positions, for every minute change.

For drawing a straight line, the end point is when the mouse button is released.

```
canvas.create_line((x,y,event.x,event.y),fill=outline, width =
sizeVal)
```

Finally, let's update the x and y values with the event's x and y values. We especially need this for the free-hand drawing, so we can start over.

```
x,y = event.x,event.y
```

Let's run our program now.

When we try to draw on the screen as such, nothing happens. Why? Well, we haven't activated any of the options yet. But, if I select either pen or line (from the menu), I can draw on the canvas (Figure 18-5).

Figure 18-5. *Free hand and straight lines*

Squares and rectangles!

Let's draw our squares and rectangles now. The process is similar. You have a create_rectangle method in canvas. Give the start and end coordinates within a tuple again. In this case, you can mention two kinds of colors, outline and fill colors, and finally the width of the shape.

Then, let's assign the current event's x and y values (mouse release) to the first x and y values (left mouse click).

```
def draw_square(event):
    global x,y,sizeVal
    canvas.create_rectangle((x,y,event.x,event.y),
    outline=outline, fill=color, width = sizeVal)
    x,y = event.x,event.y
```

That's it! Let's run our program now. Select "Square", hold your mouse button down, drag it to the point you want, and release the button. You'll get yourself a square or a rectangle. Try and see! 😊

This is what I did (Figure 18-6). :P

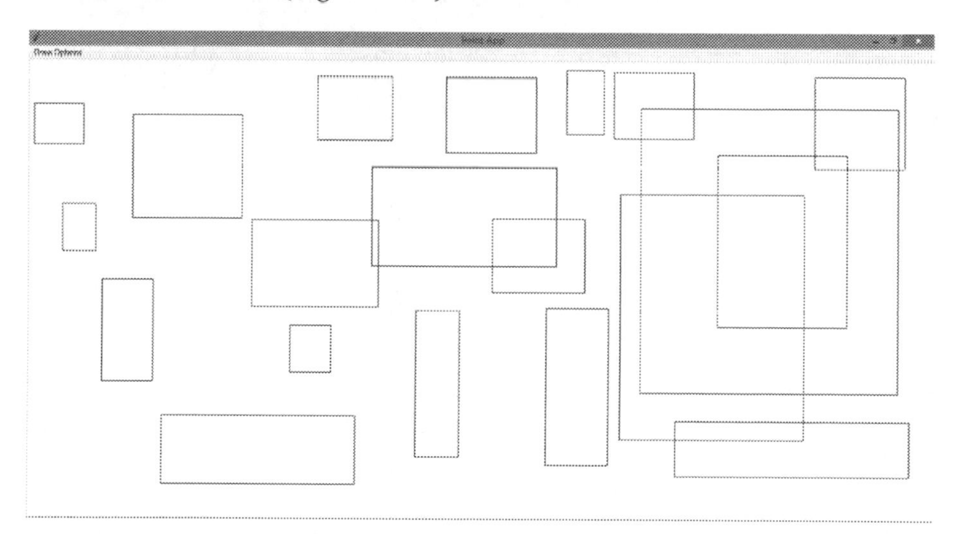

Figure 18-6. *Squares and rectangles*

Beautiful squares and rectangles! 😊

Circles and ovals!

Finally, let's draw circles and ovals. There's another method called create_oval. A perfectly formed oval is a circle, am I right? You need to give the start and end points for this method as well.

Your start point is when you pressed the mouse button, and the end point is the x and y value of the point where you finally released the mouse button (mouse release event).

```
def draw_circle(event):
    global x,y,sizeVal
    canvas.create_oval((x,y,event.x,event.y), outline=outline,
    fill=color, width= sizeVal)
    x,y = event.x,event.y
```

Let's run the program, and we get this (Figure 18-7).

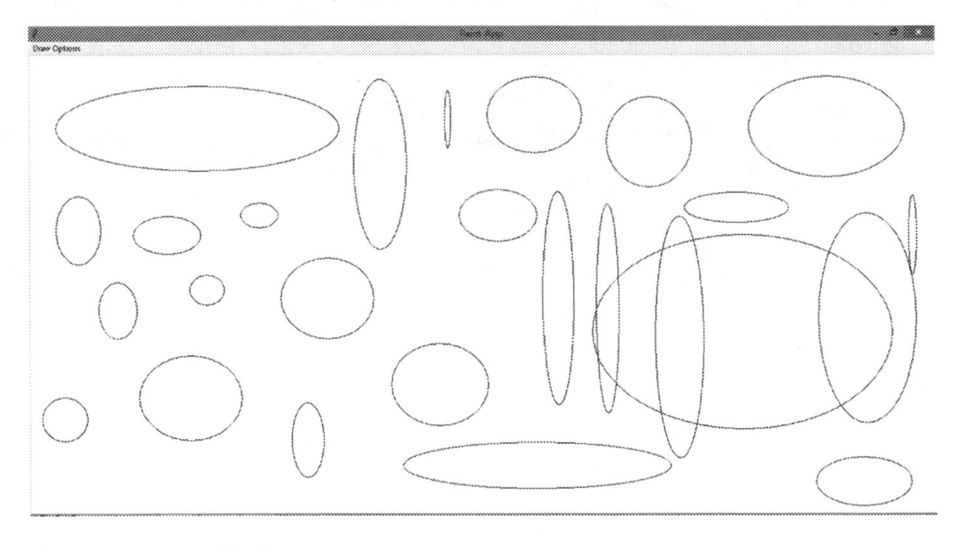

Figure 18-7. *Circles*

Nice! We've finished all our draw functions. We're almost there! 😊

Select size!

Now, let's move on to the second menu in our program. So far, our lines and the outlines of our shapes are too narrow in width. What if we want them to be thicker? We need options for that as well. Let's create them! I'm going to create sizes from 1, 5, 10, to 30. 1 is the default we've set.

Let's create a new submenu, menu2, for the sizes. Place this after the menu1's code, but before the menu configuration line of code. Every option is going to be a size, and I'm going to call the changeSize function for every option click. We'll be sending the size as the parameter to this function.

```
menu2 = Menu(main)
main.add_cascade(label='Select Size', menu = menu2)
menu2.add_command(label='1', command=lambda: changeSize(1))
menu2.add_command(label='5', command=lambda: changeSize(5))
menu2.add_command(label='10', command=lambda: changeSize(10))
menu2.add_command(label='15', command=lambda: changeSize(15))
menu2.add_command(label='20', command=lambda: changeSize(20))
menu2.add_command(label='25', command=lambda: changeSize(25))
menu2.add_command(label='30', command=lambda: changeSize(30))
```

Now, define the function to change the size. You can place this function after the select() function, or anywhere you want, as long as it's above menu2's lines of code (function calls).

This is a very simple process. Let's receive our size, load the global sizeVal, and assign our size to sizeVal. That's it! Since sizeVal is global and loaded into all our draw functions, once we change the size, the next time we draw something, the new size will reflect in that drawing.

```
def changeSize(size):
    global sizeVal
    sizeVal = size
```

Let's check if this works! I'm going to draw a bunch of lines after changing the size to 15 (Figure 18-8).

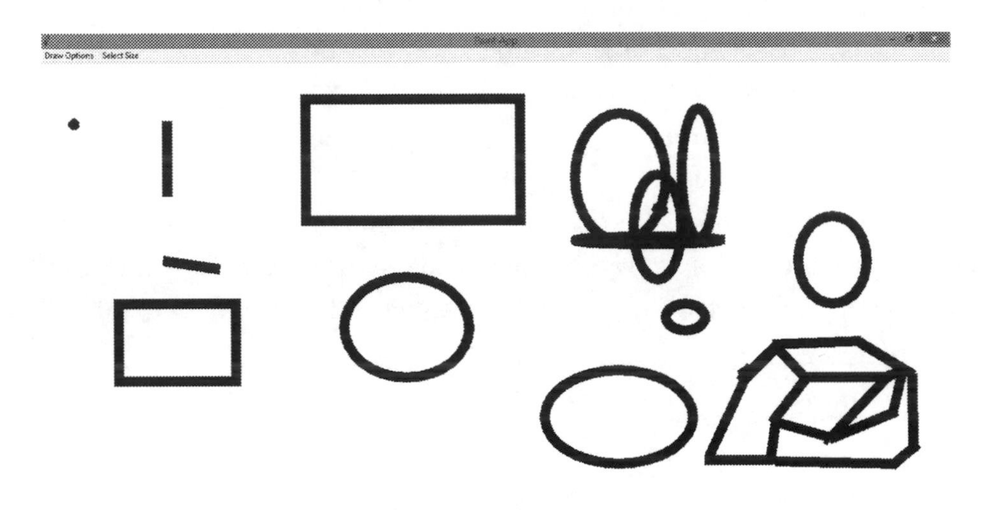

***Figure 18-8.** Change the width of your outlines*

Those are some thick lines. :D

Lots and lots of colors!

Now, let's create the third menu that'll let us change the outline and fill colors of our drawings.

Let's create a menu3 that holds just two options, one to change the line color and the other to change the fill color, each calling their respective functions.

```
menu3 = Menu(main)
main.add_cascade(label = 'Choose Color', menu = menu3)
menu3.add_command(label='Line Color', command = set_line_color)
menu3.add_command(label='Fill Color', command = set_fill_color)
```

Now, let's define those functions. We're going to use our colorchooser to create our color palettes. There's an askcolor method in colorchooser that opens a palette when we need it (in this case, when the "Line color" option is clicked). This opens in a new window. Let's also set a title for that window: Choose color.

```
def set_line_color():
    global outline
    getColor = colorchooser.askcolor(title="Choose color")
```

Now, you can't just use getColor as it is. When we choose a color, let's say red, this is the format in which it gets registered in getColor:

```
((255.99609375, 0.0, 0.0), '#ff0000')
```

The first value in the tuple contains another tuple that holds the rgb color value (red, green, and blue shades of our color). The second value in the tuple contains the hexadecimal value of the color we just chose. They're both the same, and you can just write it as "red". These are just different formats in which you can mention a color. You don't really need to know about them or memorize them. Just know that every shade there are hexadecimal and rgb values you can use and your computer recognizes.

Now, we can't use the entire tuple. We just need one of its values. Let's just retrieve the second value and use it, shall we?

```
outline = getColor[1]
```

Now, every time we change the "Line color", the value of "outline" changes and it'll be reflected in our next drawing.

Now, let's do the same for fill color.

```
def set_fill_color():
    global color
    getColor = colorchooser.askcolor(title="Choose color")
    color = getColor[1]
```

That's it for our colors! Let's check if it works, shall we? Let's click "Line color" to see if the color palette opens up (Figure 18-9).

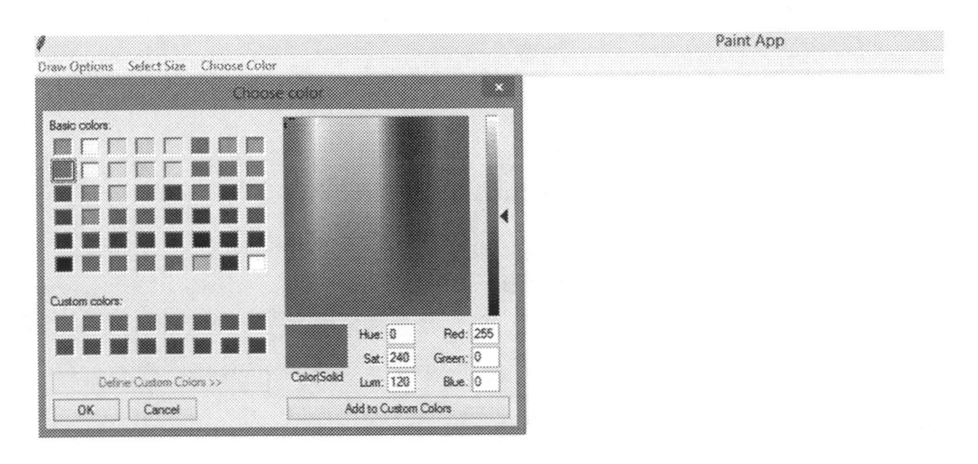

Figure 18-9. *Colors!*

It works! 😊

Now, let's choose our colors (Figure 18-10).

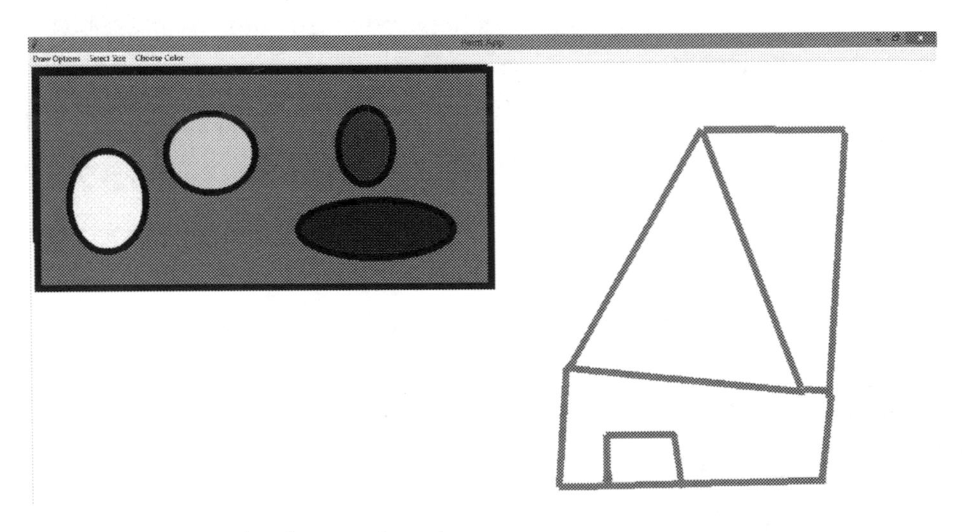

Figure 18-10. *Final app, done!*

All our colors work perfectly!

I've finished drawing!

Okay, we have our little paint app. We've drawn to our heart's content! But what if we want to start over? We need an option to clear the canvas. Let's create that!

First, the menu.

```
menu4 = Menu(main)
main.add_cascade(label = 'Clear', menu = menu4)
menu4.add_command(label = 'Clear', command = clear_screen)
```

Now, the clear_screen() function. We just need a single line of code: canvas.delete('all'). This will delete everything on the canvas.

```
def clear_screen():
    canvas.delete('all')
```

This is how the option will come up (Figure 18-11).

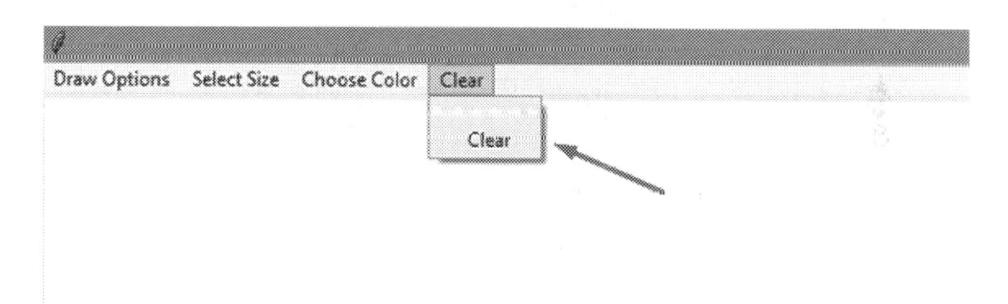

Figure 18-11. *Clear*

Draw something and select the clear option to see everything disappear! Take a screenshot before you do though!

We've finished our paint app! :O Finally, if you haven't written it already, write the mainloop line of code, and we're done.

```
w.mainloop()
```

Entire program

Now, the entire program in the order it should be created:

```
from tkinter import *
from tkinter import colorchooser

x, y = 0,0
color = None
outline = 'black'
sizeVal = 1

w = Tk()
w.title('Paint App')
w.state('zoomed')
w.rowconfigure(0,weight=1)
w.columnconfigure(0,weight=1)

#create a canvas
canvas = Canvas(w, background='white')
canvas.grid(row=0,column=0,sticky="NSEW")

def draw_line(event):
    global x,y,sizeVal
    canvas.create_line((x,y,event.x,event.y),fill=outline,
    width = sizeVal)
    x,y = event.x,event.y

def draw_square(event):
    global x,y,sizeVal
    canvas.create_rectangle((x,y,event.x,event.y),
outline=outline, fill=color, width = sizeVal)
    x,y = event.x,event.y
```

```
def draw_circle(event):
    global x,y,sizeVal
    canvas.create_oval((x,y,event.x,event.y), outline=outline,
    fill=color, width= sizeVal)
    x,y = event.x,event.y

def select(options):
    if options == 1:
        #selected Pen, create bind
        canvas.unbind("<ButtonRelease-1>")
        canvas.bind('<B1-Motion>',draw_line)
    if options == 2:
        #selected line, create bind
        canvas.unbind("<B1-Motion>") #so pen is no longer
        active
        canvas.bind('<ButtonRelease-1>',draw_line)
    elif options == 3:
        #selected square, create bind
        canvas.unbind("<B1-Motion>")
        canvas.bind('<ButtonRelease-1>',draw_square)
    elif options == 4:
        #selected circle, create bind
        canvas.unbind("<B1-Motion>")
        canvas.bind('<ButtonRelease-1>',draw_circle)

def position(event):
    global x,y
    x,y = event.x,event.y

def changeSize(size):
    global sizeVal
    sizeVal = size
```

```
def set_line_color():
    global outline
    getColor = colorchooser.askcolor(title="Choose color")
    outline = getColor[1]

def set_fill_color():
    global color
    getColor = colorchooser.askcolor(title="Choose color")
    color = getColor[1]

def clear_screen():
    canvas.delete('all')

canvas.bind('<Button-1>',position)

#options
main = Menu(w)
menu1 = Menu(main)
main.add_cascade(label='Draw Options',menu = menu1)
menu1.add_command(label='Pen', command=lambda: select(1))
menu1.add_command(label='Line', command=lambda: select(2))
menu1.add_command(label='Square', command=lambda: select(3))
menu1.add_command(label='Circle', command=lambda: select(4))

menu2 = Menu(main)
main.add_cascade(label='Select Size', menu = menu2)
menu2.add_command(label='1', command=lambda: changeSize(1))
menu2.add_command(label='5', command=lambda: changeSize(5))
menu2.add_command(label='10', command=lambda: changeSize(10))
menu2.add_command(label='15', command=lambda: changeSize(15))
```

```
menu2.add_command(label='20', command=lambda: changeSize(20))
menu2.add_command(label='25', command=lambda: changeSize(25))
menu2.add_command(label='30', command=lambda: changeSize(30))

menu3 = Menu(main)
main.add_cascade(label = 'Choose Color', menu = menu3)
menu3.add_command(label='Line Color', command = set_line_color)
menu3.add_command(label='Fill Color', command = set_fill_color)

menu4 = Menu(main)
main.add_cascade(label = 'Clear', menu = menu4)
menu4.add_command(label = 'Clear', command = clear_screen)

w.config(menu=main)
w.mainloop()
```

Summary

In this chapter, we learned about "drawing" on our *Tkinter* screen using "canvas" and used that to make a paint app. We drew with a pen and drew circles/ovals, straight lines, and squares/rectangles. We also changed the size of your pen and our shapes' outline colors and fill colors.

In the next chapter, let's go back to our original package, the *Turtle* package. Let's create a full-blown snake app with *Turtle*, scoreboards, and all. It's going to be a fun and interesting ride. Buckle up!

CHAPTER 19

Project: Snake Game with *Turtle*

In the previous chapters, we took a deep dive into *Tkinter*. We learned all about creating widgets in *Tkinter*, styling them, making them do things when events are performed on them, and also drawing on canvases. We also looked at creating two big projects – a tic-tac-toe game and a paint application.

In this chapter, let's go back to *Turtle*. We've worked on *Turtle* all these chapters, but we never created a real-world application. So, let's create a snake game in this chapter.

Snake game

A. Elumalai, *Introduction to Python for Kids*, https://doi.org/10.1007/978-1-4842-6812-4_19

It's a very simple game. You have your snake, which is drawn as a square in our game. We start with just its head, and when you press any of the arrow keys, the head moves in the direction the arrows are pointing to.

Then, you have a red, ripe apple that's the exact size of your snake head. It appears in random positions, enticing your snake head to eat it.

Whenever your snake comes in contact with the apple (we're assuming it ate the apple then), your apple disappears into the snake's stomach. The snake grows by one part (it just ate, so it should grow, right?). Another apple appears in yet another random position on the screen.

The scoreboard increases by 1 every time the snake eats an apple.

But if the snake head collides with any of the four walls of the screen or with its own body (it grew so big!), game over! ☹

Simple enough game, isn't it? Have you ever played it? Our final game will look something like this (Figure 19-1).

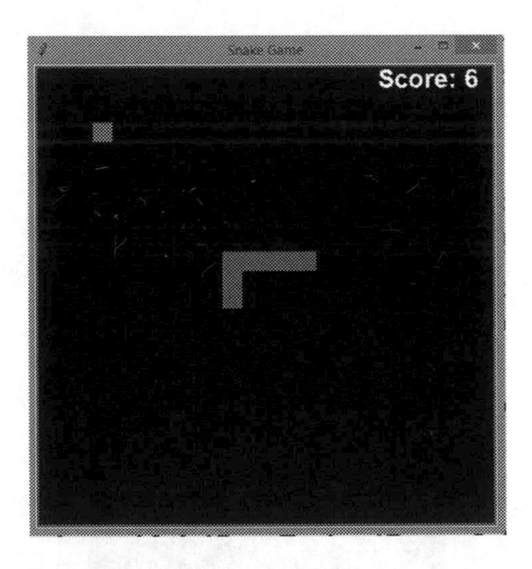

Figure 19-1. *Snake game*

Our snake had eaten six apples at that point and grown by six body parts (seven including the head).

Alright then. Now that you know how the snake game works, you must have a brief idea of what we need to code to make all of this happen. Don't worry. I'll explain everything in detail.

Also, don't get confused about the order in which you need to write every piece of code. While I explain things, it might look jumbled, but I've included the entire code in the correct order at the end of the chapter. You can refer to it while coding your own game.

Let's get started! This is going to be a slightly long, but very rewarding journey! 😊

Import the required modules

You need three modules for this game. You need the turtle package to draw the snake, score, and apple. You need the random package to make the apple appear in random positions, which is one of the main aspects of the game.

Finally, you need the "time" package. We've seen this package before, and it makes a loop or function pause for a specified amount of time. We need that now to make our snake move in a controlled pace. If we don't pace things, our snake will just move off the screen in a blink of an eye.

```
import turtle
import time
import random
```

Set up the turtle screen

We're going to set up a turtle screen with the same steps as we usually use. Make the title 'Snake Game' and the background color 'Black.'

```
s = turtle.Screen()
s.title('Snake Game')
s.bgcolor('Black')
```

But in this case, we're going to use the setup() function to set up a width and height (in pixels) for our screen. We need a specified width and height so we know where everything is on the screen, so we can specify the exact coordinates to move our snake around.

```
s.setup(width = 500, height = 500)
```

Finally, let's get rid of the animation that happens whenever we draw something on the screen. Animations are pretty, yes, but we're going to be drawing so many things so fast that animating every piece of drawing is not going to work out well for our game.

You can use the tracer() method (of our screen) and give an input of 0 to make this happen. Look at that! You've already learned a bunch of new things in *Turtle*. 😊

```
s.tracer(0) #gets rid of animation
```

Now, run the program and you'll get a black screen like this (Figure 19-2).

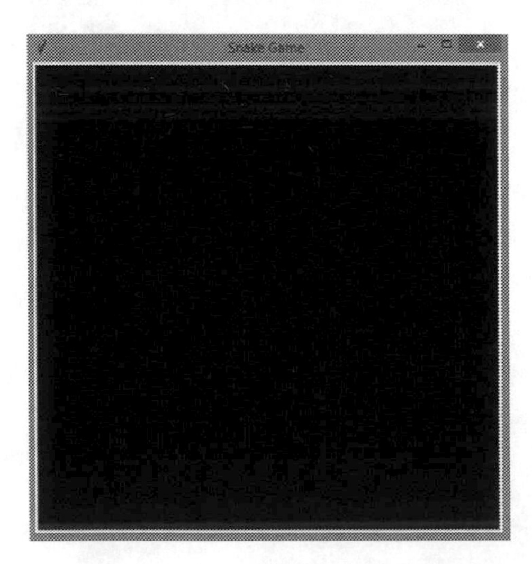

Figure 19-2. *Game screen*

Create and initialize the required variables

We've seen this in our *Tkinter* programs already. Whenever you create a program, you need some "global" variables that'll be used throughout the program. We have some too.

There's the "snake" list that's going to contain the "turtle" of each of our snake's part. Every time we draw a snake part (including the head), we're going to create a new turtle so all of those turtles can work together to draw the entire snake at the same time. By storing these turtles in a list, we can access them whenever we want and get their positions (you'll see how).

```
snake = []
```

We're going to make the size 20. This is the width and height of your squares (snake head, snake parts, apple). I'm going to make this value a constant.

```
size = 20
```

Let's also create a variable "key" that stores which key is pressed: "u" for up arrow key, "d" for down arrow key, "l" for left arrow key, and "r" for right arrow key. When we start the game, this value is going to be an empty string.

```
key = ''
```

Finally, let's make a "score" variable and initialize its value to 0 when we start the game.

```
score = 0
```

Draw the head

Now that we've initialized the variable, let's draw our head and make it appear on our screen.

We're going to create a new turtle (head) for this. Make its speed 0, shape square, and color green. Finally, move it to the position 0,0 (center of the screen).

```
#Draw head
head = turtle.Turtle()
head.speed(0)
head.shape('square')
head.color('Green')
head.penup()
head.goto(0, 0)
```

Let's also append this head to the "snake" list. Since the list is empty, it'll occupy the first position in the list.

```
snake.append(head) #get the first head
```

Run the program and tell me what you see. Is it still a blank screen? :O Where's our turtle?!

Ah well, I guess we can't see anything because of the tracer. We got rid of the animation, remember? We need a game loop to make things right this time.

You'll learn more about game loops in *Pygame*, but for now, just know that every game needs a never-ending loop (usually a while loop) that runs while the game is still "on".

Let's create such a loop now and use the update() method (of our screen) to update the screen every time the loop is executed.

```
while True:
    s.update()
```

That's it! Now run the program again, and you'll see a cute little snake head on the middle of your screen (Figure 19-3).

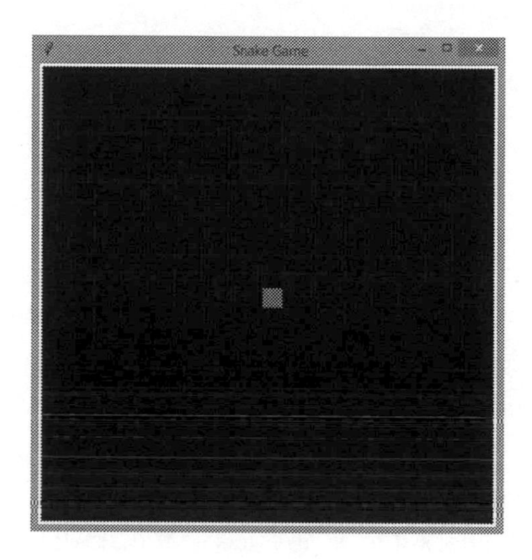

Figure 19-3. *Snake head*

Draw the first apple

Now that we've drawn our snake, let's draw our first apple at its first random position. We need another turtle for this, and we're going to name it "apple".

```
#Draw first apple
apple = turtle.Turtle()
apple.speed(0)
apple.shape('square')
```

Make its color red, and let's move it to a random position.

```
apple.color('Red')
apple.penup()
```

Read the following line of code. We're generating a random number between -11 and 11 and multiplying that by 20. If you multiply something by 20, you're creating multiples of 20, which is exactly what we want because our snake head is going to move 20 points forward every time it moves.

If our snake has to win, it should be able to superimpose the apple completely, so the apple should appear in the same line of movement as the snake. We need a multiple of 20 to make that happen.

Why a range of -11,11? Well, you can make it a little bigger, maybe -11,12 so the actual range is -11 to 11, but the entire premise is that the apple should appear within the screen.

-11 * 20 is -220. That's the x,y position of the top-left corner of our square, and then comes the square, which is of size 20. So, the top-right corner of our square will be at -240, right?

That's where it should end. If we move even further to the left, our apple might disappear.

```
aX = random.randint(-11,11)*20
aY = random.randint(-11,11)*20
```

Finally, let's go to the random x and y coordinates we just created.

```
apple.goto(aX,aY)
```

Did you notice that our pens (head and apple) are always "up"? Well, that's because we aren't going to draw with them. The turtles(pens) are going to be the game characters this time, not their drawings.

Let's run the program, and we get this (Figure 19-4).

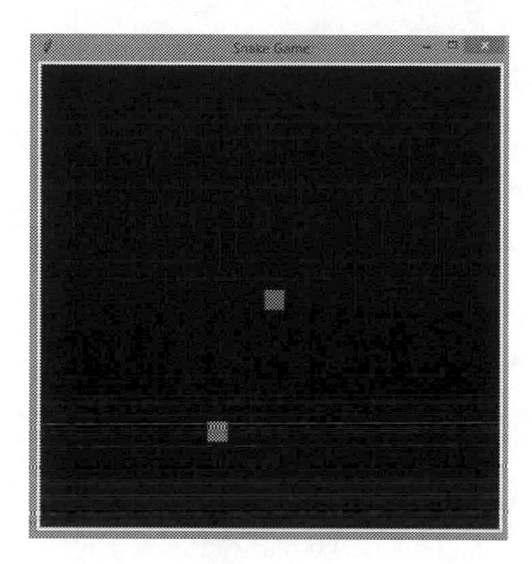

Figure 19-4. *Head and first apple*

Great! We have a snake head, fixed at the middle of the screen, and an apple that appears at a random position within the screen.

Run the program multiple times and you'll notice that the apple gets drawn in a different position every time. Cool right? 😊

Now, at the very end of the program (add the next lines of code before this line), add the following:

```
s.mainloop()
```

This is to make sure that the screen is open until we close it, so the prompt doesn't come up in the Shell while we're playing the game.

Is my screen registering my arrow presses?

Most games have movement controls. We either use a joystick or keyboard keys. Ours is a simple game, so we're going to stick to keyboard keys.

Shall we make our snake move when we press the arrow keys? Up, Down, Left, or Right arrow keys.

To make your screen "listen" to keyboard key presses, that is, to know that keys are being pressed, use your screen's listen() method. Now, your screen is listening. Place these lines of code after you draw your first apple and snake head, but before the while loop (game loop).

```
#Listen to the events and act
s.listen()
```

Now, you can use the onkeypress() methods to call user-defined functions when key presses happen. This works similar to how we did things in *Tkinter*, with the only difference that our function call comes before the "event" we're looking for.

Our events are 'Up', 'Down', 'Left', and 'Right'. These are values your onkeypress() function is expecting, so place them within quotes and write them without changing case. Your functions can be anything. I've made mine set_up, set_down, set_left, and set_right.

```
s.onkeypress(set_up,'Up')
s.onkeypress(set_down,'Down')
s.onkeypress(set_left,'Left')
s.onkeypress(set_right,'Right')
```

Now that we've called our function, we need to create them (or we'd get an error). Let's define our functions above the onkeypresses. Each function will load the global "key" variable, and change the value to 'up', 'down', 'right', or 'left'.

But we need to keep track of something here. In the snake game, snakes can't move backward, or they'll just hit their own body (which ends the game), so we need to check if the user is trying to move back.

For example, if the current value of key is 'down', then we shouldn't change the value to 'up' next. Ignore that particular key press and so on.

```
def set_up():
    global key #so the global variable key can be used in a
               local context here
    if(key != 'down'):
        key = 'up'
def set_down():
    global key
    if(key != 'up'):
        key = 'down'
def set_left():
    global key
    if(key != 'right'):
        key = 'left'
def set_right():
    global key
    if(key != 'left'):
       key = 'right'
```

Alright, we've officially changed direction. But if we run the program now, we wouldn't see a difference. Press keys. Does anything happen? Nope. We haven't written the code to make our snake move yet! Let's do that next.

Make our snake head move

So, in a snake game, once we set a direction, the snake will move in that direction automatically, until we change the direction again. So basically, once the snake starts moving, it'll continue to move until it collides with something.

To create this automatic movement, we're going to call a moveHead() function from within our game loop.

```
while True:
    s.update()
    moveHead()
```

But, we aren't going to stop there. We're going to run the while loop at a delay of 0.2 seconds for every iteration, so that the human eye can actually see the snake move.

Every iteration of a loop gets executed in microseconds. That's how powerful and fast Python and your computer are. But, this is a game. We need something the human eye can see, so let's slow down our program, shall we? Make it sleep for 0.2 seconds after every iteration.

```
time.sleep(0.2)
```

Okay, now that we're done with the "while" loop, let's create the moveHead() method to set the x and y coordinates of the head.

We're going to continuously change the x and y coordinates of the head by 20 points for every function call (which happens at a 0.2-second delay), so the head moves forward by 20 points every 0.2 second (Figure 19-5).

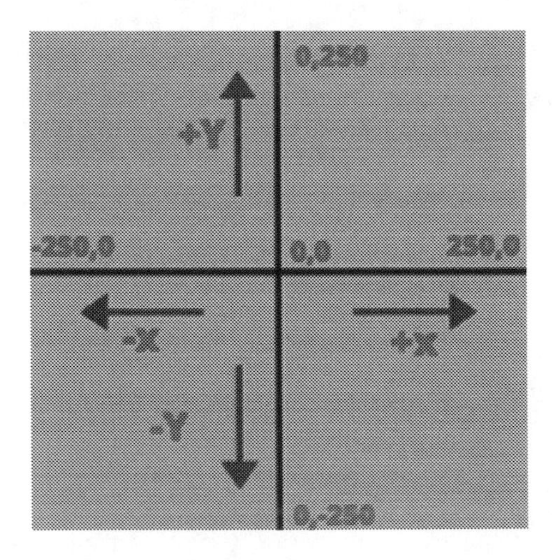

Figure 19-5. *Game screen coordinates*

Look at the preceding illustration. If you want to move your snake to the left, decrease the value of X while keeping the value of Y the same. To move to the right, increase the value of X. To move up, increase the value of Y (X remains the same). To move down, decrease the value of Y.

Simple enough? Let's apply this to our code now!

```
#Make it move based on the set direction
```

We don't need to load "key" in this function because we aren't changing/re-assigning its value. We're just retrieving its value. Retrieve the current x or y coordinates of the "head" turtle (snake's head in our game) using the xcor() and ycor() methods. Now you know why we stored the entire turtle in our list. This is so we can use it to get a lot of information about it (like its position).

Increase or decrease the x or y coordinate by "size" (20 pixels) because that's our measurement. Our apple is going to appear along one of these points as well.

```
def moveHead():
    if key == 'up':
        head.sety(head.ycor() + size)
    if key == 'down':
        head.sety(head.ycor() - size)
    if key == 'left':
        head.setx(head.xcor() - size)
    if key == 'right':
        head.setx(head.xcor() + size)
```

Now, run the program and try to make the snake move (Figure 19-6). It will!

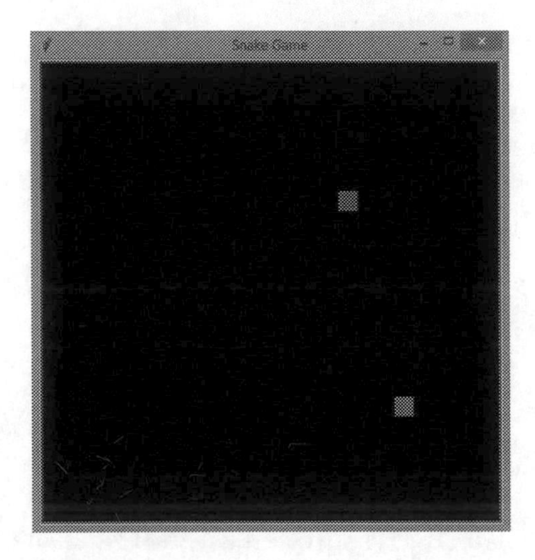

***Figure 19-6.** Move the snake head*

If you try to move it backward, it wouldn't. Why don't you try and see for yourself?

Get the scoreboard going

Now that our snake's head is moving around, we need to start scoring. Before we grow our snake every time it "ate" an apple, let's draw the scorecard at the top-right corner of the screen, so we can keep track of the code. Place this piece of code right below the code where you drew the first apple. Don't worry about the order. I'll paste the entire code in the right order at the end of the chapter.

I'll be creating another turtle for the scoreboard because I want it to "draw" the score while the other turtles are working. I'm positioning it at the point 120,120 (toward the top-right corner).

```
#Draw the score
sc = turtle.Turtle()
sc.speed(0)
sc.pencolor('White')
sc.penup()
sc.goto(120,220)
```

To start with, let's write 'Score:0' in Arial, 20 points, bold format. We'll be updating the value as the game progresses.

```
sc.write('Score:0',font=('Arial',20,'bold'))
```

Let's finally hide this turtle because we only need what it draws (unlike the "apple" and "snake" turtles).

```
sc.hideturtle()
```

Run the program, and you get this (Figure 19-7).

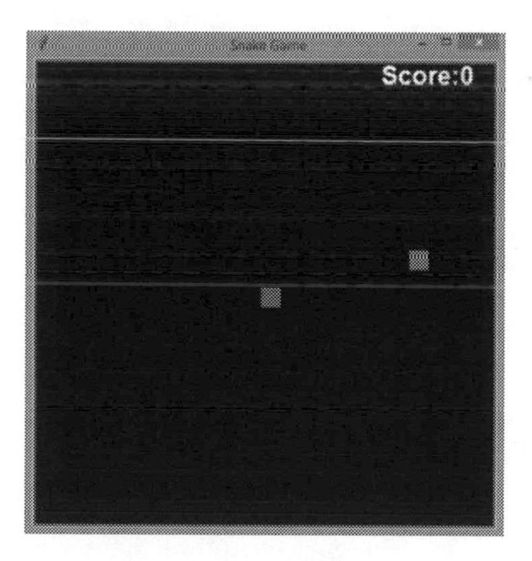

Figure 19-7. *Create the scoreboard*

Yep, we have our scoreboard! 😊 We're almost there, people!

Our snake's eating!

Now that we have our scoreboard done, let's make our snake eat. Right now, if our snake touches the apple, nothing happens. It'll just pass right by it. It won't grow and our apple won't disappear either.

Place the next few lines of code (before the function definitions) inside the "while loop", right after the s.update() method.

So, we're going to check the distance between our snake's "head" and apple. If that distance is less than or equal to 0, that is, if the snake head completely merges with the apple, then we want two things done:

1. A new apple drawn in another random position. We'll be creating a drawApple() function that does this.

2. One more body part added to the end of the snake. We'll be creating a new "turtle" as our head's body part(s). Let's create a drawSnake() function that does this.

Turtle has a distance() method that checks if an object is in a particular distance from another object. In our case, we're going to check if our object has no distance from the other object (completely superimposed).

```
#check for eating
if head.distance(apple) <= 0: #completely superimposed
    drawApple()
    #Create a new body part
    drawSnake() #keep the tail - old head
```

Let's also increase the value of score by exactly 1 and call the changeScore() method and send it the current value of score. This method will update the scorecard.

```
score += 1
changeScore(score)
```

Alright, that's it for our while loop (for now). We need to define three functions now (above the calling "while" loop): one to draw a new apple, one to change the score, and the next to draw the new snake body part since it has to grow (it just ate, didn't it?).

```
#Draw apple function
```

Follow the same procedure as before, when we drew our first apple, to get the next x and y coordinates, and move the "apple" turtle to that point. That's it!

```
def drawApple():
    aX = random.randint(-11,11)*20
    aY = random.randint(-11,11)*20
    apple.goto(aX,aY)
```

Now, let's draw our snake body part. We're going to create a new turtle every time our snake head eats an apple. So, every time our drawSnake() function gets called, a new turtle "sBody" is going to be created. It's going to be square in shape and green in color just like our snake "head". Let's also append the new part to the "snake" list.

```
#draw snake
def drawSnake():
    sBody = turtle.Turtle()
    sBody.speed(0)
    sBody.shape('square')
    sBody.color('Green')
    sBody.penup()
    snake.append(sBody) #insert at the end
```

Now, let's work on the changeScore method. Let's make the score "turtle" sc go back to its 120,220 position (starting position). Let's clear what's currently there using the clear() method, create a new string with the current score, and rewrite the text. Since the speed is 0, you won't see any of this happening in real time, so for our human eyes, it'll look like the scoreboard is updating itself seamlessly.

```
def changeScore(score):
    sc.goto(120,220)
    sc.clear()
    string = 'Score: {}'.format(score)
    sc.write(string,font=('Arial',20,'bold'))
    sc.hideturtle()
```

Let's run the program and try eating some apples (Figure 19-8).

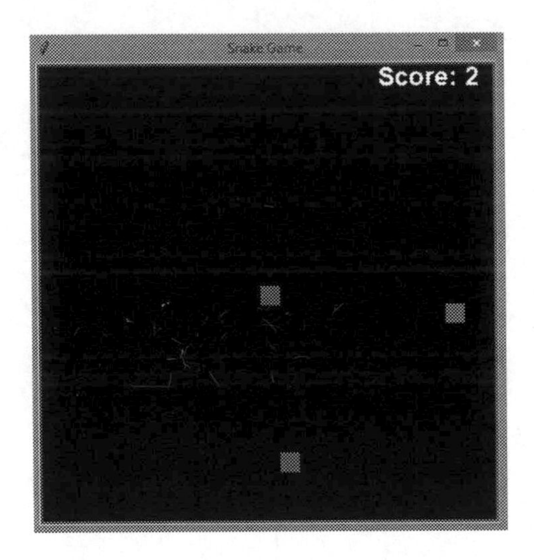

Figure 19-8. *Create new snake parts (snake eats)*

Well, the scoreboard seems to be updating properly. The apples do disappear and appear in a new position. And we do seem to get new "body parts" every time our snake eats, but they're not joined together, and they don't move together. And, it looks like the new body parts are appearing on top of each other (in the middle of the screen), so to our eye, we only see one body part, while there should be two by now (since the score is 2).

Why? Well, we haven't asked them to do that yet. As you know, in programming, you need to give detailed instructions for every little thing. So, let's do just that, shall we? 😊

Make the entire snake move

Let's update the while loop with a call to the moveBody(). This function will attach the snake body parts to the head and make the body parts move along with it.

Our while loop will look something like this once we're done:

```
while True:
    s.update()
    #check for eating
    if head.distance(apple) <= 0: #completely superimposed
        drawApple()
        #Create a new body part
        drawSnake() #keep the tail - old head
        score += 1
        changeScore(score)
    moveBody() #RIGHT HERE!
    moveHead()
    time.sleep(0.2)
```

Make sure the call to the moveBody() function is **BEFORE** the moveHead() function so they moves before the new head is drawn so it looks like actual movement.

Now, let's define the moveBody() function. We're basically going to switch coordinates.

Since we appended "head" at the start of the program, the 0th index of the "snake" list is going to have our "head" turtle, am I right? Then, we've appended other body parts, also turtles after the snake head. So, to simulate movement, we need these body parts to shift their coordinates.

Right now, only "Head" moves because that's the only code we've written (moveHead() function). So, every time "head" moves to a new coordinate, the body part right next to it (in the "snake" list) should move to the head's old coordinate. Now, the body part next to the first body part should move to the first body part's old position and so on until all the parts of the snake have shifted 20 pixels forward.

How can we make that happen? In programming, whenever you want to exchange values, you need a temporary variable that'll hold the old values.

So, we're going to create a temporary list temp that's going to store all the current x and y coordinates of the snake's body parts.

We're going to create a "for" loop that loops through the "snake" list to do this.

```
def moveBody():
    temp = []
    #create a list of the current positions
```

Let's store just the x and y coordinates of each snake part in one "item" of the list. We're going to create dictionaries within a list.

```
for i in snake:
    x = i.xcor()
    y = i.ycor()
    temp.append({'x': x, 'y': y})
```

Now that we have our temporary list, let's do our exchanges. We don't need to change the position of the item in the zeroth index (which is our head, which moves on its own), so let's create a for loop that loops from 1 through the length of the snake (1 – (len–1)), which is just the body parts.

```
#Move entire body
for i in range(1,len(snake)):
```

Since “temp” already has the “old” x and y coordinates of the entire snake (including the head), we’re just going to use that. So, let’s make the turtle in the ith position (starting at the first index) go to the x and y coordinates of the turtle in the i–1th position (which is our head, to start with).

That’s it! Since we used a dictionary to store our values in temp, we need to access them as such. So, the x value of the first item in “temp” would be temp[0]['x'] and so on.

```
snake[i].goto(temp[i-1]['x'],temp[i-1]['y'])
```

Let’s check if our snake moves now (Figure 19-9).

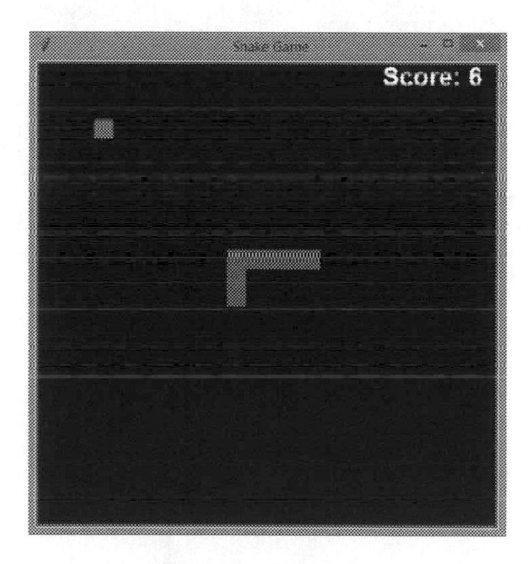

Figure 19-9. *Make the entire snake move*

It moves and grows perfectly. Whohoo! 😊

Now, for the final part of the game. Collision check!

Collision check

Before moving the head for the next time sleep, we need to do the collision check, so the next movement does not happen. We're going to call the checkCollision function, which is going to return a True if there's a collision, and if the result of the function call is indeed a True, we're going to break the game loop (while loop). The updated while loop is this:

```
while True:
    s.update()
    #check for eating
    if head.distance(apple) <= 0: #completely superimposed
        drawApple()
        #Create a new body part
        drawSnake() #keep the tail - old head
        score += 1
        changeScore(score)
    moveBody()
    moveHead()
    #Before moving the head for the next round, check for collision
    if checkCollision():
        break
    time.sleep(0.2)
```

If we place the collision check anywhere else, before the body moves, for instance, we might see inconsistencies in our game. For instance, try placing the collision check between moveBody() and moveHead(). This might seem logical at a first glance, but by doing this, you're creating a body, moving it, but then immediately checking for collision ***before*** you move the head. This will cause a body collision because right now your first body part and your head are in the same position.

So, let's move our snake completely, before checking for collision.

Now, let's define the collision check function. This function is going to load the global "key" variable because we are going to change it back to an empty string, so the movement stops temporarily.

We're also going to create a variable "collision" and make its default value False.

```
def checkCollision():
    global key
    collision = False
```

Let's check for wall collision first. It's quite simple, really. If the head's x or y coordinates are either greater than 240 or lesser than -240, then collision is True.

```
#wall collision
if head.xcor() < -240 or head.xcor() > 240 or head.ycor() < -240
or head.ycor() > 240:
    collision = True
```

Now, for body collision, let's loop through 1 to length of the snake list again (only the body parts, not the head). If the head's x and y coordinates are the same as the x and y coordinates of any of the snake's body parts, then a body collision has occurred, and collision is True again.

```
#body collision
for i in range(1,len(snake)):
    if head.xcor() == snake[i].xcor() and head.ycor() ==
    snake[i].ycor():
        collision = True
```

Finally, if collision is True, then make key an empty string again (pause movement). The game is essentially over. If collision wasn't True, then nothing will happen, and the next iteration of the "while" loop will continue.

```
if collision == True:
    key = '' #pause the movement
```

We need to do three things next:

1. Pause the program for 1 second so the user realizes that the game is over.
2. Move the snake (all its parts) and apple off the screen so it essentially "disappears".
3. Draw a "Game Over" message. We need a new turtle to do this. We're going to keep the scorecard so the user knows what they scored last.

```
time.sleep(1) #pause for a bit so user registers what happened
```

Let's loop through "snake" and move all its parts to 2000,2000 (essentially off the screen). Let's move apple to a farther position as well.

```
for s in snake:
    s.goto(2000,2000) #make it go off the screen
apple.goto(2500,2500)
```

We're going to create an ordinary *Turtle*, move it to the point -170,0 and draw 'GAME OVER' in white.

```
#game over message
game = turtle.Turtle()
game.penup()
game.goto(-170,0)
game.pencolor('white')
```

```
        game.write('GAME OVER!',font=('Arial',40,'bold'))
        game.hideturtle()
return collision
```

Finally, let's return collision back to the calling function. That's it! We've finished our game! ☺

Let's check if the collision works, shall we?

Let's check for wall collision first (Figure 19-10).

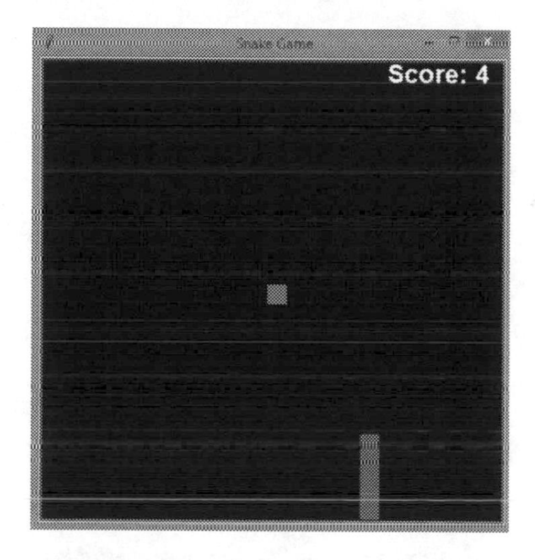

Figure 19-10. *Wall collision*

Yup, it works.

Now for body collision (Figure 19-11).

Figure 19-11. *Body collision*

That right there is a coiled-up snake!

And after the mentioned 1-second delay, everything disappears, and we're left with just the scoreboard and the "GAME OVER" message. If the user wants to play again, they'll have to run the program again (Figure 19-12).

Figure 19-12. *Game Over message*

Whew! That was long, but certainly worth it! I hope you had a lot of fun creating this game with me. I know I did! ☺

Entire code

Now, the entire code, as promised:

```
#import the required modules
import turtle
import time
import random

#setup the screen
s = turtle.Screen()
s.title('Snake Game')
s.bgcolor('Black')
s.setup(width = 500, height = 500)
s.tracer(0) #gets rid of animation

#create and assign the required variables
snake = []
size = 20
key = ''
score = 0

#Draw the head
head = turtle.Turtle()
head.speed(0)
head.shape('square')
head.color('Green')
head.penup()
head.goto(0, 0)
snake.append(head) #get the first head
```

```
#Draw the first apple
apple = turtle.Turtle()
apple.speed(0)
apple.shape('square')
apple.color('Red')
apple.penup()
#generate a random integer that's a multiple of 20
#multiples of 20 that doesn't go beyond the screen (250,-250)
aX = random.randint(-11,11)*20
aY = random.randint(-11,11)*20
apple.goto(aX,aY)

#Draw the scoreboard at the beginning
sc = turtle.Turtle()
sc.speed(0)
sc.pencolor('White')
sc.penup()
sc.goto(120,220)
sc.write('Score:0',font=('Arial',20,'bold'))
sc.hideturtle()

#Change the direction of the snake
def set_up():
    #so the global variable key can be used in a local
    context here
    global key
    if(key != 'down'):
        key = 'up'
def set_down():
    global key
    if(key != 'up'):
        key = 'down'
```

```
def set_left():
    global key
    if(key != 'right'):
        key = 'left'
def set_right():
    global key
    if(key != 'left'):
       key = 'right'

#Make the snake move based on the set direction
def moveHead():
    if key == 'up':
        head.sety(head.ycor() + size)
    if key == 'down':
        head.sety(head.ycor() - size)
    if key == 'left':
        head.setx(head.xcor() - size)
    if key == 'right':
        head.setx(head.xcor() + size)

#make the new snake body move (if the snake has grown)
def moveBody():
    temp = []
    #create a list of the current positions
    for i in snake:
        x = i.xcor()
        y = i.ycor()
        temp.append({'x': x, 'y': y})
    #Move entire body
    for i in range(1,len(snake)):
        snake[i].goto(temp[i-1]['x'],temp[i-1]['y'])
```

```
#Draw apple function
def drawApple():
    #generate a random integer that's a multiple of 20
    #multiples of 20 that doesn't go beyond the screen (250,-250)
    aX = random.randint(-11,11)*20
    aY = random.randint(-11,11)*20
    apple.goto(aX,aY)

#Create a new snake part
def drawSnake():
    sBody = turtle.Turtle()
    sBody.speed(0)
    sBody.shape('square')
    sBody.color('Green')
    sBody.penup()
    snake.append(sBody) #insert at the end

#Update the score
def changeScore(score):
    sc.goto(120,220)
    sc.clear()
    string = 'Score: {}'.format(score)
    sc.write(string,font=('Arial',20,'bold'))
    sc.hideturtle()

#Check for collision - wall & body
def checkCollision():
    global key
    collision = False
    #wall collision
    if head.xcor() < -240 or head.xcor() > 240 or head.ycor()
    < -240 or head.ycor() > 240:
        collision = True
```

```
    #body collision
    for i in range(1,len(snake)):
        if head.xcor() == snake[i].xcor() and head.ycor() ==
        snake[i].ycor():
           collision = True
    if collision == True:
        key = '' #pause the movement
        time.sleep(1) #pause for a bit so user registers
        what happened
        for s in snake:
            s.goto(2000,2000) #make it go off the screen
        apple.goto(2500,2500)
        #game over message
        game = turtle.Turtle()
        game.penup()
        game.goto(-170,0)
        game.pencolor('white')
        game.write('GAME OVER!',font=('Arial',40,'bold'))
        game.hideturtle()
    return collision

#Listen to the events and act on the required key presses
s.listen()
s.onkeypress(set_up,'Up')
s.onkeypress(set_down,'Down')
s.onkeypress(set_left,'Left')
s.onkeypress(set_right,'Right')

#The main game loop that keeps the game running
while True:
    s.update()
    #check for eating
```

```
    if head.distance(apple) <= 0: #completely superimposed
        drawApple()
        #Create a new body part
        drawSnake() #keep the tail - old head
        score += 1
        changeScore(score)
    #Move the body first, and then the head to the new position
    moveBody()
    moveHead()
    #Before moving the head for the next round, check for collision
#If there's a collision, stop the game loop - no more movement
    if checkCollision():
        break
    #A delay of 0.2 seconds before each movement
    time.sleep(0.2)

#Keep the screen open until the user closes it
s.mainloop()
```

Summary

In this chapter, we created a snake game with our *Turtle* package. We learned a bunch of new things, like using the time module to pause your program for a while, creating game loops, getting the positions of your turtles, moving your game characters, collision check, score keeping in a 2D game, and so much more.

In the next chapter, let's learn all about *Pygame*. We'll learn how to create simple 2D games in *Pygame*, which was created especially to make games.

CHAPTER 20

Become a Game Developer with *Pygame*

In the previous chapter, we created a snake game with *Turtle*.

In this chapter, let's learn get an introduction *Pygame*, a platform that's been extensively used for 2D game development. Let's learn all about creating our characters, using images as characters, setting up your screen and modifying it, making your characters move, collision detections, shooting bullets out of guns, scores, text, and so much more!

What is *Pygame*?

A. Elumalai, *Introduction to Python for Kids*, https://doi.org/10.1007/978-1-4842-6812-4_20

Pygame is a cross-platform platform that consists of multiple Python modules. It was designed for writing video games. It might seem simple when you get started, but once you go deep into it, it's quite powerful, and you can create anything from simple text-based games to complicated, sophisticated, multi-player world games with it.

In this chapter, let's learn the basics of *Pygame* because exploring the entire extent of its features and capabilities is beyond the scope of this small chapter.

Install and import *Pygame*

Anything that's beyond the standard Python code needs to be installed, am I right? That holds true for *Pygame* as well.

But the problem is unlike *Tkinter* and *Turtle, Pygame* doesn't come installed in your standard Python installation. So, you need to install it separately.

To install *Pygame* in your Python installation, go to your command prompt and to the folder in which you've done your Python installation (Figure 20-1).

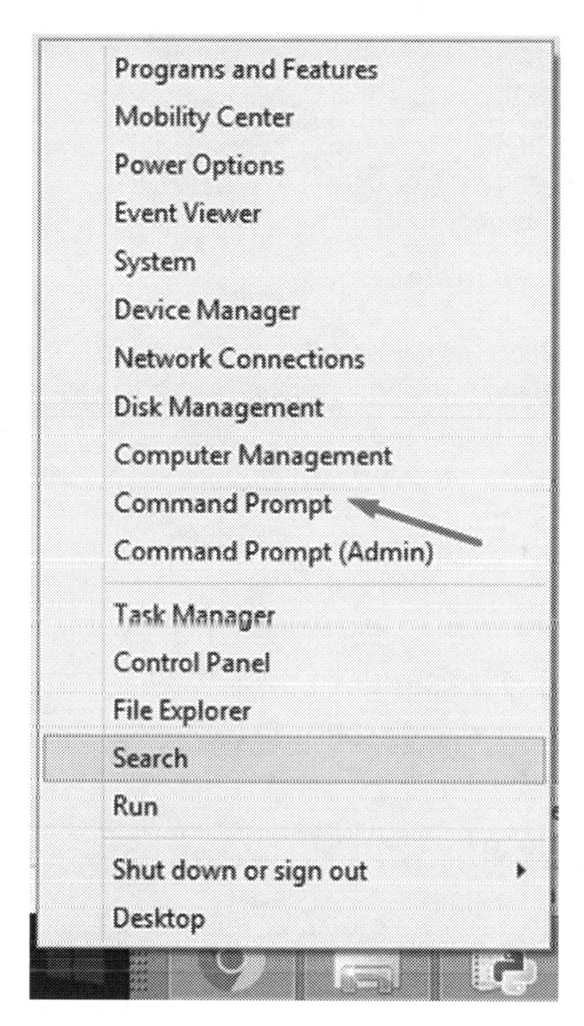

Figure 20-1. *Open command prompt*

In your command prompt, type the following:

```
pip install pygame
```

Press Enter and wait for a few seconds. You should get a message like this (Figure 20-2).

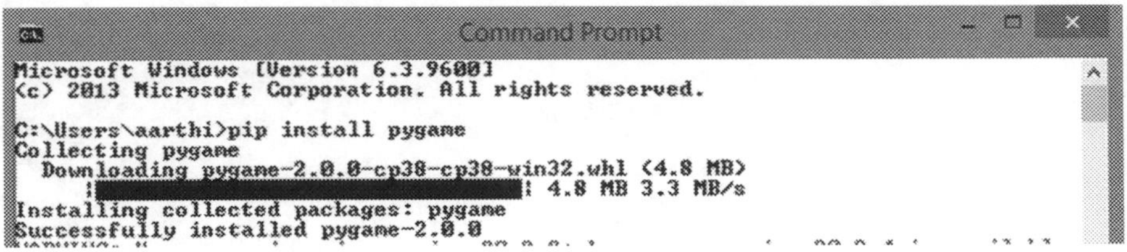

```
Command Prompt
Microsoft Windows [Version 6.3.9600]
(c) 2013 Microsoft Corporation. All rights reserved.

C:\Users\aarthi>pip install pygame
Collecting pygame
  Downloading pygame-2.0.0-cp38-cp38-win32.whl (4.8 MB)
     |████████████████████████████████| 4.8 MB 3.3 MB/s
Installing collected packages: pygame
Successfully installed pygame-2.0.0
```

Figure 20-2. *Install Python*

That's it! *Pygame* is installed in your system now. Let's use it in our program next. Open your Python Shell and create a new script. Name it whatever you want, just not pygame.

Unlike *Tkinter* and *Turtle,* you can't just import pygame and be done with it. You need to initialize the library as well. Use the init() method to do that. Your program wouldn't work until you initialize.

```
import pygame
pygame.init()
```

That's it! We've imported *Pygame,* and we're ready to go!

Set up your gaming screen!

What's the next step in creating a game? You've created many so far, so why don't you guess? Yes! A screen. We need a screen where everything happens.

Let's do that now. I'm going to define a variable "screen" (you can name yours anything you want) and use the display.set_mode method to create my screen with the dimensions I want.

You need to give the width and height of your screen inside a tuple or a list though. You'll get an error otherwise.

```
screen = pygame.display.set_mode((500,500))
```

Now, let's run our program and see what we get (Figure 20-3).

Figure 20-3. *Python window*

We have our screen. Whoo!

But try closing your screen, and you'll find that you can't. That's because unlike the other packages, *Pygame* needs special instructions to close your screen. So, we're going to comb through all the events happening on the screen, choose the event that corresponds to a left mouse button click on the "x" (close) button, and ask *Pygame* to "QUIT" when that click happens.

Simple enough? Let's do that!

As you know, every game needs a game loop. A never-ending loop that only ends when the game ends. *Pygame* is no exception. We're going to create a "while" loop that becomes false when the close button is clicked.

```
game = True
```

Now, we're going to use a "for" loop to comb through all the events happening on the screen. You can use the pygame.event.get() method to get a list of the events, and you can iterate through them. For every iteration, check if your event.type is pygame.QUIT (the close button click we're looking for). If it is, make "game" False so the while loop stops executing.

```
while game:
    for event in pygame.event.get():
        if event.type == pygame.QUIT:
            game = False
```

Once we're out of the game loop, we're going to use the pygame.quit() method to close the screen.

Now try closing the screen. Does it close? Yup! 😊

Make your screen pretty

Now, let's make our screen pretty! Why don't we start with changing the caption (title) of the screen?

You need to use the display.set_caption method to do that. Place these lines of code below the line where you created the screen (above the game loop).

```
pygame.display.set_caption('My first game')
```

Run the program, and see what you get (Figure 20-4).

***Figure 20-4.** Customize your screen*

Our title has changed!

Our screen is black in color right now. Why don't we change colors? To set our colors, we're going to be using RGB values.

R stands for Red, G stands for Green, and B stands for Blue. These three colors are called primary colors, and different shades and combinations of these three colors form the rest of the colors you see everywhere.

So, with these three values, we can come up with pretty much any color. The values go from 0 to 255 for each of the three colors, where 0 is an absence of any color and 255 is the presence of color.

Naturally, (0,0,0) is a complete absence of colors, which will give us black, and (255,255,255) is a complete presence of colors, which will give us white.

You can use the following website to find the RGB color codes of any shade you want to use in your program:

```
https://htmlcolorcodes.com/
```

There are plenty of other websites out there that give you the same information. Search for "color picker" or "rgb color codes" online to look them up.

Now that we've learned how colors work, let's fill our screen with red color. That'd be 255,0,0 (complete presence of just Red).

Inside the "while" loop, below the for loop where we look at the events, add the following lines of code:

```
screen.fill((255,0,0))
```

But if you run the program now, you won't see the change. Why is that? Well, the screen isn't being updated for every iteration. You need to use the display.update() method to update your screen.

```
pygame.display.update()
```

Now, run your program again, and you'll get this (Figure 20-5).

Figure 20-5. *Change screen background*

Our color has changed! Whoo! 😊

Create your characters on the screen

You can use the draw methods to draw lines, rectangles (or squares), circles, or polygons. These can be your game characters.

It's quite easy to draw a line. The syntax is as follows:

```
pygame.draw.line(screen,color,(x1,y1),(x2,y2),width)
```

You need to specify where you want the line drawn (the screen), the color (in RGB), the x and y coordinates of the starting and ending points of the line (each pair within a tuple), and, finally, the thickness of the line.

Let's try this in our program. Place this line of code above the display.update() method so the line gets updated to the screen:

```
pygame.draw.line(screen,(255,255,0),(50,50),(100,150),10)
```

Run the program, and you'll get this (Figure 20-6).

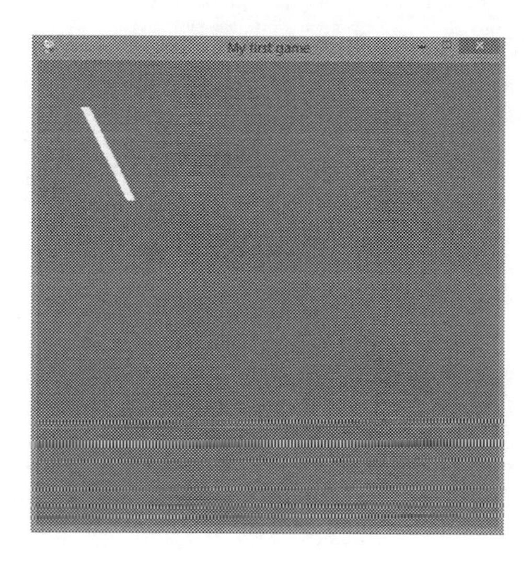

Figure 20-6. *Draw line*

We have our line in the exact position we wanted!

Next, let's look at a rectangle. The syntax is this:

```
pygame.draw.rect(screen,color,(x,y,width,height),outline)
```

We need to specify the x and y position of the top-left corner point of the rectangle and its width and height. If you mention the same width and height values, you'll get yourself a square. The final value mentions whether you want a fill or an outline. If you mention the outline as 0, you'll get a completely filled rectangle. Any other value will get an outline. Let me show you examples of both:

```
pygame.draw.rect(screen,(153,255,102),(100,200,100,100),0)
```

Run the program, and you'll get this (Figure 20-7).

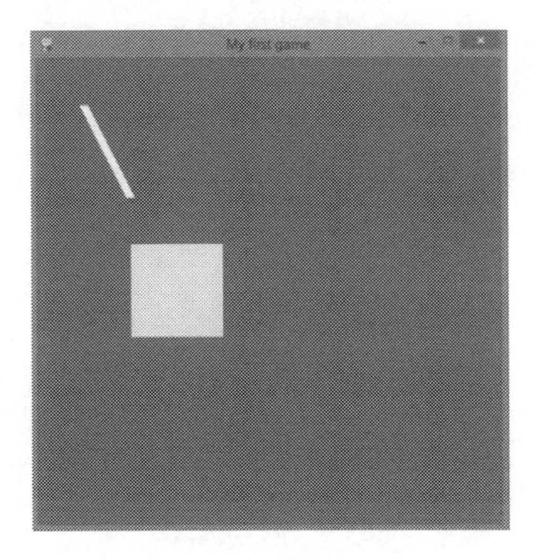

Figure 20-7. *Draw rectangle*

Now, let's give the outline as 50 (50% fill) (Figure 20-8).

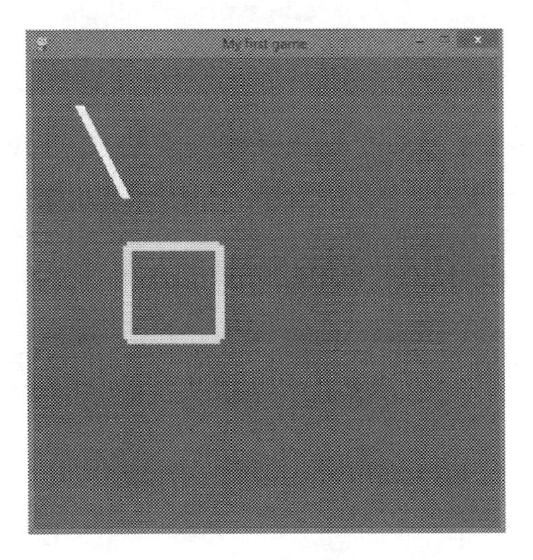

Figure 20-8. *50% fill*

Now, let's draw a circle. The syntax is this:

```
pygame.draw.circle(screen,color,(x,y),radius,outline)
```

The x and y points are the x and y coordinates of the circle's center. Then, mention the radius and the outline (if you don't need a complete fill).

```
pygame.draw.circle(screen,(0,102,255),(300,200),50,0)
```

Run the program, and you'll get this (Figure 20-9).

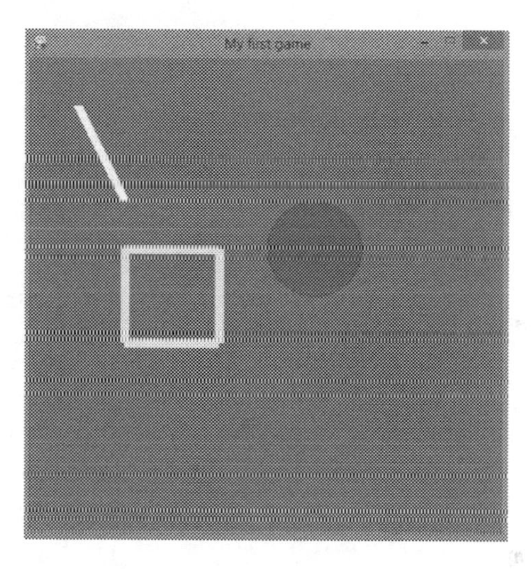

Figure 20-9. *Draw circle*

Nice! 😊

Finally, you can draw polygons (any number of lines).

```
pygame.draw.polygon(screen,color,((x1,y1),(x2,y2)...(xn,yn)))
```

Let's draw a triangle first.

```
pygame.draw.polygon(screen,(128,0,0),((150,350),(50,450),
(250,450)))
```

Maybe a five-sided polygon, next?

```
pygame.draw.polygon(screen,(253,0,204),((400,300),(300,300),
(350,450),(450,450),(450,350)))
```

Run the program, and you'll get this (Figure 20-10).

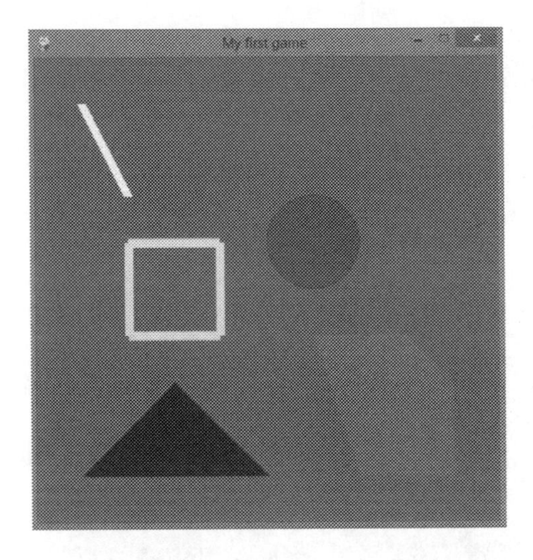

***Figure 20-10.** Draw polygons*

That's it for the shapes! Now, let's look at images.

Let's start from scratch for our images. It's a very simple process. You need to load your image (once, outside your game loop) and "blit" it inside the game loop in the exact coordinate you want it to appear in, so it gets updated on the screen.

Specify the exact path you have your image in. If you don't want to complicate things, place your image in the same folder as your Python file, and you'll just have to mention the name of the file, and be done with it. 😊

```
image = pygame.image.load('ball.png')
```

Then, use "blit" to display it on the screen.

```
while game:
    for event in pygame.event.get():
        if event.type == pygame.QUIT:
            game = False
    screen.fill((255,0,0))
    screen.blit(image,(200,150))
    pygame.display.update()
```

Run the program, and you'll get this (Figure 20-11).

Figure 20-11. *Draw images*

There you go! Our image is here. 😊

Move your characters

It's quite easy to move our characters. You just need to change the x and/or y coordinates of your character, and you're done. If you want continuous movement, keep changing it for every iteration of the game loop.

Let's try moving our ball, shall we?

I want it to move down, until it reaches the y value of 400 (since our image is of height 100, when its y reaches 400, its bottom will touch the screen), and then stop, okay? Let's do that.

Let's import pygame and time. We need the time module here because we're going to slow down our iterations so the human eye can see the movement of the ball.

```
import pygame
import time

pygame.init()
screen = pygame.display.set_mode((500,500))
image = pygame.image.load('ball.png')

game = True
```

We're going to create a "y" variable that holds the first value of 150.

```
y = 150
while game:
    for event in pygame.event.get():
        if event.type == pygame.QUIT:
            game = False
    screen.fill((255,0,0))
```

Let's blit the image.

```
screen.blit(image,(200,y))
```

As long as y is not 400, let's increment the y value by 1 for every iteration of the loop.

```
if y != 400:
    y += 1
```

Let's update the screen and make the program sleep for 0.005 seconds between every iteration of the loop.

```
    pygame.display.update()
    time.sleep(0.005)
pygame.quit()
```

That's it! Run the program (Figure 20-12), and you'll see a smooth downward movement until the ball touches the bottom end of the screen.

Figure 20-12. *Move your characters*

Keyboard press events

Alright, we can move our ball now. But what if we want to move it based on user input, maybe a keyboard press event?

Let's say I want to move my ball in all four directions based on which arrow key my user presses on their keyboard. How would I do that?

Remember the events we were looping through while looking for the QUIT event? We can use the same loop for our key press events too.

Look for the KEYDOWN event, which registers **only** when a key is pressed down while the user is on our game screen. You'll get a dictionary of events when you look for KEYDOWN. Get them in a variable. Let's name ours "keys".

To register the left arrow key, search for keys[K_LEFT]. If the value of this is true, move left (decrease x by 1).

To register the right arrow key, search for keys[K_RIGHT] and increase x by 1 if that's true.

To register the up arrow key, search for keys[K_UP] and decrease the y value by 1 if that's true.

To register the down arrow key, search for keys[K_DOWN] and increase the y value by 1 if that's true.

To get continuous movement, introduce directional variables, that'll continuously increment or decrement your x or y value based on the direction you've set.

Let's set a starting value for x and y and the directional variables at 0 because at the moment, our ball isn't moving.

```
x = 200
y = 150
xd = 0
yd = 0

while game:
    for event in pygame.event.get():
        if event.type == pygame.QUIT:
            game = False
```

Now, let's look for our events. If the user wants to set the direction to left, then xd should become -1, while yd stays the same. Follow the same logic for the rest of the directions.

```
    if event.type == pygame.KEYDOWN:
        if event.key == pygame.K_LEFT:
            xd = -1
            yd = 0
        if event.key == pygame.K_RIGHT:
            xd = 1
            yd = 0
        if event.key == pygame.K_UP:
            yd = -1
            xd = 0
```

```
        if event.key == pygame.K_DOWN:
            yd = 1
            xd = 0
screen.fill((255,0,0))
```

Now, before you blit the image and update the screen, add the xd and yd values to the current x and y values.

```
    x += xd
    y += yd
    screen.blit(image,(x,y))
    pygame.display.update()
    time.sleep(0.005)
pygame.quit()
```

Now, when you set a direction, the ball will continue to move in that direction until you change it (just like in our snake game).

But what if we only want the screen to move along with the keyboard presses. When we stop pressing on the arrow keys, we want the ball to stop moving.

There's a KEYUP event that'll help you with that. Inside the for loop, check if the KEYUP event has happened, and in an inner "if" statement, check whether the current events are either the LEFT, RIGHT, DOWN, or UP events.

If so, stop changing both the xd and yd values (make them 0), and you'll stop the movement.

```
if event.type == pygame.KEYUP:
    if event.key == pygame.K_LEFT or event.key == pygame.K_RIGHT
    or event.key == pygame.K_UP or event.key == pygame.K_DOWN:
        xd = 0
        yd = 0
```

That's it!

Mini project – bouncing ball

In this project, we're going to create a bouncing ball that bounces up and down the screen. When it hits either the top or the bottom of the screen, it should reverse direction and continue like that. Simple enough? Let's do this with pygame.

1. Let's import pygame and time to start with.

```
import pygame
import time
```

2. Then, let's initialize pygame and create our screen. It's going to be of width and height 500 each.

```
pygame.init()
screen = pygame.display.set_mode((500,500))
```

3. Now, let's create a variable y and make it 0 to start with. This is because with and up and down bounce, the only value that'll change is the y value.

```
y = 0
```

4. We also need a "game" variable that's currently True but will turn False when the user closes the screen.

```
game = True
```

5. Let's also create a directional variable "d" that'll be 1 by default. We're going to increment the y value of the ball by 1 (to move upward) and -1 (to move downward). This variable is going to change our ball's direction.

```
d = 1
```

6. Now, let's create our game loop.

```
while game:
```

7. To start with, let's create the quit condition. If the event type is pygame.QUIT, make game false.

```
for event in pygame.event.get():
    if event.type == pygame.QUIT:
        game = False
```

8. Then, let's fill our screen with white color.

```
screen.fill((255,255,255))
```

9. Then, let's use the draw.circle method to draw a red ball in the position 250,y (to start with, 250,0). Its radius is going to be 25 and is going to be a circle that's entirely filled, so 0 for the last attribute.

```
#draw a ball
    #circle draw function
    #where you want to draw it, color of the
    circle, position, width
    pygame.draw.circle(screen,(0,0,255),
    (250,y),25,0)
```

10. Let's use the display.update method to ensure that the screen gets updated every time the loop runs.

```
pygame.display.update() #update the screen
in the output window
```

11. If we leave the game as it is, our ball would move too fast to be seen by the human eye. So, let's slow the iterations of the loop down. There'll be a delay of 0.005 seconds after every iteration.

```
time.sleep(0.005)
```

12. Now, let's set the wall collision conditions. When y is 488 (since our ball has a diameter of 25, and we need the other half of the ball to be visible, we're setting it at 488 and not 500), let's reduce the value of y, because we need the ball to move up. So, d is going to be –1.

```
if y == 488:
    d = -1
```

13. If y is 12, then increase the value of y. "d" is going to be +1.

```
elif y == 12:
    d = 1
```

14. Finally, once we're out of the if elif statement, let's add "d" with the current value of "y".

```
    y += d
pygame.quit()
```

That's it! Run the program, and you'll have yourself a bouncing ball (Figure 20-13).

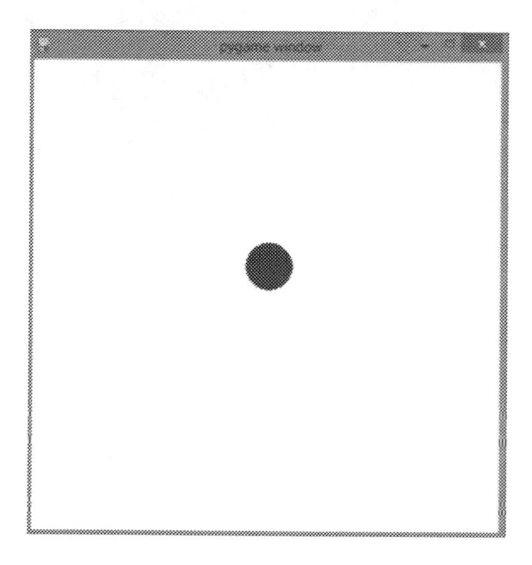

Figure 20-13. *Bouncing ball*

Summary

In this chapter, we learned the basics of pygame. We learned how to set our gaming screen, set up a game loop, create our characters (shapes and images), make them move, detect wall collision, and detect keyboard events.

In the next chapter, let's apply what we learned in this chapter, and a little more, to create a space invaders game!

CHAPTER 21

Project: Space Shooters with *Pygame*

In the previous chapters, we learned the basics of *Pygame*. We learned all about creating your game screen, closing the screen, beautifying it, creating your characters, moving your characters, and more.

In this chapter, let's apply what we've learned so far, and more, to create a space shooter game. You'll also learn how to create text and scorecards for your game.

Space shooter game

A. Elumalai, *Introduction to Python for Kids*, https://doi.org/10.1007/978-1-4842-6812-4_21

It's a very simple game. You have a spaceship that's more like a gun. It can move left or right when you press on your left and right arrow keys.

Then, you have your enemies. Three rows of enemies, totaling 21, and they'll move down towards that spaceship. If they hit the spaceship, game over!

To prevent that, the spaceship can shoot at the enemies. It has one bullet to shoot at a time. The bullet reloads after every shot (when it hits the enemy or the upper wall of the screen), so the spaceship can shoot again.

Every time the bullet hits the enemy, you gain a point and the enemy it hits disappears. If you finish killing all the 21 enemies, they'll reload, and you'll get a new set of 21 enemies in three rows. Start shooting again until you lose!

Look at that (Figure 21-1). The enemy is almost near, so we need to clear that row to stay alive. We've hit two enemies already, and our score is 2.

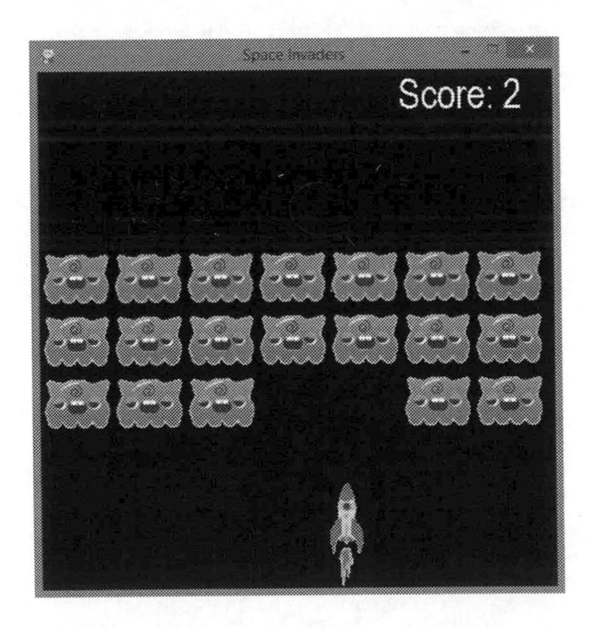

Figure 21-1. *Final game*

It's a simple enough game with a lot of potential for improvement (more levels, increased speed, more bullets, more enemies), so let's get started!

Import the required modules

We need the pygame module to create the game as such and the time module to slow down the characters enough that it's visible to the human eye.

```
import pygame
import time
```

Initialize everything

Let's initialize *Pygame* and its font package (to write the scoreboard).

```
pygame.init()
pygame.font.init() #To use text
```

Next, let's create our game screen and set the caption to 'Space Shooters.'

```
screen = pygame.display.set_mode((500,500))
pygame.display.set_caption('Space Shooters')
```

Let's also create a "font" variable that'll store the font we need used, which is font type "Arial" and size 40.

```
font = pygame.font.SysFont('Arial',40)
```

We need two game conditions: an "over" that turns True when the game is over (enemy hit the spaceship) and a "game" that turns False when the user closes the window.

```
over = False #Game over
game = True #Closed the game window
```

That's it! Let's run the program, and we get this (Figure 21-2).

Figure 21-2. *Game screen*

We have our screen! 😊

Game loop

Next, let's create our game loop.

```
while game:
```

Let's create the window "close" condition first. You already know how to create that.

```
#Close window condition - Quit
for event in pygame.event.get():
    if event.type == pygame.QUIT:
        game = False
```

Let's also fill the screen with black while we're at it. Of course, this wouldn't make much of a difference because the default color of a pygame screen is black.

```
screen.fill((0,0,0))
```

After the program is out of the game loop, close the window:

```
pygame.quit()
```

Don't worry about the code sequence. I'll paste the entire code in the order it should be written at the end of the chapter.

Now, run the program again and try to close the window. It'll work!

Create the spaceship

Now, let's create our spaceship and make it appear on the screen.

Place these lines of code above the game loop.

```
#Create the spaceship
```

I'm going to load the spaceship.png image I've gotten for this project. It's a nice little spaceship, pointing upward.

```
spaceship = pygame.image.load('spaceship.png')
```

Now, let's set preliminary positions for the spaceship. Mid-way horizontally, at an x position 250 and a y position of 390 (toward the bottom of the screen). Let's also set the direction at 0 as default. We can increase or decrease it later when we make the spaceship move.

```
sp_x = 250
sp_y = 390
sp_d = 0
```

To make the spaceship appear on the screen, in the game loop, below the for loop, include the following lines of code:

```
if over == False:
    screen.blit(spaceship,(sp_x,sp_y))
```

If the game is still true, then blit the image to the x and y coordinate positions we set.

Finally, update the display:

```
pygame.display.update()
```

Let's run the program, and we get this (Figure 21-3).

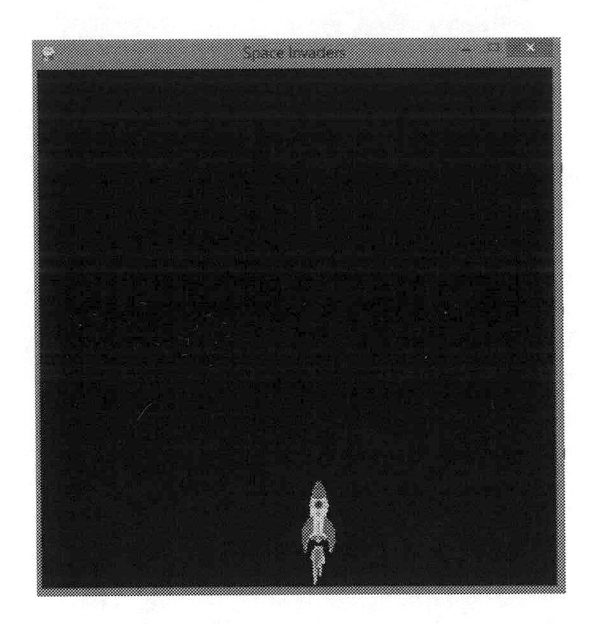

Figure 21-3. *Position your spaceship*

We have our spaceship. Yay! 😊

Move the spaceship

You already know how to make characters move, am I right? We need the following done:

1. Move the spaceship right or left depending on which arrow key is pressed.
2. When the user stops pressing on the arrow key, stop moving the spaceship.

We need to look for two events in this case: KEYUP and KEYDOWN.

Within KEYUP, we need to look for two keys: K_LEFT and K_RIGHT.

Let's go back to our game loop and the for loop where we iterated through all the events happening on the screen and include the next two conditions.

Look for the KEYDOWN condition, and if the key pressed in the "down" event is the left key (left arrow key), then decrease the space direction by 1, which means the spaceship will move toward the left (horizontally).

If the key pressed is the right arrow key, then increase the space direction by 1, which means the spaceship will move toward the right (horizontally).

```
if event.type == pygame.KEYDOWN:
    #Make spaceship move
    if event.key == pygame.K_LEFT:
        sp_d = -1
    if event.key == pygame.K_RIGHT:
        sp_d = 1
```

Now, let's make the spaceship stop moving if the arrow keys are let up. Let's look for a KEYUP event and check if the keys released are the left and the right arrow keys.

```
#Make spaceship stop if not moving
if event.type == pygame.KEYUP:
    if event.key == pygame.K_LEFT or event.key == pygame.K_RIGHT:
```

If they are, bring the spaceship direction back to 0, so there's no change in position, and it just stops where the user leaves it.

```
sp_d = 0
```

But we can't stop there. We need to add the sp_d value to the sp_x value, out of the for loop, if we want it to move for every iteration of the game loop.

```
#Spaceship move condition
sp_x += sp_d
```

Place the preceding lines of code above the spaceship blit and "update" lines of code.

Now, run the code and try moving the spaceship. Whoa! That was fast. I can't really control my spaceship. Why is that?

Well, we aren't spacing the game loop iterations, are we? Let's pause the program (game) 0.005 seconds after every iteration. Place this line of code above the "display" line of code.

```
time.sleep(0.005)
```

Now, run the entire program, try to move your spaceship left and right, and you'll get this (Figure 21-4).

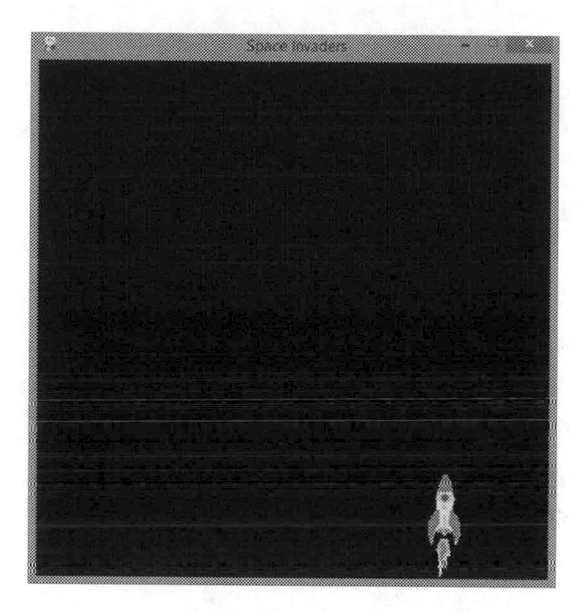

Figure 21-4. *Make spaceship move on arrow presses*

It works. Yes! ☺

Create and move the enemies

Now let's move the enemies! We need three rows of seven enemies, totaling 21. They're going to have the same properties (image), but the only difference is their positions.

Let's create lists that hold all of our values. One that holds the images so it can be blit in the game loop, one that holds all the "x" positions, one for all the "y" positions, and, finally, one for the enemy movement (direction).

```
#Create enemy
enemy = []
enemy_x = []
enemy_y = []
enemy_d = []
```

Let's also keep track of the number of enemies alive. The counter will start at 0 and increase by one for every enemy being shot down. When the number reaches 21, we're going to reset everything, draw three rows of new enemies again, and make them fall down to continue the game.

```
enemy_count = 0
```

Now, let's set the x and y positions for our enemies. We're going to create a for loop that runs from 0 to 20 (range of 21) for this.

For the first row (from iterations 0 through 6), the x positions are going to start at 0 and increase in multiples of 70 – 0, 70, 140, 210, 280, and so on.

The y positions are going to be at –60 (away from the screen, at the top), but still near the visible portion since this is the first row.

The distance value is going to be 0.5 throughout, for every enemy, because that's the speed at which they're all going to fall.

```
for i in range(21):
#Row 1
if i <= 6:
    enemy.append(pygame.image.load('enemy.png'))
    enemy_x.append(70 * i)
    enemy_y.append(-60)
    enemy_d.append(0.5)
```

Look at that! To create multiples of 70, I just multiplied 70 by "i" since "i" is going to take values from 0 through 6 anyway.

Now, the second row is a little tricky. We still need multiples of 70 for the x values, but we can't use "i" as it is again, because, for the second row, "i" is going to go from 7 through 13. So, let's subtract "i" by 7 while multiplying it by 70.

The y value for this set of enemies is going to be –120, a little behind the first row.

```
#Row 2
elif i <= 13:
    enemy.append(pygame.image.load('enemy.png'))
    enemy_x.append(70 * (i-7))
    enemy_y.append(-120)
    enemy_d.append(0.5)
```

Similarly, let's multiply 70 by i – 14 for the x value of the third, and last row, and place the y value at -180.

```
#Row 3
else:
    enemy.append(pygame.image.load('enemy.png'))
    enemy_x.append(70 * (i-14))
    enemy_y.append(-180)
    enemy_d.append(0.5)
```

That's it! We've positioned our enemies now. Let's make them appear and fall next.

Inside the game loop (while loop), and after you've "blit" the spaceship, let's create yet another "for" loop that runs 21 times (0 to 20).

Just like we did with our spaceship, we're only going to draw the enemies if the game is still not over.

We need to check for two conditions here:

1. If the enemy's "y" position is more than 500 (it has reached the end of the screen), then make it go back to a "y" of -60. That's enough. Why? Well, the first row will disappear first, then the second, and finally the third. Everything is continually moving too, so if we just move each row back to -60, the movement of the previous row will compensate for the appearance of the next row in the same point.

2. If the y position is not yet 500, then we need to move the enemy down. Add the enemy_d value to the enemy_y value and blit that particular enemy to the screen.

```
#Draw enemies and make them move
for i in range(21):
    if over == False:
        #enemy wall collision
        if enemy_y[i] >= 500:
            enemy_y[i] = -60
        else:
            #Draw enemies
            enemy_y[i] += enemy_d[i]
            screen.blit(enemy[i],(enemy_x[i],
            enemy_y[i]))
```

That's it! Our enemy should move now. Let's check (Figure 21-5).

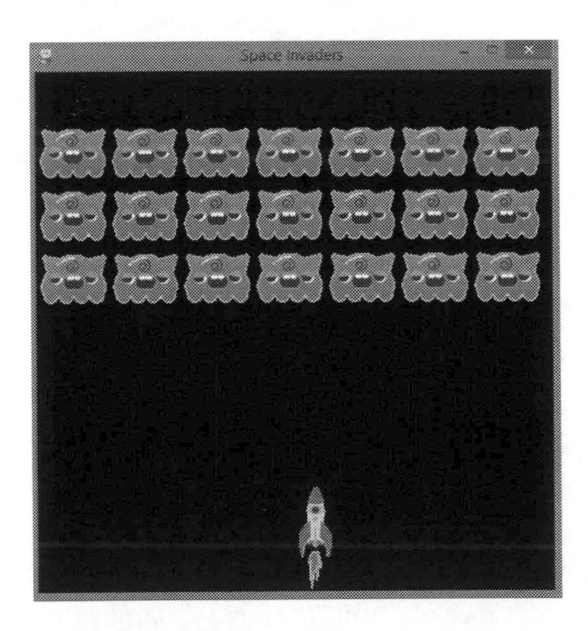

Figure 21-5. *Create the enemies*

Yes! We have three rows of moving enemies!

Fire the bullet

Next, let's fire the bullet. We need to do three things here:

1. Create the bullet outside the game loop, but not blit it until the user fires (presses the spacebar).
2. Check for the "space" press event inside the game loop (in the for loop that iterates through all the events, and inside the "if" statement where we did the KEYDOWN event check), and if it happened, set the bullet's x and y positions and change its direction.
3. Finally, outside the events "for" loop, but inside the game loop, blit the bullet to the screen (if it was fired). Let's also check for the wall collision while we're at it and bring the bullet back to its original position if it hits the wall.

Alright. Now that we know what we need to do, let's write the code for the same.

We're going to load the "bullet.png" image, and that's going to be our bullet. To start with, we're going to set the x and y position of the bullet at –100 so it's off the screen, unseen by the gamer. Let's also set the movement value, bullet_d, to 0 so there's no movement.

```
#create the bullet
bullet = pygame.image.load('bullet.png')
#place it off the screen to start with
bullet_x = -100
bullet_y = -100
bullet_d = 0
```

Finally, we're going to create a variable "fire" that's going to hold the state of the bullet. If the user has fired the bullet, this variable's value is going to change to True from False (its default value).

```
fire = False
```

Now, let's register the "space" key press. Go to the game loop, and inside the for loop where we iterate through all the events, look for the "if" statement where we registered the KEYDOWN event. Inside that statement, type the following:

Register the K_SPACE press event. As long as the "fire" value is False (bullet hasn't been fired previously), if the user clicks the space button, let's make the bullet move.

Make "fire" True now (because the bullet has been fired). Position the x and y values of the bullet to the current x and y values of the spaceship. Finally, make the bullet_d value -2, so it moves upward.

```
#Make bullet fire
if event.key == pygame.K_SPACE:
    if fire == False:
        fire = True
        bullet_x = sp_x
        bullet_y = sp_y
        bullet_d = -2
```

Now, let's blit the bullet.

Outside the for loop and above the code where we blit the spaceship, but after we've changed the spaceship's x value (so the new x value is assigned to the bullet), blit the bullet if "fire" is True and "over" is False (game is still live).

```
#Fire bullet
if fire == True and over == False:
```

We've set the x value to bullet_x+12 so it disappears behind the spaceship to start with.

```
screen.blit(bullet,(bullet_x+12, bullet_y))
```

Next, let's increase y value of the bullet by the bullet_d's value (decrease, in this case, since the bullet_d value would be -2).

```
bullet_y += bullet_d
```

Finally, let's check for wall collision. Once the bullet reaches the top of the screen (y is 0 or less), if the "fire" value is still True (still fired), let's change the x and y values of the bullet back to the x and y values of the spaceship and make the bullet_d value 0, so it starts moving. Let's also make the value of "fire" False so the bullet is no longer "blit" into the screen until it is fired again.

```
#bullet wall collision
if bullet_y <= 0 and fire == True:
    bullet_x = sp_x
    bullet_y = sp_y
    bullet_d = 0
    fire = False
```

Run the code, and you'll get this (Figure 21-6).

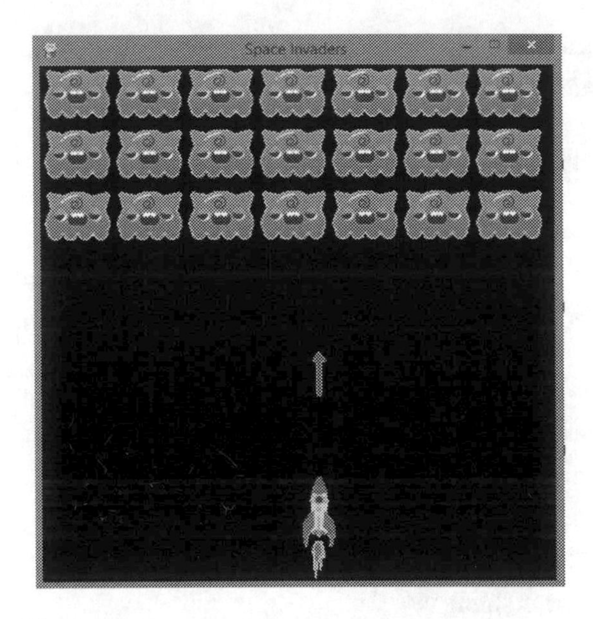

Figure 21-6. *Shoot the arrow*

Our bullet works now! 😊

Create and display the scoreboard

Now that we have all our characters, and they're moving as we want them to, let's create our scoreboard so we can display scores as we shoot at our enemies.

Let's create our scoreboard first.

```
#Create scoreboard
```

The value of "score" is going to be 0 to start with.

```
score = 0
```

Next, let's create another variable score_text that stores the string we want displayed when the game starts, which is Score: 0.

```
score_text = 'Score: {}'.format(score)
```

Finally, let's render this score_text using the "font" option in *Pygame*. The text color is going to be (255,255,255), which is white. This is RGB. We've already talked about that.

```
score_board = font.render(score_text,False,(255,255,255))
```

If we run the program now, we can't see anything because we haven't rendered the scoreboard inside the game loop yet. Let's do that now.

```
screen.blit(score_board,(350,0))
```

Place the preceding code above the time.sleep line of code.

Let's run our code, and we'll get this (Figure 21-7).

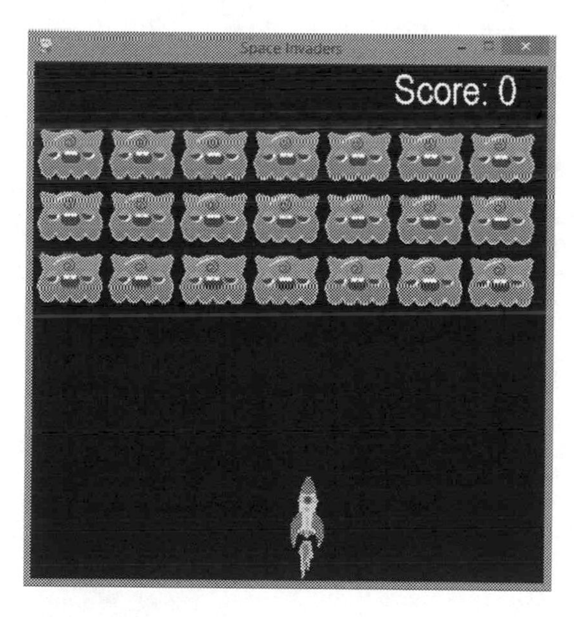

Figure 21-7. *Scoreboard*

We have our scoreboard, yay! 😊

Kill the enemies

Now, let's create the lines of code that kill the enemies when the bullet hits it. For every iteration of the loop, we're going to continuously look for collision between our bullet and all 21 of our enemies.

So, let's open a "for" loop to do that. Place this in the game loop, below where you "blit" all the enemies.

```
for i in range(21):
```

Now, we need the collision condition. It's going to be pretty simple. If the distance between the bullet and the enemy (the top-left-most corner position) is less than or equal to 55, we have a collision. This'll cover the bullet hitting any point from the top-left-most corner to the rest of the parts of the enemy.

To do this, let's subtract the coordinates of the bullet (which are higher since they are at the bottom of the screen) from the coordinates of the enemy. Let's get the absolute value of this subtraction so that no matter where the two characters are, we just get the "difference" value we need, without the sign.

```
if abs(bullet_x+12 - enemy_x[i]) <= 55 and abs(bullet_y -
enemy_y[i])
```

Why bullet_x+12? That's because we "blit" the bullet at that "x" point.

If there's a collision, we need to bring the bullet back to position and make the bullet movement value, bullet_d, 0.

```
#bring bullet back to position
bullet_x = sp_x
bullet_y = sp_y
bullet_d = 0
```

Let's also make "fire" False because we're done firing the bullet. It did what we sent it to do.

```
fire = False
```

Now, within the same "if" statement, let's open more if and else statements to bring that enemy back to position (and not move). It'll just wait in that position until all the enemies in the current set are killed so the three rows of enemies are formed again.

Remember the conditions we used while positioning the enemies? Let's use the same to position them now so they'll be ready to go once all 21 enemies have been killed.

```
#bring enemy back to position
if i < 7:
    enemy_x[i] - 70 * i
    enemy_y[i] = -60
elif i < 14:
    enemy_x[i] = 70 * (i-7)
    enemy_y[i] = -120
else:
    enemy_x[i] = 70 * (i-14)
    enemy_y[i] = -180
```

Finally, let's make the enemy movement value 0, to stop its movement (waiting for the rest to join it), and increase the enemy_count by 1.

```
enemy_d[i] = 0
enemy_count += 1
```

What happens when the bullet hits an enemy? The enemy dies and goes back to its original position. The bullet also goes back to its original position, but the score increases as well!

Let's do that next. Let's increase the score and render it again.

```
#increase score
score += 1
score_text = 'Score: {}'.format(score)
score_board = font.render(score_text,False,(255,255,255))
```

That's it! We can kill enemies now. Let's see if it works, shall we? (Figure 21-8)

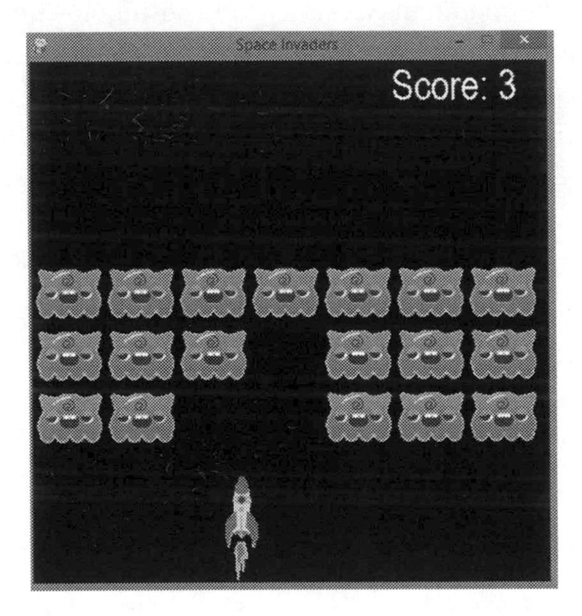

***Figure 21-8.** Kill the enemies*

Whohoo! We can kill our enemies now, and our score increases accordingly! 😊

Kill the spaceship!

Finally, let's create a collision condition for the spaceship and the enemies, so we can end the game. Place these lines of code below the code where you wrote the enemy-bullet collision lines of code.

The process is the same. For every iteration of our game loop, we're going to loop through all the enemies and check if one of them hit our spaceship.

```
#Enemy-spaceship collision
for i in range(21):
```

The collision condition is going to be a difference between the x and y values of the spaceship and the enemies, and if they are less than or equal to 50, game over.

```
if abs(sp_x - enemy_x[i]) <= 50  and abs(sp_y - enemy_y[i]) <= 50:
    #game over
```

Make "over" True. If over is True, then we won't blit the spaceship and the enemies (not to mention the bullet) to the screen, remember? That means they'll disappear from the screen and we'll be left with just the scoreboard.

```
#make everything disappear
over = True
```

Let's try that now (Figure 21-9).

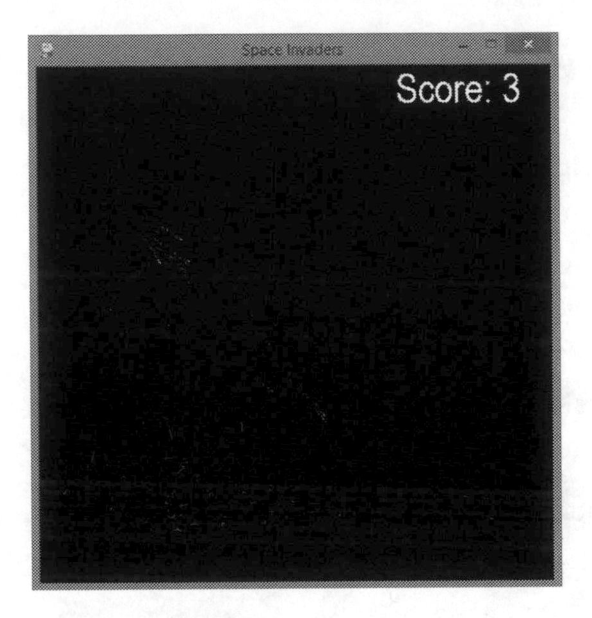

Figure 21-9. *Kill the spaceship*

Yup, it works! 😊

Re-draw the enemies

After the collision checks, we need to check if the user is done killing all the enemies. If all 21 are gone from the screen, we need to reset the enemy_count value back to 0 and make them fall from the top of the screen again.

```
#Set enemy move condition
if enemy_count == 21:
    for i in range(21):
        enemy_d[i] = 0.5
    enemy_count = 0
```

Let's run the program, and check if this works (Figure 21-10).

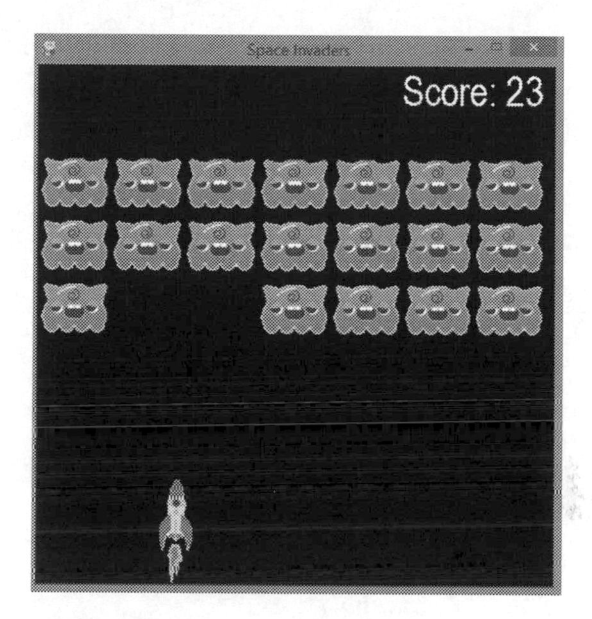

Figure 21-10. *Re-draw the enemies*

Look at that! We got our second row of enemies, and our score is 23 now! :O

Game over!

Finally, let's write "GAME OVER" when the enemy hits the spaceship. Write "GAME OVER" when "over" is True, which means there's been a collision.

```
#Game over
if over == True:
    #Draw game over text
```

Let's create a new game_over_font and make it font type Arial and font size 80. Let's render that font over our desired text. Make the color white. Finally, "blit" it into the screen in the position 50,200 (around the center of the screen).

```
game_over_font = pygame.font.SysFont('Arial',80)
game_over = game_over_font.render('GAME
OVER',False,(255,255,255))
screen.blit(game_over,(50,200))
```

Let's run our code, and we get this (Figure 21-11).

Figure 21-11. *Game over screen*

Whohoo! Our game's over! 😊

It was quite simple, wasn't it? Try it out, and maybe try improving it (more levels, more difficulty, etc.).

Entire code

Now, here's the entire code, as promised:

```
import pygame
import time

pygame.init()
pygame.font.init() #To use text

screen = pygame.display.set_mode((500,500))

pygame.display.set_caption('Space Invaders')

font = pygame.font.SysFont('Arial',40)

over = False #Game over
game = True #Closed the game window

#Create the spaceship
spaceship = pygame.image.load('spaceship.png')
sp_x = 250
sp_y = 390
sp_d = 0

#Create enemy
enemy = []
enemy_x = []
enemy_y = []
enemy_d = []

enemy_count = 0
```

```
#Position enemies - 3 rows of enemies
for i in range(21):
    #Row 1
    if i <= 6:
        enemy.append(pygame.image.load('enemy.png'))
        enemy_x.append(70 * i)
        enemy_y.append(-60)
        enemy_d.append(0.5)

    #Row 2
    elif i <= 13:
        enemy.append(pygame.image.load('enemy.png'))
        enemy_x.append(70 * (i-7))
        enemy_y.append(-120)
        enemy_d.append(0.5)

    #Row 3
    else:
        enemy.append(pygame.image.load('enemy.png'))
        enemy_x.append(70 * (i-14))
        enemy_y.append(-180)
        enemy_d.append(0.5)

#create the bullet
bullet = pygame.image.load('bullet.png')
#place it off the screen to start with
bullet_x = -100
bullet_y = -100
bullet_d = 0
fire = False
```

```
#Create scoreboard
score = 0
score_text = 'Score: {}'.format(score)
score_board = font.render(score_text,False,(255,255,255))

while game:
    #Close window condition - Quit
    for event in pygame.event.get():
        if event.type == pygame.QUIT:
            game = False

        if event.type == pygame.KEYDOWN:
            #Make spaceship move
            if event.key == pygame.K_LEFT:
                sp_d = -1
            if event.key == pygame.K_RIGHT:
                sp_d = 1
            #Make bullet fire
            if event.key == pygame.K_SPACE:
                if fire == False:
                    fire = True
                    bullet_x = sp_x
                    bullet_y = sp_y
                    bullet_d = -2
        #Make spaceship stop if not moving
        if event.type == pygame.KEYUP:
            if event.key == pygame.K_LEFT or event.key ==
            pygame.K_RIGHT:
                sp_d = 0

    screen.fill((0,0,0))
```

```
    #Spaceship move condition
    sp_x += sp_d

    #Fire bullet
    if fire == True and over == False:
        screen.blit(bullet,(bullet_x+12, bullet_y))
        bullet_y += bullet_d

    #bullet wall collision
    if bullet_y <= 0 and fire == True:
        bullet_x = sp_x
        bullet_y = sp_y
        bullet_d = 0
        fire = False

    if over == False:
        screen.blit(spaceship,(sp_x,sp_y))

    #Draw enemies and make them move
    for i in range(21):
        if over == False:
            #enemy wall collision
            if enemy_y[i] >= 500:
                enemy_y[i] = -60
            else:
                #Draw enemies
                enemy_y[i] += enemy_d[i]
                screen.blit(enemy[i],(enemy_x[i],enemy_y[i]))

        #Bullet-enemy collision
    for i in range(21):
        if abs(bullet_x+12 - enemy_x[i]) <= 55 and
        abs(bullet_y - enemy_y[i]) <= 55:
            #bring bullet back to position
```

```
            bullet_x = sp_x
            bullet_y = sp_y
            bullet_d = 0
            fire = False

            #bring enemy back to position

            if i < 7:
                enemy_x[i] = 70 * i
                enemy_y[i] = -60
            elif i < 14:
                enemy_x[i] = 70 * (i-7)
                enemy_y[i] = -120
            else:
                enemy_x[i] = 70 * (i-14)
                enemy_y[i] = -180

            enemy_d[i] = 0
            enemy_count += 1

            #increase score
            score += 1
            score_text = 'Score: {}'.format(score)
            score_board = font.render(score_text,False,
            (255,255,255))

    #Enemy-spaceship collision
    for i in range(21):
        if abs(sp_x - enemy_x[i]) <= 50  and abs(sp_y -
        enemy_y[i]) <= 50:
            #game over
            #make everything disappear
            over = True
```

```
    #Set enemy move condition
    if enemy_count == 21:
        for i in range(21):
            enemy_d[i] = 0.5
        enemy_count = 0

    screen.blit(score_board,(350,0))

    #Game over
    if over == True:
        #Draw game over text
        game_over_font = pygame.font.SysFont('Arial',80)
        game_over = game_over_font.render('GAME OVER',
        False,(255,255,255))
        screen.blit(game_over,(50,200))

    time.sleep(0.005)

    pygame.display.update()

pygame.quit()
```

Summary

In this chapter, we created a space shooter game with *Pygame*. We applied what we learned in the previous chapter in our game, and we also learned all about collision detection and rendering text on our game screen.

In the next chapter, let's look at an overview of web development with Python. We'll get a brief look at creating web pages with HTML, designing them with CSS, making them dynamic with JavaScript, and creating your very first program in Python's very own *Flask*.

CHAPTER 22

Web Development with Python

In the previous chapter, we learned how to create a space shooter with *Pygame*. We learned all about shooting at characters, collision detection, rendering text on a *Pygame* screen, and so much more.

In this chapter, let's look at web development with Python. Let's have a brief look at creating websites with HTML, CSS, and JavaScript and creating your very first program with Python's *Flask*.

Python and web development

A. Elumalai, *Introduction to Python for Kids*, https://doi.org/10.1007/978-1-4842-6812-4_22

What is web development? Do you visit websites? Facebook, Netflix, Amazon, and so on? Anything that you use online comes under web development.

They are created and maintained with their own unique set of technologies that fall under web development. How does that work, and where does Python come in here?

Well, before we get into that, let's talk a little bit about the staple technologies of web development. There's HTML, CSS, and JavaScript.

HTML is the building block of a website. What does that mean? Well, everything you see online was created by HTML. The images, the text, the buttons, everything came from HTML.

Now CSS styled all of it. It's called "Cascading Style Sheet", and the elements (building blocks) that you create with HTML can be designed (colored, aligned, etc.) using CSS. JavaScript makes everything dynamic. When you click a button on a site, something happens right? Maybe another site opens up, or maybe you just get a popup that gives you some information. JavaScript lets you do things like that on your site.

But what about Python? Where does it come in web development? To understand Python's role in web development, you need to understand the difference between front-end and back-end web development.

Front-end web development is what we talked about just now: HTML, CSS, JavaScript, and all together we get the user-facing end of your website; that is, what the user sees.

Back-end web development is just the opposite. It's what the user does not see: server-side development. Most applications need a lot of information transfer and retrieval, am I right? You have an account on a site, and when you log in to that site, your account detail should be retrieved. You search for something on Google, and they give you a list of related websites that pertain to your search.

All of this information retrieval and transfer (you send a chat message or email to someone) comes under back-end web development, and you need to use a back-end technology like Python to make that possible.

Python has a "file" feature, remember? That's just the start. You can create databases and connect them to your web applications and so much more with the help of Python.

Let's quickly look at what each of these technologies has to offer us. This is not a comprehensive chapter. Web development, especially full-stack web development, is a huge topic that requires a book of its own to cover completely. I'm just going to give you some examples of how each of these technologies works to give you an idea. If you're interested in the subject, you can choose to read up on it in the future.

Building blocks – HTML

As I told you earlier, HTML, which stands for Hyper Text Markup Language, is used to create the building blocks of your web applications. You can write your HTML code in notepad (or notepad++), but when you save the file, save it as filename.html or filename.htm, and not filename.txt.

A HTML code has two parts, a head and a body. The "head" contains the code that's not visible to the user, like the title, while the "body" contains all the visible parts of the page, like the paragraphs, images, and buttons.

Let's create a simple HTML file now. Open a notepad, and maybe name your file website.html, or anything you want to name it as. While you save your file as a html file, you'll notice the icon changing from a notepad icon to your default browser's icon.

```
<!DOCTYPE html>
<html>

</html>
```

The preceding code is the skeleton of a html file. A HTML code contains tags, some of them empty and some of them with starting and ending tags (the ones that are written like this: </tag>). `<!DOCTYPE html>` specifies that we're using HTML5, the latest version of HTML, in our code.

<html>...</html> is the root tag. It encompasses the entire code.

```
<!DOCTYPE html>
<html>
        <head>

        </head>

        <body>

        </body>
</html>
```

So, that's your head and body tag. Now, let's add a title inside our <head> tag.

```
<!DOCTYPE html>
<html>
        <head>
                <title>My first website</title>
        </head>

        <body>

        </body>
</html>
```

Open the file in your browser, and you'll see the screen shown in Figure 22-1.

Figure 22-1. *Basic HTML website*

We have our title. Perfect!

If you want to add text or elements, you need to use the <body> tag. Let me quickly list some of the important tags so we can use them in our website.

`<h1> </h1>` is used to create primary headings.

`<h2> </h2>` is used to create sub-headings.

You can create more headings that decrease in size (h3, h4, h5, h6), but the commonly used ones are h1 and h2.

`<p> </p>` is used to create paragraphs.

`<button> </button>` is used to create buttons.

`<a> </a>` is used to create the hyperlinks (linking to other websites and pages) you see online.

`<img>` is used to create images. It's an empty tag, but it'll take attributes to specify the image location.

So, that's enough for now, I guess. Let's use them in our program. Let's create an introduction page for Susan.

```
<body>
        <h1>My introduction</h1>
        <p>Hello there! I'm Susan. I'm 8 years old. I have a
        puppy named Barky. I love him so much! :) </p>
        <button>Click Me!</button>
        <a href='google.com'>Look me up!</a>
        <img src='susan.png'>
</body>
```

We've created a heading, a paragraph (you can create more if you want), a button (doesn't work yet, but it's been created), and a link to Google (you can link anywhere you want), and finally, we've displayed Susan's pic.

Let's open our website now, and we see this (Figure 22-2).

Figure 22-2. *Various elements added to our website*

We have the makings of our web page! Of course, the button doesn't work (wait for JavaScript), and things aren't pretty yet (CSS!), but we have our building blocks! 😊

Pretty things up – CSS

If you want to pretty things up: add colors, align things, and so on, you need CSS. But CSS is a vast topic, so I won't be covering everything here. Let me just show you a bunch of examples.

To write your CSS stylings, you need to open and close a <style> tag inside the <head> tag.

Call the element you want styled, and mention the style attributes and values within it, like background color: blue, like that. You need to end every attribute-value pair with a semicolon, unlike Python's lines of code where the indent (or the next line) marks the end of a line of code.

Let's change the background color of our entire page light gray. We're going to call the html element (the entire page) for that (Figure 22-3).

Figure 22-3. *Add background color*

Next, let's change the heading color to dark green and the paragraph color to dark red. You need to use the "color" attribute to do that.

```
<head>
      <title>My first website</title>
      <style>
            html {
                    background-color: lightgray;
                 }

            h1 {
                    color: darkgreen;
               }

            p {
                    color: darkred;
              }
      </style>
</head>
```

Refresh your web page, and you'll see this (Figure 22-4).

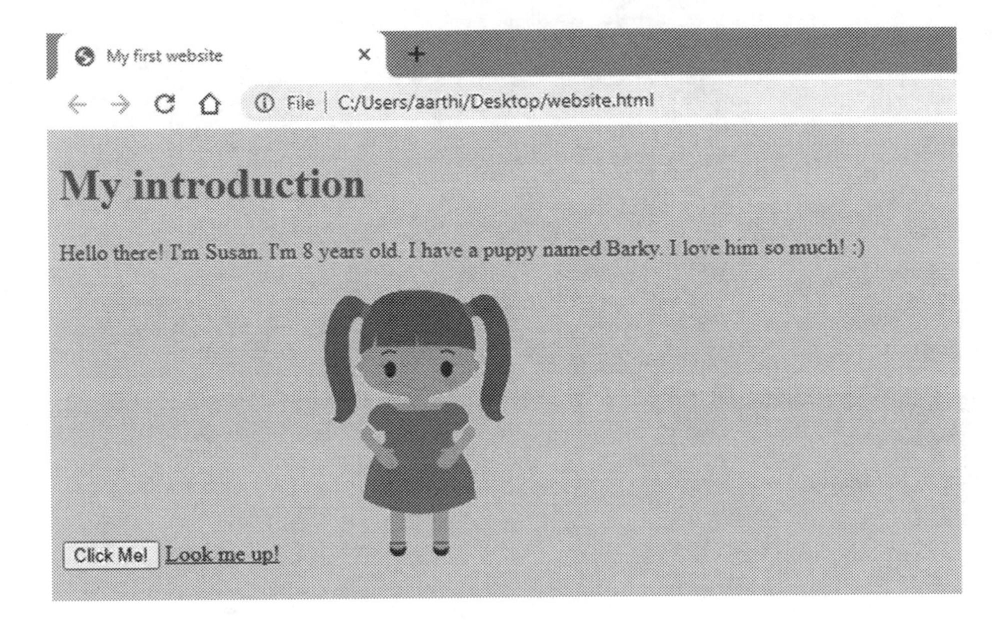

Figure 22-4. *Customize (design) your website with CSS*

So that's basic CSS. As I said, it's a vast topic, so I can't cover it completely in here.

Front-end dynamic – JavaScript

Let's try to make our button dynamic in this section. JavaScript is a scripting language, just like Python. The only difference is that JavaScript is used in the front end and Python is used in the back end.

You can use the `<script></script>` tag to write your JavaScript code, usually within the <body> tag, so the entire website loads before the dynamic features are loaded.

```
<body>
        <h1>My introduction</h1>
        <p>Hello there! I'm Susan. I'm 8 years old. I have a
        puppy named Barky. I love him so much! :) </p>
        <button>Click Me!</button>
        <a href='google.com'>Look me up!</a>
        <img src='susan.png'>

        <script>

        </script>
</body>
```

JavaScript has variables, numbers, strings, Booleans, if else statements, for and while loops, objects, and lot of other concepts that we've just covered in Python. But there are differences between the two languages, especially in the syntax and how these are written or used. We won't be looking at all of them here, but let's just look at a couple.

You can create variables using the keyword "let".

```
let variableName;
```

Just like with CSS, every line of code in JavaScript needs to end with a semicolon.

You can assign values to these variables as well. But let's not look at the mundane stuff. Let's look at the true power of JavaScript, which is manipulating your HTML elements (changing their styles, making them do things, etc.) right from within your JavaScript code.

To do that, let me first assign a unique "id" to my element, like this:

```
<button id='btn'>Click Me!</button>
```

This is a unique id and can't be assigned to any other element. I can use this id to style this specific element or to retrieve it using JavaScript, like this:

```
<script>
    let button = document.getElementById('btn');
</script>
```

I've created a variable "button", and I've retrieved the element with the id "btn" from my document (HTML document) and placed it inside the variable. JavaScript is case sensitive, so the capital letters should be retained as such.

Now, I can listen for events in this element. Shall we listen for a "click" event? Shall we make an alert box (just like the message box in *Tkinter*) pop up whenever you click the button?

You need to add an event listener on the element that you just retrieved. This listener will listen for the "click" event and call the buttonClick() function when the event happens.

```
<script>
    let button = document.getElementById('btn');
    button.addEventListener('click',buttonClick);
</script>
```

Now, define the function above the call. In JavaScript, we don't use "def", we use "function" to define a function. To create an alert, use something like this: alert('Your message');

```
<script>
    let button = document.getElementById('btn');
    function buttonClick() {
    alert("Hello there! I'm Susan!");
    }
    button.addEventListener('click',buttonClick);
</script>
```

Now, let's refresh our page and see if our button works (Figure 22-5).

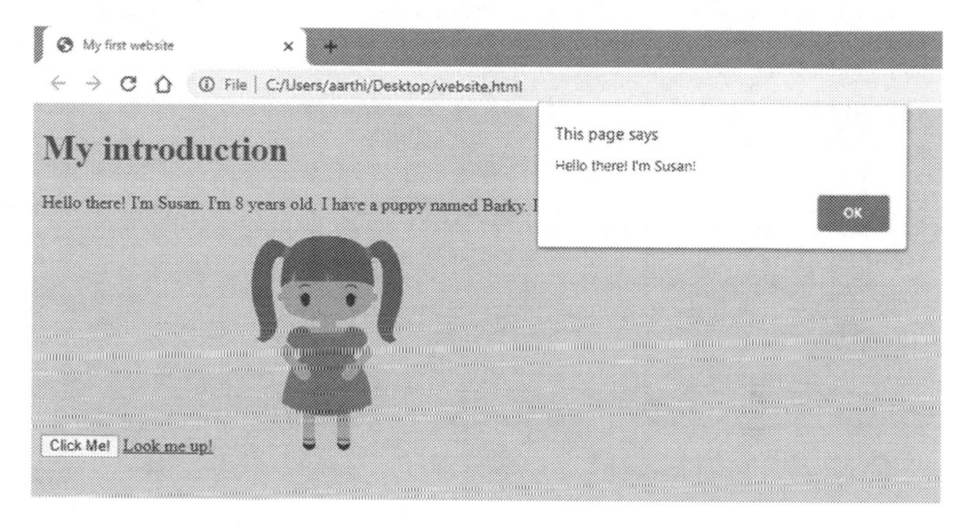

Figure 22-5. *Make websites work with JavaScript*

Look at that! I clicked my button, and an alert box popped up, with the message "Hello there! I'm Susan!". Perfect, isn't it? 😊 That's the power of JavaScript.

Python's *Flask*

To create the back end with Python, you're better off using a framework. We've already looked at Python's packages and libraries like *Turtle*, *Tkinter*, and *Pygame*. We know how useful they are and how much they enhance the original Python code. The same goes for the web frameworks.

The most famous ones are Django and *Flask*. Let's look at a brief example of *Flask* before ending this chapter. You can't use *Flask* as such. You need to install it.

To install it, open your command prompt, and type the following:

```
pip install Flask
```

Press enter and wait for some time. You should get a success message like this (Figure 22-6).

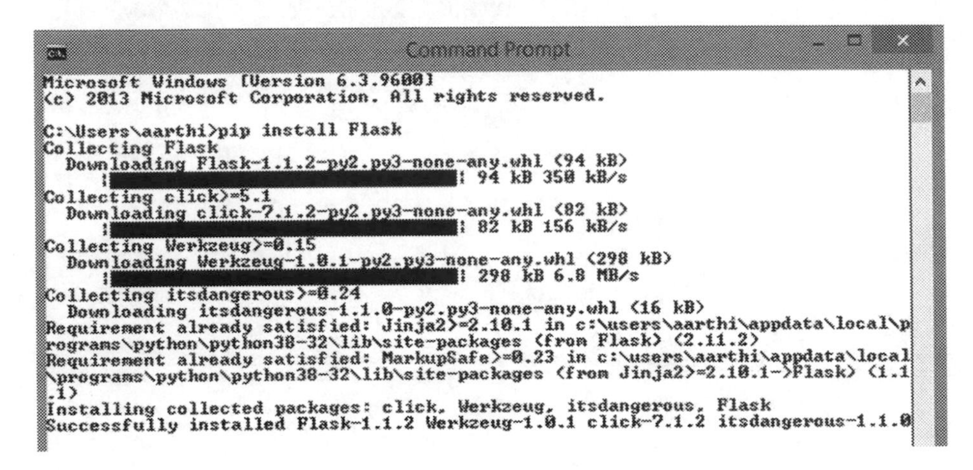

Figure 22-6. *Install Flask*

Now, let's create a simple program that displays our introductory message on screen. Open a script and name it. Let's name ours hello.py. Start by importing the *Flask* class from our "flask" framework.

```
from flask import Flask
```

Then, let's create an instance of that class in the variable "app".

```
app = Flask(__name__)
```

Now, we need to create a route. We want our page to appear on the "root" of the website, you know when you type `http://websitename.com` or something like that, so my route is going to be '/'. You can make yours '/introduction' or something.

```
@app.route('/')
```

Now, create a function, introduction, and return what you want displayed on the screen. You don't need to call this function.

```
def introduction():
    return "Hello, there! I'm Susan! I'm 8 years old. I have a
    puppy named Barky. I love him so much! :)"
```

Finally, let's set a host and port for our website. This is how web developers test their websites locally (without Internet) before deploying them online (Internet with actual website names). The commonly used host is 0.0.0.0 and port is 5000.

```
app.run(host='0.0.0.0', port=5000)
```

We're done! Let's run our program.

The file should be saved in the same folder as the folder your command prompt opens in. Mine is C:\Users\aarthi so I'm going to save hello.py there.

Now, go to your command prompt and type python hello.py in the Shell prompt and press Enter, and you'll get this (Figure 22-7).

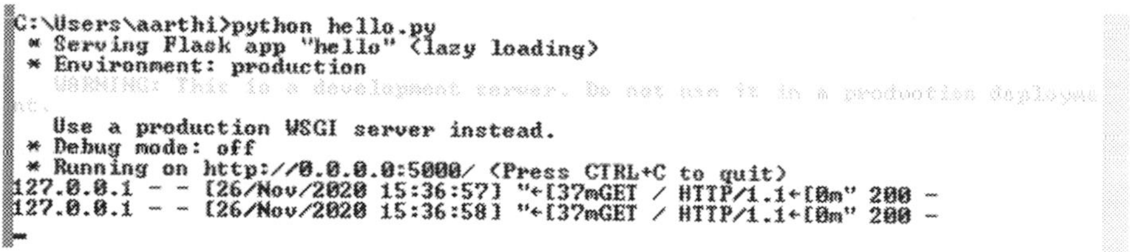

```
C:\Users\aarthi>python hello.py
 * Serving Flask app "hello" (lazy loading)
 * Environment: production
   WARNING: This is a development server. Do not use it in a production deployme
nt.
   Use a production WSGI server instead.
 * Debug mode: off
 * Running on http://0.0.0.0:5000/ (Press CTRL+C to quit)
127.0.0.1 - - [26/Nov/2020 15:36:57] "←[37mGET / HTTP/1.1←[0m" 200 -
127.0.0.1 - - [26/Nov/2020 15:36:58] "←[37mGET / HTTP/1.1←[0m" 200 -
```

Figure 22-7. *Run your Flask code*

Now, you can see your website by clicking this link: `http://127.0.0.1:5000/` (Figure 22-8).

127.0.0.1:5000
127.0.0.1:5000
Hello, there! I'm Susan! I'm 8 years old. I have a puppy named Barky. I love him so much! :)

Figure 22-8. *Your Flask website*

Yay! Our very first *Flask* program. 😊

Summary

In this chapter, we looked at web development with Python. We had a brief look at creating websites with HTML, CSS, and JavaScript and creating your very first program with Python's *Flask*. In the next chapter, let's create some more mini projects with the Python concepts you've learned in this book.

CHAPTER 23

More Mini Projects

In the previous chapter, we learned about web development with Python. We took a brief look into HTML, CSS, and JavaScript, and we created your first program with *Flask*. In this chapter, let's create some more mini projects with the Python concepts you've learned in this book.

Project 23-1: Calculator with *Tkinter*

In this project, we're going to create a calculator app like the one you see on your computers and mobiles with *Tkinter*. Let's get started!

1. Let's import *Tkinter* first and create our window. I'm going to set the resizable option to 0 and 0, so the window can't be resized. I'm also going to set the title as 'Calculator.'

A. Elumalai, *Introduction to Python for Kids*, https://doi.org/10.1007/978-1-4842-6812-4_23

```
from tkinter import *
w = Tk()
w.resizable(0,0) #cant resize
w.title('Calculator')
```

2. Now, I'm going to create a string variable (*Tkinter* variable) that will hold our expression (that needs to be calculated). I'm also creating an empty string that'll initially hold the expression. We'll later set the *Tkinter* variable with the value in the "string". Now, we're making this a string and not an integer or float because we can use the eval() method in Python to evaluate mathematical expressions, and the expressions can be in the form of a string.

```
e = StringVar()
calc = ''
```

3. Now, let's create our buttons.

   I'm going to create an "entry" button to start with. It's going to hold "e", our *Tkinter* variable, and let's justify the text to "right" and pack it at the top with enough outer padding (padx, pady) and inner padding height-wise (ipady).

```
entry = Entry(w,font=('Arial',14,'bold'),
textvariable = e, justify= RIGHT)
entry.pack(side=TOP, ipady = 7, padx = 5,
pady = 5)
```

4. Next, let's create a frame, "buttons", that'll hold all of our buttons. Let's pack that as well.

```
buttons = Frame(w)
buttons.pack()
```

5. Now, let's start creating all of our buttons. They're going to be of width 13 and height 2, and we're going to call the clear_entry() method for the clear button, get_answer() method when the "answer" or equal to button is clicked, or the button_click() method that'll add either a number or an operator to our expression.

```
clear = Button(buttons,text='c',width=13,
height=2,font=('Arial',10,'bold'),
command=lambda:clear_entry())
clear.grid(row=0,column=0,padx=5,pady=5,
columnspan=2)

answer = Button(buttons,text='=',
width=13,height=2,font=('Arial',10,'bold'),
command=lambda:get_answer())
answer.grid(row=0,column=2,padx=5,pady=5,
columnspan=2)

num7 = Button(buttons,text='7', width=5,
height = 2, font=('Arial',10,'bold'),
command=lambda:button_click('7'))
num7.grid(row=1,column=0,padx=5,pady=5)

num8 = Button(buttons,text='8', width=5,
height = 2, font=('Arial',10,'bold'),
command=lambda:button_click('8'))
num8.grid(row=1,column=1,padx=5,pady=5)
```

```
num9 = Button(buttons,text='9', width=5,
height = 2, font=('Arial',10,'bold'),
command=lambda:button_click('9'))
num9.grid(row=1,column=2,padx=5,pady=5)

num_div = Button(buttons,text='/', width=5,
height = 2, font=('Arial',10,'bold'),
command=lambda:button_click('/'))
num_div.grid(row=1,column=3,padx=5,pady=5)

num4 = Button(buttons,text='4', width=5,
height = 2, font=('Arial',10,'bold'),
command=lambda:button_click('4'))


num4.grid(row=2,column=0,padx=5,pady=5)
num5 = Button(buttons,text='5', width=5,
height = 2, font=('Arial',10,'bold'),
command=lambda:button_click('5'))
num5.grid(row=2,column=1,padx=5,pady=5)

num6 = Button(buttons,text='6', width=5,
height = 2, font=('Arial',10,'bold'),
command=lambda:button_click('6'))
num6.grid(row=2,column=2,padx=5,pady=5)

num_mul = Button(buttons,text='*', width=5,
height = 2, font=('Arial',10,'bold'),
command=lambda:button_click('*'))
num_mul.grid(row=2,column=3,padx=5,pady=5)

num1 = Button(buttons,text='1', width=5,
height = 2, font=('Arial',10,'bold'),
command=lambda:button_click('1'))
num1.grid(row=3,column=0,padx=5,pady=5)
```

```
num2 = Button(buttons,text='2', width=5,
height = 2, font=('Arial',10,'bold'),
command=lambda:button_click('2'))
num2.grid(row=3,column=1,padx=5,pady=5)

num3 = Button(buttons,text='3', width=5,
height = 2, font=('Arial',10,'bold'),
command=lambda:button_click('3'))
num3.grid(row=3,column=2,padx=5,pady=5)

num_sub = Button(buttons,text='-', width=5,
height = 2, font=('Arial',10,'bold'),
command=lambda:button_click('-'))
num_sub.grid(row=3,column=3,padx=5,pady=5)

num0 = Button(buttons,text='0', width = 13,
height = 2, font=('Arial',10,'bold'),
command=lambda:button_click('0'))
num0.grid(row=4,column=0,padx=5,pady=5,
columnspan=2)

num_dot = Button(buttons,text='.', width=5,
height = 2, font=('Arial',10,'bold'),
command=lambda:button_click('.'))
num_dot.grid(row=4,column=2,padx=5,pady=5)

num_add = Button(buttons,text='+', width=5,
height = 2, font=('Arial',10,'bold'),
command=lambda:button_click('+'))
num_add.grid(row=4,column=3,padx=5,pady=5)
```

6. Now that we've created our buttons, we should have something like Figure 23-1.

Figure 23-1. *Calculator app – the layout*

7. Now, let's create our buttons above the function calls (widgets). First, the button_click method. Let's load our global "calc" variable and just concatenate the number or operator clicked (we sent them in the form of a string, remember) with the current value of "calc". That's it!

```
def button_click(n):
    global calc
    calc = calc + n
```

8. Finally, set the *Tkinter* variable with the current value of calc. This'll make the expression appear on the entry box of your app.

```
e.set(calc)
```

9. Next, for the clear_entry method, we're just going to make "calc" an empty string again and set "e" to that string.

```
def clear_entry():
    global calc
    calc = ''
    e.set(calc)
```

10. For the get_answer method, let's import "calc", create a variable "ans" that'll use the eval() method to calculate the expression inside "calc", and set that answer to "e", so the expression is replaced with the answer.

```
def get_answer():
    global calc
    ans = eval(calc)
    e.set(ans)
```

11. Finally, let's convert "ans" to a string (it'll be an integer or floating-point value after evaluation) and replace the expression in "calc" with the answer so we can continue calculating.

```
calc = str(ans)
```

Run the program, and you'll get this (Figure 23-2).

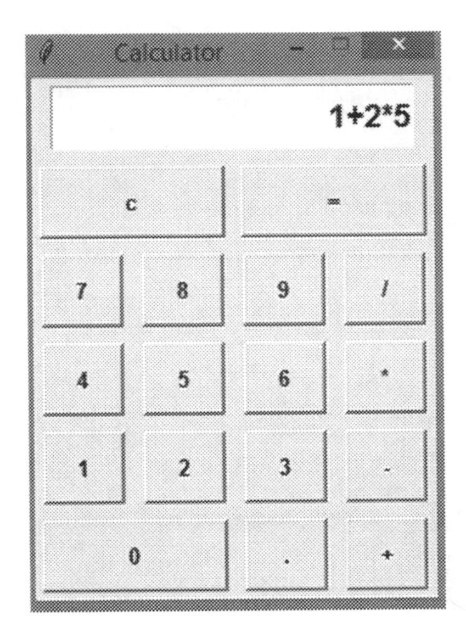

Figure 23-2. *Final calculator app*

That's it! A very simple calculator. You can actually do a lot to make this better. Maybe add some colors, iron out a couple of kinks, or add more features. For example, as of now, you can click two operators, one after the other, and that'll get you an error. Why don't you create an "if" condition that prevents that from happening?

Have fun! 😊

Project 23-2: Random story generator

In this project, let's create a simple random story generator. We're going to have a bunch of options for "when" our story happened, who our "character" is, who our "enemies" are, what's the "attribute" of our character, and pronoun (he or she or it). Finally, we're going to write a story that chooses from these options, and every time we create a new story, we get completely new characters, events, and timeline. Interesting enough? Let's get to it!

1. Let's import our random module first.

```
import random
```

2. Then, I'm going to create my options.

```
when_ch = ['Once upon a time,','A long time
ago,','Thousands of years ago,','Long long
ago,']
character_ch = ['dragon','unicorn','fairy',
'elf']
pronouns_ch = ['he','she','it']
attributes_ch = ['brave','courageous',
'strong','smart','intelligent']
enemy_ch = ['witches','warlocks','dark
elves']
saved_ch = ['the world', 'the Kingdom',
'everyone', 'the village']
```

3. Finally, let's define a generate_story() function that loads all of our options in. Then, let's use the choice() method in the random module to choose our option for that particular story.

```
def generate_story():
    global when_ch,character_ch,pronouns_ch,
    attributes_ch,enem_chy,saved_ch
    when = random.choice(when_ch)
    character = random.choice(character_ch)
    pronouns = random.choice(pronouns_ch)
    attributes = random.choice(attributes_ch)
    enemy = random.choice(enemy_ch)
    saved = random.choice(saved_ch)
```

4. Also, if our character is an elf, we need to address it with "an" and "a" for the rest of the characters.

```
if character == 'elf':
    a = 'an'
else:
    a = 'a'
```

5. Finally, let's create our story with a multi-string.

```
story = '''{} there lived {} {}. {} was
very {}. {} fought against the {} and
saved {}'. '''.format(when,a,character,
pronouns.capitalize(),attributes,pronouns.
capitalize(),enemy,saved)
```

6. Now, let's print it.

```
print(story)
```

7. Now, for the function call, I'm going to create an infinite while loop that asks the user if they want to create a new story or not. If they typed 'Y' or 'y', then let's call our generate_story function. Otherwise, let's stop the program.

```
while True:
    create = input('Shall we create a new
    story? Y or N: ')
    if create == 'Y' or create == 'y':
        generate_story()
    else:
        break
```

Simple enough, right? Why don't we generate a bunch of stories now?

```
= RESTART: C:\Users\aarthi\AppData\Local\Programs\Python\
Python38-32\story_generator.py
Shall we create a new story? Y or N: Y
Thousands of years ago, there lived a unicorn. She was very
strong. She fought against the dark elves and saved the world'.

Shall we create a new story? Y or N: Y
Thousands of years ago, there lived a dragon. She was very
intelligent. She fought against the witches and saved the world'.

Shall we create a new story? Y or N: Y
Once upon a time, there lived an elf. It was very smart. It
fought against the dark elves and saved the Kingdom'.

Shall we create a new story? Y or N: N
```

Nice! Very simple though. I'm sure you can add a lot more options and make these stories bigger or more random. Have fun! 😊

Project 23-3: Rock Paper Scissors game

Let's create a Rock Paper Scissors game for this project!

1. Let's import the *Tkinter* and random packages first.

```
#Rock, paper, scissors
from tkinter import *
import random
```

2. Now, let's create our window, configure its background color to white, and make it non-resizable.

```
w = Tk()
w.configure(bg='white')
w.resizable(0,0)
```

3. To start with, we need a label that holds the title.

```
title = Label(w,text='Rock Paper Scissors',
fg='red', bg='white',font=('Arial',45,'bold'))
title.pack()
```

4. Let's also create a u_option variable that's empty right now, but will hold the user's option later.

```
u_option = ''
```

5. Let's also create a list with our three options.

```
options = ['rock','paper','scissors']
```

6. Now, let's create the rest of our widgets. We need another label that says 'Choose one'.

```
label = Label(w,text='Choose one', fg='green',
bg='white',font=('Arial',25,'bold'))
label.pack()
```

7. Below that, we need a canvas that'll hold our rock, paper, and scissors. Let's make it so that the cursor turns to a "hand" when the user hovers over the canvas.

```
canvas = Canvas(w,width=500,height=150,backg
round='white')
canvas.pack()
canvas.config(cursor='hand2')
```

8. Next, let's load our image using the PhotoImage method. You can use any image you want. I've used illustrations of a rock, paper, and scissors.

```
img1 = PhotoImage(file="rock.png")
```

9. Next, let's draw our image into the canvas, in the X,Y coordinate position we want.

```
rock = canvas.create_image(50,20,anchor=NW,
image=img1)
```

10. Then, let's create a tag_bind on that image. We need tag_bind, instead of bind, for canvas items. Ours is going to be a <Button-1> bind, for left mouse button click, and let's call the chose() method with the argument being the item that was just clicked.

    We're going to use lambda here, and since binds need events in their function definition, and lambda is essentially a function definition, include "event" as the lambda's attribute here.

```
canvas.tag_bind(rock,'<Button-1>',lambda
event:chose('rock'))
```

11. That's it! Let's repeat the process for the next two images.

```
img2 = PhotoImage(file='paper.png')
paper = canvas.create_image(200,20,anchor=NW,
image=img2,)
canvas.tag_bind(paper,'<Button-1>',lambda
event:chose('paper'))
img3 = PhotoImage(file='scissors.png')
scissors = canvas.create_image(350,20,
anchor=NW,image=img3)
canvas.tag_bind(scissors,'<Button-1>',lambda
event:chose('scissors'))
```

12. Now, let's create labels that'll initially be empty, but will later hold the messages we want, about the user's choice, the computer's choice, and the winner.

```
you_chose = Label(w,text='', fg='blue',
bg='white',font=('Arial',25,'bold'))
you_chose.pack()
c_chose = Label(w,text='', fg='blue' ,
bg='white',font=('Arial',25,'bold'))
c_chose.pack()
winner = Label(w,text='', fg='brown',
bg='white',font=('Arial',45,'bold'))
winner.pack()
```

13. Now, let's create our chose() function above the widgets. Let's import the u_option variable.

```
def chose(option):
    global u_option
```

14. If u_option is empty, that means the user is selecting an option for the first time, and we're ready to play. Let's assign the option to u_option.

```
if u_option == '':
    u_option = option
```

15. Let's also choose a random option for our computer and place that in c_option.

```
c_option = random.choice(options)
```

16. Now, let's configure you_chose and c_chose with our choices.

```
you_chose.config(text='You chose {}'.
format(u_option))
```

```
c_chose.config(text='Computer chose {}'.
format(c_option))
```

17. Next, let's check who won. If both u_option and c_option have the same value, it's a draw. If u_option is rock, then the user wins if c_option is scissors and loses if c_option is paper. Similarly, let's create our other conditions and also configure "winner" for every outcome.

```
if u_option == c_option:
    winner.config(text='Draw!')
elif u_option == 'rock':
    if c_option == 'paper':
        winner.config(text='You lose :(')
    elif c_option == 'scissors':
        winner.config(text='You win!')
elif u_option == 'paper':
    if c_option == 'rock':
        winner.config(text='You win!')
    elif c_option == 'scissors':
        winner.config(text='You lose :(')
elif u_option == 'scissors':
    if c_option == 'paper':
        winner.config(text='You win!')
    elif c_option == 'rock':
        winner.config(text='You lose :(')
```

18. Finally, let's create our 'New Game' button.

```
new = Button(w,text='New Game',font=('Arial',
20,'bold'),command=new_game)
new.pack()
```

19. Above the button, define the new_game() function. Let's load u_option first. Now, let's configure our labels so they become empty again, and let's empty u_option so the user can play again.

```
def new_game():
    global u_option
    you_chose.config(text='')
    c_chose.config(text='')
    winner.config(text='')
    u_option = ''
```

20. That's it! Let's end the program with a main loop.

```
w.mainloop()
```

Now, let's run the program (Figure 23-3).

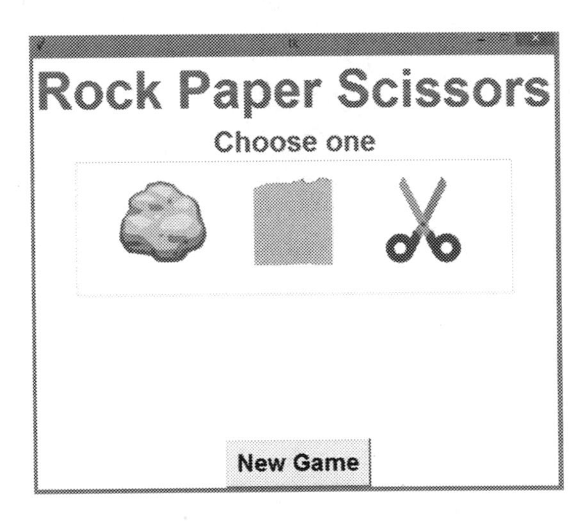

Figure 23-3. *Rock Paper Scissors game*

When the user clicks an option, they'll see this (Figure 23-4).

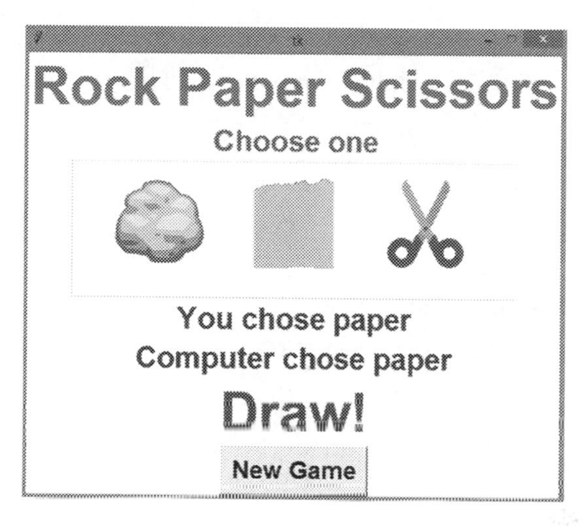

Figure 23-4. *User chose an option*

Works perfectly! 😊

Project 23-4: Bouncing ball (off the four walls) with *Pygame*

In this project, we're going to create a bouncing ball that bounces randomly off the four walls of the screen. When it hits any of the four walls of the screen, it should reverse direction and continue like that. Simple enough? Let's do this with pygame.

1. Let's import pygame, random and time to start with.

```
import pygame
import random
import time
```

2. Then, let's initialize pygame and create our screen. It's going to be of width and height 500 each.

```
pygame.init()
screen = pygame.display.set_mode((500,500))
```

3. Now, let's create a variable x and make it 250 and a variable y and make it 0 to start with. This is because we want to start the bounce from the point 250,0.

```
x = 250
y = 0
```

4. We also need a "game" variable that's currently True but will turn False when the user closes the screen.

```
game = True
```

5. Let's also create x and y directional variables "xd" and "yd" that'll be 1 by default. We're going to increment the x or y value of the ball within the range (1 to 2) (to move upward) and (–1 to –2) (to move downward). This variable is going to change our ball's direction.

```
xd = 1
yd = 1
```

6. Now, let's create our game loop.

```
while game:
```

7. To start with, let's create the quit condition. If the event type is pygame.QUIT, make game false.

```
for event in pygame.event.get():
    if event.type == pygame.QUIT:
        game = False
```

8. Then, let's fill our screen with white color.

```
screen.fill((255,255,255))
```

9. Then, let's use the draw.circle method to draw a red ball in the position 250,y (to start with, 250,0). Its radius is going to be 25 and is going to be a circle that's entirely filled, so 0 for the last attribute.

```
#draw a ball
    #circle draw function
    #where you want to draw it, color of the
    circle, position, width
    pygame.draw.circle(screen,(0,0,255),
    (250,y),25,0)
```

10. Let's use the display.update method to ensure that the screen gets updated every time the loop runs.

```
pygame.display.update()
#update the screen in the output window
```

11. If we leave the game as it is, our ball would move too fast to be seen by the human eye. So, let's slow the iterations of the loop down. There'll be a delay of 0.005 seconds after every iteration.

```
time.sleep(0.005)
```

12. Now, let's set the wall collision conditions. When x is greater than or equal to 488 (since our ball has a diameter of 25, and we need the other half of the ball to be visible, we're setting it at 488 and not 500), let's reduce the value of x by a random value between 1 and 2, because we need the ball to move toward the left (back inside the screen). So, xd is going to be -1.

```
if x >= 488:
    xd = -(random.randint(1,2))
```

13. If y is >= 488, similarly, reduce the value of yd.

```
elif y >= 488:
    yd = -(random.randint(1,2))
```

14. If x is <= 12, increase xd, and increase yd if y is lesser than or equal to 12.

```
elif x <= 12:
    xd = (random.randint(1,2))
elif y <= 12:
    yd = (random.randint(1,2))
```

15. Finally, once we're out of the if elif statement, let's add "d" with the current value of "y".

```
    x += xd
    y += yd
pygame.quit()
```

That's it! Run the program (Figure 23-5), and you'll have yourself a bouncing ball that's bouncing off all the four walls of the screen. Yippee!

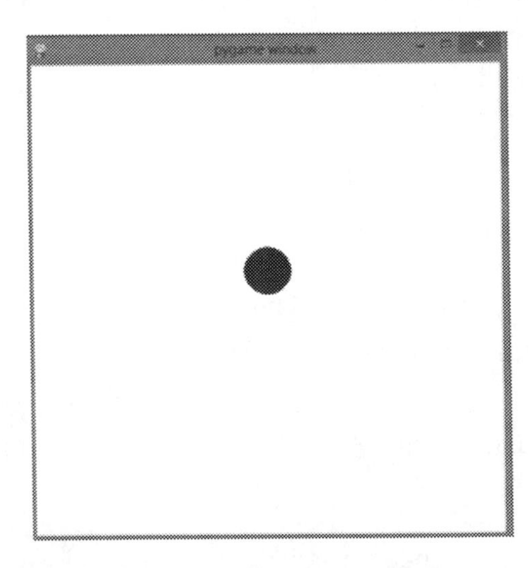

Figure 23-5. *Bouncing ball (off the four walls)*

Project 23-5: Temperature conversion app

For this project, let's create a temperature conversion app. Our app will have two features, a "Celsius to Fahrenheit" converter and a "Fahrenheit to Celsius" converter.

1. Let's import tkinter and set up our screen.

```
from tkinter import *
w = Tk()
```

2. Now, let's design our app. It's going to be a very simple design. We're going to create two frames, one for each converter.

```
frame1 = Frame(w)
frame1.grid(row=0,column=0,padx=10,pady=10)
```

3. Let's create a label, an entry box for the Celsius value, and a button that does the conversion on click and another entry box to get the result (Fahrenheit value).

```
#Celsius to Fahrenheit conversion
label1 = Label(frame1,text='Celsius to
Fahrenheit conversion',font=('Arial',15,'bold'))
label1.grid(row=0,column=0,columnspan=3)
entry1 = Entry(frame1)
entry1.grid(row=1,column=0)
button1 = Button(frame1, text='Convert to
Fahrenheit',command=find_fahrenheit)
button1.grid(row=1,column=1)
entry2 = Entry(frame1)
entry2.grid(row=1,column=2)
```

4. Let's repeat the same for the next converter.

```
frame2 = Frame(w)
frame2.grid(row=1,column=0,padx=10,pady=10)

#Fahrenheit to Celsius conversion
label2 = Label(frame2,text='Fahrenheit to
Celsius conversion',font=('Arial',15,'bold'))
label2.grid(row=0,column=0,columnspan=3)
entry3 = Entry(frame2)
entry3.grid(row=1,column=0)
button2 = Button(frame2, text='Convert to
Celsius',command=find_celsius)
button2.grid(row=1,column=1)
entry4 = Entry(frame2)
entry4.grid(row=1,column=2)
```

5. Run the program, and you'll get this (Figure 23-6).

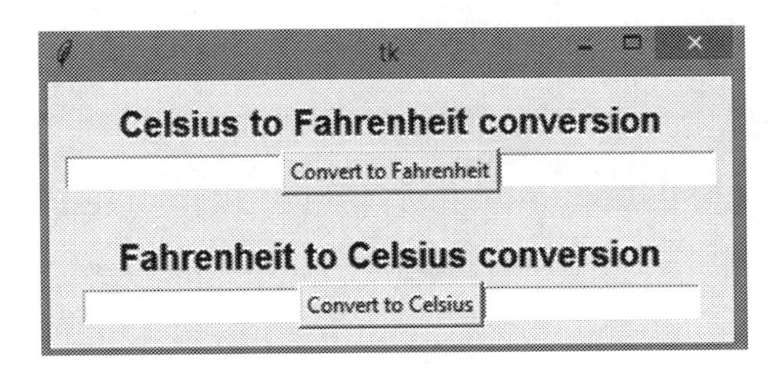

Figure 23-6. *Temperature converter*

6. Now, let's create our functions above the widgets. The find_fahrenheit() function to convert Celsius to Fahrenheit.

```
def find_fahrenheit():
```

7. There's a formula to do the same, and that's given as follows:

```
#Formula is F = ((9/5)*C)+32
```

8. Let's delete the second entry box (the result box) in case the user already made a conversion and this is a new conversion.

```
entry2.delete(0,END)
```

9. Now, let's get the first entry box's value in "C" and convert that into an integer.

```
C = entry1.get()
C = int(C)
```

10. Now, let's calculate "F" and insert that into the second entry box. That's it!

```
F = ((9/5)*C)+32
entry2.insert(0,F)
```

11. Let's repeat the same for our find_celsius function.

```
def find_celsius():
    #Formula is C = (5/9)*(F-32)
    entry4.delete(0,END)
    F = entry3.get()
    F = int(F)
    C = (5/9)*(F-32)
    entry4.insert(0,C)
```

Let's run our program, and we'll get this (Figure 23-7).

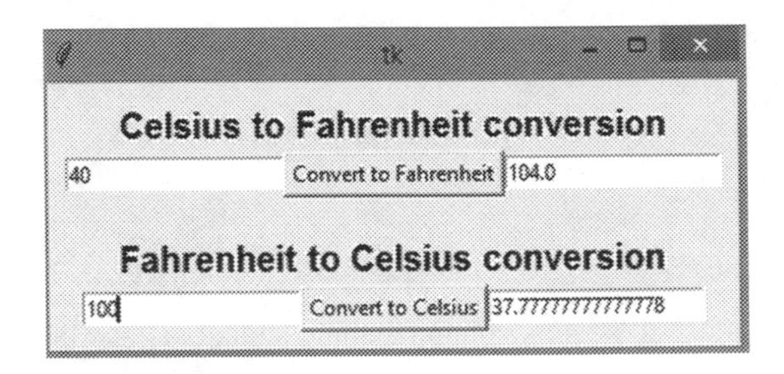

Figure 23-7. *Conversion*

It works! 😊

Project 23-6: Introduce with files and *Tkinter*

This is going to be a simple project. We are going to create a text file called introduction.txt in a folder of your choice. We are going to write our introduction to that file via our Python code, and finally, we're going to create a simple text application that accepts the file name (complete file path) and prints out the contents of that file in a text box.

Shall we get started?

1. Before we get started, let's import *Tkinter* and create our screen.

```
from tkinter import *
w = Tk()
```

2. I'm going to create my file in the following path: `G:\\Python\introduction.txt`

3. I can also use "x", but I'm using 'w' so I wouldn't have to open the file in write mode again.

```
f = open('G:\\Python\introduction.txt','w')
```

4. 4. Then, I'm going to write Susan's introduction to it:

```
f.write('''Hi, I'm Susan.
I'm 9 years old.
My puppy's name is Barky.
He loves me very very much! :)''')
```

5. Now, I'm going to create a global variable that'll store the content of my file whenever I press Enter on my entry box. Let's store an empty string in it for now.

```
f_content = ''
```

6. Now, let's create our widgets. I want a label that is on the left of my entry box. I've hence placed it in row 0 and column 0.

```
label = Label(w,text='File name',font=('Arial',
12,'bold'))
label.grid(row=0,column=0,padx = 5, pady=5)
```

7. I'm going to place my entry box in row 0 and column 1, make it sticky in all four directions, and give everything padding. All the values I've chosen (width, padding, etc.) are arbitrary. You can test different values and choose the ones you like.

```
entry = Entry(w,width=65)
entry.grid(row=0,column=1,sticky='nsew',
padx = 5, pady=5)
```

8. Finally, let's create a bind for my entry. Whenever I press the Enter button on my keyboard (command in Mac), I want to call my get_file function. You need to use the '<Return>' condition to make that happen.

```
entry.bind('<Return>',get_file)
```

9. Finally, let's create our text widget. I'm going to give my text some default stylings and place it in row 1, column 0 and make it span two columns (so it takes up the entire width of the first two widgets).

```
text = Text(w,font=('Arial',14,'bold'))
text.grid(row=1,column=0,columnspan=2)
```

10. Alright, now that we're done with the widgets, let's define our get_file function. Define it above the calling function, okay?

    Since we created a bind, our function needs to receive the "event". Load f_content into the function.

```
def get_file(event):
    global f_content
```

11. To start with, get the file name from the entry box. Then, open that file in read mode, and store its contents in f_content (f.read()).

```
file = entry.get()
f = open(file,'r')
f_content = f.read()
```

12. Finally, insert whatever's in f_content into the text box. We're using 'end' so the entire content gets inserted.

```
text.insert('end',f_content)
```

That's it!
Let's run our program now (Figure 23-8).

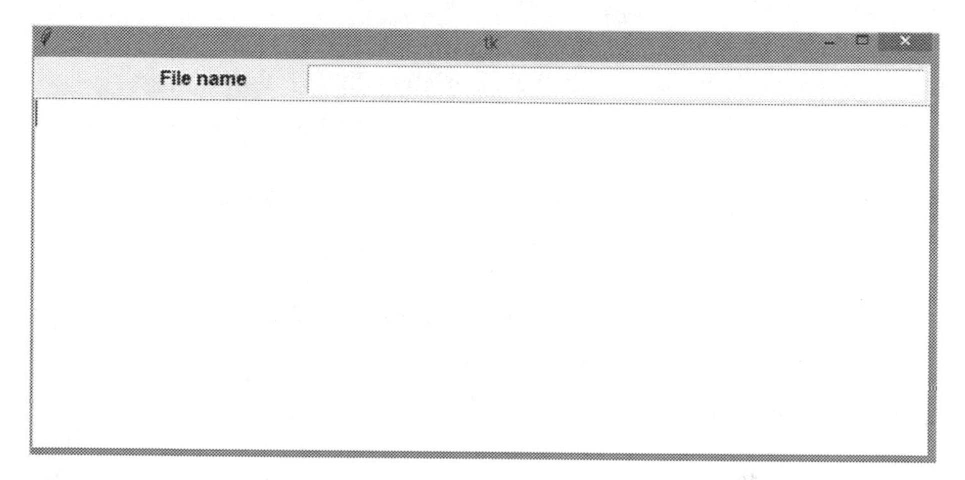

Figure 23-8. *Tkinter app layout*

We have our widgets right where we want them! Let's see if our program works now (Figure 23-9).

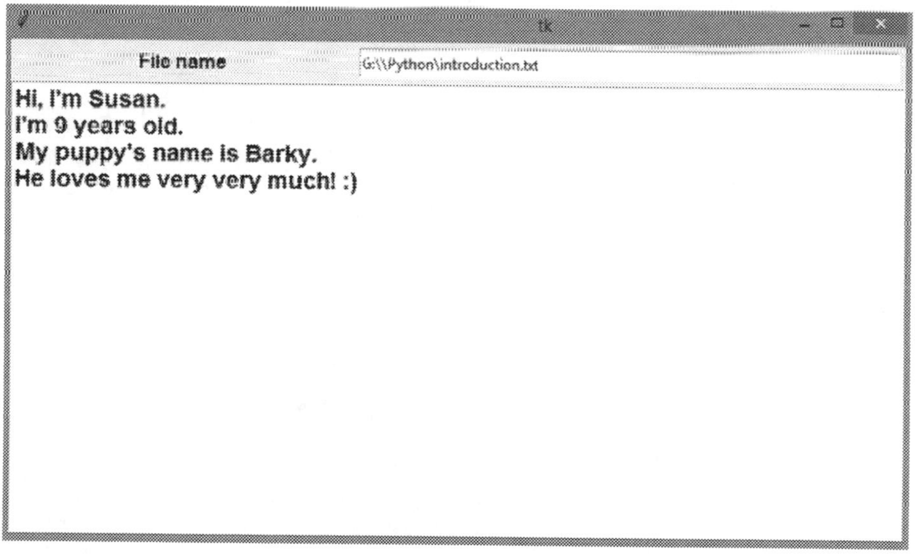

Figure 23-9. *Import the file contents*

Yes, it did. I entered my file path (the exact path) and pressed Enter, and my file's content's being displayed on my text box. Perfect! 😊

Summary

In this chapter, we created six apps using either *Tkinter* or *Pygame*. We created a calculator, a random story generator, a Rock Paper Scissors game, a file uploader app, a temperature conversion app, and a bouncing ball.

In the next chapter, let's talk about what's next in your Python journey. I'll give you some ideas on what you need to learn about next, and I'll also give you some ideas on more mini and capstone projects you can work on your own.

CHAPTER 24

What's next?

In the previous chapter, we created more fun little mini projects with Python. In this chapter, let's look at what's next. I'll give you more mini and capstone project ideas to try, and let's briefly discuss how you can continue your Python journey from here.

Mini project ideas you can try

Python is a very interesting programming language where you can do pretty much anything you set your mind to.

Mini projects and puzzles are a great way to build your expertise in Python. You've already created plenty of mini projects in this book. Why don't I give you some ideas to create your own mini projects?

Currency conversion app

You could use *Tkinter* for this project. Try creating conversion options for as many currencies as you can.

You can make this a single-line app with drop-downs against text boxes (like you see in the currency conversion app on Google). The drop-downs will list all the currency options. Based on what's selected on both sides, make the conversion.

Simple, right? Automate as much as possible, that is, reduce as many lines of code as possible.

A. Elumalai, *Introduction to Python for Kids*, https://doi.org/10.1007/978-1-4842-6812-4_24

Race in *Pygame*

We created a *Turtle* race in one of our mini projects, remember? Why don't you try the same with *Pygame*, but make it better this time? Create proper racetracks with lines and place your colored players (could be rectangles) at the start of the tracks.

Maybe you could create a start button too, and on clicking that, make your players race (make them move randomly), and finally, based on who wins, create a "Game over" screen in the player's color.

Simple, isn't it? Try it out!

More patterns in *Turtle*

Do you remember the mandala patterns we created in our earlier project? Why don't you try creating more patterns like those? Make them more complicated. You already know that you can use for loops to automate patterns.

You can create different patterns (circular and square) and combine them together randomly (using function calls).

Capstone project ideas you can try

We've already seen how to create the snake game in *Turtle*, but as you can see by now, *Pygame* is more suited for, well, any game really, so why don't you try creating the same in *Pygame*?

Snake game in *Pygame*

It should be pretty simple to create. Draw rectangles for the snake heads and body parts, including the apple, make them move (you already know how), create a scoreboard when the snake head superimposes the apple while growing the snake by one body part, and finally end the game if there was a collision (wall or body collision).

Dodge the bullet

Why don't we create a reverse of the space game we created with *Pygame*? Instead of shooting the aliens, you have a bunch of aliens shooting at you. You're out of ammunition, and the only thing you can do now is dodge the raining bullets (randomly fired from each alien ship so you don't know which one is going to shoot at you), and that's exactly what you're going to do.

You have, let's say, ten lives, and every time a bullet hits you, you lose a life. The more time you hold out, the higher your score. Quite interesting, but simple, don't you think? Make the game as easy or tough as you want it to be.

Memory game in *Pygame*

This is a fun little game you probably played at arcades. Create even numbered boxes. Each of these boxes is hiding an image behind them, but there's a catch. There are two of each image, and you need to match them.

When the user starts the game, reveal all the images hidden behind the boxes for a specified time limit (maybe 5–10 seconds), so the user can see where they are. Then, hide them again, and the game starts. Now, the user needs to match the images.

The first time the user clicks one of the boxes, the image behind it will be revealed to them. They have to click the box with the same image the next time. If they don't, and if the next image being revealed is a different image, both images will be hidden again, and they can start over.

If they click the same boxes hiding the same image, one after the other, then the boxes will not be hidden again, and they gain a point.

They need to match all the boxes like this within the given time limit (usually 30 seconds for a set of ten images).

Interesting? Try it! 😊

Looking ahead

Alright, we're at the end of our book. So far, you've learned the basics of Python, all about *Turtle*, *Tkinter*, and *Pygame*, and you've also created projects to familiarize yourself with the topics. What's next? How should you continue your journey? Let me give you some ideas.

OOPs in detail

We did learn about objects and classes, but we didn't delve deeper into the topic, not by a long shot. If you want to do proper real-world programming, OOPs is going to help you a lot. It's also a valuable skill to have in your arsenal for any programming language, let alone Python.

So, why don't you start by using classes in more of your projects and see how they transform your code? Next, pick up a good object-oriented programming with Python book and continue your journey.

Regular expressions

Regular expressions is a very interesting, albeit advanced, topic in any programming language, especially Python. It's basically pattern matching with a twist.

Have you wondered how programs knew how your password didn't have the specified number of letters, numbers, and special characters and how they were able to point out whether one of the characters were a capital letter or not? Magic? Nope, that's your regular expression pattern matching at play.

Research on the topic. I'm sure you'll find it interesting.

Web development

I've given you a basic introduction to web development already, but as you probably guessed already, we've barely scratched the surface. There's a lot more to learn and a lot more to do.

The world is your oyster, as far as web development is concerned. Delve deeper into HTML, CSS, and JavaScript and learn more about website design and development. Then, look into Django or *Flask* for back end and MongoDB for creating and maintaining databases for your program. Once you've learned the subject, try creating projects (maybe a social media site or a shopping cart). It's a vast topic that'll take months to learn. Take it one step at a time.

Packages in detail

Yes, we have looked at *Turtle*, *Tkinter*, and *Pygame* to an extent. But there's still a lot more to learn. So, I'd recommend creating more projects (not just the ones mentioned in this book), and as you encounter more problems, you'll look for more solutions (or syntaxes) to solve them, and you'll delve deeper into each package you're working with.

Have fun! 😊

Summary

In this chapter, I gave you more ideas on mini and capstone projects you can try creating yourself. Then, I gave you directions on what you can learn next.

That's it! We've come to the end of the book. I hope you had fun learning Python with me. Don't stop learning and creating, but more important than that, never stop having fun! 😊

Index

A. Elumalai, *Introduction to Python for Kids*, https://doi.org/10.1007/978-1-4842-6812-4

I

J, K

L

M

N

O

P, Q

R

S

T, U, V

W, X, Y, Z

Printed in the United States
by Baker & Taylor Publisher Services